THE IRISH IN VICTORIAN BRITAIN

The Irish in Victorian Britain

THE LOCAL DIMENSION

Roger Swift *&* Sheridan Gilley

EDITORS

FOUR COURTS PRESS

Set in 11 pt on 13 pt Ehrhardt by
Carrigboy Typesetting Services for
FOUR COURTS PRESS LTD
Fumbally Court, Fumbally Lane, Dublin 8, Ireland
e-mail: info@four-courts-press.ie
and in North America for
FOUR COURTS PRESS
c/o ISBS, 5804 N.E. Hassalo Street, Portland, OR 97213.

A catalogue record for this title
is available from the British Library.

ISBN 1-85182-403-0 hbk
ISBN 1-85182-444-8 pbk

Printed in Great Britain
by MPG Books Ltd, Bodmin, Cornwall

Contents

INTRODUCTION   7
Roger Swift and Sheridan Gilley

A regional perspective: the Famine Irish in south Wales   14
Paul O'Leary

Irish immigrants in Cornwall: the Camborne experience, 1861–82   31
Louise Miskell

'Sturdy Catholic emigrants': the Irish in early Victorian Birmingham   52
Carl Chinn

Irish settlement in the north-east and north-west of England in the
    mid-nineteenth century   75
Frank Neal

Catholic education in Victorian Hull   101
Marie McClelland

Mayhew's Irish: the Irish poor in mid nineteenth-century London   122
Jacqueline Turton

Migration, 'community' or integration? Irish families in Victorian Stafford   156
John Herson

Class, creed and country: the Irish middle class in Victorian Liverpool   190
John Belchem

Nationalists in exile: the National Brotherhood of St Patrick in
    Lancashire, 1861–5   212
Gerard Moran

Alternative historiographies of the Irish in Britain: a critique
    of the segregation/assimilation model   236
Mary J. Hickman

The Gaelic revival in London, 1900–22: limits of ethnic identity   254
John Hutchinson and Alan O'Day

From Victorian 'Little Ireland' to heritage trail: catholicism, community and   277
    change in Liverpool's docklands
Frank Boyce

SELECT BIBLIOGRAPHY   298

NOTES ON CONTRIBUTORS   314

INDEX   315

Introduction

Roger Swift and Sheridan Gilley

This volume follows two books of essays, *The Irish in the Victorian City* and *The Irish in Britain, 1815–1939*, which appeared under our editorship in 1985 and 1989. The first of these works was a collection of national and regional studies, and reflected the consensus on the subject by describing both the degree of demoralisation and disadvantage experienced by Irish immigrants into Britain in the Victorian era, and the positive aspect of the Irish Catholic achievement in creating enduring religious and political communities by the end of the nineteenth century. Our second volume was an assemblage of revisionist essays which attempted to show the extent to which some of these more traditional emphases in the historiography of Irish immigration into Britain required modification and reinterpretation. We also tried to identify gaps in the scholarly knowledge of the subject, thereby suggesting the need for more local and regional studies.

This third volume goes further by presenting the fruits of the more recent research in this area, some of it by established historians, some by a younger generation. In particular, the collection illustrates the diversity of Irish experience in recent studies of specific towns and regions. Thus in the first essay, Paul O'Leary argues that the generally hostile reception of the Famine Irish in South Wales, and the attacks on the Catholic priest and chapel in Cardiff in 1848, are best interpreted in terms of a strong sense of regional identity, and of the social and economic problems of the region, which is a more useful unit for understanding the immigrants' experience and reactions to them than the smaller entities of town and city. Within this framework, the argument is illustrated by a vivid narrative of the sheer shock to individuals, institutions and communities of the sudden impact of the mass of impoverished and disease-ridden immigrants, desperate for survival, in a disaster not of their own making, and of the kinds of resentment, frustration and sheer inhumanity to which this gave rise.

This regional study balances Louise Miskell's account of one small Cornish town, Camborne, and its Irish community, the largest in Cornwall, where the Irish can be shown to have been directly affected by their immediate setting and surroundings. Most of them settled not in the town centre but in the surrounding hamlets where housing was poorer and cheaper, so that these came to be considered Irish areas, even though their Irish residents were never more than a minority of the population. Because of the local mix of agriculture and

industry, they had an interesting range of occupations apart from their major
one of tin mining. The anti-Irish riot of 1882 was the product of a local popular
tradition of protest against injustice by authority, in this case, the perception of
a too-lenient sentence for an assault by Irishmen on a Cornishman, and was
part of a Cornish pattern of riotous behaviour which took the form not so
much of actual violence as of mob intimidation.

In a larger urban study, of the Birmingham Irish, Carl Chinn stresses the
strength and complexity of the extended family networks, often occupying whole
lodging houses, through which Irish immigrants remained supportive of one
another. While not living in ghettos, they were still concentrated in particular
areas of the city. The links of family were supplemented by those of work.
Chinn shows that the Birmingham building trade was the largest employer of
Irish labour, but that there were also a range and variety to the work undertaken
by the Irish, some 765 jobs in all, right down to different kinds of button maker,
reflecting 'Birmingham's multiform industrial structure and the large number
of sub-divisions in certain trades'. Also important were the ties of the immigrants' Irish township and county: the poorer Connacht immigrants crowed
into the old city centre, while the better-off Dubliners and immigrants from
Cork lived on the periphery. Here both Irish background and the economic,
social geographic structure of the host city gave a shape and structure to Irish
settlement and determined the character of Irish communal life.

There are some interesting contrasts both of patterns of settlement and of
employment in Frank Neal's comparison, based upon a study of the materials
provided by the 1851 census, of Irish immigrant experience in the north-east
and north-west of England. Irish settlement was concentrated in the dockland
areas of Newcastle and Tynemouth and along the south banks of the Tyne, but
the immigrants were also widely scattered in the furnace towns and pit villages
of county Durham, where their exceptional mobility suited the sudden growth
and decline of local mines and iron works. Their female dependants lacked the
employment opportunities available in domestic service and in the textile mills
in Lancashire, though these last employed fewer of the Irish than might be
expected, and even those employed were not in the best-paid positions. The
Irish were still at the bottom of the occupational heap in both places, but the
labour needs of the eastern and western counties still made a striking difference
to their fortunes, perhaps most strikingly manifest in the differing opportunities for women. Neal also suggests the wider theme of how large immigrant
households containing three generations of a family and their lodgers could
make a difference to their survival.

While most of the essays in this volume are only indirectly concerned with
the development of Irish institutions, Marie McClelland demonstrates the part
played by the Catholic educational system in the emergence of the Irish
Catholic community in Hull, especially through the schools and teacher
training college created by the Irish Sisters of Mercy, who within a few decades

of their foundation in Dublin had colonised the English-speaking world. The essay tells us something of one of nineteenth-century Ireland's more successful exports, the entrepreneurial nun, intent upon building convents, schools and hospitals among the Irish abroad, sometimes in the teeth of opposition from both Protestants and the Catholic clergy. The difficulties of the Sisters in Hull, which included local councillors, a major scandal and hostile priests, were those of their own and other orders elsewhere, but the strength of the Protestant tradition in Hull gave a particular piquancy to their success.

The largest population of Irish immigrants settled in London. Jacqueline Turton re-evaluates Henry Mayhew's celebrated portrait of the mid-Victorian London Irish street folk. Her account stresses again the importance of the networks of place of origin, family, work and church in ensuring daily survival, and generally confirms the historical evidence discovered by contemporary scholars in other ways. She also emphasises that Mayhew's own attitudes to the Irish were mixed, both sympathetic and unfavourable. He tried to let the poor speak for themselves through their own voice, even though his interviews were structured by his questions, so that despite his shortcomings as a reporter, in part the consequence of the rushed character of his journalism as well as of the general restriction of his material to the street Irish, his work retains its value both as external description and as a pioneering form of oral history. The essay also testifies to his humanity, a quality sometimes lost in the severer sort of statistical study.

John Herson's depiction of the Irish in Victorian Stafford paints a very different picture from the one sometimes given of a stream of isolated transitory drifters, by demonstrating the existence of a large number of stable Irish Catholic families who experienced a measure of integration and even of upward social mobility, some of them through what looks from the outside like an explicit 'strategy' of integration into British society, partly by intermarriage with the English, both Catholics and non-Catholics. Again, Herson charts the fortunes of the significant number of Irish Protestants, and indicates the importance of further out-migration, with the changing fortunes of Stafford itself. His essay suggests the subtle interplay of the processes which are sometimes regarded as simply polarised, of integration and separation, accommodation and assertion, and the poignancy of the ways in which some prospered while others decayed or perished. Like Carl Chinn, Herson shows how the study of extended and intermarried families and of their occupations and professions within the social and communal activity of the town in which they lived can paint a vivid miniature of Victorian life.

Something of the same vividness is part of John Belchem's account of the Irish middle class in Victorian Liverpool, the entrepôt for Ireland, with its flourishing Catholic Church and its republican conspirators and other leaders and moulders of the large working-class Irish Catholic community. Professor Belchem also describes a significant Irish Protestant commercial presence, but his overall argument is still that Liverpool remained in many ways *sui generis*, especially in the fierceness of its religious and political divisions, though it should perhaps be noted that Dr MacRaild has recently found a similar ferocity of sectarian conflict among the Irish immigrants in Victorian Cumbria.[1] Professor Belchem's essay also identifies an element in the development of Irish Catholic community consciousness, the self-interest of the more prosperous, merchants, shop-keepers, publicans, politicians, policemen and journalists within a complicated body of social and religious institutions, in creating and sustaining positions of leadership among their fellow-Irish, and winning respectability and acceptability for their co-religionists and fellow-countrymen and fame and fortune for themselves. It is a paradox of Irish nationalism and Catholicism that they succeeded by adopting some of the very Protestant and bourgeois Victorian values which they were widely thought to reject.

All students of the Irish in mid-Victorian Lancashire owe a debt to W.J. Lowe for his monograph on the subject, with its demonstration that in spite of their poverty, poor housing, unskilled occupational status and general poverty, the immigrants succeeded in creating strong religious and political communities, with, paradoxically, a degree of assimilation into the life of the people around them.[2] These communities, however, had their own inner tensions, and Gerard Moran's account of the Lancastrian dimension of the Brotherhood of St Patrick in the early 1860s demonstrates the difficulties of an apparently innocuously cultural nationalist movement, exposed to the suspicion of the Church and of moderate nationalists on the one hand and of entryism by revolutionary Fenians on the other. In its rhetoric and organisation, however, the Brotherhood anticipated the more successful nationalist movements later in the century, when the Irish Parliamentary Party and the Catholic Church achieved a *modus vivendi* on the basis of a moderate Catholic nationalism, so that Catholicism and nationalism reinforced each other within the constitutional movement for Home Rule.

This is a rather different view to Mary Hickman's, in the most iconoclastic essay in this volume, which the editors commend for its sharpness of statement and clarity of argument. Her principal point is that the experience of Irish Catholic immigrants was conditioned by the policies of the British State, and that the Catholic Church, the chief institution involved with the immigrants, especially through its system of schools, was to a remarkable degree a government instrument in both controlling the immigrants' conception of their own identity and 'incorporating' them into British life. This resulted, if not in the

---

1   Donald M. MacRaild, *Culture, Conflict and Migration: The Irish in Victorian Cumbria* (Liverpool, 1998).
2   W.J. Lowe, *The Irish in Mid-Victorian Lancashire: The Shaping of a Working Class Community* (New York, 1989).

dehibernicisation of the immigrants, at least in the modification and moderation of their Irishness into something acceptable to the British. Dr Hickman's essay is therefore something of a counterargument to this volume as a whole, in suggesting that the general overall setting for the migrants – the British State and the English Catholic Church – have been much more important to their destiny than any local or regional considerations. Dr Hickman does not deny that such considerations were important, but she assigns them a second place. She also counters the argument made by many scholars, including Lowe, that communal attachment to the Catholic Church was the basis for the Irish involvement in nationalist politics; and that a sense of nationality would hardly have survived without the social cement of Catholicism. Hers is an argument that would also have astounded a great many Victorian Protestants and Conservatives, for whom the very existence of Irish Catholicism represented disloyalty to the British Empire and the Protestant religion.

A degree of Irish 'incorporation' into British society is, however, a demonstrable fact, and is one theme of the essay by John Hutchinson and Alan O'Day on the Gaelic Revival in London, which was sustained in the 1890s by a new generation of immigrant Irish journalists, civil servants, teachers, clerks, post office officials and younger priests, who were seeking a redefined cultural identity in a revival of Irish culture, sport and language. The movement was at odds with the older generation of nationalist politicians, and its resurgence after their eclipse through the Easter Rising, in the form of the Irish Self-Determination League, gave a new form to London Irish politics. This, however, collapsed in turn, with the emergence of an independent Ireland and the divisions created by the Treaty, with the return or deportation of leading activists to Ireland and with the reversion to conventional politics of most of their supporters, even in London. The implication is that the general choice of Irish immigrants was in the end 'incorporation' rather than sharp separation, and that they found a wholly distinctive Irish culture and identity less attractive than an unassertive one.

The concluding essay, by Frank Boyce, recalls what was one of the largest concentrations of the Irish in Britain, the north dockland area of Liverpool, where between the two world wars, some seventy to seventy-five priests served a population of a 100,000 Catholics. Boyce describes the transformation of the area since the 1950s, with the loss of industry and population and the closure and merger of its Catholic parishes and schools. The paper is the recreation of a world now almost as lost as Lyonesse, and addresses the problem of what in this 'heritage' can now be salvaged from the wreck, as the old British working class also disappears into history. The skilful use of taped interviews binds past and present, as has been shown on a much larger scale by Dr O'Dowd's recent history of the seasonal migration of agricultural workers from Ireland to England.[3]

---

3 Anne O'Dowd, *Spalpeens and Tattie Hokers: History and Folklore of the Irish Migratory Agricultural Worker in Ireland and Britain* (Dublin, 1991).

All these essays are pieces of original research, but they generally confirm the picture painted by Dr Steven Fielding in his recent book on the Irish in Britain, based on his Warwick doctoral thesis on the Irish in Manchester, of a progressive accommodation by immigrants to their host society, which was compatible with the retention of loyalties to Catholicism and Irish nationalism, so that even the mass of poor Irish became an accepted part of the wider working class.[4] Not all Catholic immigrants were or remained Catholic, and only a minority were politically active. None of their attachments was unproblematic, but all had some basis in loyalties to both nuclear and extended families, and the historian may well be more impressed by the persistence of a people and its traditions and their remaking according to new needs and pressures, than by the many who abandoned them altogether.

The reader will note the mass of recent publications on the Irish in Britain in both the footnotes to the articles and in our bibliography, and in recording them we hope to assist and to inspire others. Yet we are also aware that much scholarly research is required before the definitive history of the Irish in Victorian Britain can be written. For example, the experiences of Irish migrants in Britain before 1841 still require further detailed investigation, although Ruth-Ann Harris has recently made a significant contribution to the study of this earlier period.[5] We need to know much more about Irish urban and rural settlement and demography during the Victorian period, especially in regard to in and out migration, residential and social mobility, and male and female employment patterns. Until this is achieved, in part through the diachronic analysis of census data, it is difficult to assess how static or dynamic Irish communities actually were; in many towns the 'Little Irelands' of the 1840s and 1850s had disappeared by the end of the nineteenth century in the wake of slum clearance programmes, yet many of the districts where the Irish resettled still await scholarly study. We also need to know much more about the internal dynamics of Irish communities, both clerical and lay, community organisations and cultural and recreational provisions. The economic, social, cultural and political roles of Irish women, Irish Protestants, and the Irish middle class remain similarly obscure.[6] The relationship between the Irish and other ethnic minorities during the period is also worthy of further study. Thus much remains to be achieved if we are to understand how and in what ways Irish migrants were shaped by and shaped their Victorian environment.

4 Steven Fielding, *Class and Identity: Irish Catholics in England, 1880–1939* (Buckingham, 1993).

5 Ruth-Ann Harris, *The Nearest Place That Wasn't Ireland: Early Nineteenth-Century Labour Migration* (Ames, Iowa, 1994).

6 For further discussion of these, and other issues, see Roger Swift, 'The historiography of the Irish in nineteenth-century Britain', in P. O'Sullivan (ed.), *The Irish World Wide: History Heritage, Identity*, vol. 2, *The Irish in the New Communities* (Leicester, 1992), pp 52–81.

In this context, the recent publication of a massive and majestic study of the Irish in one city, New York, edited by Ronald Bayor and Timothy Meagher,[7] reminds us that the academic study of the Irish in Britain continues to lag far behind its counterpart in the United States[8] and for reasons that are well known. Nevertheless, the essential agenda that underpins *The New York Irish*, as well as the various themes addressed and methodologies which it employs, are clearly of relevance to scholars with an interest in the history of the Irish in Britain, not least because it serves to remind us that there is considerable scope for detailed scholarly studies of the Irish immigrant experience in specific British towns and cities during the Victorian period and beyond. Three British cities in particular might well benefit from such treatment. Liverpool, the most Irish of British cities, is an obvious candidate; an extensive local historiography already exists, including important studies by Frank Neal[9] and John Belchem[10] The recent doctoral thesis by Caroline Scott comparing Liverpool with Manchester and Newcastle shows something of what can be achieved by such further study.[11] Glasgow is surely another candidate, as is demonstrated by the extensive historiography created by Tom Gallagher[12] and by some of the contributors to Tom Devine's edited collection of essays on the Irish in Scotland.[13] Arguably, however, it is London, the city with the largest Irish-born population during the nineteenth and twentieth centuries, that would benefit most of all from intensive scholarly study; nearly twenty years have elapsed since the appearance of the pioneering study of the city's Irish by Lynn Lees,[14] and there has been little published on the subject since. These reservations and suggestions notwithstanding, this volume is offered as a further contribution to a burgeoning historiography, and as an example of the 'state of the art' in the late 1990s of the study of the Irish in Britain.

7   Ronald H. Bayor and Timothy J. Meagher (eds), *The New York Irish* (Baltimore and London, 1996).

8   See especially Donald Harman Akenson, 'The historiography of the Irish in the United States', in P. O'Sullivan (ed.), *The Irish World Wide: History Heritage, Identity*, vol. 2, *The Irish in the New Communities* (Leicester, 1992), pp 99–127.

9   Frank Neal, *Sectarian Violence: The Liverpool Experience, 1819–1914* (Manchester, 1987).

10 John Belchem (ed.), *Popular Politics, Riot and Labour: Essays in Liverpool History* (Liverpool, 1992).

11 C.L. Scott, 'A Comparative Re-examination of Anglo-Irish Relations in Nineteenth-Century Manchester, Liverpool and Newcastle-upon-Tyne' (University of Durham PhD thesis, 1998).

12 Tom Gallagher, *Glasgow: The Uneasy Peace – Religious Tension in Modern Scotland, 1819–1940* (Manchester, 1987).

13 T.M. Devine (ed.), *Irish Immigrants and Scottish Society in the Nineteenth and Twentieth Centuries* (Edinburgh, 1991).

14 Lynn Lees, *Exiles of Erin: Irish Migrants in Victorian London* (Manchester, 1987).

A regional perspective: the Famine
Irish in south Wales

Paul O'Leary

Recent research on the industrial revolution in Britain has emphasised its distinctively regional character. It has been shown that a nuanced picture of social and economic change requires generalizations about country-wide developments which must be counter-balanced with detailed studies of regional variations. The historiography of the Irish in nineteenth-century Britain has not suffered from an excess of broad generalizations at the expense of local studies, but rather the opposite. In one sense, it could be said that there has been a surfeit of town and city studies which, in their determined particularity, have failed to address the broader picture. The gap between J.A. Jackson's pioneering study of the Irish in Britain, published in 1963, and the next single-author book-length study by Graham Davis in 1991 is telling, encompassing as it did more than a quarter of a century during which studies of the Irish in particular localities proliferated.[1]

For most social historians, individual towns or cities were (and remain) the most attractive scale of analysis for understanding Irish settlement and social life and the migrants' interaction with the host society. There are many compelling reasons for following this route, both in terms of the concerns and methodologies of social history and the institutional realities of Victorian society. The town or neighbourhood is a convenient scale of analysis for marshalling and manipulating the large volume of data about settlement patterns, family structure and occupations available in the census enumerators' books which has done so much to deepen our knowledge of emigrant communities. In addition, Poor Law records, with their wealth of information about the most destitute in society, are most easily accessible on the level of individual parishes. Also, some of the key questions about the experience of Irish migrants as a group, such as the extent to which they were segregated from or integrated into the host population, would seem to be best addressed at the micro-level of an individual town or neighbourhood where the dynamics of social interaction are

---

1 J.A. Jackson, *The Irish in Britain* (London, 1963); Graham Davis, *The Irish in Britain* (Dublin, 1991). See also Roger Swift, 'The historiography of the Irish in nineteenth-century Britain' in Patrick O' Sullivan (ed.), *The Irish in the New Communities: The Irish World Wide*, vol. 2 (Leicester and London, 1992), pp 52–81.

most easily detectable.[2] Yet, as J.D. Marshall has argued persuasively, the study of towns and their regions should not be separated out and examined independently;[3] his point is an important reminder that individual towns or cities are not the only meaningful locales for studying the Irish.

Although few historians have explored the regional dimension to Irish migration to Britain, it has been claimed that in the century following 1750 'the region was a powerful focus of social and political identity across the social spectrum'.[4] The implications of this comment for Irish immigrants has yet to be fully understood. Attempting an understanding of regional variations among Irish immigrants requires a perspective somewhat different to that of the individual town study, entailing a search for the linkages between places as much as the close analysis of individual towns. Not the least of the challenges facing the historian is deciding which geographical areas constitute a meaningful regional entity in any particular period.

Some of the early writers on labour migration in Britain had a much sharper grasp of the significance of regional identities and differences. A regional analysis was implicit in Arthur Redford's study of migration, first published in 1926, in which he attempted to identify the causes and volume of population movements between different parts of the United Kingdom. He drew attention to the existence of three principal streams of Irish immigration to Britain, consisting of the movement from the northern counties of Ireland to the west of Scotland; the migration principally from Dublin and the central and western counties of Ireland to Liverpool and its hinterland; and the stream from the south-western counties of Ireland to south Wales, Bristol, and on to London.[5] This chapter is concerned with the tributary of migrants which flowed to south Wales during the Great Famine.

In terms of its physical geography, south Wales is composed of a narrow coastal belt which broadens out into the Vale of Glamorgan to the west of Cardiff before narrowing again near Bridgend, together with a mountainous

---

2 See, for example, Roger Swift and Sheridan Gilley (eds), *The Irish in the Victorian City* (London, 1985); Roger Swift and Sheridan Gilley (eds), *The Irish in Britain, 1815–1939* (London, 1989).

3 J.D. Marshall, 'Why study regions?' *Journal of Regional and Local Studies*, vol. V (1985), p. 25; see also Marshall's article, 'Why study regions? (2)', *J.R.L.S*, vol. VI (1986) pp 1–12.

4 Pat Hudson (ed.), *Regions and Industries: A Perspective on the Industrial Revolution in Britain* (Cambridge, 1989), p. 2. However, see also the essays by Malcolm Chase, 'The Teesside Irish in the Nineteenth Century', and Frank Neal, 'English-Irish Conflict in the North-east of England', in Patrick Buckland and John Belchem (eds), *The Irish in British Labour History* (Liverpool, 1993), pp 47–58; 59–85.

5 Arthur Redford, *Labour Migration in England, 1800–1850*, third edition (Manchester, 1976). The study was originally published in 1926.

hinterland known as 'the Hills' in the first half of the nineteenth century but which later became known as 'the Valleys'[6] with the rapid growth of the coal industry from the mid-nineteenth century and the settlement of many valley bottoms. During the early modern period the two areas were separate in terms of their economies, social structures, and often languages. From the late eighteenth century, transport connections increasingly united them as first canals and then railways defied the sharp elevations between coast and interior in order to permit the export of heavy goods like iron and coal. The Glamorganshire Canal connecting Cardiff on the coast with the iron-manufacturing town of Merthyr Tydfil inland in 1799 was a notable triumph of engineering, and one which was consolidated when the Taff Vale Railway connecting the same towns opened in the 1840s.[7]

The four principal themes studied here demonstrate the usefulness of examining linkages between individual towns and the wider regional context. Firstly, there is a consideration of transport communications and their impact upon the character of immigration along the south Wales coast; secondly, there is an assessment of the strategies employed by the authorities throughout the region to stem immigration; thirdly, an attempt is made to evaluate the impact of social problems – such as disease – which were attributed to the Irish; and, fourthly, the impact of popular disturbances at the local and regional level is considered.

The close proximity of Ireland and Wales ensured contacts between the two countries from the earliest times, but geographical proximity was not enough in itself for a port to attract and retain Famine refugees – the means of transport available to them was a factor of even greater importance. Unlike Liverpool and the west of Scotland, the ports of south Wales lacked a direct steam link with Ireland (a fact which complicated attempts by the Poor Law authorities in the region to return paupers to that country). Consequently, the chief mode of travel for migrants to south Wales was a by-product of trade between the region and southern Ireland. Colliers – ships exporting coal to Ireland – frequently returned empty as there was relatively little trade in the other direction and so the captains were more than happy to obtain a little extra money for what otherwise would have been an unremunerative trip in ballast.[8]

6   When used in this way 'the Valleys' refers specifically to the industrial valleys of the south Wales coal field. It is not a generic term.

7   A.H. John, *The Industrial Development of South Wales, 1750–1850* (Cardiff, 1950); W.E. Minchinton (ed.), *Industrial South Wales, 1750–1914: Essays in Economic History* (London, 1969); Neil Evans, 'Two paths to economic development: Wales and the North-east of England' in Pat Hudson (ed.), *Regions and Industries: A Perspective on the Industrial Revolution in Britain* (Cambridge, 1989); and various articles in A.H. John and Glanmor Williams (eds), *Glamorgan County History*, vol. V (Cardiff, 1980).

8   For the background, see T. Boyns and C. Baber, 'The supply of labour, 1750–1914' in John and Williams (eds), *Glamorgan County History* (1980), pp 311–62.

This practice came to light in 1836 when R.M. Muggeridge, migration agent to the Poor Law Commissioners, was faced with a conundrum: how to explain why the number of passengers departing Bristol for Ireland exceeded the number travelling in the opposite direction, when all other evidence pointed to large numbers of Irish men and women migrating to Britain. The reason, he discovered, was that many Irish seasonal workers entered Britain cheaply via small ports on the Welsh coast in colliers returning in ballast from Ireland. After gathering the harvest in England they had more money at their disposal and hence were able to return via Bristol on the more comfortable and costly packets.[9] Such practices, designed to reduce the cost of seasonal migration, increased the migrants' familiarity with the industrial developments taking place in south Wales. In this respect, they acted as conduits of information about job opportunities for those who remained at home. This method of migration intensified and became more widespread under the exceptional conditions of the Famine years.

The Irish were present in Wales in sufficient numbers to establish their own ethnic institutions in all the major urban settlements before the Great Famine of 1845–9 occurred, but it is clear that the immigration during the crisis years of the late 1840s and early 1850s was on a greater scale than ever before.[10] Between the censuses of 1841 and 1851 the number of Irish-born in Wales increased by 153% (compared with an increase in the population as a whole during the same decade of only 11%), and the flood continued well into the 1850s.[11] The newcomers were described in a tragically evocative phrase as bringing with them nothing but 'pestilence on their backs, famine in their stomachs'.[12]

Among the earliest ships bearing refugees to arrive in South Wales was the *Wanderer* of Baltimore, west Cork. It had left Ireland on 23 December 1846 and spent more than five weeks at sea in inclement weather before arriving at Newport on 1 February 1847. Captain Casey delivered 113 destitute men, women and children to the town, some 26 of whom were dying. 'Human conception can scarcely reach the depth of misery in which a large number of them appeared', commented a local newspaper, and Sir Benjamin Hall brought the case to the

9 Parliamentary Papers (hereafter P.P.), 1836, XXIX, Poor Law Commissioners Report, Part I, Appendix B, p. 419.

10 For the pre-Famine migration to Wales, see my forthcoming *Immigration and Integration: the Irish in Wales, 1798–1922* (University of Wales Press).

11 On the Famine immigration to Liverpool and the west of Scotland, see Frank Neal, *Sectarian Violence: The Liverpool Experience, 1819–1914* (Manchester, 1988), pp 80–124; Frank Neal, 'The Famine Irish in England and Wales', in Patrick O'Sullivan (ed.), *The Irish World Wide*, vol. 6, *The Meaning of the Famine* (London and Washington, 1997), pp 56–80; James E. Handley, *The Irish in Scotland* (Glasgow, 1964), pp 177–98.

12 T.W. Rammell, *Report to the General Board of Health on a Preliminary Inquiry into the Sewerage, Drainage and Supply of Water, and the Sanitary Condition of the Inhabitants of the Town of Cardiff* (London, 1850), p. 41.

attention of parliament.[13] A fortnight later a newspaper editorial remarked upon the 'alarming and lamentable appearance' of the streets of Newport, crowded as they were with 'many hundreds' of famishing Irish.[14] It was believed that many of the men had been lured to the town by promises of work on the railways and in the ironworks at wages of four shillings per day, while the women were promised washing and domestic work 'in whatever numbers they please' for between two shillings and half a crown per day. It was also claimed that handbills had been distributed to this effect in Ireland and that a bellringer had been engaged to spread the message at the markets of county Cork. In reality, the vision of waged work as the escape route from starvation and destitution was no more than a cruel chimera. With this misplaced hope in mind, 'hosts of squalid beings' were 'induced to embark on board filthy hulks, totally unsuited for a living freight, the miseries of whom, densely stowed upon damp ballast, suffering from famine and sickness during this tempestuous season, are almost beyond human expression'.[15]

During the first six weeks of 1847 Newport's Refuge for the Destitute provided food and temporary accommodation for 369 men, 360 women and 402 children, quite apart from the aid distributed to 'an enormous extent' by the Poor Law Union. It was hoped that it would be possible to take care of 'these miserable strangers' until better times arrived. Great pride was taken in this philanthropy and especially in the local relief fund which exceeded £1000. Sharp criticisms were aimed in particular at the 'local committees' in Ireland who, it was believed, were paying the cost of paupers' passages to Wales in order to alleviate their own burden.[16] During April and May 1847 the influx intensified. In addition to the 1000 Irish recently relieved by the Poor Law authorities at Newport, an additional 'several hundred' Irish entered the town during the second week of April. Even before their arrival the Refuge for the Destitute, a temporary hospital and the old lock-up had been filled by previous arrivals.[17] As the town's limited resources were stretched to breaking point, anxiety turned to anger. When another two ships carrying more than 200 Irish paupers docked at Newport, the *Monmouthshire Merlin* began to suspect 'obdurate landlords' of trying to avoid their legal responsibility by shipping the Irish poor to Wales. By this time the municipal authorities were taking a stern attitude to the newcomers and summarily sent 100 of them back to Ireland. When another 500 men, women and children arrived during the first week of

---

13 *Monmouthshire Merlin*, 6 Feb. 1847; *Hansard's Parliamentary Debates*, 3rd Series, vol. XCI (1847), cols 269–71.
14 *Monmouthshire Merlin*, 20 Feb. 1847.
15 Ibid.; *The Times*, 19 Feb. 1847. On the Famine in Cork, see James S. Donnelly, *The Land and the People of Nineteenth-Century Cork* (London, 1895), pp 73–131.
16 *Monmouthshire Merlin*, 20 Feb. 1847.
17 Ibid., 10 April 1847.

May they, too, met with a harsh response. After being provided with nothing more than temporary relief these unfortunates were ordered to leave the town.[18] The sense of deep shock and concern felt by the inhabitants of Newport early in 1847 was a product of the strain placed upon the town's institutions and an *ad hoc* response to the desperation and helplessness of the continuously-arriving contingents of famished Irish. At the same time, attitudes to Irish beggars inland at Merthyr Tydfil had begun to harden, to the extent that some of them resorted to acting dumb when begging in an attempt to disguise their origins.[19]

Other ports along the coast also experienced a Famine influx, although Newport probably suffered more acutely than did any of the others. Both Swansea on the coast and Merthyr Tydfil inland also received large numbers of poor Irish. The impact of the inundation was particularly severe at Cardiff because it was such a small settlement at this time, and consequently found it difficult to absorb or simply cope with the numbers landing there. Recalling the first ships to arrive, Jeremiah Box Stockdale, the superintendent of Police, stated that many passengers were 'apparently starving' and in an 'advanced stage of disease', while there were numerous deaths shortly after landing.[20] Stockdale maintained that in 'hundreds of instances' he had been told that a specific, although unnamed, landowner near Cork city had paid 2*s*. 6*d*. for the passage of each Irish man and woman. On receipt of this report in March 1847, the marquis of Bute informed the Secretary of State of the matter before instituting his own enquiries as to whether relief funds were the source of passage money. By April he was suggesting that the mayor address an official complaint to the Secretary of State in order to bring the landowners and authorities of south-west Ireland 'to a proper sense of their duty', and that a complaint should be made directly to the Kinsale poor union in particular about its behaviour in allegedly shipping destitute families to Wales.[21] The claim that the government's Relief Committees were diverting funds to under-write the cost of sending paupers to Britain was first drawn to the government's attention in February 1847. An investigation into the matter revealed only one documented case of this happening, when those in charge of the relief depot at Skibbereen in west Cork sent destitute paupers to Newport. It was generally

18 Ibid., 17 April, 8 May 1847.
19 Ursula Masson, 'The Development of the Irish and Roman Catholic Communities of Merthyr Tydfil and Dowlais in the Nineteenth Century' (University of Keele MA thesis, 1975), p. 62.
20 P.P., 1847–8, vol. LIII, Reports and Communications on Vagrancy, p. 31.
21 Bute to James Lewis, 27 March 1847, National Library of Wales (hereafter NLW) Bute Collection, box 70, letterbook dated 1 January 1847–18 March 1848; Bute to Lewis, 23 April 1847, ibid.; Names of those supplying passage money are given as Mr. Stewart and the Revd. M. McGrath, Bute to Lewis, 15 April 1847, ibid.

believed that the practice was more widespread, but Sir Randolph Routh concluded that 'the more usual course is for the landlord to pay these expenses.'[22]

Of all British ports only Liverpool collected systematic data about the numbers
and type of immigrant arriving from Ireland from 1847, although Newport did
record the overall numbers of annual Irish arrivals from 1849 to 1853.

Table 1: Irish arrivals at Newport, 1849–53

Year	Number	Year	Number
1849	1720	1852	3052
1850	2140	1853	4812
1851	3739		

Source: P.P. (1854), LV. The Number of Passengers Landed at this Port from the Coast
of Ireland, 1849–53.

Although these figures show a steady rise in arrivals from 1849, it is impossible
to tell whether this is indicative of a constant increase from 1847 or whether
there was an earlier peak in immigration to the town in 1847–8. Anecdotal
evidence gleaned from the local press suggests that the numbers of arrivals in
1847 were in excess of those recorded for 1849 and thus the figure for 1849
would appear to represent a decline after the large influx of 1847–8.

In the absence of synchronic data it is difficult to make an accurate estimate
of the numbers passing through the ports, partly because so many of them
clearly moved on to other places shortly after arriving and partly because of the
routes by which many entered the country. Vessels disgorging the starving and
diseased along the coast from Milford Haven in the west to Newport in the east
often did so away from the larger and busier ports, preferring instead clandestine
landings in order to avoid the attentions of officialdom and the hostility of the
Welsh. This coast, indented with many small, sheltered bays, was conducive to
unnoticed landings. But disembarking in this manner was a hazardous exercise
for passengers offloaded unceremoniously at a small inlet or in the shallows of
a beach, as shown by the horrific fate of an Irishman who drowned by sinking
in a mudflat in the face of an oncoming tide at Penarth in May 1847.[23]

The municipal authorities in Welsh towns were faced with a daunting
problem beyond their experience and comprehension, that is an influx of

22 Correspondence between Mr Hughes and Sir Randolph Routh, 12 February 1847; Mr
    Stephen to Mr Trevelyan, 16 February 1847, and Sir Randolph Routh to Trevelyan, 20
    February 1847, all printed in P.P., 1847, vol. LII, *Correspondence Relating to the Measures
    Adopted for the Relief of Distress in Ireland (Commissariat Series), Second Part*, pp 130,
    159–60.
23 *Monmouthshire Merlin*, 1 May 1847.

destitute people they could not halt or regulate, which showed no signs of abating. Poorly equipped to meet the demands now made upon them, local authorities in Wales directed their energies towards deflecting the newcomers or compelling them to return home. Unfettered and uncontrolled immigration spurred on the authorities to explore methods whereby the influx might be stemmed. They were provided with leadership in December 1847 when the coal and iron masters at Newport resolved to punish the captains of vessels which had carried Irish refugees to the port by refusing to send freight in their ships, an act which led to a temporary lull in the influx.[24] In the longer term, an unbending enforcement of the law concerning the carriage of passengers at sea was the preferred strategy at Newport, where it was reported in July 1848 that while many captains possessed licences to carry up to ninety passengers, a large number were willing to risk illicit landings of larger numbers on the mudflats below the entrance to the harbour.[25] In February 1849 the master of a vessel was fined £5 at Newport for exceeding the terms of his passenger licence, and the penalties for infringing such regulations became progressively harsher during the year. After landing destitute Irish immigrants at Cardiff and Newport in March 1849, William Sutton, the master of the *Mary* of Cork, was imprisoned for two months in default of payment of a £50 fine, while in June Robert Travers, captain of the schooner *Two Friends*, was fined £10 with 15s. costs for the illegal carriage of Irish immigrants from Courtmacsherry to Newport. In a vain attempt to deter captains from carrying immigrants the most trivial contravention of regulations was punished. An example of this occurred in July 1849 when William Shea, the master of the *Purilla*, was charged with failing to display sufficiently clearly on his vessel a copy of the Passenger Act.[26]

Other towns in the region looked on with great interest. In April 1848 the Swansea press commended the zeal with which captains were prosecuted at Newport, suggesting that 'their example ought to be followed by all others'.[27] For those bewildered by the seemingly unstoppable inundation, the prospect of controlling and ultimately stopping the influx of immigrants by enforcing regulations governing the carriage of passengers helped to identify a tangible cause of their confusion and held out the seductive possibility of a panacea for their problems. Writing to the mayor of Newport in June 1849, the Revd G.A. Cockburn, the incumbent of a small parish near Milford Haven in Pembrokeshire, requested precise information about the legislation 'whereby these rascally captains might be laid hold of', adding that 'it would not be permitted to remain inactive by me'.[28] This is a concrete example of how the press in the

24 *Cambrian*, 3 Dec. 1847.
25 *Monmouthshire Merlin*, 15 July 1848.
26 Ibid., 3 March, 10 March, 9 June, 21 July 1849.
27 *Cambrian*, 14 April 1848.
28 *Monmouthshire Merlin*, 16 June 1849.

region provided a network for disseminating information about policies and practices relating to the treatment of Irish refugees in nearby areas.

In spite of this public enthusiasm for enforcing the law more punctiliously, few towns prosecuted captains as systematically or as successfully as at Newport and, as has been seen, even there it is questionable whether court action succeeded in deterring captains or merely encouraged them to seek landfall on more secluded parts of the coast where their actions might go unnoticed. Admitting the failure to prosecute captains docking at Cardiff, the chairman of the Cardiff Board of Guardians informed the Secretary of State that paupers were deposited clandestinely on the coast near the port while vessels continued on their journey to Newport; those who landed in this way made their way to Cardiff where relief had to be provided. In an attempt to assuage local anxieties the Secretary of State acceded to a request in July 1849 that the coast guards along the south Wales coast would be instructed to report any infringements of the laws on carrying passengers to the authorities at Cardiff, although once again the efficacy of this action is in some doubt.[29] After all, as H.J. Paine of Cardiff succinctly pointed out, the continuation of this traffic was ensured by the grim economic rationale of supply and demand: 'The captains, it appears, find it cheaper to ship and unship this living ballast than one of lime or shingles'.[30]

Starvation and illness went hand-in-hand as lack of food increased the susceptibility of the poor to disease. The winter of 1846–7 in Ireland brought with it an epidemic of 'famine-fever' – in reality the two diseases of typhus and relapsing fever – rapidly followed by dysentery and scurvy. Confined in large numbers in the small holds of sailing ships, often in close proximity to livestock, emigrants found themselves in an ideal environment for the spread of disease; upon landing many were enfeebled and dying. The manager of the tramp house at Newport estimated that 40% of the Irish in the town in 1847 suffered from fever, while nearby at Chepstow the comparable figure was 20%.[31] Dysentery was common and frequently fatal. During these years the self-sacrifice of many Catholic priests in an attempt to alleviate the plight of the diseased Irish was proverbial; two of them died from typhus in 1847.[32]

As fear of contagion gripped the citizens of the ports a variety of schemes to control the influx was hastily mooted. In April 1847 the Marquis of Bute, the

29 Public Record Office H.O. 100/257, 34303, Charles Williams to Sir George Grey, 7 June 1849; *The Times*, 2 July 1849. With his letter to Sir George Grey, Charles Williams enclosed a copy of a poster offering a £10 reward for information leading to the conviction of a captain illegally landing Irish passengers between Aberthaw and the River Rumney. As late as 1854 coal ships returning in ballast were landing large numbers of starving Irish on the South Wales coast. See P.P., 1854, vol. XVII, pp 434–5.
30 Rammell, *Report to the General Board of Health* (1850), p. 41.
31 P.P., 1847–8, vol. LIII, p. 37.
32 *Catholic Directory*, 1848, p. 91; *Monmouthshire Merlin*, 5 June 1847; *Catholic Opinion*, 25 September 1869.

most powerful landowner in south Wales, advised the mayor of Cardiff to place all vessels from Ireland under quarantine so that the state of health of the passengers could be ascertained. He drew up a detailed plan to detain all vessels offshore in Penarth Road under the yellow flag and their passengers were to be deposited at 'a place … fitted up out of the Town in the nature of a Lazaretto', which would have meant the use of Flat Holm island as an off-shore quarantine station.[33] Nearly a year later a Poor Law official stressed the suitability of islands off the Welsh coast as reception points where the Irish could quarry rock for repairing roads, thereby easing the financial burden which had descended willy-nilly upon the ports.[34] Whether the impetus derived from a desire to isolate diseased incomers or concern about the cost of relieving the poor, it was an idea which was not acted upon. However, similar plans were put into operation in North America, on Grosse Isle in the St Lawrence River for Quebec, on Deer Island for Boston, and Staten Island for New York.

The depth of anxiety about the threat to public health posed by the Famine immigrants was matched by an equally persistent concern about the cost of relieving the starving and destitute who became chargeable to the receiving parishes. Although the statistics of those being relieved at Houses of Refuge do not differentiate between the Irish and other nationalities there can be little doubt but that the sharp upturn in numbers observed at this time was a result of the Irish influx. The numbers receiving relief at the Newport House of Refuge in January 1847 was quadruple the figure for the previous January. The numbers peaked in April 1847, but they continued at an exceptionally high level well into 1848. Rural Poor Law unions were particularly fearful of the increase in the numbers of Irish vagrants and expressed alarm at the prospect of having to provide them with poor relief for an indefinite period. The increase in their financial burden was substantial. Of those paupers not belonging to a parish in the Chepstow union there were more in the first six months of 1847 than in the previous eighteen months taken together, while the numbers relieved in the Brecknock union increased threefold during 1847.[35] The Poor Law system was simply sagging under a weight of numbers it had not been designed to assist.

Most of the Irish were categorised as 'tramps' or vagrants and were thus usually ineligible to be admitted to the workhouse. The nature of the accommodation made available to them varied widely from one parish to another. At Swansea there existed provision for only thirty vagrants, while at Neath the relieving officer simply provided each applicant with sufficient money for

33 NLW Bute Collection, box 70, letterbook dated January 1847 to March 1848, pp 14–15. Bute to James Lewis, 15 April 1847.
34 P.P., 1847–8, vol. LIII, p. 13.
35 P.P., 1847–8, vol. LIII, pp 29–30, 95. The Monmouth Union demanded a change in the law to solve the problem, ibid., p. 78.

lodging and bread. At Newport, Cardiff and Chepstow, Irish applicants for poor relief were lodged in buildings under the control of officers employed by the Guardians but separate from the workhouse. Accommodation at the tramp house at Newport was typical of that provided elsewhere. The lodgings consisted of two large rooms on the ground floor of the old workhouse, both floored with brick, and the occupants slept on rugs on the ground. According to the matron, Mrs. Huxtable, straw was not provided because 'if we did, we could not keep the place free from vermin'. Upstairs, was a room containing twelve beds for tramps suffering from minor ailments 'and any other clean persons who may occasionally come'. Even this limited and primitive provision was considered a magnet for paupers by some magistrates who wished to see the refuge closed on that account.[36] Strenuous attempts were made to deter the able-bodied from applying for poor relief. Mr Bentley, the relieving officer at Neath, threatened those who came more than once a month with the police, a stratagem which was not always successful. 'Some will not be frightened', he complained, '*and will have money*, which I am obliged to give, to get rid of them, and for the sake of peace'.[37] At Cardiff, vagrants applied directly to Superintendent Stockdale, who had been delegated the responsibility of relieving the able-bodied, while the sick were referred to the workhouse. Stockdale's policy for dealing with Irish vagrants was to send them back to Ireland as soon as possible. A barracks which had been used as a hospital and a night-asylum had both been discontinued during the previous twelve months and the only accommodation available for the destitute at Cardiff was a room with straw for bedding.[38] It would appear that the use of a police officer in the administration of poor relief was a favoured method of deterring able-bodied Irish vagrants from applying for assistance. The authorities at Newport copied the example to great effect.[39]

The Poor Law authorities took a stern attitude to those individuals applying for relief who were shown to be less than utterly destitute by prosecuting vagrants who possessed the means to purchase their own food who persisted in demanding alms. The experience of John Collins, 'a forbidding looking Irish vagrant', illustrates this clearly. One Sunday in June 1847 Collins visited the village of Llandaff on the outskirts of Cardiff pleading that he was starving. However, upon being searched it was found that he had ample amounts of bread, cheese, meat and money in his pockets to maintain himself, and a constable escorted him out of the village, instructing him not to return. Nevertheless, Collins 'lounged about' until Monday morning when he began

---

36 Ibid., pp 26–9.
37 Ibid., p. 46.
38 Ibid., pp 30–1.
39 P.P., 1854, vol. XVII, *Select Committee on Poor Removal*, p. 494.

begging again. He was arrested and committed to gaol for one month.[40] When, in 1848, an Irish family applying for assistance at Newport was searched and found to have £3 of their own money they were sent home at their own expense.[41] Similarly, when an Irish vagrant was searched at Merthyr Tydfil in May 1850 and found to have money on his person, a portion was taken from him and paid to the treasurer of the Board of Guardians.[42]

Even those who were sent away could return within a matter of weeks, as Superintendent Stockdale readily conceded. Some sought work inland at the ironworks while others trekked further afield to English cities. As the local economy was unable to absorb all of the immigrants the women, children and aged members of many families remained at the port of entry, maintained by the Poor Law, while the men travelled in search of work elsewhere. 'Some of the Irish families', opined the master of the Chepstow workhouse, 'appear to be making for no place, and we see them often in their rounds'.[43] The Poor Law inspector W.D. Boase summed up the evidence collected from officials throughout south Wales when he reported in 1848 that 'by far the greatest proportion of Irish vagrants in Wales were women with small children, old men apparently feeble, pregnant women, and girls and boys about 10 years old'.[44] Boase proceeded to contrast the nature of Irish immigration to south Wales with that of Liverpool. Those arriving at Liverpool were predominantly able-bodied young men who had tramped long distances across Ireland from western counties such as Mayo, Roscommon and Sligo to board ship at Dublin or Drogheda on the east coast. Their ability to make this arduous journey on foot suggested that they were fit enough to earn their own livelihood and support themselves without recourse to charity, a characteristic which Boase believed was not evident in south Wales. There, in his view, the Irish were 'nearly all helpless and burdensome to the community'.[45]

It is clear that responses to refugees were conditioned by the cost of providing relief and medical services, responsibilities which strained the resources of small towns and gave rise to a mixture of outrage and anxiety. The following table gives some indication of the dimensions of the problem.

40 *Cardiff and Merthyr Guardian*, 26 June 1847.
41 P.P., 1847–8, vol. LIII, pp 23–4.
42 Glamorgan Record Office, U/M Merthyr Board of Guardians Minute Book, 1849–51, p. 210; the incident was also mentioned in the *Morning Chronicle's* report on the town.
43 P.P., 1847–8, vol. LIII, p. 17.
44 Ibid.
45 Ibid.

Table 2: Numbers and cost of relieving Irish paupers, 1848

Place	Individuals	Amount
Cardiff	2,063	£868 14s. 7d.
Newport Union	12,661	£184 15s. 7d.
Merthyr Tydfil Parish	1,346	£212 8s. 0d.

Source: P.P. (1849), XLVII: Numbers of Irish Poor Relieved during 1848.

As Frank Neal has suggested, the average cost of relief per head of 3½d. indicates that the casual Irish poor predominated in Newport, whereas in Cardiff the cost was 8s. 5d. per head, suggesting that more permanent Irish paupers predominated in that town.[46] Among those relieved, Boase identified a large number of widows with small children who came over 'to get a bit for the children', married women whose husbands had preceded them, young girls and boys in search of parents, brothers and uncles, and numbers of old women. Initially, the last had attempted to earn a living by street-selling, but had found it unprofitable. Influenced by prevailing ideas about the existence of a hereditary 'dangerous class' of paupers, Boase was inordinately exercised by the fear that should the Irish settle they might produce a new generation of dependants.[47]

Popular reaction to the famine immigrants varied from the all-too-rare cases of sympathy to the more common response of overt hostility. The typical response was reported by the government Commissioners enquiring into the state of education in Wales in 1847 when they noted that 'the prevailing sentiment' among the people of the mining areas of Monmouthshire was that 'if the Government wanted to mend their condition, it had better "tackle their masters", and stop the Irish coming among them'. This comment arose specifically out of a strike against the employment of Irish labourers who, it was claimed, had caused a reduction in wages. Anticipating a major disturbance, a local magistrate was preparing to read the Riot Act at Pontypool.[48] That this incident was representative of a deeper and more widespread hostility in the region is demonstrated by events in the following year.

Tensions arising from the cumulative impact of heavy immigration, epidemics and the disruption attendant upon railway construction precipitated numerous instances of ethnic conflict in the towns along the South Wales coast, culminating in a particularly serious anti-Irish riot in November 1848. In May

---

46 Frank Neal, 'The Famine Irish', in O'Sullivan, *Meaning of the Famine*, p. 79, n. 44. In making this distinction, however, he reminds us that we do not know precisely what expenditure was included in the overall figures.
47 Ibid.
48 P.P., 1847, vol. XXVII, *Reports of the Commissioners into the State of Education in Wales*, Pt. II, p. 293.

of that year two Welshmen were murdered at a beer-house near Swansea by a group of Irish navvies working on the South Wales Railway, an event which sent a frisson of horror through the local populace. Anonymous threatening letters were sent to members of Swansea's Irish community and rumours of assaults on the Irish abounded in the press.[49] Later that year, in June, the houses of the well-established Irish community in the village of Llantrisant near Cardiff were attacked, 'without any provocation, and in the dead of night', with the aim of driving the Irish away. The cause of the outbreak remains a mystery and there was no attempt to invoke the customary justification of a reduction in wages. Nevertheless, it was reported that colliers in the neighbouring Rhondda valley had expressed a willingness to complete the work begun by the locals but were frustrated from carrying out their threat by the intervention of the police. Further trouble in the locality was anticipated and magistrates swore in thirty special constables, whose presence in the village for the best part of a week succeeded in preventing more violence.[50] Coverage of these events in the local press occurred at the same time as reports of the arrival of Famine refugees and contributed to a composite picture of the Irish as a diseased and destitute group of lawless individuals whose presence inexorably led to disturbances of the peace. In one sense, therefore, the riot at Cardiff in November 1848 can be seen as both a product of local circumstances and a culmination of the year's hostilities in the region.

In the early hours of Sunday, 12 November 1848 a Welshman was stabbed by an Irishman in an altercation in Stanley Street, at the heart of an area with a large Irish population. A police constable was quick to appear on the scene of the crime, but was too late to prevent John Connors, the murderer, from slipping away into the darkness and eluding arrest. The police failed to discover Connors' whereabouts, even though he remained in the vicinity for the whole of Sunday before escaping, a fact which enabled the press to accuse the Irish as a group of harbouring a murderer and thus of being equally culpable of the crime. 'He knew he was safe enough', thundered the *Cardiff and Merthyr Guardian*, 'and why should he conceal himself? His secret was in good hands. No one knew it but the Irish; and they never betray murderers – never'.[51] As a result, the newspaper felt justified in broadening the scope of its invective to encompass all Irish immigrants who were, in its opinion, 'the worst specimens of Irish barbarism'. Such intemperate language did nothing to mollify the Welsh, but it has to be seen as a reflection of popular hostility rather than a contributor to its cause, because by the time these words appeared in print a crowd had attacked the Catholic church and the priest had fled the town.

At the Sunday evening service at St David's Roman Catholic chapel on the corner of Stanley Street and David Street Fr Millea had exhorted anyone in the

49 *Cambrian*, 12, 19, 26 May 1848.
50 *Cardiff and Merthyr Guardian*, 24 June 1848.
51 Ibid., 18 Nov. 1848.

congregation with knowledge of the murderer's whereabouts to give him up to the police, an appeal which made a favourable impression upon a number of the Welsh people present. However, during the afternoon of the following day Millea observed an ominous scene as three horse-drawn carts deposited their loads of stones in the street opposite the chapel and small groups of bystanders gathered nearby. Shortly after six in the evening a large crowd, which Millea estimated at 9000, but more realistically put at 2000 by another source, gathered outside the chapel.[52] Following an exchange between Millea and a few individuals in the crowd two police constables and three other men were permitted to search the premises for the murderer. The search was unsuccessful and there is no evidence to suggest that Connors had been given refuge there, but the crowd smashed a few windows before attacking the houses of Irish immigrants close by, breaking their doors and smashing windows and furniture. Fr Millea seized this opportunity to flee to a safe house outside the town before moving on to the bishop's house at Chepstow. Following his departure, the crowd returned to smash the windows of the chapel and the priest's house, causing considerable damage. Hundreds of Irish people were seen thronging the roads hurrying away from the town.[53]

Although by no means all of the immigrants were practising Catholics, they were, nevertheless, provided with a rallying point for defending themselves as a group. This became apparent on Tuesday, 14 November, when 300 Irish navvies working on the South Wales Railway entered the town determined to protect the priest and the chapel 'with their lives'. In response, the magistrates posted bills warning against any further violent attacks on people or property. Thereafter, riotous behaviour subsided, although it was an uneasy peace for as long as the murderer remained at large.[54] That the events at Cardiff reverberated throughout the region is demonstrated by the contents of an advertisement placed in the *Cardiff and Merthyr Guardian* by the parish priest of Dowlais and Merthyr Tydfil publicising the resolutions of a public meeting of the Irish which unanimously declared their abhorrence of the murder in Cardiff and their determination that the accused would not find sanctuary in their midst. A resolution deploring the attack on the Catholic chapel and the priest's house was sweetened by a collection of £2 for the dead man's widow. The conduct and resolutions of the meeting were welcomed by the newspaper which hoped it would have 'a beneficial effect upon the public mind'.[55]

John Connors was finally arrested ten miles away at the town of Pontypridd on 19 November after the police had kept Irish lodging-houses in the area under surveillance.[56] However, the fact of his capture did not signify the end of

52 *The Tablet*, 18 Nov. 1848.
53 Ibid.
54 *Monmouthshire Merlin*, 18 Nov. 1848.
55 *Cardiff and Merthyr Guardian*, 25 Nov. 1848.
56 Ibid.

ethnic conflict. The Irish lodging-house keeper at Pontypridd where Connors was taken had the windows of his house smashed, despite the fact that he had alerted the police to the murderer's presence, and three Irishmen working in the Rhondda were chased down the valley by a large crowd of colliers. The grim legacy of the event continued until the end of the year: during December there were reports of Irish people being attacked or killed at Cardiff and Newport.[57]

The navvies' action in defence of the church had held out the prospect of an escalation of the conflict and brought into sharp focus the signal failure of the police to intervene to prevent the destruction of property. While it could be argued that the local police were unable to call upon sufficient numbers to make a decisive intervention in events, it was also the case that the mayor had refused to authorise the use of a contingent of sixty-five soldiers billeted in the town. Official inaction prompted an anonymous writer in the Catholic press (probably Bishop T.J. Brown, Vicar Apostolic of the Welsh District) to accuse the civil authorities in Cardiff of criminal misconduct originating in 'disgraceful anti-Irish feeling'. He insisted that there was sufficient evidence of dereliction of duty to warrant a government investigation.[58] As E.J. Hobsbawm pointed out in his study of the 'city mob', there existed a potential body of rioters in all important pre-industrial cities where the police and military were slack. Although Cardiff in the late 1840s did not feature all the characteristics of a 'pre-industrial city', it is possible nevertheless to discern here some of the key characteristics of the city mob as described by Hobsbawm,[59] especially the complicity of the police in assisting members of the crowd to search the Catholic chapel, and, by their inaction, the tacit acceptance by the mayor and magistrates of the validity of communal justice until the prospect of a counter-disturbance by the navvies materialised. The riot was a manifestation of popular anger, representing both a severe warning to the Irish and a stern reproach to the authorities for failing to arrest the murderer.

However, despite the importance of the specific urban context in the development of the riot, its consequences were not confined to Cardiff, as was shown by the ripples of hostility to the Irish which spread out to other towns in the region in the wake of the murder. At the end of November 1848, Irish people leaving Sunday Mass at the Catholic chapel in Dowlais, near Merthyr, were attacked 'by a party of idle fellows', forcing them to flee for shelter; the clash was attributed to a combination of factors, including the murder in Cardiff and a reduction of wages in the iron industry, for which the Irish were

57 Ibid.; *Monmouthshire Merlin*, 2 Dec. 1848; *The Tablet*, 23 Dec. 1848.
58 *The Tablet*, 18 Nov. 1848.
59 E.J. Hobsbawm, *Primitive Rebels* (Manchester, 1959); Gwyn A. Williams has written that the city mob existed in 'close symbiosis' with city government, 'The Primitive Rebel and the History of the Welsh' in G.A. Williams, *The Welsh in Their History* (London, 1982), p. 4.

blamed.[60] This incident was closely followed by the attempted murder of an Irish girl at Cardiff and the manslaughter of an Irish hawker at Newport, allegedly simply because he was Irish.

These disturbances underline the interplay between local grievances and wider regional developments. They took place against a background of large-scale immigration, an acute strain on the Poor Law, the severe overcrowding of lodging-houses, and an increasing awareness of the dangers to public health posed by overcrowding and insanitary living conditions. Moreover, the situation was further complicated by the disruption resulting from the construction of the South Wales Railway along the south Wales coast – another regional development with far-reaching implications for social relations in particular localities – and the presence of a large body of mobile Irish navvies. Under these circumstances the Irish became a focus for the tensions generated by a sudden increase in population and rapid urbanisation.

Of course, regional analysis of the Famine Irish should not be carried out at the expense of studying the particularity of their experience in individual towns, but it should also be remembered that during the Famine years and their immediate aftermath there were clear linkages between urban and regional developments which ensured that no locality existed in isolation. By the same token, the mere presence of Irish immigrants was a reminder that no region existed in isolation either, especially those regions with direct access to the sea. There is no simple, unproblematic narrative of Irish immigration and settlement in mid-Victorian Britain, nor is the challenge of attempting a meaningful overall understanding which also pays due attention to the plurality of regional differences unique. Other historians have attempted to confront the implications of regional diversity in their own ways. In the context of the social history of nineteenth-century Wales, for example, one historian has written that systematic analysis from the perspective of the region is an important step towards constructing a 'coalescing and conflicting totality' from a plurality of regions and communities.[61] In a similar way, the history of the Irish in mid-nineteenth-century Britain can be seen as a patchwork of different experiences refracted through the prism of regional economies and social structures. The terms on which the Irish experienced British society (if such a phrase is at all meaningful during this period) varied from one town and region to another, depending on the numbers employed and the kind of employment they entered, as well as cultural factors deriving from religion and received attitudes to outsiders. Only when the regional dimension is fully recognised can we begin to construct a broader picture revealing the 'coalescing and conflicting totality' of Irish immigration to Britain.

60 *Cardiff and Merthyr Guardian*, 8 Dec. 1848.
61 Neil Evans, 'Writing the social history of modern Wales: approaches, achievements and problems', *Social History*, vol. 17 (1992), p. 489.

Irish immigrants in Cornwall: the Camborne experience, 1861–82

Louise Miskell

Cornwall is one corner of the country which has been largely untouched by the burgeoning historiography of the Irish in Britain. In one sense its absence is understandable: the county was home to only 1693 Irish-born residents in 1881 (0.5% of the population).[1] The far greater numerical strength of Irish communities elsewhere promised much richer rewards for historians engaged in the study of the Irish immigration. This explains its absence from modern Irish immigrant historiography, but interestingly, the subject has also been overlooked in other quarters. John Denvir gave little more than a passing mention to the Irish in Camborne in his survey of the Irish in Britain conducted at the end of the nineteenth century.[2] Likewise, few historians of Cornwall have regarded the Irish immigrant population of the county worthy of detailed study. Instead, the relative absence of migration of any kind into Cornwall has been held up as a feature of the county's image as insular and peripheral to social and economic developments elsewhere in Britain.[3] As a result of this dearth of interest, Cornwall's role as a destination for Irish immigrants to Britain is almost unknown.

Given its anonymity in terms of Irish immigrant history, it comes as quite a surprise to find that the town of Camborne, at the centre of Cornwall's tin mining region, presents a challenge to much of the received wisdom of Irish immigrant historiography. Camborne was home to the largest Irish contingent of any town in Cornwall and, as such, was recognised within the region as an important destination for Irish immigrants.[4] For this reason alone it merits study, but closer examination further reveals that the settlement patterns of the Irish who lived there in the second half of the nineteenth century present a contrast to the conventional image built up from studies of larger Irish

1 Census of England and Wales, 1881, *Ages, Civil Conditions, Occupations, Birthplaces* (London, 1883), p. 207.
2 J. Denvir, *The Irish in Britain from the Earliest Times to the Fall of Parnell* (London, 1894), p. 402.
3 See for example, W.M. Brayshay, 'The Demography of Three West Cornwall Mining Communities, 1851–1871: A Society in Decline' (University of Exeter PhD thesis, 1977), p. 226; P. Payton, *The Making of Modern Cornwall* (Redruth, 1992), p. 109.
4 See *Cornish Telegraph*, 27 April 1882, p. 4.

immigrant populations. According to this view the Irish in Britain were a largely unskilled group, primarily based in built-up urban areas near the centre of towns and often residing in housing built by their employers. The Camborne Irish, in contrast, were resident mainly in hamlets on the outskirts of the town in cottages they had built for themselves. They worked in agricultural as well as industrial jobs and were to be found at all levels of the occupational ladder. Perhaps most intriguingly, this small Irish population was the target of rioting in 1882. The timing of this incident upsets the favoured chronology of anti-Irish rioting in Britain, which sees disturbances concentrated around the middle-decades of the nineteenth century, declining thereafter along with the falling rate of Irish immigration into Britain after 1861.[5] A further problem is posed by the difficulty of interpreting the anti-Irish outbreak in Camborne as a labour dispute or a religious riot, the two most popular causes ascribed to anti-Irish riots in Britain.[6] Instead the Camborne riot makes sense only in the context of traditional Cornish patterns of protest.

This said, the aim of this chapter is not to attempt to knock down all of the carefully constructed images of the Irish in Britain based on big-city studies or British-wide surveys, even if that were possible. Rather, the intention is to add diversity to the picture by widening the net of Irish immigrant history to include the likes of the Camborne Irish. Moreover it will be argued that the models of settlement and host-immigrant relations which apply to other, bigger centres of Irish immigration, should not necessarily be regarded as typical of the Irish experience in all parts of Britain.

SOCIAL AND ECONOMIC BACKGROUND, 1860–80

Camborne was located at the heart of Cornwall's metal mining region which, by the second half of the nineteenth century, was experiencing an economic crisis. There was a general decline in the state of the industry after the mid-1860s when the copper lodes, which had sustained Cornish mining for decades, were gradually exhausted and the exploitation of the deeper tin seams became the new focus of production. The extraction of tin from the deeper levels was a costly process. Many of Cornwall's smaller and less profitable mines could not afford to adapt and were forced to close. Compared to some towns Camborne fared relatively well during the crisis years of the copper collapse. Several of her mines had plentiful reserves of tin which could be exploited, but by the latter decades of the nineteenth century the town's economic security became increasingly linked to the fortunes of Dolcoath, her largest and most

5 See for example, G. Davis, *The Irish in Britain* (Dublin, 1991), p. 121.
6 See for example A. O'Day, 'Varieties of anti-Irish behaviour in Britain, 1846–1922', in P. Panayi (ed.), *Racial Violence in Britain, 1849–1950* (Leicester, 1993), p. 32.

prosperous mine. Contemporaries saw little future for the town without it: 'The prosperity of Camborne does almost entirely depend upon Dolcoath. If Dolcoath should by any chance be unbottomed and cease to work, misery and poverty would be the result in Camborne and the neighbourhood'.[7]

Given this level of economic dependency the slump in tin prices as a result of increasing foreign competition, which hit the Cornish tin industry hard from the mid-1870s, was a serious threat to the future prosperity of Camborne and other towns which had managed to survive previous economic blows. Further mine closures ensued throughout Cornwall and overall the mining industry became a less significant employer in the county. Mark Brayshay's study of the effects of the Cornish mining decline on the populations of Camborne, Redruth and St Just revealed that the proportion of the workforce employed in mining declined from 58.57% in 1851 to 49.37% in 1871.[8]

These economic factors had important implications for demographic trends in Cornwall. Friedlander and Roshier, in their work on internal migration in England and Wales in the century after 1851, categorised different counties according to their rates of inward migration and revealed the extent of regional variation.[9] Cornwall experienced a net loss in population in every decade from 1851 to 1901. In this period the collapse of the mining industry prompted mass emigration. One historian estimated that from 1866 to 1881 one-third of the mining population of the county emigrated.[10] Yet even before the mining collapse Cornwall never attracted immigrants on the same scale as other industrialised regions of Britain. Mark Brayshay regarded this lack of immigrant workers as remarkable given the established nature of the mining industry in the region, and argued that it was a consequence of the county's insularity.[11] Other historians have also identified Cornwall's geographical isolation as a factor in its failure to attract migrants. Philip Payton, for example, has argued that the 'peripheral' nature of the county had significant repercussions for economic and social homogeneity.[12] Although there was considerable population movement inside the county, migrants from other parts of Britain were scarce. Even in areas like south Wales and the Midlands which developed trading links with the Cornish mining industry, there was no significant trend of migration to the county. An analysis of birthplaces of the population resident in Cornwall illustrates this more clearly: in 1881, 89.4% of the population enumerated in

---

7 *West Briton*, 22 Feb. 1883.
8 Brayshay, p. 296.
9 D. Friedlander and R.J. Roshier, 'A study of internal migration in England and Wales: Part 1', *Population Studies*, 19, part 3 (March 1966), pp 239–79.
10 Brayshay, p. 255.
11 Ibid., pp 226–7.
12 Payton, p. 77.

Cornwall were also born there.[13] The immigrant population of the county which made up the remaining 10% was dominated by short distance migrants from neighbouring counties in the south-west of England.

Against this background of economic depression, mass emigration and demographic insularity, the presence of a small Irish contingent in Camborne can be seen as a significant immigrant minority. It is in this regional context, rather than the wider picture of the Irish in Britain as a whole, that the Camborne Irish must be examined.

PATTERNS OF IRISH IMMIGRATION AND SETTLEMENT
IN CAMBORNE, 1861–81

The Irish-born population of the town in the second half of the nineteenth century came mainly from the south-western counties of Ireland such as Cork, Waterford and Limerick which were within easiest reach of Cornwall. As might be expected, this was a characteristic shared by Irish immigrant populations in other parts of the south west such as South Wales and Bristol,[14] but it was not typical of Britain as a whole. David Fitzpatrick found that the two most popular counties of origin for Irish immigrants to England and Wales were Mayo and Kildare; Cork was only the fifth most common county overall.[15]

Many of the Irish who came to Camborne migrated in family groups in the immediate post-Famine period, at a time when Cornish metal mining was a thriving industry. This can be shown by analysing information on the ages and birthplaces of children co-resident with Irish immigrant parents.[16] Using data from the 1861 and 1881 census enumerators, books, children co-resident with Irish-born parents in Camborne were identified and divided into six age-groups: 0–5 years, 6–10 years, 11–15 years, 16–20 years, 21–25 years and over 25 years. In addition, they were divided according to their place of birth into a number of groups: those born in the town of enumeration, those born elsewhere in the same county, those born elsewhere in England and Wales and those born in Ireland. The results were arranged in tabular form (figures 1 and 2).

13 Census of England and Wales, 1881, *Ages, Civil Conditions, Occupations, Birthplaces* (London, 1883), p. 207.
14 See for example D. Large, 'The Irish in Bristol, 1851', in Roger Swift and Sheridan Gilley (eds), *The Irish in the Victorian City* (London, 1985), pp 37–58.
15 D. Fitzpatrick, 'A curious middle place: the Irish in Britain, 1871–1921', in Roger Swift and Sheridan Gilley (eds), *The Irish in Britain, 1815–1939* (London, 1989), p 19.
16 For this analysis I have followed the method used in M. Sill, 'Mid-Nineteenth Century Labour Mobility: The Case of the Coalminers of Hetton-Le-Hole, Co. Durham', *Local Population Studies*, vol. 22 (Spring 1979), pp 44–50.

Figure 1: Camborne 1861

Birthplace	Age Group						Totals
	0–5	6–10	11–15	16–20	21–25	25+	
Camborne	30	20	2	2	1	0	55
Ireland	3	5	16	30	3	4	61
Cornwall (other)	12	6	2	4	0	0	24
England & Wales	3	10	7	3	0	1	24
Total	48	41	27	39	4	5	164

Figure 2: Camborne 1881

Birthplace	Age Group						Totals
	0–5	6–10	11–15	16–20	21–25	25+	
Camborne	27	27	27	18	4	1	104
Ireland	2	3	3	3	5	1	17
Cornwall (other)	1	1	0	2	3	1	8
England & Wales	0	1	1	1	0	0	3
Total	30	32	31	24	12	3	132

Source: Census enumerators' books for Camborne, 1861 and 1881.

The results offer a number of clues to the pattern of Irish migration and settlement in Camborne. Ireland was the birthplace of the majority of children in 1861, suggesting that a high proportion of the Irish immigrant population in Camborne migrated from Ireland in family groups. There was also a clear age distinction between the co-resident children born in Ireland and those born in Camborne. The majority of the former group were between the ages of 11 and 20 in 1861, while those born in Camborne were almost exclusively younger than 10 years. This indicates that a number of Irish immigrant families in the town in 1861 may have included older children born in Ireland along with younger ones born in Camborne itself. It also suggests that few of the Irish families had been in Camborne for much longer than ten years at that time. By 1881 however, the picture had changed. The majority of children co-resident with Irish-born parents were born in Camborne. The ages of these children were evenly distributed across the age-groups, with almost equal numbers found in each age category up to 20 years. This was indicative of a well-established Irish immigrant population, the majority of whom were long-time residents of Camborne. In contrast, the number of co-resident children born in Ireland was negligible. Instead the Irish immigrant population of Camborne was by this time dominated by a well-established group of migrants who had settled and raised their families in the town.

Another important issue raised by these figures is the significance of second generation migrants as a proportion of the Irish population of the town by 1881. Most recent historical studies of the Irish in Britain acknowledge the importance of the decendants of Irish-born immigrants in Britain's Irish population by the end of the nineteenth century, but because of the difficulties of accurately enumerating those who were Irish by descent, few historians have confronted the issue head on. Steven Fielding, in his work on the Irish in Manchester and Salford, has suggested that by the latter decades of the century, the number of Irish-born immigrants in British towns should be doubled to give an estimate of the total Irish population, taking into account second generation migrants.[17] The very small Irish population such as that at Camborne, however, makes possible a more detailed analysis of the second-generation Irish contingent. On the strength of such an analysis, the second-generation Irish at Camborne emerge as an even larger proportion of the Irish population than Fielding's calculation methods would suggest. Second generation migrants who lived with their Irish-born parents are easily identifiable in the census enumerators' returns. Figure 2 shows there were 115 such children in Camborne in 1881. This figure already exceeded the number who were Irish by birth, which in 1881 was just ninety-three. In addition to this a further thirty inhabitants were identified as Irish on the strength of their surnames. These included Timothy McCarthy, a sailor, enumerated in Wellington Street, Camborne in 1881, and Edith Connor, a live-in domestic servant at the Commercial Hotel in Trelowarren Street. This brings the total number of second generation Irish to 145 and, added to the Irish-born contingent, amounts to a total Irish population of over 230. This figure should be regarded as a useful estimate rather than an accurate calculation of the total Irish population in Camborne in 1881. In particular, the identification of Irish descendants on the basis of surnames alone is far from ideal, but it is certainly more accurate to use an estimated figure for the total Irish population, than to ignore the second generation altogether. Contemporary comments show that local people drew little distinction between first and second generation migrants in identifying the Irish population of Camborne in the 1880s.[18] Perhaps historians should follow their lead.

Clues to the mobility of the parent migrants are also implicit in the figures. In 1861 the number of children born outside Camborne in other parts of

17 S.J. Fielding, *Class and Ethnicity. Irish Catholics in England, 1880–1914* (Manchester, 1992), p. 14.
18 See for example, *Royal Cornwall Gazette*, 28 April 1882.

Cornwall and throughout England and Wales was almost one-third of the total number of co-resident children. This suggested that a substantial number of Irish immigrants enumerated in Camborne in 1861 came to the town after spending time elsewhere in Cornwall or in other parts of Britain. Parts of southern England including Kent, Sussex, London, and Gloucestershire, all figured among the birthplaces of co-resident children. Those who resided elsewhere in Cornwall before reaching Camborne, did so in a handful of smaller mining towns and villages such as St Austell, St Hilary and Gwithian. On the basis of these findings, there is no evidence to support the comments of Mark Brayshay on the presence of the Irish in Cornwall, that 'The development of an Irish community in Cornwall resulted from a secondary movement of such immigrants, who may have first settled in Merseyside or the Midlands.'[19] Figure 2 however, suggests that by 1881 the movement of Irish people to Camborne through other parts of the country had declined. The likely explanation for this was the depression in the Cornish mining industry over the intervening decades which left Camborne, the centre of the Cornish mining industry, a much less attractive prospect for migrants than it had been earlier in the century with the result that fewer newcomers were attracted from outside the town. The decline in the numbers of children born outside Camborne to Irish parents who later moved to the town is indicative of this.

The structure of urban development in Cornwall's metal mining towns was quite different from other industrial areas. The copper and tin mines which provided the main source of employment were located on the fringes of the town. Dolcoath, Stray Park, Cook's Kitchen and a host of smaller mines on the outskirts of Camborne became the focus for small pockets of residential housing, including the hamlets of Coombe and Pengegon, which were between a mile and a mile and a half distant from the town centre. The result was a town with a small commercial centre which only came to life on market days when produce from the surrounding countryside was brought in and sold at the market hall. With little in the way of civic or municipal buildings and with half of its population located in these satellite villages there was little sign of a strong urban identity in Camborne. There was also a marked difference in the standard of housing found in the town centre streets and those located in the outlying hamlets. The Royal Commission on the Housing of the Working Classes heard evidence to this effect from a local resident: 'The business part of the town, which yields the best rents, belongs to Mr Bassett, as the landlord. The poorer part of the town belongs to Mr Vyall Vivian of Trelowarren. His houses are all built upon three lives.'[20]

19 Brayshay, p. 233. Although Brayshay's study area also included Redruth and St Just, there is no reason to suppose that their patterns of Irish immigration would have differed substantially from those of Camborne.

20 P.P., 1884–5, vol. XXX, *Report of the Royal Commission on the Housing of the Working Classes*, question 8028.

The 'three lives' system was the most common form of property holding in Camborne. The tenant would lease a piece of land from the landlord for the duration of three named lives, after which time the land and any property which stood on it would return to the landlord. Uncertainty over the exact length of the lease often meant that houses built on three lives were poorly maintained. Tenants were reluctant to make too many costly repairs and improvements to property which might revert to the landlord at any time.

Figure 3: Residential location of the Irish-born compared
with the total population, 1861

	Total population	% of total population	Irish-born	% of Irish-born
Town	7206	51.3	50	23.9
Outlying Hamlets	6848	48.7	159	76.1

Source: Census enumerators' books for Camborne, 1861.

Figure 4: Residential location of the Irish-born compared
with the total population, 1881

	Total population	% of total population	Irish-born	% of Irish-born
Town	7372	54.2	86	36.1
Outlying Hamlets	6274	46.1	152	63.9

* Includes first and second generation Irish.
Source: Census enumerators' books for Camborne, 1881.

Figures from the census enumerator's books, displayed in figures 3 and 4, show that the Camborne Irish lived predominantly in these satellite villages rather than in the town centre streets. While the town population as a whole was divided roughly in two between those who resided in the town centre and those who lived in the surrounding villages, for the Irish, the distribution was weighted much more heavily in favour of the hamlets. In particular, the hamlets of Brea, Coombe and Pengegon, located between a mile and a mile and a half to the south and east of the town centre, were favoured locations for Irish residential settlement. In 1861 over 50 % of the Irish-born population of Camborne were to be found residing in these three villages. By 1881, the residential patterns of the second generation Irish and the remaining migrants of Irish birth were strikingly similar to those of 1861. Again they were to be found predominantly in the satellite villages rather than in the town centre streets. There were exceptions to this of course. Some Irish lived and worked in central Camborne amongst neighbours who were almost exclusively Cornish in origin. William Cahill, a railway clerk, and his three daughters were the sole Irish inhabitants of Adelaide Street in 1881. Another exception was Bridget Jennings, an Irish-born draper who lived at 7 Union Street. In general though, the preference of the Irish was for the outlying hamlets which were convenient for the mines where many of them worked and where the typical four roomed miners' cottages could be built relatively cheaply on land leased directly from the local landlord.[21] In this they differed considerably from the typical residential arrangements of their compatriots in other British towns where Irish settlement in town centre streets and courts, often in employer-built housing, was much more the norm.

Historical work on Irish residential patterns has been dominated by the search for signs of concentration or dispersal; segregation or integration. Underpinning this whole debate was the idea of community as a residential area, but recently computer analysis of residential data from census enumerators' returns has undermined the idea of homogenous Irish residential communities.[22] As a result, historians who have continued to use the term 'community' to describe Irish settlement in nineteenth- century Britain have shifted the emphasis away from residential proximity to take into account factors such as social networks and support systems as evidence of Irish communities.[23]

In Camborne the conventional idea of an Irish residential community in the second half of the nineteenth century was statistically untenable. The Irish were comfortably outnumbered by the host population in every part of the parish. Even in the single enumeration district which encompassed Brea, Coombe and Pengegon where the Irish were at their most numerous, they still numbered fewer that 8% of the population in 1861. Despite this, contemporaries clearly identified Irish quarters in Camborne. Brea in particular was referred to as an 'Irish quarter' or an 'Irish settlement'.[24] In 1861 the concentration of over half the town's Irish-born residents in these few villages afforded some justification for the use of such terms but by the 1880s, when these comments were made, the idea of an Irish quarter in the town was numerically implausible. To explain

---

21 See M.E. Weaver, 'Industrial housing in West Cornwall', *Industrial Archaeology* 3, no 1 (1966), p. 28.

22 See for example, C. Pooley, 'Segregation or integration? The residential experience of the Irish in mid-Victorian Britain', in Swift and Gilley, (eds) *The Irish in Britain*, p. 79.

23 For example, L.H. Lees, *Exiles of Erin. Irish Migrants in Victorian London* (Manchester, 1979), p. 63.

24 See for example, *Cornish Telegraph*, 27 April 1882; *Royal Cornwall Gazette*, 21 April, 1882.

why such notions existed it is necessary to take a different approach to contemporary perceptions of the 'Irish territory' in Camborne. The fact that local people associated the Irish with particular residential areas had more to do with local memory than with statistics. An element of continuity over time in the patterns of residential settlement adopted by first and second generation Irish was probably the crucial factor in shaping local perceptions of Irish residential territory in the town. The continued preference of the Irish for the same residential areas created a long-term association between Irish inhabitants and specific districts of the town. This was sufficient to ensure that certain residential districts were identified as Irish territory despite the fact that the Irish never came close to forming a majority of the population in any part of the town.

Another aspect of Irish settlement patterns in Camborne which contrasts with the traditional image of the Irish experience in Britain is their occupational profile. John Denvir referred to his countrymen in Camborne as an 'Irish mining community'.[25] This description suggests a kind of social homogeneity by implying that the tin mining industry was the focus of their economic interests and a source of communal identity for Irish immigrants. Other contemporary accounts portrayed Irish workers in Camborne as predominantly unskilled. One Irish newspaper concluded that 'The Irishmen are merely the heavers of stone and the drawers of the burden. The Cornishmen are the skilled miners ... although there are many Irishmen skilled in the business. The young Irishmen were beginning, few as they were, to compete with the Cornishmen.'[26] In fact, this was not the case. The Irish residents of the town were engaged in a variety of occupations throughout the period under study, and never resembled an homogenous social or occupational group. It was true that the majority of the Irish engaged in the tin mining industry were employed as semi-skilled workers, either at the surface or underground, but these workers never accounted for more than one third of the Irish workforce as a whole in the period under study. Others took up non-industrial occupations. Some were employed in trades such as carpentry and drapery and others worked on the land. Census enumerators' books for Camborne commonly recorded Irish households which contained both agricultural and industrial workers. The household headed by Honora Heffin, a widowed Irish resident of Union Street in 1861, is a good example of this occupational mix. She was employed as a charwoman while her two co-resident nephews worked as miners. She also accommodated two female Irish lodgers, one a farm hand and the other a mine labourer. In other cases, whole families were employed as agricultural workers. At Rosewarne Downs in the hamlet of Tuckingmill, an Irishman and his two sons were all employed as farm labourers. In the town centre, meanwhile, Irish miners were to be found living alongside Irish shopkeepers.

25 Denvir, p. 402.
26 *Freeman's Journal*, 22 April 1882.

These diverse occupational patterns reflected the influence of Camborne's rural hinterland on its employment market. Nineteenth-century Cornwall was a strange mix of rural and urban. Industrial and agricultural interests co-existed and sometimes overlapped. It was common, for example, for workers employed in the mines to lease small plots of land on which they cultivated much of their own food.[27] Some miners also had shares in fishing boats, giving them access to an alternative source of income in the pilchard fishing season. The political representation of the Cornish constituencies reflected this balance between rural and industrial interests. The Liberal Party in the constituency of West Cornwall, was particularly sensitive to the need to appeal to both rural and industrial interests, with the result that the district's two MPs were usually an industrialist and a landowner.[28] Cornwall was not unique in preserving this close relationship between agricultural and industrial interests. Michael Anderson's description of Preston in 1851 as 'a half way house'[29] between rural, pre-industrial and urban, industrial England seems a phrase which could equally be applied to Camborne, but essentially it was an experience untypical of other industrialised regions in Britain.

Thus in their occupational patterns, as in their residential characteristics, the Camborne Irish did not conform to the traditional image of urban, industrial Irish immigrant populations in Britain. The fact that they adapted so many aspects of their settlement patterns to suit prevailing social and economic conditions in the town might be seen as a sign that they were a well-integrated group which adjusted well to the environment in which they found themselves. But it is difficult to reconcile such an image of social integration and harmony with the events of April 1882, when the small Irish population of Camborne were the target of rioting in the town.

THE ANTI-IRISH RIOT, CAMBORNE 1882

On 19 April 1882, Mr Cornish, clerk to the magistrates at Camborne, wrote a letter to the Home Secretary, Sir William Harcourt. It read: 'Sir, I regret to inform you that a riot of somewhat serious character occurred at Camborne in this division last night. The cause was apparently an ill feeling existing between

---

27 See D. Rose, 'Home ownership, subsistence, and historical change: the mining district of West Cornwall in the late Nineteenth Century', in P. Williams and N. Thrift (eds), *Class and Space. The Making of Urban Society* (London, 1987), pp 119–20.

28 E.K.G. Jaggard, 'Political continuity and change in late Nineteenth Century Cornwall', *Parliamentary History*, vol. 11, pt 2 (1992), p. 222.

29 M. Anderson, 'Household structure and the Industrial Revolution; Mid-Nineteenth Century Preston in comparative perspective', in P. Laslett (ed.), *Household and Family in Past Time* (Cambridge, 1972), p. 215.

the native and Irish population of the district in and around Camborne'.[30]
Newspapers the next morning carried alarming reports of Irish homes
'completely wrecked'[31] and of damage to the local Roman Catholic Church
where 'the windows were smashed and after repeated efforts the doors were
forced',[32] and of the fear of the town's Irish population. According to the *West
Briton*, 'Nearly all the Irish hid themselves in engine-houses. Others left for the
district of Wendron, and many it is believed, would stop out all night in some
thicket or other, rather than encounter the infuriated gangs.'[33]

The news from Camborne provoked a swift reaction from the press and the
authorities. Correspondents from *The Times*, the *Freeman's Journal* and a host
of Cornish newspapers flocked to the town; the Home Secretary faced a
barrage of questions in the House of Commons and over 100 police from the
Cornish County Constabulary, along with some 80 special constables, were
drafted in on the morning of Wednesday 19 April.

The trouble began in Camborne at the town magistrates' court where a case
against two Irishmen, Daniel Corney and John McCarthy, was being heard.
The two men who, as one newspaper pointed out, were 'said to be Irish but are
really natives of Cornwall',[34] were charged with assaulting a local man named
Richard Edwards on the evening of 3 April 1882. According to local press
reports, the incident became a topic of heated discussion in the town during the
two weeks that elapsed between the perpetration of the offence and the
appearance of the two accused in court: 'All that time the matter had been
rankling in the minds of the lower classes of the Camborne population.'[35] The
two defendants, it was said, had been part of a gang of five rough Irishmen who
had set upon the defenceless Edwards, innocently making his way home from a
public house. On Tuesday 18 April, hundreds of people crowded into the court
and the Market Square outside, interested not in hearing the evidence against
the two accused but rather in seeing that a suitable punishment was imposed on
them by the magistrates. The outcome of the trial saw Corney and McCarthy
found guilty and given sentences of two months and six weeks respectively. In
delivering their sentence, the magistrates declared that it should be sufficient
to quell the tensions that had emerged between the Irish and Cornish since the
beginning of the case: 'We believe the case to have excited a good deal of feeling
in the parish, and we trust that now we have endeavoured to deal fairly and

---

30 PRO HO144/97/A15859, 19 April 1882, letter from Mr Cornish to Sir William
    Harcourt.
31 *Western Morning News*, 19 April 1882.
32 *West Briton*, 20 April 1882.
33 Ibid.
34 *Royal Cornwall Gazette*, 21 April 1882.
35 *West Briton*, 27 April 1882.

impartially towards all concerned, the feeling will subside'.[36] Instead it had the opposite effect. Far from curtailing animosities, the conviction and sentencing of the men by the town magistrates were deemed inadequate. Had they been committed to stand trial at the next quarter sessions, a higher penalty could have been imposed.

The crowd outside the courtroom, already incensed by what they perceived as the leniency of the sentences, were further angered when one of the defence witnesses, another Irishman named Lawrence Driscoll, emerged from the court: 'There was a disposition among many in the mob to disperse without any further demonstration, but at this moment, the man Driscoll foolishly threw out a challenge to fight.'[37] In return for his defiant behaviour, Driscoll was pursued by the crowd and dealt a sound beating. One witness saw what happened after the attack: 'Driscoll was brought out of the saw mill yard and led as far as Pengegon. I saw some blood on his face. He was led by the crowd. It appeared as though they had given him a good thrashing and then led him home.'[38]

Corney and McCarthy, meanwhile, were safely conducted away from the court. The crowd dispersed from the Market Square but, still angered at the events of the afternoon, a large group set off for the villages of Coombe and Brea, two locally recognised 'Irish settlements' about a mile and a half outside the centre of Camborne. Contrary to some early reports there was no evidence of extensive damage to property or injury to persons at Brea or Coombe. Rather, the crowds who made repeated visits to these villages and also to Pengegon on the Wednesday and Thursday evenings, sought to intimidate the Irish rather than to attack them physically. One newspaper reported that the Irish were kept 'In a constant state of terror through the threats openly shouted by miners as they passed their houses. The general cry was, "Here's another Irish. We'll give 'em Camborne tonight".'[39]

On the afternoon of Tuesday 18 April, while gangs visited the outlying villages, a crowd headed for the mines around Camborne in the hope of finding more Irishmen. They went first to Dolcoath, the largest of the town's mines, where 'An Irishman named John Sullivan of good character was brutally used. He was first severely beaten, and then for the diversion of his assailants, was made to go down on his knees and say a prayer.'[40] Cook's Kitchen mine was also visited on the afternoon after the trial by, 'a strong and violent gang'.[41] There an Irishman by the name of John Murray was attacked. Another named John Gibbons was pursued by the crowd and ran into the account house in

36 *Cornish Telegraph*, 20 April 1882.
37 *West Briton*, 20 April 1882.
38 Ibid.
39 *Royal Cornwall Gazette*, 28 April 1882.
40 *West Briton*, 20 April 1882.
41 *Royal Cornwall Gazette*, 21 April 1882.

search of protection. An account of this incident was given by the mine agent, Captain Charles Thomas:

> About 4 p.m., an Irishman came into the counting house and said that the crowd were after him. I told him to sit down as no one would harm him in there … I went out, half dressed as I was, and stood on the steps outside the door … There was a crowd in front of the account house door, about 200. They were excited but not disorderly and did no harm at our mine. Eight or ten of them mounted the steps but I did not recognise one. They demanded admission into the account house, and said they were searching for Irishmen. I said they should not go in.[42]

This initiative by the mine agent not only provided protection for the Irishman, but also illustrated the respect and authority commanded by senior figures at the mines. Captain Charles Thomas, along with a number of other prominent mine managers, were sworn in as special constables to assist the police in controlling the anti-Irish disturbances. According to the *West Briton* this was 'undoubtedly calculated to have a wholesome influence on the crowd, which was mostly composed of men and boys who are under the supervision of the mines'.[43] Their enrolment as special constables was an important indication of the extent to which the riots were condemned by Camborne's 'respectable' residents. Moreover, the fact that a number of Irish sought protection in their workplaces testifies to the good relationship between the Irish and their employers. In a letter to the MP for Cornwall West, Camborne's magistrate's clerk reported that a number of them took refuge in the vicinity of the mines: 'One family spent the night in a croft, another in a quarry-pit and the Irish miners in Cook's Kitchen mine, escaping the rioters by barely a minute, hid themselves in a smithy'.[44] There seemed to be a confidence among them that in the company of their employers and in their workplaces they would be safe from attack.[45]

Two further disturbances took place on the evening of Tuesday 18 April. One occurred at the home of Major Walter Pike in Pendarves Road, in Camborne town centre. Major Pike was a long-time resident, although not a native of the town. He came to Camborne to take up a position as purser in the local mines. He was not Irish, but was one of Camborne's more prominent Roman Catholic residents. On the evening of Tuesday 18 April, his house was surrounded by a crowd of people who hurled stones, smashing several panes of glass. Further damage to the property was prevented by Major Pike's

---

42 *West Briton*, 27 April 1882.
43 Ibid., 27 April 1882.
44 PRO HO144/97/A15859, 23 April 1882, letter from Mr Cornish to Sir John St Aubyn.
45 Likewise during the Tredegar anti-Irish riot in July 1882, Irish families sought refuge in the iron works.

neighbours who stopped the crowd from entering the house and persuaded them to disperse.[46] The second was an attack on Camborne's Roman Catholic Church, situated on Beacon Hill near the town centre. The damage was described by Superintendent Miller of Camborne police: 'The windows, except the stained ones were smashed; the conservatory at the priest's house was also smashed. Inside the church, the confessional was very much broken, and some of the seats broken and thrown down. The railings around the font were torn down.'[47] An Irish woman by the name of Caroline Burns who was in the priest's house next door when the rioters entered the church, described what she saw when she went to investigate what was happening: 'I saw people throwing stones and told them to be quiet; they were from fifteen to twenty years of age and over ... They were throwing stools out of the chapel into the road.'[48]

Contemporary commentators tended to seize upon these two incidents in their search for explanations for the riot. The attack on Major Pike's home was said to have been prompted by the widely-held local belief that he was responsible for importing Irish workers into the area. The *Royal Cornwall Gazette* claimed that, 'Mr Pike had sent for 200 Irish labourers to work at 2 shillings a day'.[49] Other contemporaries also emphasised the issue of economic rivalry as the main cause of Cornish/Irish tensions. The *Freeman's Journal* correspondent noted that younger Irish workers were beginning to challenge locals for the skilled mining jobs, and concluded: 'That this was the origin of the attack upon Edwards I have no doubt'.[50] In a church sermon the vicar of St Just also suggested that economic rivalry lay at the root of the Camborne riot. He interpreted the disturbance as a wages quarrel which had got out of hand.[51] Such comments implied that the problem of Irish immigrant labour in Camborne was a contentious issue which figured highly on the list of grievances felt by locals. In fact this was not the case. The impact of immigrants on the labour market was simply not an issue in Camborne as it was in other industrialised counties of England and Wales. Instead, the presence of Irish immigrant workers by the 1880s was widely acknowledged to be crucial to the working capacity of the mines in Camborne:

> The withdrawal of the Irish from the county would, in the opinion of those experienced enough to judge, open up serious labour difficulties. The Cornish labour market is far from being abundantly supplied at the present moment. The emigration of previous years is not common at present – miners are needed.[52]

46 *West Briton*, 20 April 1882.
47 Ibid., 27 April 1882.
48 Ibid.
49 *Royal Cornwall Gazette*, 21 April 1882.
50 *Freeman's Journal*, 22 April 1882.
51 *Cornish Telegraph*, 27 April 1882.
52 *West Briton*, 27 April 1882.

Contemporary interpretations of the Camborne anti-Irish riot as a 'wages quarrel' owed more to the familiarity and convenience of the labour issue as an explanation for anti-Irish animosity. In Cornwall this was enhanced by news from overseas where the Cornish and Irish did find themselves in competition for similar jobs.[53] Similarly, the attack on the Catholic church was held up as evidence that the rioters were motivated by anti-Catholicism. Catholic churches were a common target for attack during anti-Irish riots in Britain.[54] In Cornwall, where adherence to Wesleyan Methodism was deeply rooted among the mining populations,[55] Catholicism may well have been regarded with some suspicion, even contempt. But several factors suggest that this was not the case in Camborne. No evidence exists of anti-Catholic tension in the town before the outbreak of rioting. The correspondent for the *Freeman's Journal* wrote that 'Father McKey [Camborne's Roman Catholic priest] is personally popular here, and is on the most friendly terms with people of all classes'.[56] In fact, for many local people, the attack on the church was the most regrettable part of the disturbances. On the initiative of local dignitary the earl of Mount Edgecumbe, magistrates and some of the town's more prominent residents, a meeting was held at Abraham's Hotel in Camborne, to discuss ways of making amends to the congregation of the Roman Catholic Church. As a result a fund was set up to raise money for repairs. Father McKey received numerous letters of support as well as independent contributions towards the restoration of the church. The Revd H.S. Fagan, vicar of St Just, made a collection in his church[57] and a minister from Torquay wrote sending a sovereign towards the cost of repairs.[58]

The lack of evidence of labour tensions and anti-Catholic sentiment means that the disturbances cannot be interpreted within the conventional explanatory framework of anti-Irish rioting in Britain. This is hardly surprising given the demographic profile of Cornwall in this period. The lack of immigrants meant that traditional anti-immigrant grievances which fuelled hostility in other parts of Britain, such as their impact upon local labour markets and wage rates, were not really tenable in Cornwall. The lack of immigrants in the county also affected common perceptions of outsiders. Distinctions between the inhabitants of different Cornish parishes and towns were clearer and more pronounced than

53 See G.M. Burke, 'The Cornish Miner and the Cornish Mining Industry, 1870–1921' (University of London PhD thesis, 1981), p. 433.
54 See for example, accounts of attacks on Catholic churches in Tredegar: PRO HO144/100/A18355, 13 July 1882, letter from Fr William Williams to Sir William Harcourt; Brighouse, West Yorkshire: Denvir, p. 296; and in Stockport: P. Millward, 'The Stockport riots, 1852', in Swift and Gilley (eds), *The Irish in the Victorian City*, p. 209.
55 See J.C.C. Probert, *The Sociology of Cornish Methodism* (Redruth, 1971), pp 4–5.
56 *Freeman's Journal*, 21 April 1882.
57 *Royal Cornwall Gazette*, 28 April 1882.
58 *West Briton*, 27 April 1882.

those drawn between Cornwall and other regions of Britain. Parochialism was evident in the intense local rivalries that developed between neighbouring towns and villages. Rivalry between Camborne and Redruth was especially strong, and further west residents of Newlyn and Penzance held deep native antipathies which manifested themselves as late as 1896 during the Newlyn fishermen's riot.[59] The influence of local landlords, which remained virtually unchallenged until the end of the nineteenth century, also underpinned local loyalties.[60] Most were prominent local figures who controlled the lease of land, thus ensuring that the focus of power and authority for the majority of people in Cornwall remained at a local level.

If immigrants were not the traditional focus for suspicion and tensions in Cornwall as they were elsewhere in Britain, then there is a need to look elsewhere for an explanation of the anti-Irish disturbances in Camborne in 1882. The initial grievance against the Camborne Irish was the perceived inadequacy of the punishments dealt out to Corney and McCarthy by the town's magistrates. As far as the crowd thronging the courtroom and the square outside were concerned, justice had not been done. One newspaper correspondent commented perceptively that the rioting which ensued was in part, an attempt 'to supplement the punishment awarded by the magistrates'.[61] Established legal channels were perceived to have failed and collective action was deemed necessary to restore justice.

In order to understand why this perceived failure of the magistrates to dispense justice provoked such a response in Camborne, it is necessary to examine some of the traditions of popular protest in the region and their links with public attitudes to authority. A mistrust of the police and magistrates and the gulf between their perceptions of justice and those of the public were, in fact, familiar themes of group protests in Cornwall. The long tradition of food rioting, which survived well into the nineteenth century in the south west of England, long after it had died out elsewhere, was underpinned by the notion that it was legitimate to resort to riot where there was a need to protect the fundamental right to food. Riot was regarded as a more effective means of redress against high prices and food shortages than the authority of magistrates.

On other occasions there were more direct expressions of mistrust in the effectiveness of the authorities. In Camborne in 1873, rioting broke out against the local police force. The police station was attacked and individual officers were pursued and beaten. The grievances which brought about the attack were based on a perceived misuse of police authority in the town. It was widely felt

---

59 J. Corin, *Fisherman's Conflict. The Story of Newlyn* (Newton Abbot, 1988), pp 69–70.
60 J. Rowe, *Cornwall in the Age of the Industrial Revolution* (Liverpool, 1953), p.83.
61 *Cornish Telegraph*, 20 April 1882.

in the community that overbearing police powers were infringing public rights. A number of prominent citizens refused to be sworn in as special constables to assist the authorities in quelling the disturbances.[62] Against this background of mistrust in the ability of official authorities to uphold the rights of the public, the angry response to the sentences passed on Corney and McCarthy can be seen as an attempt to impose a measure of community justice where magisterial powers had failed.

THE CAMBORNE RIOT IN CONTEXT

The analysis of the causes of the rioting in Camborne in 1882 reveals a difficulty in trying to locate the disturbances within a context of anti-Irish behaviour in Britain. In a number of respects the incident at Camborne differed from the usual pattern of anti-Irish attacks in Britain, where high injury tolls and large scale damage to Irish property was the norm. Very few Irishmen in Camborne, for instance, were physically attacked by rioters. The magistrate's clerk, Mr Cornish, reported to the Home Secretary that, 'the beating of Driscoll was the only personal violence committed'.[63] While press reports found one or two other examples, the general absence of personal attacks on the Irish at Camborne was in stark contrast to the pattern of anti-Irish rioting elsewhere in Britain. At Tredegar in Monmouthshire, where anti-Irish disturbances broke out just three months after those at Camborne, the injury toll was far higher. Fifteen Irishmen were badly hurt in the course of a weekend of rioting and some fifty houses were seriously damaged.[64] In Camborne, physical attacks on the Irish were largely avoided. Instead, protesters attacked their victims verbally, issuing threats and challenges to the Irish on their visitations to Brea and Pengegon. The intention was clearly to intimidate the occupants of the Irish homes they located and, according to reports in the local press, this end was successfully achieved. One Cornish newspaper commented that 'A disgraceful state of terrorism has existed for some days in these villages.'[65]

Compared to the high injury tolls sustained in other anti-Irish riots, the incident in Camborne could be dismissed as something of a non-event. But again traditional forms of protest in Cornwall provide a more instructive context for the interpretation of the disturbances than a comparison with anti-

---

62 For a full account of this incident see *Cornish Telegraph*, 15 October 1873.
63 PRO HO/144/97/A15859, 22 April 1882, letter from Mr Cornish to Sir William Harcourt.
64 For details of this riot see, J. Parry, 'The Tredegar anti-Irish riot of 1882', *Llafur*, vol. 3, no 4 (1983), pp 20–3.
65 *Royal Cornwall Gazette*, 28 April 1882.

Irish rioting elsewhere. The kind of unsensational crowd behaviour witnessed at Camborne was widely acknowledged to be peculiar to Cornwall, unlike the more violent and physically aggressive methods resorted to by protesters elsewhere. The Cornish novelist Henry Dawson Lowry based his last book, *Wheal Darkness*, on the events of the 1882 riot. The reviews written at the time of its publication pointed out that

> The riot is very well described, but the 'up country' reader must be warned not to expect among Cornishmen, even when angered to the point of window-breaking, the reckless ferocity of mobs in some other parts of the world. The natural courtesy of the south-western Celt makes a Cornish mob somewhat unsatisfactory to lovers of sensation.[66]

Threats and intimidation commonly supplanted physical violence against individuals in Cornish riots and disturbances. In particular, the use of intimidation against the Camborne Irish was typical of the threatening tactics employed by food rioters against grain-hoarding farmers. Food rioters in Cornwall and elsewhere in the south west commonly resorted to methods of intimidation in order to achieve their ends. Warning notices were occasionally posted, outlining to farmers the likely consequences awaiting them if they were found to be hoarding grain in order to force up prices, or arranging for it to be exported. In other cases farmers would be intimidated into signing contracts by which they agreed to sell their produce at a fixed price. Roger Wells found evidence of this tactic in his study of food rioting in Devon, Cornwall and Somerset in the 1800 to 1801 period.[67] In Wadebridge in May 1847, food rioters surrounded a cellar where grain was being stored for export, and issued a threat to magistrates that they would break into the cellar unless a guarantee could be given that the food would not be exported.[68] Other forms of intimidation were also commonly used in Cornwall as a means of regulating public behaviour. Effigy-burnings, for example, were relatively common in Cornwall throughout the nineteenth century as a way of warning people to desist from behaviour that was deemed immoral or socially unacceptable.[69] From this perspective the anti-Irish disturbances in Camborne can be seen as part of a distinctive tradition of regional protest characterized by a deep-seated mistrust of authority, a belief in the legitimacy of protest action where lawful methods of redress had failed, and a preference for intimidation rather than direct physical attack. It is against this background, rather than in the context

---

66 *Times Literary Supplement*, 10 Nov. 1927.
67 R. Wells, 'The revolt of the South-West, 1800–1801: a study in English popular protest', *Social History*, vol. 2, no 6 (1977), p. 723.
68 *Times*, 17 May 1847.
69 See *West Briton*, 5 Mar.1883, for an account of an effigy-burning in Camborne.

of anti-Irish rioting elsewhere in Britain, that the events in Camborne in April 1882 can most usefully be interpreted.

There were attempts by the press to locate the Camborne riot in a nation-wide context of anti-Irish sentiment. In the *West Briton* it was claimed that 'What has taken place at Camborne is but typical – no isolated phenomenon but a link in a chain of events'.[70] In the same report it was argued that not only was the behaviour of the Irishmen who attacked Edwards typical of incidents of lawlessness and violence in Ireland, but also that the episode would have prompted a similar response anywhere else in England. The press also drew attention to broad political issues as a source of anti-Irish grievance in Camborne. The *West Briton* alluded to 'The cry of Home Rule and the organised Irish interference in English and Scotch elections'[71] as a cause of growing anti-Irish tension in the town. Similarly, a contributor to the *West Briton's* letters section added that 'Even their members of Parliament are an eyesore and a scandal to the House of Commons, where they have obstructed the progress of the business of state.'[72] Although comments such as these illustrate a local awareness of Irish issues current on the British political agenda, they make unconvincing explanations for the anti-Irish attack in Camborne. References to Irish lawlessness, Home Rule and disruptive political tactics simply added further weight to the arguments of those intent upon justifying the anti-Irish attack.

CONCLUSION

This study of the small Irish population of Camborne in the second half of the nineteenth century reveals a picture of Irish immigration and settlement which was, in a number of key respects, different from the patterns found in larger towns and cities across Britain. The analysis of Irish settlement patterns in Camborne illustrates the necessity of taking full account of local and regional factors in achieving an understanding the nature of the Irish experience there. The decline of the mining industry, the extent to which industrial and agricultural interests co-existed and the absence of a strong urban identity in Camborne all impacted upon Irish settlement in the town, distinguishing it from the experience of Irish communities elsewhere in Britain.

The importance of the regional perspective is further underlined by the analysis of the riot in Camborne in 1882. Cornish traditions of popular protest provide a more usable interpretative framework for the pattern of disturbances

70 *West Briton*, 27 April 1882.
71 Ibid.
72 Ibid., 4 May 1882.

in Camborne, which were less violent and resulted in fewer injuries than other anti-Irish attacks in Britain. Although there were attempts by contemporary commentators to explain the disturbances in the context of traditional anti-Irish grievances such as anti-Catholicism, labour disputes and political tensions, none of these factors sufficiently explain the circumstances of the riot. Instead the customary suspicion of authority and the readiness of people to use collective action in order to assert what were perceived to be legitimate rights were reflected in the causes of the anti-Irish disturbances in the town.

In assessing the significance of this for the study of the Irish in Britain as a whole it is important to keep things in perspective. Clearly we will never find Camborne included in any lists of leading British destinations for Irish immigrants, but this does not mean that it has nothing to add to the debate. Local and regional conditions provide a much more meaningful context in which to assess the impact of immigrant populations. In Cornwall it was the general absence of immigrants from other parts of Britain or from overseas which made the small Irish contingent at Camborne more significant locally than they might appear to the quantitative historian. To recognise this is not to reject the value of larger scale studies or general surveys. Rather it adds greater diversity to the existing picture of Irish immigration and settlement in the latter half of the nineteenth century.

'Sturdy Catholic emigrants': the Irish in early Victorian Birmingham

Carl Chinn

No-one can ignore the Irish in Birmingham today. That was made clear on 15 March 1998 when at least 40,000 people flocked to the city centre to take part in or watch the annual St Patrick's Day Parade. Starting at the Catholic church of St Catherine of Siena on Bristol Street, floats, walkers, marching bands, musicians and dancers from Ireland as well as Birmingham itself made their way to Digbeth, a focal point for the city's Irish. Here they passed 'Mary Donleavy's West of the Shannon', the 'Dubliner' and the offices of the Irish Community Forum before going on towards the Irish Welfare Centre, 'The Roscommon Bar', the Irish Centre and St Anne's in Alcester Street. The committee which organised the event proudly declared that Birmingham's St Patrick's Day Parade was the third largest in the world after those of New York and Dublin.[1]

This celebration both reflected and stressed the importance of the Irish to Birmingham. With a population of over 38,000 they make up 4% of the city's people – a proportion which can be swelled greatly if the daughters and sons of emigrants are included as part of the Irish community.[2] The statistical significance of the Irish is matched by the crucial role they play in the life of Birmingham. Irish men and women are prominent as city councillors and honorary aldermen; whilst Clare Short, MP for Birmingham Ladywood and Minister for Overseas Development, is proud of her Irish heritage. Similarly, Irish journalists are noted contributors to local newspapers; Brummie Irish musicians and dancers have gained international recognition; and Irish businessmen and women are major figures in banking, the building industry, the licensed trade, the travel industry and other sectors of the city's economy.[3]

1 I thank the following people from Birmingham Library Services for their help in providing material essential to this study: Martin Flynn, Central Library Manager and Arts and Lending Services; Richard Albutt, community history development librarian; Patrick Baird, head of service Local Studies and History; and Doreen Hopwood, genealogist. My appreciation also goes to Dave Cross, curator West Midlands Police Museum; Revd T.A. Farrel, Diocesan Treasurer, archdiocese of Birmingham; Agnes and Michael Doyle; and Karen Garry.
2 Iestyn Williams, Dr Mairead Dunne, Professor Mairtin Mac an Ghaill, *Economic Needs of the Irish Community in Birmingham* (Birmingham, 1996), pp 4–5 and 10–12.
3 Of course, not all the Irish in Birmingham have been economically successful. Many are in straitened circumstances and suffer from ill health: Williams, *Economic Needs of the Irish*, pp 14–22, and 'Father Joe's Legacy of Hope', *Evening Mail*, 9 Mar. 1998, pp 6–7.

The visibility of the Irish in late twentieth-century Birmingham heightens their invisibility in the nineteenth century. In the authoritative *History of Birmingham* by Conrad Gill and Asa Briggs there is no reference to the Irish, while in the thoughtful studies of both Victor Skipp and Chris Upton they appear only briefly because of their Catholicism or the dire conditions in which many of them lived.[4] Upton does comment also upon the notorious Murphy Riots of 1867 when serious disturbances broke out between Protestant English and Catholic Irish after the visit of the rabble-rousing Protestant preacher William Murphy. It is this incident which provides the only mention of the Irish in older works such as that by Robert K. Dent.[5]

This non-appearance of the Irish in the main secondary works on the city is reflected in the meagre mention of them in the *Catalogue of the Birmingham Collection*. Brought out by the council in 1918 to assist local studies in the Reference Library by indicating the availability of primary sources, it has only three headings under 'Irish'.[6] Such inattentiveness is surprising given that the presence of the Irish in Victorian Birmingham was comparable statistically to that in the city today. In 1861 their numbers peaked at 11322, making them 3.8% of the population. Both figures dropped in the following years, and the Irish never formed as large a proportion of citizens as they did in Liverpool, Manchester and Glasgow, yet they did constitute by far the largest ethnic minority in Birmingham, and some of them had a considerable impact on local affairs.

The Revd Thomas M. McDonnell was one of those who gained the esteem of the people of Birmingham in general. When he took up his duties in 1824 at St Peter's Catholic church in Broad Street he became the first Irish priest in the town. Soon he gained a wide following both for his determination to help the poor and his fervent support of parliamentary reform. So popular was he that in 1831 he became the only Catholic on the council of the Birmingham Political Union. His forceful and outgoing style was not appreciated by his superiors and

---

4 Conrad Gill, *History of Birmingham*, vol. I, *Manor and Borough to 1865* (London, 1952); Asa Briggs, *History of Birmingham*, vol. II, *Borough and City 1865–1938* (London, 1952); Victor Skipp, *The Making of Modern Birmingham* (Birmingham, 1983), pp 90 and 115; and Chris Upton, *A History of Birmingham* (Sussex, 1993), pp 103–4.

5 Robert K. Dent, *Old and New Birmingham. A History of the Town and its People* (Birmingham, 1880).

6 William Powell and Herbert Maurice Cashmore (compilers), *A Catalogue of the Birmingham Collection Including Printed Books and Pamphlets, Manuscripts, Maps, Views, Portraits, etc.* (Birmingham, 1918), p. 511. Birmingham Libraries are striving to redress the balance and are now targeting sources on the Irish and other ethnic minorities. However, two recent studies are worthy of particular note: Judith Champ, 'Assimilation and Separation: The Catholic Revival in Birmingham, 1650–1850' (University of Birmingham PhD thesis, 1984); Kara Irene Ziesler, 'The Irish in Birmingham, 1870–1970' (University of Birmingham PhD thesis, 1989).

ten years later they transferred him to south west England. Within three days of his leaving over 7000 people – many of them Protestants – had signed petitions asking for his return.[7]

John Frederick Feeney was a contemporary of the battling MacDonnell. A Protestant Irishman, Feeney arrived in the city in 1835 to work as a journalist on a radical newspaper called the *Reformer*. Later he bought the *Birmingham Journal* and through its columns in 1850 he appealed for tolerance when the Pope's decision to set up a hierarchy in England was accompanied by anti-Catholic outbursts. Seven years later Feeney started the *Birmingham Daily Post*, which continues to carry his name on its editorial page. After his death his newspapers were run by his son, whose donations to Birmingham's Museum were so great that a gallery was named after the family.[8]

Sir Charles Haughton Rafter was another Protestant Irishman who had a deep effect on Birmingham and its people. Born in Belfast, he was appointed as Chief Constable to the city's police force in 1899. He held the post for thirty-six years and was praised widely for his excellent police work and for his concern for the welfare both of his men and local children. When he died in 1935 he was acclaimed as 'a great citizen' and as 'one of the finest police officers this country has ever known'.[9] Other outstanding Irishmen included Daniel J. O'Neill, to whom the citizens of Birmingham presented an illuminated address in 1913 recognising his efforts to strive for the social and moral advancement of the people; the Revd Canon O'Sullivan, Vicar General of St Chad's, who was 'deeply beloved by those of his own nationality and faith' and who headed the poll for the first elections to the Birmingham School Board in 1871; Vernon Rigby, a famous singer born in Dundalk but raised in Birmingham; and Dr Murphy, whose medical care was focused on the poverty-stricken and largely English working-class neighbourhood of Floodgate Street in which he 'was loved by all'.[10]

7 Eileen L. Groth, 'The politics of the Bible: radicalism and non-denominational co-operation in the Birmingham Political Union', in R.N. Swanson (ed.), *Unity and Diversity in the Church* (Oxford, 1996), pp 387–97. See also Judith Champ, 'Priesthood and Politics in the Nineteenth Century: The Turbulent Career of Thomas McDonnell', *Recusant History*, vol. 18 (May, 1987), pp 289–303.

8 John Alfred Langford, *Modern Birmingham and its Institutions. A Chronicle of Local Events from 1841 to 1871*, vol. 2 (Birmingham, 1871), pp 337–8; Carl Chinn, 'John Frederick Feeney', *Old Brum Magazine*, 13 Oct. 1997, pp 2–3.

9 'Unstinted Tributes', *Evening Despatch*, 23 Aug. 1935, p. 5.

10 Joseph McKenna, 'The Irish in Birmingham' (unpublished ms, 1991), p. 47.; 'Rev. Canon O'Sullivan', *Birmingham Faces and Places. An Illustrated Local Magazine*, vol. II (Birmingham, 1890), pp 27–9; Thomas McTiernan, 'Integration or Segregation amongst Irish Migrants in Nechells and Duddeston' (University of Birmingham BA Hons dissertation, 1997), p. 5; and Mary Elizabeth Shott, *Brum and Candlelight. A Walk Down Memory Lane* (Studley, 1995), p. 22.

To their number could be added well-known people of Irish descent such as Charlie Mitchell, a celebrated British boxing champion of the late 1800s who fought the famous American, John L. Sullivan; and the Catholic Byrne brothers.[11] Their father had come to Birmingham at least in the 1860s and had been involved in the manufacture of gutta percha and then rubber. He was followed by his sons and in 1896 the tyre-making business of the three younger brothers was bought out by the forerunner of the Dunlop Rubber Company. It is apparent that with their advice and expertise they played a crucial role in the emergence of that enterprise. Indeed the Irish Protestant owners of Dunlop, the Du Cros family, acknowledged that they served their apprenticeship as rubber makers at the works of the Byrnes.[12]

It was Birmingham's reputation as an expanding, industrial city which drew to it Irish migrants. There is little evidence about the pioneers of this movement, although the certificates of settlement for the forty years from 1686 do mention the arrival of a James Wright from Dublin in 1723.[13] He is a solitary figure until the early nineteenth century when the Irish in Birmingham become more apparent. On 12 May 1805 the Franciscans of St Peter's recorded the baptism of Lucia, the daughter of Bartholomew and Catherine Robinson of Ireland. Between then and 25 April 1826 the christenings occurred of a further twenty-four children whose parents came from many parts of Ireland: Carlow, Derry, Donegal, Dublin, Kildare, King's County (Offaly), Leitrim, Limerick, Mayo, Queen's County (Laois), Tipperary, West Meath and Wicklow. Two couples appear twice, suggesting longer-term residence. They were Thomas and Elizabeth Maccormick of Luxlip, Kildare on 19 May 1811 and 1 August 1813; and Michael and Catherine MacDonnel of St Jacob's, Dublin on 29 November 1812 and 13 November 1814. None of these people is listed in contemporary trades directories and as the baptismal registers do not give occupations there is no knowledge of their employment.[14]

The Maccormicks and MacDonnels were part of a small community. Giving evidence to the Select Committee on the Irish Poor in 1834, the Reverend Edward Peach stated that he had ministered to no more than 100 Irish when he took up his post as priest of St Chad's in Bath Street in 1807. This position was transformed about 1826 when 'a vast increase took place so that my chapel

11 A.G. Hales (compiler), 'The Life of Charlie Mitchell (triple champion of the world)' (no date), p. 1 (manuscript supplied by Sam Gregory and Bill Matthews).
12 Joan Skinner, 'Dunlop in Birmingham: the making of an industrial empire', in Barbara Tilson (ed.), *Made in Birmingham*, pp 213–15.
13 W.H.B. Court, *The Rise of the Midland Industries 1600–1838* (London, 1938), p. 49.
14 'The Franciscan Register of St Peter's 1657–1830', in W.P.W. Phillimore and others (eds), *Warwickshire Parish Registers. Baptisms*. vol. II (London, 1904), 12 May 1805 to 25 April 1826. Throughout this article I have adhered to the spelling of personal names as found in the primary documents.

could not hold my congregation by many hundreds'. Peach believed that there
were now at least 5000 to 6000 Irish under his charge. Father McDonnell
challenged this figure. He gave the total Irish population of Birmingham as
about 6000 – of whom between a sixth and a third came under the ministry of
his church, St Peter's.[15] McDonnell's lower estimate is supported by the
comments of the acute French social observer Alexis de Tocqueville, who
stated that there were 'at the most' 5000 Irish in Birmingham in 1835.[16] It is
difficult to decide who is the more accurate. The lack of reliable statistics from
the period is compounded by the likelihood that the Irish population of
Birmingham fluctuated with the season. Yet the evidence would seem to favour
McDonnell, especially as the 1841 Census counted 4683 Irish in Birmingham.

In a difference to the earliest Irish settlers, those who arrived in Birmingham
from the 1820s tended to come from a distinct part of Ireland – Connacht and
its counties west of the Shannon. McDonnell himself declared that chiefly they
came from Mayo and Roscommon.[17] This influx was prompted by the rapidly
worsening rural conditions in Connacht, and agricultural labourers were
noticeable amongst the Irish of Birmingham. During the 1830s John Thomas
had a farm four miles from the town on the Warwick Road and each year he
employed Irishmen at harvest time, after which they would move on to work on
the land in Staffordshire and 'get back in time for their own harvest'.[18] In the
course of his work for the Birmingham Town Mission, Thomas Finigan, a
Catholic turned Protestant evangelist, met a group of such labourers on 27
August 1837. With their hooks in hand they were ready to fight 'thoughtless
young men who insulted them and cast reflections on these poor shoeless and
shillingless bogtrotters from Connaught'.[19]

The 1851 census confirms the continuing presence of agricultural labourers
in the industrial city of Birmingham. There were 136 of them, making them
one of the largest groups of Irish workers in the town. The enumerators listed
the place of birth of ten of them: one each from Cork, Armagh and Monaghan;
and three each from Galway, Roscommon and Mayo. This last county was well-
known for its *spalpeens*, or seasonal migrants.[20] Marrie Walsh came to Birmingham
in the 1950s from Treanoughter, Mayo and emphasised the economic pressures
under which her people had suffered for over a century. The land they farmed

---

15 'State of the Irish poor in Birmingham', in *Royal Commission on the Conditions of the Poorer Classes in Ireland*, Appendix G, *Report of the Select Committee on the State of the Irish Poor in Great Britain*, P.P., vol. XXXIV (1836), p. 1.

16 Alexis de Tocqueville, *Voyages en Angleterre et Irlande* (Paris, 1967) p. 185.

17 'State of the Irish Poor', p. 1.

18 Ibid., p. 7 .

19 Thomas Finigan, *Journal of Thos Augtn Finigan Missionary. Birmingham Town Mission 1837–1838*, 27 Aug. 1837, p. 79 (Birmingham Reference Library, 312749).

20 *Census* (1851).

'was poor and little of it was suitable for growing crops, surrounded as we were by bogs, hills and water'. As a result her father, brothers, uncle and many other men annually went to England in the summer to earn money, leaving their wives and children 'to work the farms as best they could'.[21] They followed a practice that was established firmly in the 1820s and 1830s, although unlike them it appears that an increasing number of agricultural workers decided not to return home. Peter Lawless was one of those who stayed in Birmingham throughout the year. A sixty-three year old widower, he originated from Killcommon, Mayo – as did his four adult children who lived with him in Henrietta Street. The two daughters were button makers, whilst one son was a bricklayer's labourer and the other a spoon maker. In a court off Edgbaston Street, Patrick Jennings was another Mayo farm labourer. His wife Jane was a washerwoman from Galway, whilst their son and daughter had been born in Birmingham. Aged thirteen and nine, both were wire workers. Former seasonal workers such as Lawless and Jennings were joined by their country folk who had left the west of Ireland intending a permanent settlement. Together they provided the core of the Irish in Birmingham.

A snatch of further evidence about some of these early migrants is provided by the 1851 census. It recorded a forty-year-old blacksmith called John Noon living at 24 Smallbrook Street with his wife, Jane, and two cousins. All were from Roscommon. Three other cousins lodged at the house: Mary Noon, aged fifteen; the twenty-eight year old John, and the twenty-seven year old Thomas Noon. These were born in Birmingham, suggesting that members of the Noon family had moved from Roscommon sometime in the early 1820s. Margaret Wire of Alcester Street (back) must have migrated in the same years. A forty-three year old widow and worker in bone buttons, she came from Galway and had a son aged twenty-four who was born in Birmingham. It is apparent that she maintained contact with her countyfolk as she provided lodgings for John Cronin, a twenty-seven year old grate fitter also from Galway.[22]

It seems that following the great increase of the Irish in Birmingham, their population stabilised until the late 1840s when it rose dramatically by at least 60%. In April 1847 alone the town's poor law authorities reported that '1761 Irish persons were relieved in the short space of 21 days'.[23] There is no doubt that the great majority of these were new to Birmingham, nor about the reasons for this sudden increase. Father Bowen was the priest in charge of a Catholic

---

21 Marrie Walsh, *An Irish Country Childhood. Memories of a Bygone Age* (London, 1996 edition), pp ix, 78 and 112. Migrant Irish agricultural workers were still coming to Warwickshire in the late 1800s and early 1900s; see Flora Thompson, *Lark Rise to Candleford* (London, 1973 edition), p. 235 and Angela Hewins (ed.), *The Dillen. Memories of a Man of Stratford upon Avon* (Oxford, 1982 edition), p. 96.

22 *Census* (1851)

23 *Report of the Select Committee on Poor Removal*, P.P., vol XIII (1854–5), 308, p. 2.

mission in the very poor Inkleys neighbourhood and in 1856 he wrote that the local 'streets, courts and squalid squares were densely packed with labourers', a large proportion of whom were 'sturdy Catholic emigrants, driven out by the late "Potato Famine", from Mayo and elsewhere in Ireland'.[24]

According to the tabulations of Irish-born people living in principal British towns, these fresh migrants boosted the Irish population of Birmingham to 9341.[25] I have scoured this census and found 7981 Irish living in Birmingham and that part of Aston within the borough of Birmingham. It is certain that I have missed some people, and I did not look at the returns for Edgbaston. Still, it is unlikely that the discrepancy between the two numbers can be accounted for by these factors. I do not believe that I have overlooked over 1300 people, and it is improbable that such a number of Irish people lived in Edgbaston, a prosperous middle-class area which was never associated locally with the Irish and had a population of only 9269. Accordingly, whilst not dismissing the figure of 9341 my analysis is based on my own count of 7981 Irish in Birmingham.[26]

This research suggests that whilst Irish people were found in all parts of the city there were pronounced differences in their concentration. In Aston within Birmingham there were 854 Irish, representing 1.7% of the people; whilst in the more recently urbanised western wards of All Saints and Ladywood they totalled just 242, or 0.7% of the inhabitants. It is difficult to ascertain the exact Irish presence in the rest of Birmingham's wards as in the most populous, central part of the town the 1851 census returned figures for parishes which overlapped municipal boundaries. Together these had 140,190 residents, amongst whom there were 8873 Irish. At 4.9% of the total they were a more obvious presence here than in outer Birmingham. Despite the difficulties of interpretation, within the large central area further differences are clear. In the newer, northern streets which radiated from Summer Lane there were 578 Irish, while in the freshly cut streets off Holloway Head there were 249. Both were expanding districts and it seems that in each of them the Irish would have made up the same low proportion as they did in Aston within Birmingham.

If these latter two localities are included then there were 1923 Irish in outer Birmingham, or 24% of the total. Their fellows were packed into the older, over-crowded and central localities of the town: 1106 Irish lived in the neighbourhood north west of the Town Hall and in the Jewellery Quarter – although 642 of these were found in Livery Street and two small streets which

24 'Account of Father Bowen', in Father H. Barnett, *The Story of St Catherine's in the Horse Fair* (Birmingham, 1971), p. 1.
25 Colin Pooley, 'Segregation or integration? The residential experience of the Irish in mid-Victorian Britain', in Roger Swift and Sheridan Gilley (eds), *The Irish in Britain 1815–1939* (London, 1989), pp 61–6.
26 *Census* (1851). Because I did not look at the returns for Edgbaston its population is excluded from all of my analysis.

ran off it; 787 had homes in just fourteen streets of the Gun Quarter; 134 made their base close by across Lancaster Street; 1138 gathered in a small stretch of streets, alleys and courts east of Bull Street, the main shopping thoroughfare of Birmingham's middle class; 1089 lived in streets flowing down the hill south west from the Town Hall; 912 were drawn nearby to the markets' quarter; and 892 had their dwellings across the way in the streets south east of High Street. Within this area, eleven streets stand out as having a major Irish presence, as is made plain in Table 1.[27]

Table 1: Streets of highest Irish population in Birmingham, 1851

Street	Total population	Irish population	% Irish
Edgbaston	574	214	37.5
Green's Village	372	189	51
Henrietta	466	131	28
John	748	261	35
Livery	1592	394	25
London Prentice	768	357	46.5
Myrtle Row	150	118	78.5
Old Inkleys	708	228	32
Park	842	388	46
Slaney	688	356	51.5
Water	451	117	26

Source: Census of Great Britain (1851).

In these streets, as elsewhere, the Irish community could be expanded largely if the English-born children of migrants were included. For example, in Water Street this exercise would advance the Irish from a quarter of the residents to over a third, while in London Prentice Street it would augment them from almost a half to near two-thirds.

This last street had been associated strongly with the Irish since the inflow of the 1820s. Short and narrow, it ran between two more important roads and was close to the middle-class dwellings of Old Square. Unlike them, the properties of London Prentice Street were old and decaying. Many were lodging houses, five of which were operated by Irish people. Two of them were women – Eleanor McNally and Mary Kielty, a sixty-nine year old widow. Of the three

27 Ibid.

others, John Ratakin and his wife were a young couple from Roscommon who had eight lodgers, five of whom shared their name; Thomas Doherty was a widower from Tubercurry, Sligo; while Patrick Barnwell was from Queens County and judging by the age of their daughter, he and his wife had been in Birmingham for at least twelve years. Together these people rented accommodation to forty-three Irish, yet their official lodging houses did not account for the majority of lodgers in the street.

Of a further fifty-one homes headed by Irish, only twelve were occupied by single families. The remainder had a substantial number of lodgers, visitors or relatives. Excluding two houses in which adult English lodgers were also present, 325 Irish and their English-born children were crowded into 37 dwellings – an average of almost nine people to each. The most overcrowded was 7 house 10 court where James Garry, a general labourer, his wife and five children gave lodgings to Mary Crosby and her two adult children; Patrick Keely; Thomas and Bridgett Morton and their two youngsters; and Bridget Farrall, a fifty-year old widow, and her four daughters.[28]

London Prentice Street was in the area assigned to Finigan and his comments emphasise that the dire situation of too many packed into too little space was long-standing – and not just for the Irish. On 15 September 1837 he commented that the street had 'on the whole 119 or 120 houses' in the majority of which 'there are from 12 to 16 persons lodging or living, in others it is less, but I never found it any under six – except in two or three cases'. He estimated that the population was at least 850, of whom half were Catholic and by inference Irish. Despite his sometimes disparaging comments about Catholicism, Finigan recognised that poverty forced many of the Irish into dreadful living conditions. In early February 1838 he passionately wrote that throughout his area the 'human misery, wretchedness and want even to almost starvation were truly appalling'. Everyone was affected by the bad winter yet 'the English poor were not wholly left without some small assistance from the Parish officers – but the unfortunate natives of Ireland who had the temerity to present themselves and crave even a mouthful of bread at the workhouse door were spurned away with contempt and inhuman scorn'.[29]

Finigan's insight and sympathy were not shared by Dr John Darwall who blamed the Irish poor for the terrible environment in which they had no choice but to live. As the 1820s waned he noted that there was 'a large class of Irish, who are said to be seldom less than 5000 in number, but who are perpetually changing'. He acknowledged that few of them were employed in manufactories and instead were mason's labourers 'or follow whatever other casual occupation

28 Ibid.
29 Finigan, *Journal*, 15 Sept. 1837, p. 113; Friday 9 Feb., p. 25. For an inquiry into the relief of the Irish poor in Birmingham see *Report of the Select Committee on Poor Removal*, pp 1–22.

they can obtain'. His understanding of the meagreness and precariousness of their earnings did not stop him from declaring that 'their habits, morals, and conditions are very far inferior to those of the native artisans'. Badly clothed, miserably fed and miserably lodged, they 'exhibit a striking contrast to their more fortunate neighbours'.[30] His derogatory opinions were mirrored by those of John Mouchet, surgeon of the General Dispensary and the Town Infirmary of Birmingham. In 1836 he commented on the overcrowding of the Irish locally and declaimed them as 'the very pests of society' who 'generate contagion' through fevers and other infectious diseases. He exclaimed that ill health was caused by 'not by poverty' but by 'the want of ventilation and the cleanliness of person'.[31] Such an attitude betrayed an ignorance of the vile surroundings of the poor. Those in poverty did not open the windows of their homes simply because they were desperate to keep in what heat there was, while they were unable to clean themselves effectively because of a lack of running water in dwellings, polluted wells, an inability to afford utensils and no changes of clothing.[32]

In his major report of 1849 Robert Rawlinson graphically laid out the severe difficulties faced by the poor in Birmingham. Without judgement he explained that there were 'about 2000 close courts undrained, many unpaved and where privies exist they are a source of nuisance'. Of those he had inspected personally, large numbers had 'a want of water of water, privies and cesspools which were crowded against the houses, and a deficiency of light and ventilation'. Joseph Hodgson, a surgeon, submitted a statement to Rawlinson which pointed out that in the poorest parts off the town privies were too few and where present they were too conspicuous and missing doors. This meant that 'ordure' was often kept in households and emptied anywhere at nightfall. Elsewhere, such as the Inkleys and other Irish quarters, 'the door is opened, and it is thrown out without the least reference to the spot where it falls, or anything else'.[33]

Appalling and insanitary conditions characterised most of the streets of heavy Irish settlement, and it was the Irish poor whom medical practitioners condemned as having an aversion to vaccination against smallpox. Given the

30 John Darwall, 'Observations on the medical topography of Birmingham and the health of the inhabitants', in *Midland Medical and Surgical Reporter and Topographical and Statistical Journal*, vol. 1 (1828–9), p.109. cited in T.P. Heslop, 'The medical aspects of Birmingham', in Samuel Timmins (ed.), *Birmingham and the Midland Hardware District. A Series of Reports* (London, 1866), p. 696.

31 'State of the Irish poor', p. 6.

32 For insanitary conditions in central Birmingham see Carl Chinn, *Homes for People: 100 Years of Council Housing in Birmingham* (Exeter, 1991), pp 1–21.

33 Robert Rawlinson, *Report to the General Board of Health on the Sewerage, Drainage and Supply of Water and the Sanitary Condition of Birmingham* (1849), cited in John Thackray Bunce, *History of the Corporation of Birmingham with a Sketch of the Earlier Government of the Town*, vol. 2 (Birmingham 1885), pp 322–4.

contemporary middle-class preoccupation with public health and the fear of the spread of disease, the Irish mostly featured negatively in sanitary reports. In 1841 local physicians and surgeons stated that the lowest lodging houses in Birmingham could be categorised into three kinds: mendicants; prostitutes; and Irish – of whom 252 were known to the police. In some of these Irish lodging houses the inhabitants were 'beggars and trampers, but the majority of them are resident labourers, employed by the builders and in various occupations'. Such premises were found 'principally in the old streets of the town' but especially in Slaney Street and London Prentice Street. The latter was 'almost occupied by the low Irish' and was rated as 'one of the filthiest streets in the town'; whilst Slaney Street, 'which furnishes the largest amount of febrile disorder, is inhabited by the lowest class of Irish'.[34]

If the Irish poor were castigated by many commentators for their bad housing and unhealthy environment, then the streets with which they were associated were also condemned as dangerous. One author welcomed the late nineteenth-century disappearance of London Prentice Street as the sweeping away of a 'nasty, dirty, stinking street' in which children could learn lessons of depravity, while Park Street was vilified as having 'a mixture of the worst class of Irish and regular thieves'.[35] Similarly, writing in 1885, John Thackray Bunce was delighted by the cutting of the John Bright Street and other alterations behind New Street Station for 'they swept away a series of narrow streets, close courts and confined passages, shut out from fresh air, imperfectly lighted, fetid with dirt, ill-supplied with water, and so inhabited that at one time – in the flourishing days of the Inkleys and Greens Village, and the like – the police could not venture into them single-handed; while no family could dwell there without destruction to the sense of decency, or peril to health and life'.[36]

It was the supposedly notorious Green's Village which was the focus of the 'sturdy Catholic emigrants' from Ireland mentioned by Father Bowen. Nearby in Smallbrook Street he set up Saint Patrick's day school in 1856. The premises were 'a large and lofty upper room with unsealed floor up steep and dark wooden steps over a storehouse for vegetables with skylight and 2 small windows behind'. Two years later a night school was established for girls. The curriculum was 'very primitive'; 'the first elements of writing, and sums of addition, interspersed with a "Daily, daily, sing to Mary" and a Catechetical

34 *A Committee of Physicians and Surgeons, Sanitary Inquiry – England. Report on the Public Health in the Borough of Birmingham* (Birmingham, 1841), pp 2 and 13–14; see also 'State of the Irish poor', p. 6.

35 T.T. Harman, *Showell's Dictionary of Birmingham. A History and Guide* (Birmingham, 1885), p. 138; 'Dark Side of Birmingham', Letter signed by 'English Catholic', in *Birmingham Daily Gazette*, 1 July 1867, cited in Raphael Samuel, 'The Roman Catholic Church and the Irish Poor', in Roger Swift and Sheridan Gilley (eds), *The Irish in the Victorian City* (London, 1985), p. 273.

36 Bunce, *History of the Corporation*, pp xiv–xv.

Instruction, formed the attraction'. Father Bowen was helped in his work in this 'infamous and fearful' locality by Mrs Powell, the Misses Maher and other ladies from wealthy English Catholic families, and by the Sisters of Mercy.[37] Based in Alcester Street, they had since 1846 run a Sunday School in a loft in Park Street, whilst priests from Saint Chad's provided schools in a seven-roomed warehouse in London Prentice Street.

Along with so many other poorer neighbourhoods throughout urban Britain, behind the disreputable image of Green's Village and the Inkleys was a community bonded by powerful ties of kinship and common place of origin. Of the total Irish population in Birmingham, enumerators recorded the county of birth of 1312, or 16.5%, of them in the 1851 census. The results are striking and corroborate the impressionistic evidence from the 1830s about the conspicuousness of folk from Connacht.[38] People from Roscommon accounted for 24% of the total; those from Mayo came to 13.5%; and migrants from Galway and Sligo made up 7.5%; and 5% respectively. With only two people, Leitrim was the only county from the province which had no impact. In all, 50% of the Irish whose birth place was noted came from Connacht. This province was the stronghold of the Irish tongue and migrants from the west continued to speak it in Birmingham. Early in his missionary work, Finigan went into the back streets of his district and 'addressed one woman in her native language, & we instantly obtained not only a hearing, but this woman went out unto her neighbours and informed them that an Irish Clergyman was in the court'. Later that day he conversed with a woman 'near 80 years of age who could scarce understand a word of English'; whilst on another occasion he addressed a group of women 'in the well known Irish salutation whenever any of them enter a strange house, the English of which is "God save all here". I was received with "*twugalthew*". You are welcome.'[39] These Irish speakers were reinforced at the time of the Great Hunger. John Denvir described how Father Sherlock had been taught colloquial Irish by his old nurse, a knowledge which helped him when ministering in the Black Country to west of Ireland migrants 'who could speak nothing but Irish'. Such a skill must have been as useful to him when he moved to the Well Street mission in one of Birmingham's poorest neighbourhoods where Connacht people were widespread.[40]

The migrants from this province gathered mostly in the older, central parts of Birmingham such as Green's Village. According to the 1851 census, this collection of decrepit houses had 189 people who were born in Ireland. They formed 51% of the population and if their English-born children were added

---

37 'Account by Father Bowen', pp 1–3.
38 *Census* (1851).
39 Finigan, *Journal*, 5 July 1837, p. 3; and 26 July 1837, p. 17.
40 John Denvir, *The Irish in Britain from the Earliest Times to the Fall and Death of Parnell* (London, 1892), pp 259–60.

to the total then the Irish community in the street swelled to more than 60%. The places of birth of forty-one of these folk are recorded: twenty-six were from Roscommon, five of whom originated in Strokestown; eight came from Mayo; and three had roots in Galway. A similar pattern of settlement was apparent in London Prentice Street where 357, or 47%, of the inhabitants were Irish-born. There is information about the origins of 116 of them: 44 came from Mayo, 34 from Roscommon, 22 from Sligo and 3 from Galway. Just 13 had moved from other parts of Ireland. As is seen in table 2, folk from Connacht were dominant in the streets of highest Irish concentration from which there is information about counties of birth.

Table 2: Presence of Connacht people in streets of highest Irish presence in Birmingham, 1851

Street	*Number of Irish-born*	*Number with county of Birth*	*Number from Connacht*	*% from Connacht*
Edgbaston	214	24	24	100
Green's Village	189	41	36	90.5
Henrietta	131	111	88	79
John	261	133	97	80.5
Livery	394	0	0	0
London Prentice	357	116	103	86.5
Myrtle Row	118	0	0	0
Old Inkleys	228	0	0	0
Park	388	7	5	sample too small
Slaney	356	18	15	sample too small
Water	117	89	47	51.5

Source: Census (1851).

In only one Birmingham street did the enumerator regularly note the actual parish of birth of a meaningful number of Irish migrants. This was Henrietta Street, just to the north west of the city centre, which had 131 Irish-born residents. They accounted for 28% of the total population and of these five were from Galway, thirteen hailed from Mayo and seventy came from Roscommon. Amongst these latter, people from Elphin, Jalsk, Kilkeeven, Oran and Rathcarn stood out. Connacht folk were as evident in nearby Water Street, where it is apparent that established families played a crucial role in providing a base for newer migrants from their own county. This seems to be the case with Barnard Lerry of number 15. A twenty-nine year old bootmaker from

Tune in Galway, he was married to Jane from Down in Ulster. They had three children under five, all of whom had been born in Manchester, and gave lodgings to Michael Miland. Another bootmaker, he and his wife Alis were also from Tune. There were two other lodgers: Patrick Farry, again a bootmaker, and his wife Ann, both of whom came from Borle, Roscommon.

Nearby in 4 court Henrietta Street there was an outstanding example of the connection between county, township and kinship networks. This was the home of Batly Keegan, a thirty-two year old bricklayer's labourer from Roscommon. His wife Margaret was from Castlerea, Mayo, but their seven-year old oldest daughter had been born in Kilkeeven, Roscommon. This was also the place of birth of Batly's cousin and lodger, Patrick Haban a shoemaker. Other lodgers included Edward Pathan, another cousin; John Greyham, an uncle; John and Ann Nigan; and Catron Carney, a servant. The three men were bricklayers labourers whilst all five were from Oran, Roscommon.

Kinship was as vital in the emergence of an Irish community in other parts of central Birmingham. At 131 Howard Place lived Michael Kelley, a farm labourer, his wife Catherine, their six children and two male relatives who followed his occupation. Close by at 19 Norfolk Street, the labourer James Quirk, his wife and two children were joined by five of his Flynn cousins and two other lodgers; while at 5 Green's Village the labourer Bryan Gerarty and his Roscommon wife Mary gave lodgings to Michael Gerarty, a relative from the same county. Seven doors up lived another labourer, James Moran. He and his wife and children gave lodgings to Catherine Moran and Mary Brennan. Both were his relatives and were labourers from Roscommon. The household was completed by four other lodgers, three of whom were from that county and the other was from Mayo

Green's Village was a first-rate example of a community bound fast by kinship, for out of thirty-nine Irish households there were seven in which the lodgers were related to the head. In other parts of central Birmingham there was an indication of larger gatherings of kin. For example in 15 court Edgbaston Street there were two households of Drurys, both of which were headed by labourers from Mayo; and four families of Tulleys living in two households. Similarly in 14 court Thomas and Bridget Welch lived next door to James and Ellen Welch. The same circumstance was evident in 25 court Livery Street. Here Thomas Clark, a twenty-three year old farm labourer, was joined by his wife and ten adults and children with the same name, whilst further up the terrace was Michael Clark. A grocer's porter, he and his wife gave accommodation to seven others with the same surname.

If kinship, township and county ties were vital in the emergence and stabilisation of the Irish community in Birmingham, then so too were occupational networks. In John Street there were two households of hat makers, one of which was headed by Edward Groke of Mayo. His two teenage children were from the same county and were also hat makers, as were his lodgers, the Killasan family from Sligo. At the head of the other household was Edward Carr, a hawker also from Sligo. So too were his wife Mary and their two daughters, all of whom were hat makers. Running off John Street was London Prentice Street. Charles Miller another Sligo hat maker, lived at number 44 and gave lodgings to three others in the same trade. The two men were from his county, whilst the wife of one of them originated from Mayo. In the rest of the street there was a single female hat maker from Galway and seven more hat-making families, five from Mayo and two from Sligo.

John Street was cut across by Lichfield Street where the occupations of eighty-one Irish people were noted. Nineteen of them were shoemakers. One lived in a lodging house and another was a woman whose husband was in the gun trade. The remainder belonged to nine households. Unfortunately there is no indication as to their counties of origin but other evidence suggests that sometimes occupational ties may have overlain those of county and kin. This was exemplified at 10½ Rope Walk where Michael Farrey, a tailor from Sligo, rented rooms to a tailor from Wexford and another from Tipperary; and the household of 32 Henrietta St, which was headed by Patrick McGovern, a nailmaker from Ballurbet, Cavan. Lodging with him were nailmakers from Castlebar, Mayo, Cork, Tipperary Town, and Gory, Wexford.[41]

In particular, Irish policemen were bonded by their job. There were thirty-six of them locally, for eight of whom the enumerators noted the place of origin. Although one was a Dubliner the rest came from counties whose people had a tiny numerical presence in Birmingham: two were from Wicklow and Down, with one each from Clare, Donegal and Kings County. Three of the men were sergeants.[42] Out of a force complement of 26 they represented 11.5% – the exact proportion of the 33 Irish constables to the total of such officers. Remarkably this figure was almost four times that of the Irish in the general population. Irish police officers remained prominent throughout Victorian Birmingham. Amongst them was Inspector Kelly, who distinguished himself by his attempts to keep the peace during the Murphy Riots and their tense aftermath; and Michael McManus. Brought up in Mayo he joined the force in 1873 and retired in 1918 as Deputy Chief Constable.[43] McManus and many other Irish police officers passed into local working-class folklore as 'big, broad, blokes' who could carry out a job, and bring 'a bit of order'.[44]

The significance of occupational networks was as marked among the Irish of outer Birmingham as it was for their fellows in the central areas. In a court yard

41 *Census* (1851).
42 Ibid.
43 Total figures for the Birmingham Borough Police Force relate to 1852 and are in Bunce, *History of the Corporation*, p. 293.
43 'Demonstration in Birmingham', *Birmingham Daily Post*, 25 Nov. 1867, p. 8; and 'Michael McManus Warrant Number 4754, PC 197', Record of Service (30 June 1918).
44 'Carl Chinn Interviews', no. 2 Walter G. Chinn (1980) p. 30.

in Ward Street, Summer Lane lived Patrick Grogan a fifty-year old oil cloth japanner from Mayo. His wife was from Roscommon as was their oldest child, also an oil cloth japanner. With them lodged Elizabeth Perry, an unmarried table cove dealer from Mayo. The household next door was headed by another Patrick Grogan, a linen weaver from the same county. His teenage son shared his place of birth and was another oil cloth japanner. Not far away in St George's Street were John and Mary Sherlock, a button turner and button cutter. Both came from Dublin, as did their neighbour Joseph Maker who made metal buttons. In the same neighbourhood there were two more households of Dublin button workers in number 2 court, Great Hampton Street. Kinship ties were also apparent amongst the folk from Ireland's capital, as with Thomas Moffitt of Dartmouth Place A twenty-eight year old glass blower married to Sarah from Shropshire, he gave lodgings to his brother and another person from his town of birth. Across Birmingham in number 8 court Cheapside, James Drisdall, a Dubliner, was also married to a Shropshire woman. James Drisdall was a brushmaker, like his lodger David Drisdall.[45]

Aston within Birmingham had several, distinct collections of workers. The largest number were 111 soldiers, most of whom were based at barracks in Vauxhall with the 4th (The Queen's Own) Regiment of Light Dragoons.[46] The regiment's headquarters was in Dublin and in 1854 its men took part in the charge of the Light Brigade in the Crimean War. One of the survivors was Private Henry Keegan, a native of Kildare. After his discharge, Keegan settled in Birmingham where he died in Adderley Street.[47] Further out towards Saltley and the railway carriage works of Joseph Wright were nineteen men involved in coach making, two of whom were from Belfast, while there were twenty-three brickmakers and brick labourers, most of whom were part of family groups and worked in the clay pits close to Garrison Lane and Highgate Street. In the Holloway Head area and the western wards of All Saints and Ladywood, the most remarkable set of workers were glass cutters. They lived in six households, five of which were headed by men from Cork City or from the county Cork towns of Douglas and Riverstone.

Across Birmingham, 5231 Irish were recorded with 765 occupations. They ranged in economic status from John Ryland, an Armagh accountant who lived in prosperous Ashted Row with his family and a servant, to James Foy of 6, Park Street. He, his wife and their five children aged three and upwards were all beggars. Overall there were few Irish who could be regarded as middle class. Depending upon the interpretation of jobs and without any knowledge of income, at the most they formed 2% of the total. This small group included

45 *Census* (1851).
46 Counties of birth are recorded for most of these soldiers and their wives, but I have excluded them from my analyses. I thank John Bourne for the details about their regiment.
47 Newspaper cutting supplied by Robert Steele.

professionals, clerks, teachers and actors. More discernible were those who sold things. Although there were just 58 retailers, there were also 99 dealers, 95 hawkers, 28 travellers and 12 merchants. Together they constituted 5.5% of the Irish noted with occupations. Once again there are problems with assigning them to a class. Some were well off, like Robert Twinem. A provision dealer at 69 Digbeth, he had a wife and two young children and employed Joseph Harvey as an errand boy/servant with eleven-year old Jane Harvey as a general servant. In contrast to him were two middle-aged widows, Bridget Haley and Catherine Carly, who gathered old clothes and lodged with the Flanagans in Carey's Court, Castle Street. Overall, most hawkers, dealers and travellers did live in working-class streets. The great number of jobs in which the Irish were involved reflects both Birmingham's multiform industrial structure and the large number of sub-divisions in certain trades. This feature was renowned in button making, in which the Irish were recorded as holding forty-three types of job. Similarly the enumerators listed twenty-seven kinds of labourers, in addition to which were errand boys, porters, excavators, navigators and coal heavers. Taking these sub-divisions into consideration and excluding those who were retired, pensioners or on the parish, then the Irish of Birmingham can be regarded as taking part in 334 distinct occupations. These have been grouped under relevant headings in table 3. It highlights that although they were spread across a wide range of trades, there were 1393 Irish working in metal, the button trade and other manufactures. They comprised 26.5% of the total. Another 9% were involved in shoemaking, tailoring and the manufacture of some form of clothing, with 2% finding employment in miscellaneous trades.[48]

Table 3: Chief occupations of the Irish in Birmingham, 1851

Occupations	Numbers
Labourers	1,769
Metal trades	697
Servants, charwomen, laundresses, housekeepers and washerwomen	616
Manufacturing, various	450
Selling	292
Clothes making	290
Button trade	246
Shoemaking	191
Building trade	163
Soldiers and police officers	152
Miscellaneous trades	115
Others	250

Source: Census (1851).

48 *Census* (1851).

Contemporary observers disregarded the variety of occupations with which the Irish were connected. In 1834 George Redfern, prison keeper and Deputy Constable of Birmingham, recounted that most Irishmen locally 'are employed as builders or plasterer's labourers'. His opinions were supported by William White, a builder, and James Holmes, a plasterer who praised his Irish employees for their hard work, honesty and ingenuity. During the winter he paid them between 12s. and 13s. for a six day week, a sum which could be increased in the longer days of the summer. Because the English Brummies preferred factory jobs, Holmes was of the firm opinion that 'if it was not for the Irish we could not get the work done'.[49] Twenty-one years later and as clerk to the poor law guardians of Birmingham, James Corder told the Select Committee on Poor Removal that very few of the Irish locally were artisans. He believed that they were generally employed as hard-working labourers.[50] This was a view held strongly by A.M. Sullivan in 1856 when he wrote in *The Nation* that the Irish of Birmingham 'are poor to a man, and chiefly bricklayers' labourers'.[51]

They and their fellow labourers did make up the largest group of workers amongst the Irish locally, but they were not the majority. The 1851 Census included 1769 of them, or 34% of the total for whom occupations were inserted. There is ground to suppose that those who migrated specifically for employment as builders' labourers were joined by former agricultural workers. There was plenty of opportunity for them to do so, for in that decade alone the number of houses in Birmingham increased spectacularly from 21345 to 29397. Again the 1851 Census provides some support for this proposal. For example, at 12 Slaney Street there lived Mrs Clane, a fifty-two year old widow from Mayo where *spalpeens* were so common. She was joined by her two teenage daughters and several lodgers, all of whom were from Mayo. Three of them were day labourers. Further south in number 17 court Park Street lived James Gavan, a hawker. His wife was from Mayo as were their two sons and two lodgers, all of whom were mason's labourers.

Excluding porters, errand boys and others, actual labourers numbered 1647 and were divided by the enumerators into twenty-seven types. The greater part of them could be assigned into three main categories: 1022 labourers (including day, general and jobbing labourers); 321 bricklayer's, building, mason's or plasterer's labourers; and 135 agricultural labourers. These latter were most recognisable in Park Street and the adjacent Park Lane. It is obvious that they were as much part of an occupational network as were hat makers, shoemakers and coachmakers. Unfortunately the enumerators for this locality did not

49 Ibid.
50 *Report of the Select Committee*, p. 1151.
51 Denvir, pp 258–9.

record either the county or parish of origin of the agricultural workers, but there is some evidence of the influence of kinship amongst them. Martin MakDonal was a farmer's labourer at the head of 8 Park Lane. Among his lodgers were Michael and Patrick MakDonal and an elderly couple, John and Mary MakDonal. All five were also agricultural labourers. The two streets had a further eight households headed by such men and one lodging house in which there were fourteen of them. Overall these farm labourers totalled fifty eight, meaning that of their complement in Birmingham 43% lived in either Park Street or Park Lane.[52]

The incidence of all types of labourers was at its highest in the 'most Irish' and 'most Connacht' streets, as is made plain in table 4. The exception was London Prentice Street where hawkers and dealers were perceptible. They accounted for 8% of those for whom occupations were given. Their presence had been noticed in 1837 when Finigan visited a house in the street which was 'wholly inhabited by Irish pedlars and mendicants many of such character I have heretofore found, as in the present instance to possess much shrewdness, keen intellect and argumentative faculty'.[53] Labourers also formed less than

Table 4: Percentage of Connacht people and labourers in streets of highest Irish population in Birmingham, 1851

Street	% Irish-born	% Connacht-born (when county of origin recorded)	% Labourers
Edgbaston	37.5	100	41
Green's Village	51	90.5	42.5
Henrietta	28	79	39.5
John	35	80.5	41.5
Livery	25	ncr	42
London Prentice	46.5	86.5	31
Myrtle Row	78.5	ncr	48.5
Old Inkleys	32	ncr	49
Park	46	sample too small	48
Slaney	51.5	sample too small	43
Water	26	51.5	37

Source: Census (1851). ncr = no counties recorded

52 *Census* (1851).
53 Finigan, *Journal*, 26 July 1837, p. 22.

40% of the recorded workforce in Henrietta Street and Water Street, in both of which those in the button trade were noteworthy.

Compared to the 'most Irish' streets, labourers were less numerous in outer Birmingham. In the Holloway Head district they made up 11.5% of the total of Irish people for whom occupations were recorded; in the western wards they were 21.4%; in the Summer Lane district they were 25.5%; and in Aston in Birmingham they were 17.7%. The Irish of outer Birmingham differed from those in the central areas in another aspect: they were more likely to be married to an English or Scottish person. If one combines the four areas, there were 502 marriages in which one person was Irish. In 58% of them the other partner was English. Contrarily in the eleven 'most Irish' streets there were 558 marriages with one Irish person, only 17% of whom had an English partner.

The occupational heterogeneity of the Irish of outer Birmingham was equalled by the variety in their place of origin. From a combined population of 1212 such information is available for 280 of them. In a sharp contrast to the Irish of central Birmingham, only 19% were from Connacht. Interestingly 16.5% came from Ulster, four times the proportion in the rest of Birmingham; 17% hailed from Cork; and 21% were from Dublin. In general people from Ireland's capital were well-represented everywhere – even in central Birmingham, where they made up 14% of the total Irish population.[54] Like Connacht, the capital of Ireland had experienced serious economic difficulties. By the end of the 1820s its textile industry had all but collapsed, destroyed by the effects of free trade following the Act of Union. Although Birmingham was not a town associated with the rag trade, it would have appealed to Dubliners as a manufacturing centre. It is worth noting that the MacDonells, those early pioneers of Irish migration, were from Dublin along with five more of the twenty-three couples who had their children baptised at St Peter's before 1826.[55]

Although censuses consistently under-recorded women workers, their presence is marked wherever the Irish lived – varying from a low of 20% of the stated workforce in Park Street to a high of 36% in Water Street. The oldest of them was ninety-one year old Bridget Divine, a widowed hawker – as was Mary Keeley. Like Bridget, she and her three children lodged with the widowed charwoman Mary Gray in a back house in London Prentice Street. Indeed out of 76 people stated as hawkers, 48 were women, and a third of those were widows. Such women were as prominent amongst lodging-house keepers: from a total of 33 they contributed 15, while another 7 were married or single. Older females, whether married or widows, were also predominant as charwomen, laundresses and washerwomen.

The largest portion of female workers was that of servants. In total, 461 were in some form of service and of these 251 were single women 'living in'

54 *Census* (1851).
55 'The Franciscan Register', 12 May 1805 to 25 April 1826.

with English or other non-Irish employers. The youngest was Margaret Burns, a ten-year old working in Little Hampton Street and there were many who were aged fourteen and under. Excluding four females for whom the relevant information is not known, their average age was twenty. The place of birth was given for forty-nine of them. At 19% of the total this is a slightly higher proportion than the equivalent for the general Irish population. Interestingly the results are similar: 51% of the women came from Roscommon, Galway and Mayo, and 20.5% were from Dublin. Unfortunately, it is impossible to ascertain how many of the Irish in the 1820s and 1830s were single female servants and if so where they were from. Still, the evidence from the 1851 Census is tantalising and raises the question as to whether such women may have been as influential in the origins of the chain migration from Connacht as male agricultural labourers.

Just under half of the females giving their occupations as servants lived either with their families or were in lodgings with other Irish folk. Twelve women were also teachers of some sort, five of whom were unmarried and were based at the Catholic school in Bath Street. A few single females were also employed as shop assistants, but the greatest number of young, working women were involved in the manufacturing trades of Birmingham.[56] According to Father Bowen, many were in factories doing jobs 'mostly of the laborious and uninviting kind, such as "screw works", "umbrella wires", japanning the same, or enamelling saucepans etc'.[57] The 1851 Census indicated that they were also well represented as burnishers, polishers, spoon makers, filers, gilt toy workers, makers of hooks and eyes, japanners, penmakers and press operators. They were especially obvious in the button trade. Altogether, 246 Irish worked in some aspect of this industry, of whom 113 were unmarried women under the age of 30.[58]

Many of these occupations were harmful: the lacquering of metal objects was recognised as very unhealthy; the use of pumice stones, sand and lime dust in spoon polishing caused respiratory problems – as did the dust from the drilling of pearl and the use of mercury in the gilding of buttons; whilst the fumes from japanning made it one of the most injurious trades to women.[59] Equally the wages were low and often intermittent. In 1837 Finigan wrote of the plight of John Hannon who lived in 5 court, London Prentice Street. For eighteen months he had been afflicted by sickness occasioned by 'over working himself' and was confined to his bed. He and his wife were supported by their two daughters aged fourteen and thirteen who were pin headers, 'but for the last four or five weeks they got nothing to earn – in consequence of the bad state of the trade'.[60]

56 *Census* (1851).
57 'Account of Father Bowen', p. 2.
58 Fiona Elizabeth Terry Chandler, 'Women, Work and the Family: Birmingham 1800–1870' (University of Birmingham PhD thesis, 1995), pp 148–50.
59 *Census* (1851).
60 Finigan, *Journal*, 15 Aug. 1837, p. 51.

There were numerous younger children at work. Mary Flynn was just four and was recorded as a penmaker with her older brothers and sisters in the Park Street lodging house of their father. It is likely that she helped her siblings – as would have done Henry Durr, a seven-year old button shanker in Lancaster Street; whilst the six-year-old errand boy William Lynch must have been running messages for his parent who was a master shoemaker. Yet there is strong evidence of the full-time employment of young children outside the home, as with Peter Dunavan aged eleven of Park Street. The son of a hawker in lodgings, he was a factory boy. Two years his junior, Barbara Flin of Bull Street was in a button works, earning money to supplement the labourer's income of her father.

The industrial employment of young children was not unusual in Birmingham, but in the case of the Irish it does indicate the movement of their youth away from labouring. Gordon Smith's ancestors, the Carrs, lived in 4 house, number 8 court Dale End. The home was headed by John, a brick labourer who had been born in Ireland, as had his wife and four children. One of them was the seven-year old Dennis, who thirty years later was a 'maker of japan and every description of varnish'.[61] The Giblins exhibited a similar shift in employment. Arriving in Birmingham from Roscommon as a labourer in the 1850s, Richard Giblin met and married Ellen Cain from the same county. Their only son, Thomas, became a boot clicker, whilst his son worked as an ironplater.[62]

This trend towards the metal trades was commented upon by Hugh Heinrick in 1872 in his articles in *The Nation* on the 'Irish in England'. A journalist living in Birmingham, he explained that locally 'the great body of the people earn their bread by the severest toil', although the young chiefly 'have been trained to skilled labour'.[63] Twenty years later, Denvir stated that the sons of Irish hod carriers were 'to be found among the artizans of Birmingham and making fair progress in various other occupations', whilst their daughters 'still find employment in the manufacture of the multifarious articles fashioned from brass, iron, and other materials, for which Birmingham is world-famed'.[64] The 1851 Census points out the difference between the employment of adult Irish migrants and their English-born children. Occupations are mentioned for 451 of them: only thirteen were labourers, with just ten as servants. By contrast 256 were involved in the metal trades and sixty-five were concerned with some other form of manufacture.[65]

Overwhelmingly the Irish of early Victorian Birmingham were 'sturdy Catholic emigrants'. Their presence had been established firmly in the late 1820s when large numbers of Irish-speaking folk from Connacht made their

61 'Letter from Gordon Smith', 24 Feb. 1998.
62 'Letter from Louise Newton', Feb. 1998.
63 Alan O'Day (ed.), *A Survey of the Irish in England, 1872* (London, 1989), p. 42.
64 Denvir, p. 415.
65 *Census* (1851).

homes in the central and poorer localities of the town. At the time of the Great
Hunger these early settlers were reinforced by others from the west, ensuring
that for the rest of the nineteenth-century Birmingham's Irish were mostly
from Roscommon, Mayo, Galway and Sligo.[66] Yet the Irish of the town were
not monolithic. There was a significant and long-standing presence of Dubliners
and a noticeable number of folk from Cork. Together these groups were numerically superior to the Connacht people in the outer areas of Birmingham, where
a quarter of the town's Irish lived and were involved in a variety of occupations.
Despite the importance of labourers and servants amongst them, even the Irish
of the central localities exhibited a striking heterogeneity of employment. In
both parts of Birmingham women and children were a crucial section of the
workforce. Similarly throughout the town, the ties of occupation, kin, township
and county were major factors in the emergence and consolidation of Irish
communities. The Irish of early Victorian Birmingham had a major impact.
One of them founded the town's leading newspaper; another was a leading
reformer; large numbers were involved in certain of the trades for which the
town was celebrated; and many were amongst those who built the houses and
factories essential to Birmingham's growth.

66 In the course of his research into German-born people in Birmingham, Alan Tucker
    has so far found 2034 Irish in the 1881 Census, 707 of whom have origins recorded:
    41% of the total were from these four counties: 'Letter from Alan Tucker', 10 April
    1998.

Irish settlement in the north-east and north-west of England in the mid-nineteenth century

Frank Neal

I

Despite the considerable increase in the number of studies of the Irish in Britain over the last thirty years, North-east England has received relatively little attention. In the two important volumes of essays edited by Swift and Gilley, for example, there is not one piece on the Irish in the north-east.[1] This essay provides an interim report on some of the findings of a much larger scale

1 R. Swift and S. Gilley (eds), *The Irish in the Victorian City* (London, 1985), and R. Swift and S. Gilley (eds), *The Irish in Britain, 1815–1914* (London, 1989). There exist a number of publications, theses and articles dealing with various aspects of the Irish in the North-east and they vary considerably in quality: R.J. Cooter, 'The Irish in Durham and Newcastle, 1840-1880' (University of Durham MA thesis, 1972); R.J.Cooter, 'Lady Londonderry and the Irish Catholics of Seaham Harbour: No Popery out of Context', *Recusant History*, vol. 13, no. 3 (1976), pp 288–97; R.J. Cooter, 'On calculating the Nineteenth Century Irish Catholic Population of Durham and Newcastle', *Northern Catholic History*, no. 2 (Autumn 1975), pp 16–25; M. Chase, 'The Teeside Irish in the Nineteenth Century', in P. Buckland and J. Belchem (eds), *The Irish in British Labour History* (Liverpool, 1993), pp 47–58; S. Doherty, 'English and Irish Catholics in Northumberland, 1745–1860' (Queen's University of Belfast PhD thesis, 1987); D.C. Fox, 'The Demography of Sunderland in 1851', *Occasional Paper*, no. 1 (Department of History and Geography, Sunderland Polytechnic, 1980); J.G. Lynch, 'The Irish Population of Darlington in 1841 and 1851' (Teeside Polytechnic MA thesis, 1988); F. McConnell, 'The Irish in Durham City, 1841–61', *Durham County Local History Society Bulletin*, no. 47 (December, 1991), pp 68–82; McDermott, 'The Irish Workers on Tyneside', in N. McCord (ed.), *Essays on Tyneside Labour History* (1977); P. Norris, 'The Irish in Tow Law, County Durham, 1851–71', *Durham County Local History Society Bulletin*, no. 33 (December, 1984), pp 41–70; M. Sill, 'East Mining Colonisation and the Genesis of the Colliery Landscape, 1770–1851' (University of Durham PhD thesis, 1982); M. Sill, 'The Irish Population of Sandygate in the mid-Nineteenth Century', in M. Barke and R. J. Buswell (eds), *Historical Atlas of Newcastle-upon-Tyne* (Newcastle, 1980); H.J.Smith et al. *Crook and Billy Row in 1851: An Analysis of Census Returns* (University of Durham Department of Adult Education, 1975); L. Gooch, 'The Durham Catholics and Industrial Development, 1560–1850' (University of York MA thesis, 1984); J. Robinson, 'The coming of the Irish to Jarrow and Hebburn', *Journal of the Northumberland and Durham Family History Society*, vol. 6, no. 3 (1981), pp 70–71.

study of the Irish in the north-east, covering Northumberland and Durham and involving a database of some 35000 records of Irish-born persons and their British-born children.[2]

The most easily accessible data on the spatial distribution of the Irish-born population of Britain, from 1841 onwards, are in the published census reports and their accompanying tables. These give data, in a descending order of disaggregation, at the level of region, civil registration county, registration districts and principal towns, boroughs and cities. The following example should make clear the nature of these officially published sources of census data regarding the Irish in Britain. We shall take the case of the 1851 census reports. The Civil Registration County of Durham was numbered 38 in the various reports. This area is then broken down into registration districts; in the case of county Durham these numbered twelve (see table 3). The area covered by each of these districts was roughly identical to the corresponding Poor Law Union. In the case of both registration counties and registration districts, the officially published reports and tables give a breakdown of the birthplaces of the people counted in the census (see tables 1 and 3). Further, for each registration county, the officially published tables also record the origin of the populations in the principal towns and cities (see table 6). Each registration district is broken down further into sub-districts, townships and parishes. However, this level of disaggregation does not provide information about the birthplaces of people. For example, the registration county of Durham is number 38; the county is then broken down into twelve registration districts; and district number 545 is Durham. This district consists of four sub-districts: Tanfield (no. 1); Lanchester (no. 2); St Oswald (no. 3); and St Nicholas (no. 4). In turn, these are further sub-divided into townships. Tanfield had three townships, Lanchester had eighteen, St Oswald had twelve, and St Nicholas had fourteen. To obtain data on the Irish-born residing in the sub-districts and townships, it is necessary to extract the data from the census enumerator sheets. These are kept on microfilm in most local libraries.

The Irish-born population of Northumberland and Durham in the nineteenth century represented the fourth-largest concentration of Irish-born persons in England and Wales, following behind the north-west, London, and West Yorkshire. Though the numbers in the north-east did not approach those in these other areas, the clustering was sufficiently large as to be recognised by

2   This study includes Newcastle, Tynemouth, South Shields, Sunderland, Gateshead and a number of townships in County Durham. I am grateful to Stewart McAlister and H.M.V. Music Group Ltd, for financial assistance enabling such large amounts of census data to be extracted from the enumerators' sheets and entered up on a database.

contemporary commentators as a distinctive migrant group.[3] In the limited space available, this paper first sets out to survey the data vailable to all researchers who wish to use the official census reports and tables (see tables 1 to 6). Then a detailed examination of the Irish dispersion within selected sub-districts of county Durham will be carried out, based on data extracted from census enumerators' sheets, followed by an occupational profile of the Irish in a number of townships. Two propositions will be examined. First, that the Irish migrant economic experience was not homogeneous, but varied according to the nature of the local economy. To this end, the Irish communities in the north-east examined in this study will be compared with two towns in the Lancashire textile belt. The second proposition to be examined is that the male Irish-born population in the north-east was unequivocally concentrated in jobs involving unskilled manual labour.

II

The 1851 census revealed that the registration counties of Northumberland and Durham were home to 31167 Irish-born persons, representing 4.4% of the total population of the region. To put this population in perspective, the size of the combined Irish-born population of Durham and Northumberland was approximately one-seventh of the corresponding numbers in the north-west. However, the totals of Irish-born in any area are less significant than the statistics of the spatial dispersal of such persons.

Table 1: The Irish-born population of selected counties
of England and Wales, 1851

Counties	Total population	Irish-born	Irish as % of whole
North Western	2,490,827	214,318	8.6
London	2,362,236	108,548	4.6
Yorkshire	1,789,047	57,266	3.2
Northumb & Durham	715,247	31,167	4.4
Monmouth & Wales	1,188,914	20,738	1.7

Source: 1851 Census: Birth Places of the People: Summary Tables, no. 39.

3   The arrival of the Irish Famine refugees in the North-east from November 1846 onwards provoked a considerable response in the regional press commenting on the Irish in the area. This press coverage continued at a high level throughout the Famine crisis, particular concern being expressed over the rise of the poor rate expenditure.

If we turn first to Northumberland, the most striking feature of the data is the clustering of the Irish along the northern banks of the River Tyne. The Irish-born populations of the districts of Newcastle-upon-Tyne and Tynemouth (7152 and 2269 respectively) accounted for 74% of all the Irish in Northumberland. In the case of the Newcastle district, the Irish-born represented 8% of the total population, while in the Tynemouth district the corresponding figure was 3.5%. It is important to note that the Newcastle-upon-Tyne district included the Borough of Newcastle. This accounts for the fact that the Irish-born population of the Newcastle registration district was 7158, while in the case of the Borough of Newcastle it was 7124, or 99.6% of the district total.

Table 2: The spatial distribution of Irish-born persons in the registration districts of the registration county of Northumberland, 1851

District	District number	Total population	Number of Irish-born	Irish as % of whole
Newcastle–upon–Tyne	552	89,156	7,152	8.02
Tynemouth	553	64,248	2,269	3.53
Castleward	554	13,897	322	2.32
Hexham	555	30,436	514	1.69
Haltwistle	556	7,286	170	2.33
Bellingham	557	6,553	86	1.31
Morpeth	558	18,127	478	2.64
Alnwick	559	21122	476	2.25
Belford	560	6,871	111	0.16
Berwick	561	24,093	809	3.36
Glendale	562	14,348	174	1.21
Rothbury	563	7,431	105	1.41
Totals		303,568	12,666	4.20

Source: 1851 Census: Birth Places of the People: Division X, Northern Counties, Birth Places of the Inhabitants of Districts: Northumberland.

It is clear from the data in table 3 that the larger Irish population in county Durham was much more widely dispersed than was the case in Northumberland. Though none of the registration districts had a migrant population as large as that in the Newcastle district, there were major clusterings in Sunderland, South Shields, Gateshead, Durham and Stockton. It is interesting to observe that the Gateshead and South Shields Irish populations were on the southern banks of the River Tyne, reflecting the fact that the industries along both banks of the river provided job opportunities for the migrants. However, in the case of county Durham, outside of Gateshead, South Shields and Sunderland, the Irish were widely scattered among the furnace towns and pit villages. For example, within the registration district no. 542, Auckland, sub-district no. 1 was Bishop Auckland and sub-district no. 2 was Hamsterly. The 1222 Irish-born recorded as residing in the Auckland registration district were to be found living principally in sub-district no. 1 in such places as Seldom Seen, Byers Green, Newfield, New Hunswick, Escomb and, most of all, Bishop Auckland township. In the case of the Durham registration district no. 545 the ironworks and pits attracted the Irish, with relatively large numbers living in the townships of Conside-C-Knitsley and nearby Ivestone in sub-district no. 2, Lanchester.

Table 3: The spatial distribution of the Irish-born throughout the registration districts of County Durham, 1851

District	Number	Total population	Irish-born	Irish as % of whole
Darlington	540	21,618	534	2.47
Stockton	541	52,934	1,868	3.53
Auckland	542	30,083	1,222	4.06
Teesdale	543	19,813	228	1.15
Weardale	544	14,567	292	2.00
Durham	545	55,951	3,920	7.00
Easington	546	21,795	506	2.32
Houghton-le-Spring	547	19,564	1,052	5.38
Chester-le-Street	548	20,907	584	5.35
Sunderland	549	70,576	4,103	5.81
South Shields	550	35,790	1,164	3.25
Gateshead	551	48,081	3,028	6.30
Totals		411,679	18,501	4.49

Source: 1851 Census: Birth Places of the People, Division X, Northern Counties. Birth Places of the Inhabitants of Districts. County Durham.

Throughout the nineteenth century the north-east experienced sustained secular economic growth, based on coal, iron and shipbuilding. In all of these sectors there was a continually rising demand for manual workers who, in the case of mining, needed to be mobile. For example, from 1831 onwards, the pit villages of Durham expanded with bewildering rapidity and in some cases, declined equally rapidly as deposits of coal ran out. Thus mobility was a quality required in the labour force. There are numerous examples to illustrate the fluidity of the region's economic development, particularly in county Durham. For example, in 1841 Tow Law was a single farmhouse. By the time of the 1851 census, it was a village of nearly 2000 persons, including 202 Irish-born residents.[4] Similarly, over the period 1841–51 the increase in the population of the parish of Easington was the direct result of the opening of new pits, chiefly in Haswell township.[5] In the Durham registration district both Ivestone and Holmside townships in Lanchester sub-district no. 2, experienced population increases over the same decade, following the opening of new ironstone works and pits.[6] By contrast, Great Lumley township in the Chester-le- Street district lost population because of pits closing down, as did Harraton township.[7] Throughout the nineteenth century, the output of coal and iron increased continually and labour shortages in the later 1860s caused some Durham mine agents to again recruit miners in Cornwall.[8] The continuing attraction of the region to the Irish is illustrated by the census data in table 4 below.

Table 4: The Irish-born populations of County Durham and
Northumberland, 1841–1871

County	Population 1841			Population 1851		
	Total	Irish	Irish as %	Total	Irish	Irish as %
Durham	244,731	5,407	2.2	411,674	18,501	4.5
Northumberland	250,278	5,218	2.1	303,568	12,666	4.2
Totals	495,009	10,6225	2.1	715,242	31,167	4.4

County	Population 1861			Population 1871		
	Total	Irish	Irish as %	Total	Irish	Irish as %
Durham	508,666	27,719	5.4	685,089	37,515	5.5
Northumberland	343,025	15,034	4.4	386,646	14506	3.8
Totals	851,691	42,753	5.0	1,071,735	52,021	4.9

Sources: 1861 Census, Appendix to Report, Table 123; 1871 Census: Birth Places of the People, Table 18.

4 Norris, 'The Irish in Tow Law, County Durham, 1851–1871', *DCLHSB* (1984), pp 41–70.
5 Census Reports, 1851, Division 10, Northern Counties, Durham – Parishes and Populations (referred to from hereon as Census Parishes), Easington District, p. 19.
6 Census Parishes, Durham District, p. 19.
7 Census Parishes, Chester-le-Street District, p. 21.
8 *Newcastle Courant*, 11 Jan. 1867. This contains details of a court case at the Northumberland Epiphany assizes in which eight young Cornish miners were charged with riot.

The pulling power of county Durham's economy for the Irish is better demonstrated by the fact that in 1871, the Irish-born population of the county was seven times the number recorded in 1841. By contrast, the predominantly agricultural county of Northumberland recorded just under a threefold increase. In terms of internal migration within Britain in response to industrial development, it is instructive to place Irish migration in the context of internal, long distance migration into the North-east. With regard to Northumberland and county Durham, the convention has been adopted here of describing movement into Northumberland from county Durham, Yorkshire, Westmorland and Cumberland as *short distance* migration. In the case of county Durham, short distance migration is defined as those born in Northumberland and the other counties referred to above. Anything else, in both cases, is described here as *long distance* migration. Table 5 below gives a breakdown of the region's population in terms of their indigenous populations, short-distance and long-distance migration.

Table 5: Inward migration into Durham and Northumberland
indicating the Irish as a percentage of the
long distance migrants

Registration district	Number born in County		Short distance migrants		Long distance migrants		Irish as % of long distance migrants
	No	*%*	*No*	*%*	*No*	*%*	
Durham	279,622	68	88,094	21	43,953	11	42
Northumberland	232,826	77	31,544	10	39,198	13	32
Totals	512,448	71.6	119,638	16.7	83,151	11.7	36.5

NOTES: Short distance migrants are those born in Northumberland, Cumberland, Westmorland and Yorkshire, with respect to Durham, while in the case of Northumberland, they were born in Durham, Cumberland, Westmorland and Yorkshire.

Source: 1851 Census: Summary Tables, Table XXXIX, Birth Places of the Inhabitants.

It was to be expected, given its economic base, that county Durham should experience a higher level of inward migration compared with Northumberland. As for long distance inward migration, in the case of county Durham, the Irish represented 42% of the total, while in Northumberland 32% of all long distance immigration were Irish-born persons. In the context of economic development, it is important to note that that the level of Irish immigration into England, Wales and Scotland was rising before the onset of the Famine in 1845.

Why were the Irish emigrating to Britain? The more obvious explanations are also the most convincing. In the first half of the nineteenth century, the endemic poverty of the majority of Irish contrasted with the relative prosperity of the English, Welsh and, despite Highland poverty, the Scots. Because of this, many Irish made rational decisions to migrate in order to improve their living standards. The ordinary workings of labour markets meant that significant internal migration was taking place within the United Kingdom and the information networks existed to ensure that the Irish knew of the alternatives available to them.[9] The existence of the pre-Famine Irish communities in Britain and the annual influx of Irish harvesters meant that information was available in Ireland on jobs and conditions in Britain. The development of steam shipping after 1820 and the fierce fare competition between the steamship companies meant that moving to Britain was relatively cheap.[10] The Famine, with its horrific consequences in terms of death and destitution, made England look even more attractive.[11] The decade 1841–51 covered the Famine crisis and over this period, the Irish-born population of county Durham increased nearly three and a half times, while in Northumberland, the corresponding increase was two and a half times (see table 4). An important pull factor was the widespread knowledge that both the scale and nature of poor relief in England and Wales were superior to that available in Ireland under the Irish poor law system introduced in 1838.

Table 6: The Irish-born population of the principal urban areas
of the north-east of England, 1851–1871

Place	Total Population			Irish-born			Irish as % of whole		
	1851	*1861*	*1871*	*1851*	*1861*	*1871*	*1851*	*1861*	*1871*
Durham City	13,188	14,088	15,129	786	898	723	6.0	6.4	4.8
Gateshead*	25,568	33,587	51,903	2,195	2,299	3,276	8.6	6.8	6.3
Newcastle*	87,784	109,108	135,347	7,124	6,596	6,904	8.1	6.8	5.1
South Shields*	28,974	35239	46,949	922	1,083	1,613	3.2	3.1	3.4
Sunderland*	63,897	78,211	102,711	3,601	4,169	4,469	5.6	5.3	4.4
Tynemouth*	29,170	34,021	40,187	1,108	1,312	1,336	3.8	3.9	4.7
Totals	248,581	304,254	392,226	15,736	16,357	18,321	6.3	5.4	4.7

* Denotes Municipal Borough
Source: Census Reports: 1851, 1861 and 1871: Birth Places of the People.

9 For a recent study of pre-Famine Irish migration to Britain, see Ruth-Ann Harris, *The Nearest Place that Wasn't Ireland: Early Nineteenth Century Labour Migration* (Ames, Iowa, 1994).

10 F. Neal, 'Liverpool, the Irish Steamship Companies and the Famine Irish', *Immigrants and Minorities*, vol. 5, no. 1 (March, 1986), pp 28–61.

11 For the first detailed study of the Irish Famine refugee problem in Britain, see F. Neal, *Black '47: Britain and the Famine Irish* (London, 1998).

There is ample evidence that friends and relatives in England provided people in Ireland with information about the poor law system in Britain.[12] Despite the attractions of the coalfields and ironworks, the urban areas of the region continued to exert a strong attraction to the Irish. In Britain as a whole, Irish inward migration peaked in 1861, but with respect to the six major urban areas in the North-east, in the case of five, the total increased over the decade 1861–71, while the numbers in Durham City decreased (see table 6 above).

III

The data described above are taken from the published tables available in the various census reports. However, to establish the distribution of Irish migrants at a lower level of disaggregation, that is at the sub-district, township and street level, it is necessary to extract data from the census enumerators' sheets. This is a labourious business, but it is essential if any attempt is to be made to answer questions not only about spatial distribution but also about family structure, socio-economic status and age distributions. What follows is a detailed analysis of the spatial distribution and occupational profile of Irish migrants in two registration districts of county Durham. These are Easington (no. 546) and Durham (no. 545). The reason for the choice of these two districts is that they illustrate the type of economic forces pulling migrants into Britain during the 1840s. In the case of the townships in the west of the Durham registration district such as Consett, a major 'pull' factor was the iron industry, while in the Easington district at the opposite side of the county, the coal and coke industries and the docks attracted labour to Seaham and Dawdon.

It has already been noted that in the north-east, as in the case of the north-west of England, the Irish represented the largest proportion of long distance migrants. Reference has already been made to the fact that a particular feature of the Irish was their mobility and that in the case of the north-east, this was a particularly useful attribute as pits, ore deposits, and railway construction projects opened up and closed down with astonishing rapidity. Although this has already been referred to, it needs to be emphasised. For example, between 1831 and 1841, the population of Dawdon township in the Easington district increased significantly because of an influx of labour attracted by harbour construction works. Similarly, the population of Seaham increased between 1821 and 1831 because of harbour construction works and between 1841 and 1851 railway construction also pulled labour into Seaham.[13] In other areas such as the Houghton-le-Spring registration district (no. 547), the decade 1821–31

---

12 *Report of the Select Committee on Poor Removal, Parliamentary Papers* (1854), Minutes of Evidence, George Grey, 15 Mar. 1855, pp 460–4.
13 Census Parishes: Easington District, p. 21.

witnessed an influx of labour in the townships of Painshaw and Houghton-le-Spring, attracted by the expansion of output in the local collieries and the opening up of a stone quarry. Yet between 1831 and 1841, the populations declined as labour moved out into nearby districts where new collieries demanded labourers and presumably paid higher wages. Similarly, also in the Houghton-le-Spring district, the township of Newbottle lost population, ascribed to the opening of new pits elsewhere.[14] This same experience of labour mobility was repeated throughout county Durham. In the west of the county, in the Auckland registration district, the population of the township of Bishop Auckland increased over the years 1831 to 1841 as the direct result of new collieries opening up and the building of a railway. In this registration district, over the period 1841–51, the population of the Chapelry of Witton-le-Wear also increased because of railway works and the opening of an ironworks. Over the same decade, the population of Hamsterly township fell because a cotton mill closed down. The Irish were particularly adept at coming to terms with relatively rapid changes in the labour market, and it is against this economic environment that the data on Irish migration into the north-east needs to be interpreted.[15]

Turning first to the Easington registration district, the spatial distribution of the 507 recorded Irish-born among the nineteen townships in the district is given below in table 7. The striking feature of table 7 is the fact that the Irish were spread thinly over the whole district. Five of the townships, Kelloe, Coldheselton, Nesbitt, Seaton and Burdon had no Irish at all, while in the townships of Seaham and Dalton-le-Dale, each had only one Irish-born resident. The coalmines at Thornley and the harbour at Dawdon provided the main centres of employment for Irish-born males in 1851. However, in none of the fourteen townships in which the Irish were to be found did they represent a significant proportion of a township's total population. The largest absolute number of Irish in any township was found in Dawdon, 164, but these represented under 5% of the total population. Another noteworthy feature of the data is that among the non-Irish population the ratio of males to females was 1.1:1. By contrast, among the Irish, the ratio was 1.9:1, almost twice as many males as females. This is what one would expect on a *priori* grounds. The Irish were, at this period, more mobile than the indigenous population and so males could move around without family ties to a greater degree than was the case with the English.

14 Census Parishes: Houghton-le-Spring District, p. 21.
15 Census Parishes: Auckland District, p. 15.

Table 7: The size of the Irish-born populations of the townships
of the Easington registration district, county Durham,
as of 31 March 1851

Township	Total Population			Irish-born population			Irish-born as % of whole		
	Male	Female	Total	Male	Female	Total	Male	Female	Total
Kelloe	79	70	149	–	–	–	–	–	–
Thornley	1,423	1,317	2,740	73	32	105	5.1	2.4	3.8
Wingate	1,304	1,152	2,740	28	8	36	2.1	0.7	1.5
Castle Eden	247	244	491	2	1	3	0.9	0.5	0.8
Hutton Henry	582	485	1067	31	19	50	5.2	3.9	4.7
Sheraton-w-Hulam	74	73	147	1	–	1	1.3	–	0.7
Monk Hesleton	775	720	1495	12	6	18	1.5	0.8	1.2
Easington	475	441	916	30	15	45	6.3	3.4	4.9
Shotton	822	785	1,607	2	3	5	0.2	0.4	0.3
Haswell	2,326	2,030	4,356	37	29	66	1.6	1.4	1.5
Hawthorn	86	97	183	–	1	1	–	1.0	0.5
Coldhesleton	62	55	117	–	–	–	–	–	–
East Morton	754	633	1387	10	1	11	1.3	0.2	0.8
Dalton-le-Dale	43	40	83	1	–	1	2.0	–	1.0
Dawdon	1,750	1,788	3,538	106	58	164	6.1	3.2	4.6
Nesbitt	5	6	11	–	–	–	–	–	–
Seaham	498	231	729	–	1	1	–	0.5	0.1
Seaton	105	95	200	–	–	–	–	–	–
Burdon	56	67	123	–	–	–	–	–	–
Totals	11,466	10,329	21,795	333	174	507	2.9	1.7	2.3

Source: Census Enumerators' Sheets: 1851 Census.

When recording occupations, the census enumerators would record the job
description given. In the case of children, they would be described as 'scholars',
if attending school, or simply be described as 'at home', meaning not attending
school and not working. In some cases, no job description of any kind was
given. These I recorded as 'no data' or 'nd'. I define the economically active
section of the population to be those between ten and seventy years of age,
inclusive.

Table 8: The occupational profile of Irish-born males resident in the Easington registration district on 31 March 1851

Occupation	Thornley	Wingate	Hutton	Monk Henry	Easington Hesleton	Haswell	Dawdon	Rest	Total
Apprentice	–	–	–	–	–	–	1	–	1
Ballast weaver	–	–	–	–	–	–	6	–	6
Brickmaker	–	–	1	–	–	–	–	2	3
Cinderburner	1	–	–	–	–	–	–	–	1
Coalminer	55	17	1	8	–	29	1	6	117
Hawker	1	–	3	–	1	–	–	–	5
Agric. labourer		1 –	–	–	–	–	–	–	1
Labourer	4	1	7	3	20	68	–	3	106
Quarryman	1	–	–	–	–	–	–	–	1
Servant	1	2	1	1	–	–	1	–	6
Shoemaker	1	–	–	–	–	–	–	–	1
Tailor	–	–	–	–	–	–	4	–	4
Turner	–	–	4	–	–	–	–	–	4
Others	–	2	2	–	2	1	12	3	22
Sub-total	65	22	19	12	23	30	93	14	278
At home	1	2	6	–	3	4	8	–	24
Scholar	3	–	2	–	1	2	1	–	9
'nd'	4	4	4	–	3	2	5	–	22
Total	73	28	31	12	30	38	107	14	333

Source: 1851 Census Enumerators' Sheets.

Examining first the occupational profile of the Irish male population of Easington, the economically active numbered 307. Of this total, 278 or 91% were recorded as having an occupation. Such job descriptions do not mean that the person providing the information was in employment at the time. It simply meant that when working, the job so described was what he did. In fact, people often changed occupations throughout their life. Table 8 above lists the job descriptions for Irish-born males in the various townships of the Easington district. The importance of coalmining and dock work is immediately apparent. Of those with job descriptions, 117, or 43%, were coalminers, while 106, 38%, were labourers, the majority working in the docks at Dawdon. When the others employed in heavy manual work are included (agricultural labour, quarries, etc) then 85% of the male Irish-born were involved in manual labour. Interestingly, four were turners, a skilled engineering trade. Outside of manual work, tailoring, hawking and shoemaking were each low paid occupations. There were few barriers to entry in such trades, little capital being needed to set up in business, and together with the job of servant, such occupations added up to 17 or 6% of the total.

Table 9: The occupational profile of Irish-born females resident in the Easington registration district on 31 March 1851

Occupation	Thornley	Wingate	Hutton	Monk Henry	Easington Hesleton	Haswell	Dawdon	Rest	Total
Dressmaker	–	–	1	–	–	–	1	–	2
Housekeeper	3	–	–	–	–	–	1	–	4
House servant	–	–	–	–	1	3	6	2	12
Haberdasher	–	–	–	–	1	–	–	–	1
Hawker	1	–	–	–	–	–	–	–	1
Labourer	1	–	–	–	2	–	2	–	5
Laundress	–	–	–	–	–	–	1	–	1
Servant	1	–	2	–	–	1	2	–	6
Washerwoman	1	–	–	–	–	–	–	–	1
Weaver	–	–	–	–	1	–	–	–	1
Teacher	–	–	–	–	–	–	–	1	1
Sub-total	7	–	3	–	5	4	13	3	35
At home	2	–	8	1	4	4	8	–	27
Scholar	1	–	–	–	–	2	1	–	4
'nd' (wives)	15	4	6	4	3	7	223	2	64
'nd' (rest)	7	4	1	1	3	12	13	3	44
Total	*32*	*8*	*18*	*6*	*15*	*29*	*58*	*8*	*174*

Source: 1851 Census Enumerators' Sheets.

With regard to the census enumerators recording of female occupations (see table 9 above), the same considerations applied as those referred to above regarding males. However, in the case of those having no job description of any kind, 'nd', a large proportion of this category were wives and daughters of the heads of households. These were not contributing to household money income, but were usually providing domestic services unless, in the case of daughters, they were very young.

In the case of women in the north-east we would expect a much lower proportion of the total to have an occupation outside of the home. The pit villages and furnace towns offered little in the way of factory or domestic work. In the case of Easington, those women in the economically active age range numbered 174 or 87% of the total. Of these 35 women or 23% recorded occupations. Of this total, 24 were in the domestic service business providing such labour as housekeepers, servants and washerwomen. As for those women recording no occupation at all, significantly, 64 were married. In the pit villages, wives had a particular responsibility to wash the dirty clothes of miners and furnace workers, together with that of having meals on the table as shift workers came home. The majority of women in such communities had no opportunity to contribute to the household money income. Unlike the major urban areas, there was no large middle class demanding domestic servants and also few opportunities of factory work.

Moving across the county to its North-western border, the Durham registration district, no 545 included both coalmines and ironworks. The total Irish-born population of this registration district was, in 1851, 3920. Of this total, 786 lived in the City of Durham. The data given in Table 10 below refer to the Lanchester sub-district no. 2 of the Durham registration district. Relatively large numbers of Irish were residing in and around such villages as Leadgate, Berryedge and Consett. These in turn, were within the boundaries of Conside-C-Knitsley, Ivestone, Ebchester, and Benfieldside townships.

Table 10: The size of the Irish-born populations of the townships of Ebchester, Benfieldside, Conside-C-Knitsley and Ivestone in the Durham sub-registration district on 31 March 1851 distinguishing between males and females

Township	Total population			Irish-born population			Irish-born as % of whole		
	Male	Female	Total	Male	Female	Total	Male	Female	Total
Ebchester	324	286	610	71	44	115	21.9	15.3	18.8
Benfieldside	1,282	1,193	2,475	246	136	382	19.2	14.4	15.4
Conside-C-Knitsley	1,589	1,188	2,777	463	245	708	29.1	20.6	25.5
Ivestone	1,408	1,092	2,500	344	188	532	24.4	17.2	21.6
Totals	4,603	3,759	8,362	1,124	613	1,737	24.4	16.3	20.8

Sources: The total township population numbers were taken from the 1851 Census: Division X, Northern Counties, no 38, Durham Parishes (Areas and Houses). The numbers of Irish in each township were extracted from the Census Enumerators' Sheets, 1851.

The dispersal of the Irish between these townships illustrates that in this area, by contrast with the Easington district, the Irish represented significant proportions of the population in some townships. For example, 29.1% of all males in the township of Conside-C-Knitsley, were Irish-born. In the total population, the Irish made up 25.5%. Similarly in Ivestone township, the Irish represented over 21% of the total population. Again the sex ratios differ. In the case of the non-Irish it is 1.1:1; the Irish ratio was 1.8:1. It is noteworthy that in the four study areas, there were 284 British-born children of at least one Irish parent. If these are counted as part of the 'Irish community', then we have a total of 2021 or 24% of the total population.

The occupational breakdown of Irish-born males in table 11 again illustrates the truth of the oft-quoted assertion that Irishmen were principally occupied in heavy manual work. In Ivestone township 121 Irishmen were employed in the coalmines, while another 94 were labourers. Together with the 57 working in the ironstone mines, 93% of the Irish-born males returning occupations in the census in this township were working in heavy manual jobs. A similar situation existed in neighbouring Conside township, except that the majority worked in the iron foundry. Here, such workers, together with miners and

Table 11: The occupational profile of Irish-born males resident in the Townships of Ebchester, Benfieldside, Conside-C-Knitsley and Ivestone on 31 March 1851

Occupation	Ebchester	Benfieldside	Conside-C-Knitsley	Ivestone	Total
Coalminer/worker	22	4	65	121	212
Ironstone miner/worker	10	12	2	59	83
Labourer/general	18	154	13	94	279
Ironworker	–	8	261	13	282
Shoemaker	–	2	2	2	6
Tailor	1	–	8	–	9
Other	10	15	54	5	84
Sub-total	61	195	405	294	955
At home	6	25	225	32	88
Scholars	2	7	18	11	38
'nd'	2	20	15	7	44
Total	71	247	463	344	1125

Source: Census Enumerators' Sheets, 1851.

general labourers, accounted for 84% of all the Irish-born males returning job
descriptions in the 1851 census. Taking the four townships together, 95% of all
Irish-born males returning job descriptions were involved in heavy manual
work. Practically all of the remainder were in low paid occupations.

The occupational profile of Irish-born women in the same four townships
reveals the same lack of employment opportunities as observed in the case of
Easington (see table 12). Of the 613 females residing in the townships only 107,
or 17%, returned a job description. Of these 107 females, 62%, were described
as servants or housekeepers. It is notable that 11 of the women were labourers.
Again, it needs to be appreciated that given the dirty nature of the work in the
pits, furnaces and coke ovens, many wives had a full-time job washing and
providing meals for shift workers. For example, of the 373 women for whom no
description was given regarding occupation (no data), 223 were wives of the
head of household. These, almost certainly, ran the households.

Table 12: The occupational profile of Irish-born females resident
in the townships of Ebchester, Benfieldside, Conside-C-Knitsley
and Ivestone on 31 March 1851

Occupation	Ebchester	Benfieldside	Conside-C-Knitsley	Ivestone	Total
Dealer	–	2	–	–	2
Dressmaker	–	1	4	1	6
Hawker	1	–	2	–	3
Housekeeper	–	–	8	9	17
Labourer	–	3	6	2	11
Laundress	–	1	1	1	3
Lodg. house keeper	–	–	1	–	1
Milliner	1	–	–	–	1
Paper maker	–	–	2	–	2
Seamstress	–	–	3	–	3
Servant	6	4	26	13	49
Washerwoman	–	1	–	2	8
Rest					
Sub-total	13	13	53	28	107
At home	4	20	29	58	111
'nd' (wives)	11	51	100	61	223
'nd' (daughters)	1	21	23	13	58
'nd' (rest)	12	26	28	26	92
Scholars	3	5	12	2	22
Total	44	136	245	188	613

Source: Census Enumerators' Sheets, 1851.

IV

By 1841, Lancashire was home to a large Irish-born migrant population and their British-born children. The hinterland of the port of Liverpool, the main port of Irish entry in Britain, included the large and still growing cotton textile industry, together with other manufacturing and chemical industries as well as coalmining. The significance of the factory based industries of the north-west is that they provided job opportunities for the whole family, men, women and children. This made it almost certain that household income for the Irish in the north-west would be higher than those in the North-east. This would be especially true with respect to the Irish in the isolated pit villages of Durham.

The Lancashire civil county, no. 34, contained twenty-five registration districts. One of these was Leigh, no. 467. In turn Leigh was divided into four sub-districts, Lowton no. 1, Culcheth no. 2, West Leigh no. 3 and Atherton no. 4. Culcheth and Lowton were, and still are, principally agricultural districts, while West Leigh and Atherton were home to a rapidly growing industrial sector. To place the job opportunities available to the Irish in context, the 1851 census revealed that in the Leigh registration district, of all women aged 20 years or

Table 13: The occupational profile of Irish-born males resident
in Leigh, Lancashire, on 31 March 1851

Description	Number	Description	Number	Description	Number
Cotton Industry		**Labourers**		Grinder (factory)	1
Carder	2	Agricultural	90	Joiner	1
Grinder	1	Chemical works	5	Lodg. house kpr	7
Handloom weaver	4	General	35	Miner	4
Piecer	3	Vitriol works	5	Miller	1
Labourer	1			Painter	2
Spinner	2	**Other jobs**		Rag collector	1
Stripper	1	Baker	1	Shoemaker	12
Tenter/carder	1	Brickmaker	1	Tailor	10
Weaver	2	Cordwainer	1	Umbrella maker	1
Worker	4	Dealer (fruit)	2	Chelsea Pensioner	1
		Drawer (colliery)	1	*Total jobs*	224
Silk Industry		Factory worker	8	No data on jobs	48
Weaver	6	Farmer	1	At home	3
Worker	6	G P*	1	Scholars	4
				Overall total	280

* General Practitioner
Source: Census Enumerators' Sheets, 1851.

over, 2554 worked in the silk industry and another 1413 in the cotton mills. As
for males in the same age category, 1931 worked in the silk mills and 1523 in the
cotton textile industry. Similarly, 729 men worked in coal mines.

According to the 1841 census enumerators' sheets there were 96 Irish-born
persons in the district. By 1851 this number had risen six-fold to 570, broken
down into 280 males and 290 females. The number of economically active
Irish-born males in 1851 was 246 or 88% of the total number of Irish-born
males. Of this number 224 or 91% returned a job description (see table 13
above). Given the size of the local textile industry, cotton and silk, it is
surprising that only 33 Irish-born males worked in the industry. Similarly, only
12 Irish males described themselves as working in the coal industry. However,
not surprising is the fact that 135 or 55% of all economically active Irish males
were labourers. Significantly, four male handloom weavers were recorded, the
remnants of a once large occupational group.

Table 14: The occupational profile of Irish-born females resident
in Leigh, Lancashire, on 31 March 1851

Description	Number	Description	Number	Description	Number
Domestic &		Nurse	6	**Other jobs**	
household services		Shoemaker	1	Labourer (agric)	32
Cook	1	Seamstress	1	Chemical works	
Charwoman	2			labourer	2
Domestic duties	11	**Cotton Mills**		Factory worker	15
Housemaid	1	Bobbin winder	1	General laundress	2
Servant	24	Carder	2	Nailmaker	1
Washerwoman	17	Doubler	1		
		Hand twister	1	*Jobs total*	*181*
Other services		Piecer	2		
Assistant in		Worker	10	**No data on jobs**	
Beerhouse	1			Wife	25
Bookbinder	1	**Silk industry**		Daughters	12
Boot & Shoe binder	1	Handloom weaver	1	Lodgers	41
Dealer	3	Weaver	10	Rest	20
Dressmaker	3	Powerloom weaver	2	Scholars	7
Hawker	2	Winder	3	At home	4
Lodging house kpr	5	Worker	2		
				Overall total	*290*

Source: Census Enumerators' Sheets, 1851.

Table 15: The occupational profile of 633 Irish-born males resident in
Rochdale, Lancashire, on 31 March 1851

Description	Number	Description	Number	Description	Number
Cotton industry		**Other jobs**		**Other jobs**	
Cardroom	4	Beerseller	1	Steam engineer	1
Doffer	18	Blacksmith	2	Mechanic	4
Engraver	1	Book-keeper	1	Musician	2
Flat stripper	1	Bootmaker	1	Nailmaker	1
Fly picker	1	Carpenter	2	Outfitter	1
Fustian cutter	2	Carrier	1	Outworker	2
Jobber	2	Carter	1	Painer	1
Millworker	6	Caulker	1	Pattern maker	1
Mule piecer	1	Chair bottom maker	5	Pedlar	2
Operative	30	Coalminer	1	Pensioner	1
Piecer	4	Cooper	1	Plasterer	1
Roving carrier	1	Cordwainer	1	Printer	3
Scavenger	2	Dealer	10	Rag gatherer	1
Scutcher	2	Dyer	1	Railway porter	1
Spinner	3	Engineer	1	Ropeworks	4
Steamloom weaver	1	Factory operative	47	Sawyer	1
Stripper	1	Factory worker	9	Scavenger	1
Throstle spinner	1	Farming	3	Servant	2
Weaver	4	Fishmonger	2	Shoemaker	10
		Furniture broker	1	Showman	1
Labourers		Gardener	1	Tailor	48
Agricultural	12	Glazier	6	Tinner	3
Bricklayer	8	Grocer	1	Toymaker	1
Brick setter	2	Hatter	1	Traveller	5
Factory	2	Hawker	27	Trunk maker	1
Foundry	1	Heckler	1	Warehouse	2
Lodging house	1	Ironfoundry	3	Rest	10
Mason	2	Joiner	1	*Jobs total*	*514*
Outdoor	2			No data on jobs	34
Railway	26			Scholars	18
General	129			At home	67
				Total	*633*

Source: Census Enumerators' Sheets, 1851.

In the case of Irish-born females in Leigh in 1851 the economically active numbered 247 or 85% of the total number of Irish-born females. Of this number, 181 or 62% returned a job description. Table 14 gives a breakdown of female occupations. Despite the presence of a sizeable factory based demand for labour only 53 Irish-born females worked in cotton, silk and other manufacturing activities. By contrast, 65 worked providing domestic services, representing 34% of all those females returning a job description. The Leigh registration sub-districts of Lowton and Culcheth were the sites of a flourishing market garden industry, and this probably explains the presence of 32 women described as agricultural labourers.

The Rochdale registration district was firmly in the centre of the Lancashire cotton belt, surrounded by other textile districts, such as Blackburn, Oldham, Burnley and so on. In Rochdale, the 1851 census recorded 2058 Irish-born persons. The data used below is a sample of 1315 of these, or 64%. The main

Table 16: The occupational profile of 681 Irish-born females resident in Rochdale, Lancashire, on 31 March 1851

Description	Number	Description	Number	Description	Number
Domestic &					
household Services		Stay maker	1	Carpet weaver	1
Cook	1	Seamstress	1		
Charwoman	4	Tailoress	3	**Other jobs**	
Domestic duties	7			Caulker	1
Housekeeper	18	**Cotton mills/industry**		Factory work	39
Housemaid	1	Carder	2	Labourer	7
Housework	2	Cardtenter	1	Printer	1
Laundress	1	Copreeler	3	Rest	42
Servant	26	Drawer	9	*Jobs total*	*347*
Waiter	1	Operative	41		
Washerwoman	3	Millworker	13	**No data on jobs**	
		Piecer	9	Wife	119
Other services		Rover	5	Daughters	12
Baker	1	Slubber	1	Lodgers	45
Capmaker	1	Spinner	2	Rest	17
Dealer	10	Stocking knitter	2	Scholars	19
Dressmaker	11	Throstle piecer	9	At home	122
Hawker	50	Winder	5		
Pedlar	1	Woollen mill	11	*Overall total*	*681*

Source: Census Enumerators' Sheets, 1851.

employer was the cotton textile industry. Of all males in the district aged 20 years or above, 3743 worked in the textile factories while in the corresponding category of females, 3958 were also similarly employed. The Rochdale sample of Irish-born males used here numbered 633 and their occupational breakdown is given in table 15 above. Again in contrast to the more isolated townships of county Durham, a much wider range of job descriptions is given, in the case of Rochdale these number at least 83. However, as always, the number employed as labourer is the largest 185 or 36% of those returning job descriptions. The cotton industry and other factory work accounted for 141 Irish males, some 27% of the total. With respect to the cotton industry, it is noticeable that only 3 Irish males described themselves as spinners, the highest grade of cotton worker. As in all Irish settlements, hawkers were a noticeable presence.

Of the 681 Irish-born women in the sample (see table 16 above), 582 or 85% were in the economically active age group and of these 347 or 60% returned a job description. The cotton industry and factory work accounted for 114 of all occupations with domestic services of secondary importance, employing 64 women.

The analysis of the census data used in this essay allows some tentative conclusions to be drawn about the experience of Irish-born migrants in the north-east. The conclusions are tentative because the data used are part of a much larger study of the Irish in the north-east in which Newcastle-upon-Tyne, Gateshead and Sunderland are included. Preliminary examination of the data regarding these large urban areas suggests that the general conclusions drawn in this essay will not be significantly altered for the Irish in general.

Table 17: The numbers of Irish-born males and females returning a job description, expressed as a percentage of the total numbers

District	Total	Males No. with job description	Jobs as %	Total	Females No. with job description	Jobs as %
Easington	333	278	83	174	35	20
Ebchester	71	61	86	44	13	30
Benfieldside	247	195	79	136	13	10
Conside	463	405	87	245	53	22
Ivestone	344	294	85	188	28	15
Leigh	280	224	80	290	181	62
Rochdale	633	514	81	681	347	51

Source: Census Enumerators' Sheets, 1851.

The picture which emerges from the analysis of the census data used in this paper is fairly unambiguous. As table 17 suggests, in both the north-east and the north-west, 80% or more of all Irish-born males returned job descriptions. Also, in both regions, the majority of Irish-born males were engaged in manual labour. More specifically, in the north-east, this involved heavy labour in the iron ore and coal mines and the docks. By contrast, in the north-west, a significant number of males were employed in factories. However, it needs to be kept in mind that though factory work was less physically demanding than mining and dock work, it was dirty, laborious, and often unhealthy. Few Irish males occupied the job of spinner in the textile industry, the highest paid labour in the mills. Another difference in occupational structures of the mill towns and the Durham pit villages is that the former offered a wider range of work opportunities to Irish-born males. In both regions, hawking, shoe-repairing and tailoring were activities in which the Irish were involved in a significant way, but these were low income activities.

When we turn to the occupational profile of Irish-born women, a significant difference in the job market becomes obvious. In the case of the Durham town-ships studied, the proportion of Irish-born females returning job descriptions was much lower than in the case of the two Lancashire towns. It can be seen from table 17 that in the case of Irish women in the north-east sample, the percentage returning job descriptions varied from 10% to 30%. These figures contrast starkly with those for Leigh and Rochdale, which were 62 and 51% respectively. The explanation of such regional differences in the female labour market have already been alluded to, namely the presence of a large manu-facturing base in the north-west and the almost complete absence of such in county Durham. A common feature of both regional markets for female labour was the demand for providers of domestic services, but this was not specific to the Irish, and was true for all the female labour markets.

V

Limitations of space do not permit any analysis of Irish household structure in this essay. In this context, the issues usually addressed include such things as size of household, and whether or not it consisted solely of the nuclear family or the extended family. How important were lodgers as supplements to household income? What follows are examples of Irish households, taken from the two regions studied. These put some flesh on the statistics referred to in the essay and give some indication of the economic environment in which the migrants survived in the immediate post-Famine period.

The first case is that of the French family, who lived in James Street, Tyldsley, a district of Leigh. There were six members of the household and all were born in Ireland.

Bridget French	Widow	aged 44 years
Mary French	Daughter	aged 19 years
Bridget French	Daughter	aged 17 years
Arabella French	Daughter	aged 16 years
Fanny French	Daughter	aged 14 years
Bridget Tracy	Lodger	aged 14 years

Bridget French, the mother and head of the household, had no job, but all of the girls, including the lodger, worked in a cotton mill. The household income, including the lodger's rent, would have provided a relatively reasonable standard of living. With the exception of the lodger, the household consisted of the nuclear family. Whether or not Bridget French's husband died in the Famine or in England we simply don't know.

The second example is that of the MacNulty family, who lived in Warbarton Hill in Westleigh, a different area of Leigh to Tyldsley. There were seven members of the household.

John MacNulty	Head	aged 21 years	Labourer in chemical works
Ellen MacNulty	Wife	aged 23 years	No job
Mary MacNulty	Mother	aged 55 years	Housekeeper
Mary MacNulty	Sister	aged 17 years	Factory worker
M. MacNulty	Sister	aged 14 years	Factory worker
Margaret MacNulty	Niece	aged 21 years	No job
Ellen Doherty	Lodger	aged 28 years	No job

All members of the household were born in Mayo, and possibly this is an example of a chain of migration, though equally likely, they may have come over via Liverpool with the flood of Famine refugees. In this example, John MacNulty, the head of the household, and his wife were young and there were no childen. We do not know if his father was dead or working elsewhere at the time of the census, but it is clear that the family, from a Famine county, had made an effort to stay together. With three members in employment, household income would have ensured survival without parish relief and if the others had arrived recently, job prospects in the area were reasonable.

If we move north to Rochdale, the Kelly family lived in Hayes Street in Rochdale at the time of the 1851 census. In this case there were twelve members of the household.

Hannah Kelly	Head	aged 66 years	Widow and housekeeper
Bridget Kelly	Daughter	aged 30 years	Unmarried cotton winder
Mary Brown	Daughter	aged 28 years	Widowed cotton winder
Edmund Kelly	Son	aged 25 years	Unmarried warehouse clerk

Hannah Kelly	Daughter	aged 22 years	Unmarried cotton winder
John Brown	Grandson	aged 9 years	Scholar
James Brown	Grandson	aged 7 years	Scholar
Mary Ann Brown	Grand-daughter	aged 5 years	At home
George Brown	Grandson	aged 2 years	At home
Edmund Kelly	Bro-in-law	aged 52 years	Widower, nailmaker
Bridget Kelly	Niece	aged 25 years	Cotton winder
Ann Kelly	Niece	aged 20 years	Cotton winder

This is a clear example of the extended family household. Hannah Kelly, the head of the household, had her three unmarried children and her widowed daughter Mary living with her, together with Mary's four children. In addition, her dead sister's husband, Edmund Kelly, and his two daughters shared the household. Seven of the adults had jobs, guaranteeing a satisfactory household income, five of the women working in cotton mills. There appeared to be no need to take lodgers from outside the family. Hannah ran the household, describing herself as 'housekeeper'. All four grandchildren were born in Rochdale, suggesting that Mary had been in England before the Famine crisis years of 1845–9.

The village of Leadgate was in Ivestone township in County Durham. It was home to 410 Irish-born persons in 1851. The principal male occupations were coal and iron ore mining. The Corrigan family numbered eleven.

James Corrigan	Head	aged 54 years	Widower, ironminer
Catherine Corrigan	Daughter	aged 24 years	No job
Patrick Corrigan	Son	aged 22 years	Unmarried, miner
Ann Corrigan	Daughter	aged 19 years	No job
Susan Corrigan	Daughter	aged 16 years	No job
Mary Corrigan	Daughter	aged 13 years	No job
Charles Murphy	Lodger	aged 26 years	Married, miner
Rose Murphy	Lodger	aged 26 years	Wife of lodger, no job
Rose Murphy	Lodger	aged 1 year	
Francis Pigent	Lodger	aged 31 years	Miner
Francis Murtagh	Lodger	aged 18 years	Miner

All were born in Ireland, except for Rose Murphy, daughter of Charles and Rose, lodgers. She was born in county Durham. James Corrigan, head of the household, had four unmarried daughters at home and one unmarried son. Patrick, the son, had a job as a miner, but none of the girls worked. This lack of female employment contrasts with the situation in the Lancashire households. To supplement household income, James Corrigan had taken in five lodgers. All the male lodgers worked as miners.

On the opposite side of the county in the Easington registration district, the Henry household lived in Blandford Place, Dawdon. There were fourteen in the household, six members of the nuclear family and eight lodgers, and all were born in Ireland.

Michael Henry	Head	aged 35 years	Labourer
Anne Henry	Wife	aged 35 years	No job
James Henry	Son	aged 13 years	No job
Bridget Henry	Daughter	aged 8 years	At home
Margaret Henry	Daughter	aged 7 years	At home
John Henry	Son	aged 5 years	At home
Thomas Harris	Lodger	aged 20 years	Labourer
Michael Gannon	Lodger	aged 25 years	Labourer
Charles Gannon	Lodger	aged 20 years	Labourer
Michael Dwyer	Lodger	aged 40 years	Labourer
John Mader	Lodger	aged 25 years	Labourer
Patrick Bidiccan	Lodger	aged 20 years	Labourer
James Bidican	Lodger	aged 19 years	Labourer
John Bidican	Lodger	aged 17 years	Labourer

Michael Henry was supporting a wife and four children on a labourer's wage and so the eight lodgers were sources of extra income. With the exception of the forty-year-old Michael Dwyer, all of the lodgers were single men and all of the employed males were labourers. The fact that Michael Henry's son, John, was five years old and born in Ireland makes it highly probable that the family was part of the Famine exodus.

VI

In conclusion, I would like to refer to the issue of the degree of transiency among the Irish migrants in both regions during the period under review.[16] In a recent study of the pre-Famine Irish in Britain, Ruth-Ann Harris has argued powerfully and convincingly that the numbers of Irish in Britain on a temporary basis were much bigger than the numbers represented by the seasonal harvesters. In essence, her argument is that before the Famine, many Irish did not want to emigrate. However, the post-Napoleonic War economic depression and the subsequent run-down of Irish industry made it increasingly difficult for tenants of small holdings to maintain their rent payments. The solution was

16 For an excellent survey of this subject, see especially D. Fitzpatrick, 'A peculiar tramping people: the Irish in Britain, 1801–1870' in W.E.Vaughan (ed.), *A New History of Ireland*, vol. V (1989), pp 621–659.

temporary sojourns in Britain, earning enough money in the factories, mines, and farms to keep up rent payments in Ireland and so obviate the necessity of leaving Ireland permanently. Again, measuring mobility or transient labour is no part of this essay, but some *prima facie* evidence can be addressed regarding mobility.

The 1841 census recorded 50 Irish-born males in the Leigh registration district and 46 Irish-born females. In 1851, only 7 of the males were still in Leigh and, in the case of females, at most 12 remained. The 1861 census recorded an increase in Irish-born males, from 280 in 1851 to 587, reflecting the national trends of continuing high levels of Irish inward migration up to 1861. In this latter census, only 44 of the 280 Irish-born males resident in 1851 were still in the Leigh registration district. In the case of the 290 Irish-born females in the Leigh registration district in 1851, 54 were still there in 1861. The same picture of mobility is repeated elsewhere. The township of Southwick was in the Sunderland registration in 1851. The area was the site of lime pits and a glass bottle works, creating a demand for unskilled labour. The 1851 census recorded 128 Irish-born males living in the township. By 1861, only 18 of these were still there. In the case of Irish-born females, there were 97 in Southwick in 1851; by 1861 only 13 of these remained. Neither the evidence of Leigh or Southwick proves that the Irish leaving the districts returned to Ireland, but it does support the hypothesis that the Irish were extremely mobile. Lastly, it is interesting to note that some of the North-east disturbances between English and Irish occurred in the Ivestone area where the concentrations of Irish were relatively large.[17]

---

17 F. Neal, 'English-Irish Conflict in the North-east of England', in Buckland and Belchem (eds), *The Irish in British Labour History* (1993), pp 59–85.

Catholic education in Victorian Hull

Marie McClelland

Writing about Kingston upon Hull in 1891, Edmund Wrigglesworth was eloquent in praising the town for its deserved titles of 'The Queen of the Humber' and the 'Third Port of the United Kingdom'. At that time the government of the town was vested in 'a Corporation whose first Charter was granted in the reign of Edward I ... The Corporation now consists of a Mayor, 14 Aldermen and 42 Councillors'.[1] Hull returned three MPs to Parliament and it had its own office of Lord High Steward (held then by the marquess of Ripon). The latter post ranked among its past rolls of honour the names of 'six prime ministers, two Lord Chancellors, one archbishop of Canterbury and five secretaries of State'.[2] The port of Hull had expanded considerably since the late 1700s and by 1885 could boast nine docks occupying an area of over 145 acres and surrounded by 'spacious quays and warehouses furnished with machinery of the most modern description to facilitate the trade of the port, including enormous hydraulic cranes, some of which are capable of lifting upwards of 100 tons of dead weight'.[3]

The expansion of the docks was warranted to deal with the phenomenal 130% increase in tonnage arriving at the port between 1862 and 1882. This compared very favourably with a 97% increase in Liverpool and an 83% increase in London in the same period. While Hull could not call itself a serious manufacturing town, many significant manufacturing industries had grown out of its maritime location. Ship building, seed crushing and oil cake manufacture were of great importance. For the 80 years before 1852, Hull had enjoyed a leading position in the Greenland whale fisheries yielding an estimated 171,907 tons of oil which sold for £5,158,080. When the whaling industry was finally phased out in 1869 the fishing trade continued to prosper. The 8700 tons of fish passing through the port in 1869 was to increase to 18,981 tons by 1887. Links with other English towns and cities were guaranteed by means of fast steamers from the port or by one of the three railway connections with the town: The North Eastern Railway; The Hull & Barnsley

---

1   E. Wrigglesworth, *Brown's Illustrated Guide to Hull with A Glance at its History* (Hull, 1891), p. 5 & p. 209.
2   Ibid., p. 6.
3   Ibid., p. 209. The nine docks and their dates of erection were: Queen's 1779; Humber 1809; Prince's 1829; Railway 1846; Victoria 1850; Albert 1869; William Wright 1880; Andrew's 1883; Alexandra 1885.

and West Riding Junction Railway; and the Manchester, Sheffield & Lincolnshire Railway.

In common with most of the major towns and cities in England in the nineteenth century, Hull's population was increasing steadily and many of these newcomers were from Ireland. Table 1 provides a comparison between Hull's rising Irish population and that of Leeds, Liverpool and York, its three closest rivals.[4]

Table 1: The Irish-born populations of Hull, Leeds,
Liverpool and York, 1841–1871

	1841 Irish-born	% pop	1851 Irish-born	% pop	1861 Irish-born	% pop	1871 Irish-born	% pop
Hull	1,048	2.3	3,054	3.2	2,823	2.5	2,699	2.2
Leeds	5,027	3.3	7,795	7.6	9,468	8.0	10,128	3.9
Liverpool	49,639	17.3	70,194	27.1	66,290	24.5	76,761	15.5
York	534	1.3	2,188	3.8	2,198	3.6	1,522	3.4

Source: Census returns, 1841–1871.

The flow of Irish immigrants had become noticeable since the 1790s when openings abounded for navvies and labourers to construct the new railway lines. But from the 1840s onwards there was a veritable upsurge as victims of the Irish Famine in 1845 crowded into London and into the industrial towns of the North. Of the estimated 400,000 that had arrived by 1851, 100,000 of these were deemed to be living in London in appalling conditions.[5] Liverpool and Leeds soaked up most of the rest, while only the toughest and most determined went on to settle in Hull. Hull's Irish population trebled in that time, the majority of them coming from county Mayo in search of work on the docks. Jobs were easy enough to secure either on board ship or on the quayside or within the related industries of ship building and milling. They tended to settle in primitive hovels, huddled together in the west end of Hull. They were not markedly swift to attend church or indeed to seek out Catholic education for their children.

In his *Historical Notes on English Catholic Missions*, Bernard Kelly estimates the congregation of St Charles' Church (the only Catholic Church in Hull) as

---

4   Figures taken from the Census Returns for 1841, 1851, 1861 and 1871.
5   D. Newsome, *The Convert Cardinals: Newman & Manning* (London, 1993), p. 191.

6500 in the year 1850–1 with 240 children attending the elementary school in its basement.[6] This figure needs to be set beside the 1851 Religious Census which revealed a figure of 1200 attending Mass in the morning and 850 in the afternoon service of Sunday 30 March at St Charles. While neither figure supplies an accurate or reliable picture of the size of the mission served by Father Michael Trappes and his curate, Father John Motler, one thing is abundantly certain. The town needed more than one church and one school if it was to help and guide the immigrants to continue the practice of their faith and to develop a sense of belonging in their newly adopted country.

Father Michael Trappes came to Hull in 1848, having served as a priest in Monkwearmouth, Manchester, Rochdale, Bury, Brough Hall and Huddersfield. He was one of seven sons of a staunchly recusant family from Nidd Hall in the West Riding. He was destined to remain twenty-five years at St Charles', during which time he earned considerable respect in the town. He was a frequent lecturer at the Mechanics Institute and a subscriber to the Hull Literary and Philosophical Society. His first five years in Hull were marked with feverish activity to lay the foundation of a systematic plan for the future education of all his flock. He was a clever communicator and knew how to persuade people to do his bidding. Two years after his arrival he opened a mixed school for boys and girls in temporary accommodation in Canning Street right in the heart of the Irish settlement. This was intended to augment the provision at St Charles' school which had operated in the church basement since 1829, and to lure the Irish children into his protection. By 1855, government inspectors deemed Canning Street school to be progressing well and it was in receipt of government grants.[7] Two more projects were already in hand. One was to relocate the St Charles' school in bigger premises in Pryme Street (a street much closer to where the Irish lived), and another was to secure a site on the corner of Dansom Lane and Wilton Street in the mills and factory district of the town for a new St Mary's school-cum-chapel. The latter opened in January 1857, with accommodation in the school for 90 boys, girls and infants. The relocation of St Charles' was completed in 1859, and provision was rationalised so that the Pryme Street school concentrated on boys only and the Canning Street school provided for girls. HMI reports for 1858 singled out Canning Street for praise as one of the schools where trained and certificated teachers were being appointed.[8] Meantime, St Charles' focused its energies on

6 B. Kelly, *Historical Notes on English Catholic Missions* (London, 1907), p. 222.
7 Catholic Education Council Archives, *8th Annual Report of the Catholic Poor School Committee with extracts from HMI Reports on Schools for that year*, School no. 84, p. 249.
8 Public Record Office, Ed 17, 24, *Report of the Committee of Council on Education with Appendix 1858–9*, General report for the year 1858 by HMI of Schools, J. Reynell Morell Esq, on the RC schools inspected by him in the North Eastern Division of Great Britain, p. 206.

promoting good attendance from its first year in the Pryme Street premises. A reefer jacket and a pair of clogs were awarded to any boy who had a year's perfect attendance. Records show that this considerable incentive yielded at least 60 winners per annum. Not surprisingly, by 1861, St Charles' was listed by HMI Lynch as one of '27 of those schools of whom I can speak with unqualified praise'. Lynch was pleased with the standard of books in use in the school – mainly those published by the National Board of Education in Ireland, by the Irish Christian Brothers and by the Catholic publishers Burns & Lambert – and he was very impressed to find that one of the assistant teachers in the school had completed a year's training at St Mary's College, Hammersmith. In his report, he mentioned eight others in the Catholic schools in the town who were similarly trained.[9]

Formal training for teachers throughout the country was still in an embryo state. The Hull Catholics were impressive in having attracted school staff who were obviously eager to be as well trained as possible. The recommended route for training, according to the plan set out in 1846 by Sir James Kay Shuttleworth, Secretary of the Education Department, was a form of apprenticeship to bridge the gap between a child's completion of elementary education at about 13 and commencement at a training college at 18. During that time, a pupil-teacher would teach the younger classes in an elementary school under the supervision of the headteacher. In addition, he or she would be coached by the headteacher after school hours to prepare for the Queen's Scholarship Examination after which, if successful, the pupil teacher could enter a training college for a period of one or two years. After a training college course, the student could hope to be employed as an assistant or certificated teacher in the schools. Government grants were paid to schools receiving pupil-teachers to promote the scheme, but annual inspection of the schools and annual examination of their pupil-teachers was obligatory.

Father Trappes could not have orchestrated such a rapid and successful expansion of educational provision single-handedly. Moral support came from his curate, Father John Motler, from Lady Chichester Constable of Burton Constable Hall and from many generous parishioners. Educational expertise came in 1857 from the Sisters of Mercy of Clifford Convent, near Tadcaster. The Mercy nuns were founded in Baggot Street, Dublin, by Catherine McAuley in December 1831 to service the corporal and spiritual needs of the poor, the sick and the ignorant wherever these needs presented themselves. It was not unusual for clusters of these nuns to be sent out from Baggot Street to new parishes, new towns and new countries in response to pleas for their help. The

9 Public Record Office, Ed 17, 27a, *Report of the Committee of Council on Education with Appendix 1861–62*, General report for the year 1861 by HMI H.J. Lynch Esq on the RC schools inspected by him in Scotland and in the counties of Durham, Northumberland, Warwick and York, pp 189–91.

Mercy diaspora between 1841 and 1855 had already provided for nine foundations in addition to a cohort of eleven nuns, in 1854, for the Crimea.[10] When Father Trappes wrote to Dublin for help in 1857 his request was redirected to those Mercy nuns who had established a foundation in Clifford just two years before. They were robust and enthusiastic and had already gained considerable experience in the work of establishing and expanding their schools in Clifford. They were familiar with the requirements to qualify for government grants[11] and had already proven themselves to be careful and prudent managers. Above all, they were fired with a determination to establish their own Mother House which would both attract new nuns to them in their vocation to the religious life and would also provide a base from which new foundations could develop.[12]

Trappes' request was so cleverly tailored to meet the express needs of the Clifford nuns that they found it hard to resist. The promise of daily Mass in the convent, a furnished house free from rent or taxes, all emoluments arising from the schools including grants, fees and subscriptions, were key points at issue with their parish priest in Clifford. So attractive was the Hull offer that Mother Starr, the Mother Superior, and her deputy, Mother Kennedy,[13] came themselves with four others to establish the foothold in Hull. Their numbers gradually increased as their work in Hull took root. Understandably, relationships with the priest in Clifford became severely strained as his schools began to suffer the loss of expertise and personnel in favour of Hull. The nuns removed themselves completely from Clifford in 1867, and their work in that parish was replaced three years later by another group of nuns from the Mercy convent in Bermondsey.

To begin with in Hull, the nuns occupied the upper room of St Mary's in Dansom Lane/Wilton Street and taught the children on the ground floor.

---

10 The nine convents were: St John's Newfoundland 1842; Liverpool 1843; London 1844; New York 1846; Western Australia 1846; Dundalk 1847; Tuam 1847; Cheadle 1849; Clifford 1855.

11 Government grants were available in four categories: (1) buildings – for new schools or extensions or provision of furniture and other necessary apparatus; (2) pupil teachers – based on the number of pupil teachers being tutored by the headteacher; (3) books & educational apparatus; (4) capitation – based on numbers in attendance and on the performance of children at examination in reading, writing and arithmetic.

12 For the full story of the Hull Mercy nuns see M. McClelland, 'Early Educational endeavour: A Study of the Work of the Hull Mercy Nuns 1855–1930' (University of Hull MPhil thesis, 1993).

13 Mary Starr was appointed first superior of the Clifford convent in 1855 just two years after her final profession as a nun in Baggot Street, Dublin. She was a convert to Catholicism. Julia Kennedy, her Assistant and Bursar in Clifford, had been professed in 1854. They both became quite 'famous' because of their involvement in the Great Convent Case in 1869: see Maria G. McClelland, 'The First Hull Mercy Nuns: A 19th Century Case Study', *Recusant History* (October, 1994), pp 199–221.

Local fund-raising efforts had been spear-headed by Lady Chichester Constable since 1856 towards the cost of a suitable convent for them. When Elm Tree House – an old mansion on the corner of Anlaby Road and South Parade – with over half an acre of land presented itself as a possibility, five laymen helped Father Trappes and Father Motler to set up a weekly congregational collection with the object of paying in full its purchase price of £3800. The Catholic community endeavoured to make the site habitable, and the nuns moved in on 8 December 1857.

Over the next 16 years the nuns developed the property to include a private chapel and a pension school (i.e. a fee paying school for the daughters of the middle classes). At their own expense they had the stables converted into a temporary elementary school for girls, thus enabling Father Trappes to close down and sell the Canning Street building and to pay off some of the debt on the Pryme Street school. The crippling task of raising the £3800 for the Elm Tree property, however, continued to be a huge drain on the Hull Catholics. By 1860 only £1000 had been gathered and enthusiasm for the weekly collection was on the wane.[14] The dilemma facing Father Trappes was whether to continue his moral and munificent support for the nuns or whether to divert it to the good of his parishioners. He considered the needs of the Irish poor had to take precedence, and he was ably supported in his decision by two curates now, Father John Motler and Father Arthur Riddell.[15] The weekly collection for the nuns was replaced with one for the purpose of erecting a school-chapel dedicated to St Patrick. Trappes' aim was 'to bring God's house nearer to those who through poverty and misfortune, often stayed away from Holy Mass and neglected to send their children to school'.[16] The St Patrick's project had an instant appeal and the Irish dockworkers arranged for their employer, stevedore Mark Holland, to deduct a penny or twopence from their weekly wages towards the fund. As soon as £525 was thus saved, a site on Mill Street was bought leaving £2500 building costs still to be raised. Determination and dedication caused St Patrick's school-chapel to be opened on 7 November 1871. The premises were to be used for the next 30 years until the present St Patrick's

---

14 Middlesbrough Diocesan Archives, Sisters of Mercy Papers, 'Statement concerning the establishment of the Sisters of Mercy in Hull and the purchase of their property there', 3 March 1887, signed by Mother Magdalen Kennedy. A copy of Trappes' agreement about the property is contained within the 'Statement'.

15 John Motler was much loved by the nuns. He went as parish priest to St Joseph's, Bradford in 1865 where later as Canon Motler (1876) he invited some of the Hull nuns to run his school for boys and girls. Arthur Riddell was born of 'Old Catholic' Stapleton lineage in York. He was educated at Downside and Ushaw and ordained in 1859 at the age of 23. He moved to St Peter's, Scarborough, in 1873 and became Bishop of Northampton in 1880.

16 Endsleigh Archives, no author, 'The Story of St Patrick's School,' four typed pages, no date, p. 1.

Church was built in Spring Street in 1904. The Mill Street building was subsequently used solely as a school building until its closure in April 1965.[17] Once the project was completed, St Patrick's school was placed in the capable hands of the Mercy nuns by Father Trappes and they, in turn, accepted the added responsibility. The battles over property and money, at times acrimonious, in relation to Elm Tree House and the St Patrick's project had lasted over 10 years with neither side yielding to the other. The nuns were left with the residual bill of £2800, with an additional sum of at least £400 for the cost of converting the stables into the girls elementary school and with wounded memories of broken promises and unfulfilled expectations.[18]

By this time, Mother Kennedy had taken over as superior from Mother Starr. She decided to move swiftly to restore dignity and independence to her convent community. By effecting another property deal, with the blessing of the bishop,[19] she fulfilled her dream of establishing a genuinely independent Mother House in Hull. Her plan took everybody by surprise. The Elm Tree House estate was to be sold, £1000 of the proceeds would be returned to the Catholics of Hull (being the sum they had originally contributed) and a new purpose-built convent, chapel, pension school and elementary school would be built (and paid for by the nuns) on the opposite side of the Anlaby Road. The deal gave rise to many protestations from Hull Catholics and from their clergy on the grounds that it would have been better to retain the Elm Tree House estate as well as the new project so that a grand Catholic centre could be established. Father Riddell, for his part, envisaged a parochial church, a presbytery, schools for boys and girls and an orphanage in addition to the convent and pension school planned by the nuns. Kennedy would have none of it. The erection of their Mother House, the convent of Our Lady of Mercy, was her testament to a new self-confidence and her signal to a new era of self-determination. Hitherto, they had served in the parochial schools of St Charles, St Patrick's and St Mary's Wilton Street as if they were the sole managers but in the many heated exchanges over property and money in recent years, Kennedy realised full well that ultimate power over the schools rested with the parish priest. Worse still, she had learned that attitudes to the nuns could be affected by many things and many people and in particular by different parish

17 St Patrick's Church in Spring Street was closed officially by Bishop J. Crowley of Middlesbrough on 17 March 1998. It is scheduled for demolition.

18 The intricacies of the arguments are dealt with at length in M.McClelland, *thesis*, pp 128–44.

19 Robert Cornthwaite, a Prestonian, succeeded John Briggs as Bishop of Beverley from 1861. Cornthwaite took a very keen interest in the work of the nuns (both in Clifford and in Hull). He was a frequent visitor to their convent. When the old see of Beverley was suppressed in 1878, Cornthwaite became the first bishop of Leeds and Hull became part of the new Middlesbrough diocese under Bishop Richard Lacy.

priests and their curates assured of their male and clerical dominance.[20] In addition to their new convent on the Anlaby Road the nuns would now own their own private chapel, St Mary's High School for girls with its separate Pupil-Teacher Centre for boys and girls, and St Joseph's elementary school for girls and infants. From this secure base they were poised to expand and develop their interests in new Mercy foundations and to enter into new educational ventures at home and elsewhere, without having first to appease the local clergy or to gain approval from the leaders of the local Catholic lay community.

The Mother House was opened and blessed in 1873, the year in which Father Riddell was transferred to St Peter's Church, Scarborough and the year when Father Trappes died. Trappes was succeeded by Canon Benjamin Randerson who had also been one of Trappes' curates for a time at St Charles'. Randerson, too, was keenly interested in the welfare of his Catholic schools, and to this end set a precedent for his successors by becoming the first Catholic priest to be elected to the Hull School Board. He served as a highly respected member on the Board for over nine years.[21]

The 1870s heralded a new era for schools nationwide with the passing of the 1870 Education Act. This resulted in the setting up of locally elected School Boards whose brief was to equip, maintain and staff elementary schools for those children who were not otherwise provided for in the voluntary denominational schools. Members of Hull's Town Council were scolded in the local press for their supineness in showing no interest in the subject, and for their distinct lack of speed in applying to establish a School Board in Hull. By public demand, statistics were quickly gathered and published to reveal a school-age population for Hull of approximately 22,000. It was estimated that 20,548 of these were registered with the twenty or so voluntary schools in operation in the town, thus leaving a shortfall of about 2000 for a School Board to consider.

Canon R.E. Brooke, vicar of Holy Trinity, was to focus the minds of the town councillors on a much graver figure. He pointed out that while the voluntary schools were indeed doing a wonderful job in Hull, attendance at the schools was sometimes less than 50% of those on roll. He was, however, even more concerned about 'nearly 8000 children who ought to be at school and are not even entered on the books of any school'. A School Board with its power to compel children to attend, could begin to reach out to these children in a way

20 Mother Kennedy and Father Riddell disliked each other intensely. He liked to hold the threat of dismissal from the schools over her, and even tried to get her to sign a contract before taking up her duties at St Patrick's school. She in turn complained to Bishop Cornthwaite about Riddell's undue power in the parish. He was, she claimed, effectively in charge because Father Trappes was growing old and infirm.

21 When Randerson left Hull for St Hilda's, Whitby, in 1886, members of the School Board subscribed to a public testimonial to him for all his work. He was presented with 100 guineas and a handsome study desk and chair.

that voluntary schools could not. He was fully supported in this view by the Mayor of Hull, Robert Jameson, who believed that 'if for no other purpose than that of compelling the attendance of children, there was a necessity for the election of a School Board'.[22] The Mayor had strong views about the composition of such a Board. He deemed it 'extremely desirable that men of large and comprehensive minds who were not desirous of pushing forward any narrow bigoted views' should be on the Board. The editor of the *Eastern Morning News* urged the electorate to choose carefully 'if the country is to advance in intelligence and material prosperity'. It was hoped that when the first Hull School Board was elected on 3 February 1871, it would reflect 'representation of the leading shades of religious and political thought and of every class in the community'. The fifteen who were elected for the first three-year stint included four Anglicans, four Wesleyans, three Free Church and three Reform Church representatives and one Roman Catholic. Mr H. Lambert, a wine and spirit merchant, served for two sessions before Canon Randerson replaced him in 1877.

Following a realistic assessment and inspection of existing school places in the town in 1871, and discounting those deemed 'inefficient' by HMI in terms of eligibility for Government grants, the Board learned that 13,237 places were available in the voluntary sector. The three Catholic schools accounted for 1116 of these. The Hull Board itself faced a task of providing 7028 places in its first year. According to the Education Act, Board schools were to exist alongside the voluntary schools but were empowered to raise rates to finance their activities. As a result of this access to rate aid, they soon outstripped the voluntary schools in number, not just in Hull but throughout the country. From a perusal of the triennial reports of the School Board over a thirty-year period, it is obvious that the struggle to keep apace with the demand for school places was a formidable task. In 1889, for instance, the Board could claim that for the first time since its formation, it was within something like a reasonable distance of overtaking the deficiency of school accommodation. By 1892 it could boast having 35 schools providing for 27,767 children across the town. It forecast, too, that approximately 860 places would be needed annually to keep up with the ever growing demands for places. This was the equivalent of three good schools per triennial term 'after all arrears have been fully overtaken'.[23]

In the light of this position, it seems unreasonable that the Hull School Board should have been so 'testy' towards the denominational schools. It felt threatened from the outset by any spare accommodation in the Catholic schools. Its fear was that in the event of a Board school being full, or unavailable, non-Catholic children could be compelled to take up a vacant place in a Catholic school. Thus it kept a very close eye on all applications for extensions to

22 *Eastern Morning News/Hull Advertiser*, 16 & 17 Dec. 1870.
23 7th Triennial Report of the Hull School Board, May 1889–April 1892.

Catholic schools and it opposed all applications for new ones. All the Catholic schools were carrying some superfluous accommodation, it claimed, because average attendance figures did not match numbers on rolls. In truth, the Board was well aware of the town-wide problems of inattendance. It reported at length on 'the incorrigible Truant Class' which was becoming so characteristic of Hull. Yet the Catholic sector was expected to be free of these blemishes. Average attendance figures did not take account of absences through illness or epidemics or because of the need to withdraw children from school for seasonal work.

As a result of persistent opposition from the Hull School Board, repeated applications to the Board of Education in Whitehall for extensions to St Charles' Infants Department and to St Patrick's Girls and Infants Departments were rejected until in 1893 the situation was so desperately overcrowded that there was a need for a new school – St Gregory's in Scott Street – to relieve the strain. In the preceding years, HMI R.S. Stavelly was adamant that St Patrick's and St Charles' ran the risk of having their grants withdrawn on the grounds of overcrowding. Within a year of its opening, St Gregory's needed to expand into the chapel room upstairs with space for 226 girls, leaving the ground floor for infants alone. By December 1895 plans to erect a new church on the Boulevard for a growing community there were altered in favour of another school–cum–chapel instead. Thus approval was granted for St Wilfrid's with some reservations about the adequacy of the playground area.

Applications for expansion to each of the Catholic schools throughout the life of the Board were fairly constant. By September 1904, the records show Catholics were providing 3100 places in their six schools.[24] Approval had not yet been granted to St Vincent's School on the Queen's Road although its claim for recognition as an elementary school had been sent to Whitehall as far back as January 1901. The Hull Board had directly intervened to stop the St Vincent's venture. This was partly to protect the interests of its nearby Newland Avenue Board School where it claimed there was 'vacant accommodation for upwards of 500 children', and partly because it challenged the claims of Father J. Hall (the indomitable priest in charge of St Charles' at the time) of the existence of any Roman Catholic population in the district to warrant such a provision.[25] It was a dispute that was never properly settled, coming as it did in the transition time between the dismantling of the School Board and the setting up of the Local Education Authority under the new 1902 Education Act.

Approval for St Vincent's school was granted in January 1902 when Father Hall convinced the visiting HMI, L.T. Munro, that he had a guaranteed

24 These figures were given in the 11th Triennial Report of the Hull School Board, March 1901-September 1904, as follows: St Charles 625; St Gregory's 509; St Joseph's 666; St Mary's Wilton Street 798; St Patrick's 210; St Wilfrid's 292.

25 Public Record Office, Ed 21, 19271, Letter from C.J. O'Donoghue, Clerk of the Hull School Board, to the Secretary, Board of Education, London, 30 January 1901.

Catholic population of 136 children from the local area, together with forty orphan boys from Wright Street Orphanage which was about to be relocated to Stepney Lodge near the Queen's Road. Additionally, the inspector could speculate for himself that the considerable housing development in the area of Queen's Road and Newland Avenue would also necessitate the availability of school places for years to come. When the St Vincent's building was completed in November 1903, Father Hall applied through the new LEA for help with furnishing the school and for recognition for the Government grant. The LEA's reply was unexpected. The empty St Vincent's building could not be deemed to be a school under the meaning of the Act, because it did not have in it 'school desks, furniture or any apparatus of elementary education'.[26] Its establishment subsequently as an elementary school would be 'in the provision of a new public elementary school within the meaning of Section 8 of the Act of 1902 and public notice under that Section should have been given'.[27] The LEA added that it had no desire to re-open the question of the necessity of the school. Father Hall furnished the school on a shoestring and it was opened in May 1904. Six years later, after an inspection by HMI Leaf, the Local Authority was ordered to replace the furniture on the grounds that the desks were totally unsuitable for the children.

To those who were opposed to any kind of state aid for denominational schools, Catholics in Hull evinced at least one very irritating characteristic. They seemed to work on the principle that once they erected a school, then God would automatically provide them with the children to fill it. Their school building plans, therefore, were proactive rather than reactive. This tended to confuse government and local authority planning schemes. Catholic schools invariably started life as a *chapel-up-school-down* type of building which meant that there was always a ready-made 'adaptable' extension room when numbers increased unexpectedly. This was true for St Gregory's, for St Patrick's, for St Wilfrid's and – by 1909 – for St Vincent's. The latter school was to prove beyond doubt that far from being superfluous to needs, it had provided for, and created, a Roman Catholic population in the Queen's Road area of the city.[28]

A recurring theme that emerges from the records of the Hull School Board is its concern about the poor calibre of its pupil teachers. The Board claimed that pupil teachers were generally indifferent to the need to qualify themselves

26 Public Record Office, Ed 21, 192711, Letter from E. Laverack, Town Hall, Hull, to the Secretary, Board of Education, London, 21 January 1904.
27 Section 8 of the 1902 Act obliged LEAs to provide public elementary schools where these were deemed to be necessary.
28 The orphanage was moved again from Stepney Lodge and rebuilt beside St Vincent's school on an adjacent piece of land in 1909. Boys from all over the diocese were cared for here by the Sisters of Charity of St Vincent de Paul. The orphanage thus provided a steady population for the school.

as certificated teachers and that many were simply retaining posts to which they had been appointed several years before when they had completed their own elementary education. In 1882, the Board passed a resolution compelling all uncertificated assistant teachers 'to go forward and qualify themselves for those higher posts under penalty of dismissal'.[29] It also resolved to appoint only the best of those who qualified and to advertise for outsiders 'rather than promote those who have only just barely passed their examinations and who in many respects have shown themselves to be but inefficient teachers'. The Board felt compelled to announce that 'the Schools exist for the education of the Children, and not for the mere finding of appointments for Teachers. If the Hull Teachers, with all the inducements held out to them, will not properly qualify themselves for the higher posts as they become vacant, they and their friends must be content to see better and more competent men and women step in and fill the places which by a little more perseverance and care might have been filled by themselves or friends'.[30] The efficient training of pupil teachers was to continue to be a major concern of the Board's successors in the Local Education Authority. This issue was to highlight the very real struggles that faced the Catholics in providing for their own distinctive education in Hull.

In 1903 new regulations sought to improve the training of pupil teachers by stipulating that intending pupil teachers remain in full time education until the age of sixteen. A period of apprenticeship from 16 to 18 years would then follow accompanied by 'at least 300 hours of instruction in approved centres or classes for pupil teachers'. The Mercy nuns applied for recognition of St Mary's High School and their Pupil Teachers' Centre in Anlaby Road under the new regulations. At the same time, the LEA also applied for recognition of its High Schools and Pupil Teachers' Centre. The buildings were inspected and both parties were alerted to certain defects which had to be remedied before recognition could be granted.

On receipt of the nuns' plans on 6 February 1904, the Board of Education granted temporary recognition as long as the Hull Education Committee agreed to allow pupil teachers to attend the Catholic centre for five half-days per week. The Committee refused permission until the nuns had *completed* all their proposed improvements. It also refused to appoint probationary teachers to supply for those pupil teachers already in the Catholic system of training, thus effectively preventing them from attending *any* Pupil Teachers' Centre. This was a severe blow to the nuns because they had nearly 70 pupil teachers in training. The decision was deemed to be grossly unfair because the Education Committee clearly did not apply the same rigour to addressing the defects at its own Pupil Teachers' Centre.

29 6th Triennial Report of the Hull School Board, May 1886–April 1889, p. 31.
30 Ibid., p. 31.

The debate exploded in the local newspapers, where it inspired sharp comments on both sides of the argument. The Education Committee was accused of trying to supplant the voluntary schools and of taking undue advantage of misplaced confidence in its powers. They had acted against the spirit and letter of the 1902 Education Act wherein they were required to pay due consideration to the wishes of parents and to the cost to ratepayers. In the eyes of one contributor, the Hull Catholic community, through its many years of ratepaying, had 'contributed more than £50,000 to build Board Schools for the general public, from which schools they have not received a fraction of benefit because their conscientious convictions compelled them to send their children to their own schools'.[31] The head of the Catholic Pupil Teachers' Centre invited the ratepayers of Hull to pass judgment on 'a measure which permits the teachers of the Council schools to attend a Centre on every half day, and refuses the like privileges to the teachers in Catholic Schools, because they and their parents insist on instruction at a Catholic Centre, the cost of which Centre, is no burden to the ratepayers, being borne by the Catholic themselves'.[32] The Education Committee was unimpressed with warnings about the growth of intense indignation among Catholics in the town. It was feared that the supply of Catholic teachers would soon dry up and within a very short time school managers would be forced to employ non-Catholics in their elementary schools.

Repairs and improvements to the Catholic Pupil Teachers' Centre were completed in August 1904 and full recognition was granted by the Board of Education. The Hull Education Committee had to drop its opposition and to accept the new status quo. The Committee concentrated its energies instead on another weak link in the Catholic chain. In order to qualify for government grants, all schools had to be inspected regularly and, from 1902, inspection reports were monitored by the local education authorities. Three deficiencies were highlighted in the 1904 report on St Mary's High School, and some members of the Hull Higher Education Sub-Committee relished the opportunity thus presented to exclude St Mary's from its list of 'efficient' schools. St Mary's was deemed 'inefficient' because: (a) building work for renovations and extensions at the school meant that the playground space was temporarily limited; (b) practical science instruction had not yet commenced at the school and science was still being taught by a visiting teacher; (c) aspects of the English, the History and the Literature syllabi needed to be altered.[33] The problems were not insurmountable. Building work ended speedily and a grand 'official opening', involving the Bishop and civic dignitaries, was held in

31 (Hull) *Daily Mail*, Letter from F.W. Morrisey, 18 May 1904.
32 *Eastern Morning News/Hull Advertiser*, Letter from E.E. Shiels, 14 June 1904.
33 Minutes of the Proceedings of the Hull Higher Education Sub-Committee, 10 Jan. 1905, pp 52–3.

September 1905. A Science teacher from the LEA's Boulevard School, Joseph W. Marshall, joined the staff of St Mary's from 1 April 1905, despite the efforts of some Higher Education Committee members to prevent the nuns from securing his services. Changes to the syllabus for specific subjects took longer to effect. The school was re-inspected on 20 October and on 19 December 1905 and was granted 'efficient' status in March 1906.

The debate over the inefficiency of St Mary's High School was brought to a head by what is now referred to as 'the Bursaries Affair'. In an attempt to attract good entrants to the teaching profession, the Hull Education Committee offered 125 scholarships worth £10 a year for two years to intending pupil teachers on the basis of success at an examination held on 25 June 1904. Twelve Catholics qualified for these scholarships but were denied the bursaries when they asked that they to be tenable at St Mary's High School. The inefficiency of the school was the first reason given for the refusal, but it soon became obvious that other issues were at stake. Representations made on behalf of the twelve candidates provoked heated debates not just at Higher Education Sub-Committee level but at a variety of Council meetings, at public gatherings and in the local press. Alderman Alfred Gelder led the case against the Catholic claims. He resolved to protest emphatically 'against the granting of educational bursaries for sectarian purposes' in the belief that 'granting public monies should only be where there is the fullest representative control'.[34] Councillor S. P. Wood claimed that, if awarded, the bursaries would not benefit the candidates but the coffers of the nuns, who were 'already in receipt of approximately £3196 a year in salaries for the 73 nuns who were working in the Hull schools'. Wood was determined to pin the inefficiency tag on the nuns' schools for as long as possible in order to prevent ratepayers money being expended 'on Popish institutions'. The Chairman of the Higher Education Sub-Committee, Canon Joseph Malet Lambert, argued openly with Wood about the injustice of his obsession with the inefficiency tag. 'With the possible exception of the Girls' High School, the Roman Catholic Secondary School and the Technical School', Lambert declared, 'there is not a single properly equipped and efficient secondary school in the city. The people are being deceived into believing that the schools are efficient but they are not'.[35] He warned that if Wood and his supporters on the Committee were not checked, Hull would soon become 'a byeword and a reproach among the other large English cities' for not organising secondary education on a grand scale. The Girls' High School referred to was, in fact, a Church of England school. As it did not include a Pupil Teachers' Centre it posed no threat to the LEA's Centre. Bursaries were tenable at the Girls' High School.

34 Collected Minutes of Council 1904–1905, Minutes of Hull City Council, 2 Feb. 1905, p. 68.
35 (Hull) *Daily Mail*, Letter from J. Malet Lambert, 25 May 1906.

Some councillors argued at length about the loss in grants the authority would suffer through not having the training of those Catholic children in its own Centre. Their arguments, according to Councillor R. Galloway, were based on a false premise.

How on earth could the authority suffer any loss when they:

> never were likely to have the training of the Catholic children? Who provided the bursaries? Did not the Catholic ratepayers who had built a centre at their own cost to the amount of about £8000, also pay their share towards the bursaries for the whole of the children in the city? Why then should not the Catholic children be allowed participation in them?[36]

The consensus of public opinion in the local press was that if Catholics were not intended to participate then the original advertisement for the scholarships examination should have stated quite clearly 'No Catholics need apply'. Twenty-nine of the sixty members of the Higher Education Committee favoured the Catholic claims to the bursaries but, on a majority of two votes, none of the twelve Catholic girls received their award. The parents of the twelve continued to write to the Sub-Committee from 1904 until 28 March 1906, for the recovery of what they felt was rightly theirs, but to no avail. Eight of the girls persisted in their training without financial help, while the others were forced to abandon their studies. The wound inflicted on the Catholic community over the bursaries affair was to give birth to a new kind of public consciousness.

In his Lenten Pastoral for 1905, Bishop Lacy of Middlesbrough[37] devoted his full theme to the inalienable rights of parents to educate their children in their own faith. He left his flock in no doubt that he viewed the actions of the Hull Higher Education Committee as an 'attack on our cherished convictions, which if pressed home, will mean religious persecution'. The Hull Committee had not done itself justice, he claimed, 'nor has it quite risen to the dignity of its responsible position' in the way it had dealt with St Mary's High School. He pointed out that the nuns had been running a Pupil Teachers' Centre in Hull 'ever since 1857, at a time when neither School Board nor Education Committee existed' and they had been eminently successful in their work as evidenced by HMI reports. To ignore 'valuable educational forces such as these ready to

---

36 *Eastern Morning News/Hull Advertiser*, 30 Dec. 1904. Extensive report on the meeting of the Education Authority held on 29 December.

37 Born in Navan, county Meath, Lacy was educated at Ushaw and the English College, Rome. He was ordained for the Beverley diocese in 1867 and worked in parishes in Bradford and Middlesbrough before he became bishop of Middlesbrough in 1879. His episcopate endured for fifty years. He was revered within his diocese and regarded as 'cultured, dignified and eloquent'.

hand, and that too at a time when throughout the country there is such an alarming dearth of teachers', warned the bishop, was unwise, unfair and unjust: 'Education without religion is the most powerful dissolvent of Christianity and the supernatural order, and it is not the kind of education which we desiderate for our children'. The Bishop ended his Pastoral with a rallying cry that was not to fall on deaf ears in Hull:

> We call upon Catholic parents everywhere, irrespective of party, to show a united front in defence of their educational rights. They should see to it that they are not penalized because they choose for their children the advantages of a Catholic education … The Penal Laws are a thing of the past. Let them not be dug up again in this twentieth century.[38]

The opening of St Vincent's School in May 1904 provides a useful starting point for the charting of the new public consciousness referred to above. Catholics were beginning to appreciate the efficacy of collective effort and support. A strongly-worded lengthy letter of congratulations 'to the Irishmen of Hull' appeared in the *Daily Mail*. They were praised for waking up at last 'to the unquestionable attitude of determined hostility to their schools on the part of an intolerant and narrow-minded section of the Hull Education Committee'. They were urged to recognise that the time was ripe 'to combine in the formation of a Citizens League whose aim would be the protection of their just and sacred interests against the unjust encroachments of the Compulsory Secular Educationalists'.[39] They were reminded of the power of the ballot box to effect a change in the people who represented them in public office. They could make 1 November 1904 – local election day – a day of reckoning in Hull. Father Hall acted quickly to ensure that all Hull Catholics engaged in active preparation for that election. A Citizens' League prototype was already *in situ* in the shape of the Hull Catholic Union[40] and he sought to re-juvenate this body by calling representatives from every parish to a meeting at St Charles. He set before them the confident scene of 20,000 Hull Catholic ratepayers contributing approximately £3000 a year for schools. They had a reasonable claim to decide on how this money should be spent and to having

---

38 Bishop Lacy's *Pastoral* was read in every Catholic church in Hull and throughout the diocese. It was published in full in the Hull newspapers under the title 'The Bishop of Middlesbrough & The Education Committee'.

39 (Hull) *Daily Mail*, Letter from F.W. Morrissey, 6 May 1904.

40 The Hull Catholic Union was the local branch of the National Consultative Body entitled 'The Catholic Union'. Under the stewardship of the Duke of Norfolk, this was a 'non-political association of members of the Catholic laity to watch over Catholic interests, especially in matters arising from Government action, proposed legislation or the activities of local authorities and other public bodies'. Before the bursaries affair, the Hull Catholic Union did not enjoy full representation from all the parishes of the city.

some of it spent on their own schools. The Catholic Union formulated a five-point questionnaire based on the recognition and protection of the rights of Catholics in education matters. The questionnaire was to be issued to all candidates who presented themselves for election to Hull City Council and Catholics were urged to vote for those who favoured Catholic interests.[41] The Hull Irish National Club, writing 'on behalf of the Irish and Catholic rate-payers of the city', petitioned the local members of Parliament, each member of the City Council and of the Education Committee for help to 'rescind the resolution refusing to recognize a Catholic (Pupil Teachers') Centre'. Likewise, a fund-raising gathering of 700 Catholics in St George's Hall in the city on 16 February 1905 registered a public thank you to the twenty-nine councillors who had supported the Catholic claim to the bursaries. The crowd called for the remaining councillors to reverse their decisions in the interests of true justice. It was reported that Father Hall, with his hands in the air, shouted, 'Are we downhearted? Are we united?' When election day came (1 November) the true weight of the Catholic consolidation was recognised. The *Catholic Herald* picked up the flavour: 'The Catholic vote has come to be recognised at its proper worth in many quarters of the city. Councillor Cooper, the well-known electioneering expert, says that more than one councillor may attribute his return to the Catholic Union. Councillor Grindell admits that his re-election for Drypool Ward is due in a large measure to the same influence. Councillor Hanger has written to Canon Griffin[42] expressing his appreciation of the valuable assistance he received from the Catholics in Southcoates Ward'.

While lay Catholics were developing a new public image of strength, the Mercy nuns were registering their new confidence as educators in a much quieter way. In a letter dated 30 June 1904, application was made for permission to open a training college for girls in Hull. This was to become the Endsleigh Training College, the only Mercy training college in England. The college was to be housed on the Beverley Road in the large Endsleigh mansion bought from Mr Glossop in 1899. The nuns had operated St Anthony's select school for boys and girls from the suburban neighbourhood on that site since 1901, and

41 The five questions were: (1) In the appointment of an Education Committee, will you support the co-option of a Catholic representative? (2) Will you support the administration of the Education Acts in such a way as to give fair and equal treatment to all schools under your authority, especially as to staff, teachers' salaries and the provision of necessary equipment? (3) Will you oppose any proposals which would impair the denominational character of Catholic schools or which would interfere with the facilities for religious instruction previously enjoyed by them? (4) Will you recognise and support the Catholic Pupil Teachers' Centre for Girls at Anlaby Road Convent on an equal footing with the Council's P.T. Centre? (5) Will you vote that the bursaries for secondary instruction granted by the LEA and earned by Catholic scholars may be tenable at the Anlaby Road Catholic P.T. Centre?

42 Canon James Griffin was priest in charge of St Wilfrid's Church since 1886.

had gradually developed the property and its five acres with a training college in mind. Plans and photographs were submitted to the Board of Education together with an assurance that Endsleigh mansion could house 25 students to begin with, and new buildings could be erected to cater eventually for up to 200.

The training college venture was spearheaded by Mother Stanislaus Dawson who had become Mother Superior on the death of Mother Kennedy in 1894. Dawson was an indigenous nun – born in Epworth – but she had been expertly groomed and moulded by the founding group of Irish nuns. Like them, she was in a hurry to forge ahead with her plans in the belief that once she had permission to start a training college, God would help her with the rest! In her determination to extract an official starting date, she grew impatient with every request from the Board of Education for fine details about staffing, qualifications, courses of instructions, lecture rooms, school-practice arrangements, entry requirements and fees. To many of these queries her stock answer was that she would follow, as far as possible, the routines and practices adopted by Mount Pleasant Training College, Liverpool. She herself had trained as a teacher at Mount Pleasant, and she had recently despatched two Hull nuns there on a 'fact finding' visit before including their names on her first staff list for Endsleigh. Staff at the Board of Education were understandably bemused at her preoccupation with the physical growth of the college, and they were at pains to convince her that the establishment of a training college could not be sanctioned on the basis of building plans alone. The Board became quite alarmed at her stubborn disregard for serious academic qualifications among its first members of staff. In Dawson's view her proposed staff of seven for the sixteen students permitted in the first cohort was ample provision. She was assured, however, that 'in forming an opinion about the adequacy of a college staff for its duties, the Board (considered) not alone or mainly the number of persons amongst whom those duties are distributed but also the fitness of the persons chosen to discharge them'.[43] A list of staff was demanded together with their qualifications and their proposed duties and responsibilities in the new college. Of the seven names submitted only two were deemed satisfactory and their teaching duties were further refined to avoid overloading them in their first year. Dawson was reminded that at least two thirds of the staff would need to have approved academic qualifications before the college could open its doors in September 1905.

Two official visits were made to Endsleigh by HMIs to insist that Dawson adhere to government recommendations. HMI E.G. Holmes came in January 1905 to inspect buildings and lecture rooms and to visit the elementary schools selected for teaching practice. Chief Inspector T.A. Barnett came in June to

---

43 Endsleigh Archives, Hull. Letter from E.K. Chambers, Board of Education, London, 1 April 1905.

iron out the difficulties over staffing. By 10 July a new list of seven was produced and accepted, but only on the understanding that it would be recon-
sidered for the Autumn of 1906 when there would be another cohort of
students to contend with. The list consisted of three Mercy nuns: Dawson as
the Principal of the College (with managerial rather than teaching duties); Sr
Dominic Courtney as Vice-Principal (to teach Scripture and Needlework) and
Sr Alacoque Galvin (to teach English). The four lay people were: Walter Porter
(to teach Music); William Wadsley (to teach Mathematics); Joseph Marshall (to
teach Science & Geography) and Lisa Anderson – a graduate of the Royal
University of Ireland – was engaged to teach History & French. The three men
had Hull teaching pedigrees. Marshall was the Science teacher gained earlier
from the LEA's Boulevard School; Porter was choirmaster at St Mary's
Lowgate and Wadsley was Art Master at the Hull Grammar School.

Advertisements for Endsleigh Training College stated that applications
would be welcome from those who

> are qualified by having passed the following examinations: King's scholarship 1st
> or 2nd class in 1903 or 1904, Oxford or Cambridge senior locals in subjects
> required by Board, Matriculation or any examination approved by Board (see
> Code, Art 1115), Certificated teachers received for one year's training.[44]

In reality, it seems that any girl who applied was granted a place because
Dawson was insistent on recruiting her maximum numbers in order to
guarantee the survival of the college. She badgered the Board of Education
each year for an increase in intake. She succeeded first with 35, then with 57
until a ceiling of 92 altogether (i.e., including first and second year students)
was imposed in the year 1907/8. Her dream of 200 students was never to
materialize during her stewardship.

To have secured approval for 92 students was a tribute to Dawson's own
personal management skills. In its first 10 years, the college was lambasted by
successive HMI reports for its poor quality of students, its poor achievements,
its poor teaching methods and its poor staffing. Had it not been for a woman of
Dawson's calibre at the helm, it might well have been closed down in its infancy
for all of these reasons. The college had a singular difficulty in attracting bright
students from the outset, and once a poor reputation had been developed on
that front it was hard to recover from it. HMI F.H. Dale was a frequent visitor
to the college and was well placed to assess its true worth. Seeing what the nuns
could do for their poor quality students by their exemplary manner of life, Dale
realised that they could be particularly effective as teacher-trainers if they
themselves were appropriately qualified. On his retirement in May 1910 he

44 The advertisement appeared in local papers as well as in Catholic national papers.

submitted his final report on Endsleigh, and focused sharply on the three perennial problems affecting progress at the college:

(A) Work in English and Mathematics showed the students to be 'of poor calibre and little natural aptitude. So long as the material on which the College has to work is as poor as it is, really good results can hardly be expected'.

(B) The College had great difficulty in securing really competent lay teachers and had suffered badly from frequent and numerous changes of staff during the previous few years.

(C) 'The chief difficulty of the Order (i.e. Mercy) arises from its deficiency in the supply from its own ranks of teachers really well-qualified to take advanced instruction in such subjects as Maths and English'.[45]

In his address to the Governing Body of the college, Dale insisted that the future progress of the institution depended upon the development of a competent and stable teaching community. He recommended that three or four nuns be sent urgently to Oxford or Cambridge to equip them for work in the college. He resolved 'to write to the Archbishop urging upon him the necessity of having in all our Catholic Training Colleges a fair proportion of the staff with a university training'.[46] Dale's valediction was a useful spur for action. Dawson nominated two nuns to go to Cambridge in October for teacher-training studies and she applied to the Catholic Education Council for a grant of £300 to support their attendance there. A long-term plan to send two or more nuns each year to take up university or other courses was set in place. In the following year, Dawson engaged the services of the principal of a correspondence college in Sheffield to set, mark and report back on mock test papers for the students in an attempt to improve their answering skills for the real examinations. It was some time before HMI reports were able to praise real achievement at the college. When Dawson applied for permission to increase her numbers to 100 for the 1918–19 session, she was refused on the grounds that improvements 'in the general quality of the college staff' and in 'the arrangements for the school practice of the students' had not been sufficient to warrant an increase.

Mother Dawson retired in December 1919 at the age of 77. She was replaced as principal by 42-year-old Sr Anastasia O'Hara. An honours graduate of London University and one of the first Hull nuns to attend a postgraduate course in Cambridge, O'Hara had indisputable talents as a teacher and as a lecturer. Her contribution to the work of the college since 1913 had been

---

45 Endsleigh Archives, Hull, *Report on Hull Training College*, by HMI F.H. Dale after his visits on 9, 10, 11 May 1910, p. 1.

46 Endsleigh Archives, Hull, Minute Book of the Governors of the Hull Catholic Training College 1905–34, 11 May 1910. Dale was a Roman Catholic.

repeatedly praised in reports of inspectors and examiners. Having left 'the nest' to improve her academic qualifications and to gain teaching experience in places other than Hull, Sr O'Hara knew at first hand the benefits of encountering new ideas and new methods of working. In her first year as principal, she arranged for three nuns to start degree studies at Bedford College, London, and for two others to do likewise at the University of Leeds. In contrast to Dawson, who was chiefly an administrator, Sr O'Hara was the first *academic* principal of Endsleigh. She guided the college for the next twelve years through a period of rapid expansion and development which was to continue with her successors into the 1970s. Under her stewardship, the Board of Education took a new interest in Hull's training college.[47] Under her stewardship, Catholic education in Hull achieved a new respectability.

Mother Dawson's withdrawal from the education scene in 1920 marked the end of an era for Catholics in Hull. It was a period of just over 60 years and of three Mercy superiors (Starr, Kennedy and Dawson), who between them had helped to establish firm roots for denominational education in Hull and who had founded the only Mercy Teacher Training College in England. More importantly, the nuns and the clergy in their respective ways had galvanized the Catholic community into becoming a social and political unit, well-organised and conscious of its own identity, its needs and its rights, a community working in collaboration with an ecclesiastical leadership that was vibrant and energizing.

The building of the Catholic community in Hull could not have been brought about as swiftly without the presence of the Mercy nuns. In that process of community formation, the nuns, through their educational endeavours, prevented the narrow ghettoization of the Irish community that might otherwise have taken place. The process of assimilation of the immigrants with the local native Catholic population of the city was advanced, using the defence of the community as a clarion call for co-operation and joint enterprise. When the diocese of Middlesbrough was carved out of the old Roman Catholic diocese of Beverley in 1878, its first bishop was an Irishman, Richard Lacy, who was to rule the see for fifty years (1879–1929). In his hands the needs and rights of the Irish settlers were safe and carefully weighed.

47 At his behest, she met with Sir Selby Bigge and two female inspectors at the Board of Education in London, 28 April 1920, to discuss her plans for the college. The Governors' Minute Book records that she was 'given great encouragement for the future of the college'.

Mayhew's Irish: the Irish poor in mid nineteenth-century London

Jacqueline Turton

The last three decades have seen extensive inquiry into the social, religious and economic circumstances of the Irish, and those of Irish descent, living in nineteenth-century Britain. As might be expected of a capital city with a substantial immigrant population, London has figured prominently in that research.[1] It is surprising that in the course of these researches Henry Mayhew, writing on the plight of the London poor, amongst whom the Irish were well-represented, and writing within that thirty-year period which has undergone most investigation, has not received more attention. While there have been many passing references to his most significant works,[2] the lives and circumstances of those Irish men and women who appear in Mayhew's contributions to the *Morning Chronicle Survey of Labour and the Poor* and in *London Labour and the London Poor* have yet to receive systematic examination. This study, outlining and evaluating those areas of Mayhew's work in which the Irish are prominent in the light of recent investigations into immigrant communities, is intended as a first step in redressing that omission. It examines afresh both the attitudes of contemporaries (including of course Mayhew himself) towards the mid-nineteenth century Irish, and of the Irish themselves.

The *Morning Chronicle Survey of Labour and the Poor*, to which Mayhew, the metropolitan correspondent, is undoubtedly the most significant contributor,

---

1 See especially Lynn Hollen Lees, *Exiles of Erin: Irish Migrants in Victorian London* (Manchester, 1979).
2 Examples are almost too numerous to mention. See for instance, references to Mayhew in Ruth-Ann M. Harris, *The Nearest Place That Wasn't Ireland: Early Ninetenth-Century Irish Labour Migration* (Ames, Iowa, 1994); Graham Davis, *The Irish in Britain 1815–1914* (Dublin, 1991); Gerard Connolly, 'Irish and Catholic: myth or reality? Another sort of Irish and the renewal of the clerical profession among Catholics in England', Sheridan Gilley, 'Vulgar piety and the Brompton Oratory, 1850–1860', and Raphael Samuel, 'The Roman Catholic Church and the Irish poor', all in Roger Swift and Sheridan Gilley (eds), *The Irish in the Victorian City* (London, 1985). See also Roger Swift, 'The historiography of the Irish in nineteenth-century Britain', in Patrick O'Sullivan (ed.), *The Irish in the New Communities, The Irish World Wide: History, Heritage, Identity*, vol. 2 (Leicester, 1992).

appeared between October 1849 and December 1850.[3] In the late 1840s the *Morning Chronicle*, reflecting the concerns of the period, was strongly involved with social issues.[4] Chartism had collapsed, and the fear of revolution had receded. Though the ever-present and unignorable poor, particularly the urban poor, remained to evoke middle-class worries over the threat to social order and (given the overcrowded and insanitary conditions in which they lived) to public health, that fear was now tempered with compassion for their circumstances. This admixture of anxiety and sympathy was heightened by increasing numbers of Irish entering Britain in the late 1840s and early 1850s in the wake of famine at home, most of them poor, Catholic, and conspicuous.

Whereas the main aim of Mayhew's *Morning Chronicle* accounts was to highlight the circumstances of those employed (often casually) in the more conventional trades, and to reveal what he considered to be the underlying social and economic causes of poverty, *London Labour and the London Poor* is primarily a record those who made a living on the streets.[5] First published in 1851, it was extended to a four-volume edition in 1861–2. Almost one-third of the content was material incorporated from Mayhew's *Chronicle* writings; its significance to the historian is primarily as a record of the period around 1850. *The Criminal Prisons of London*, initially intended as the introductory volume of an ambitious and abortive project 'The Great World of London', was published in co-authorship with John Binney in 1862.

The relative neglect of Mayhew as a serious commentator must be in part due to his reputation for producing disorganised and incomplete work. Although the sheer volume of work produced in a relatively short period of time testifies to his enthusiasm and to his industry, it does appear that Mayhew had an innate reluctance to systematise his information. The demands of his

---

3   See for instance E.P. Thompson's remarks in the introduction to Henry Mayhew, *The Unknown Mayhew: Selections from the Morning Chronicle 1849–50*, edited by E.P. Thompson and Eileen Yeo (London, 1973), p. 24. Other correspondents covered the rural and manufacturing districts: see P.E. Razzell and R.W. Wainwright (eds), *The Victorian Working Class: Selections from Letters to the Morning Chronicle* (London, 1973), for extracts from all three contributors.

4   In early 1848 the newspaper had been sold to a liberal-conservative group including the duke of Newcastle, Sidney Herbert and A.J. Beresford Hope. See E.P. Thompson's introduction in *The Unknown Mayhew*, p. 20.

5   Though *London Labour and the London Poor* is sub-titled *A Cyclopaedia of the Conditions and Earnings of Those That Will Work, Those That Cannot Work, and Those That Will Not Work*, the first three volumes claim to address 'The London Street Folk', and the fourth, 'Those That Will Not Work'. See Henry Mayhew, *London Labour and the London Poor: A Cyclopaedia of the Conditions and Earnings of Those That Will Work, Those That Cannot Work, and Those That* Will Not *Work*, 4 vol. edn. (London, 1967, originally published 1861–62). See Anne Humpherys, *Travels into the Poor Man's Country: The Work of Henry Mayhew* (Athens, Georgia, 1977), ch.3, for an outline of the development of this work, and an analysis of its content.

profession, if not entirely accounting for this trait, must certainly have contributed to it. Mayhew may have been a social investigator, but his investigations were in the cause of journalism, upon which he depended for a (sometimes precarious) living. The need for accurate reporting, and the need to produce set-length articles with some rapidity were probably not always easy to reconcile. There are undoubtedly errors in Mayhew's reports, many of them resulting from the need to meet journalistic deadlines. E.P. Thompson has stressed the need to treat his statistical evidence with some circumspection, not because of deliberate distortion, but because the pressure of meeting weekly deadlines inevitably led to numerical and interpretative inaccuracies.[6]

Mayhew, aided by a small group of helpers, obtained information primarily from accounts given by the poor themselves.[7] There are of course the usual problems associated with oral and autobiographical records. He used no random sampling, and he was dependent upon informants from the 'respectable' ranks of society for obtaining his interviewees: though individual cases might be accurate, there is no guarantee that they are representative. As Razzell has pointed out, however, Mayhew was careful to use contacts who were particularly well-informed; he is frequently at pains to to explain his informants' credentials.[8] Though the areas of employment he investigated were limited, wherever possible he attempted to interview a representative socio–economic cross-section of the trade concerned, giving a general account of the circumstances of a particular occupation or social group, then his own or an observer's view of the circumstances, verifying his point with particular examples. None of Mayhew's original notes survive, but it is clear from the final edited versions that what are presented as uninterrupted monologues are actually responses to questions. Inevitably, this raises the problem of bias. Mayhew clearly did ask leading questions, but given that the form of the interrogation is generally transparent, they are easy to identify and allowance can be made for them. As for the risk of interviewees giving what might be deemed appropriate, rather than

6   See E.P. Thompson 'The political education of Henry Mayhew', *Victorian Studies*, 11 (1967–8), p. 58.
7   See preface in Mayhew, *London Labour and the London Poor*, vol. 1, p. iv, for Mayhew's acknowledgment of help from Richard Knight, who had worked for the London City Mission, and Henry Wood. Another aide was Mayhew's younger brother, Augustus ('Gus'): see Eileen Yeo's introduction in Mayhew, *The Unknown Mayhew*, pp 67–8. Himmelfarb has suggested that given his backing of helpers, Mayhew had less control over his material than is generally supposed, though hers is the only dissenting vioice. See Gertrude Himmelfarb, *The Idea of Poverty: England in the Early Industrial Age* (London, 1984), p. 320.
8   See Peter Razzell's introduction in Henry Mayhew, *The Morning Chronicle Survey of Labour and the Poor: the Metropolitan Districts*, vol. 1 (Firle, 1980), pp 6–7. For examples, see Mayhew, *Morning Chronicle Survey*, vol. 3, Letter XXVIII, Tues. 24 Jan. 1850, and Mayhew, *London Labour and the London Poor*, vol. I, p. 108.

truthful, responses, it was one Mayhew himself was well aware of. '[A] poor Irishman ... will far more frequently shape his reply to what he thinks will please his querist and induce a trifle for himself, than answer according to the truth'.[9]

Mayhew was not, of course, the first to investigate the circumstances of the poor. From the 1830s, government agencies and charitable organisations had collected statistical information and conducted investigative interviews to enable them to resolve the problems of poverty. For him, however, the perceptions of the poor, their opinions and their concerns, were as significant as economic facts. He wanted to show 'the importance of the poor and the working classes as members of the state'.[10] He was able to establish a sympathetic but equal relationship with his subject which left no room for sentimentality. As Humpherys observes, he recedes from the page, allowing the reader to become directly involved with the interviewee.[11] It is this aptitude for uncovering the unadorned personal histories of the poor which makes Mayhew a source worthy of deeper assessment in the study of the Irish in Britain.

EMIGRATION, MIGRATION AND SETTLEMENT

Assessing the present economic and social condition of the poor involved investigating the background to their poverty. Consequently Mayhew provides several first-hand, detailed accounts of the experience of migration from Ireland, and of the problems of settlement in a new, urban environment.

That the presence of Irish in London was no new phenomenon was something of which he was well aware. He recognised, for instance, that though the number of Irish involved in street-selling had increased markedly from the mid 1840s, Irish involvment in one of the lowest street trades, orange-selling, had been apparent from the 1820s.[12] Though a number of those Irish he came across had evidently been in the capital for several years – two women at least had been in London for half a century[13] – many of those interviewed were relatively recent arrivals, having left Ireland in the mid to late 1840s.

Mayhew gives four main reasons for the increase in numbers of Irish coster-mongers in London. These are of course factors which had a bearing on the

---

9 Mayhew, *London Labour and the London Poor*, vol. 1, p. 114.
10 From 'Answers to Correspondents', on the original wrapper of no. 10 (15 Feb. 1851) of Mayhew, *London Labour and the London Poor*, quoted in Humpherys, *Travels into the Poor Man's Country*, p. 33.
11 Ibid., p. 48.
12 Mayhew, *London Labour and the London Poor*, vol. 1, p. 105, p. 106.
13 Mayhew, *London Labour and the London Poor*, vol. 2, pp 483–4, and Mayhew, *Morning Chronicle Survey*, vol. 6, Letter LXXXI, 6 Dec. 1850, p. 230.

rising numbers of Irish poor in many parts of Britain in the late 1840s and early 1850s. Firstly, famine, or the threat of famine had driven many from Ireland. Secondly, the scale of evictions had given many no option but to leave. Thirdly, though many of the 'better class' of small farmers had gone to America, many Irish had remained in Britain.[14] Fourthly, given the economic circumstances in Ireland, many of the traditional migrant workforce who would normally have returned at the end of harvest saw little future there, and had remained in Britain. Though the factors associated with the collapse of the potato harvest were by no means the only ones to have a bearing on Irish emigration,[15] famine was a catalyst, which reinforced a pre-existing trend, and greatly increased the rate of exodus from Ireland. London, with its status as a capital city, with its large population, its variety of trades and an established Irish presence, attracted a significant proportion of those leaving their homeland.

Though the south and west of Ireland, with the lowest family incomes and the greatest dependence on the potato as a subsistence crop, suffered the worst ravages of famine, emigration from these areas was not particularly high. In county Cork, the figure for 1841 to 1851 was between 10% and 12% (as opposed to losses through starvation and disease), considerably less than the 20% of some more affluent, and less badly-hit areas.[16] For many in the south west, emigration was not an affordable option. Nevertheless, those Irish poor whom Mayhew encountered were overwhelmingly, though not exclusively, from county Cork. Mayhew's findings confirm those of Lynn Lees, who, in her analysis of Irish communities in five London districts also found evidence of a high number of Munster Irish.[17] The fact that at least some of the (exclusively Irish) female porters of Covent Garden, and a high proportion of the recently-arrived women Mayhew found in lodging-houses, were Gaelic-speaking (often with little or no English) is also indicative of their being from south west Ireland:[18] the 5% of the Irish population which remained Gaelic speaking in 1851 was largely in that region.[19] It is interesting that although Mayhew comments on the numbers of Irish-speakers, his specific references are only to Irishwomen. Given the well-established seasonal exodus of Irish migrant labour (predomi-

14 Mayhew, *London Labour and the London Poor*, vol. 1, p. 105.

15 Roger Swift summarises these factors in 'The historiography of the Irish', in O'Sullivan (ed.), *The Irish in the New Communities*, pp 53–4.

16 See Davis, *Irish in Britain*, p. 16; 35–6, citing the research of S.H. Cousens and O. MacDonagh. Emigration rates in some midland counties were considerably higher than in the south and west.

17 Lees, *Exiles of Erin*, p. 51.

18 Mayhew, *Morning Chronicle Survey*, vol. 6, Letter LXXXI, 5 Dec. 1850, p. 227; Mayhew, *London Labour and the London Poor*, vol. 1, p. 111.

19 Davis, *Irish in Britain*, p. 41.

nantly male) through Cork, there was perhaps a greater incentive, and more opportunity, for men to gain some fluency in the English language.[20]

Though their circumstances had varied, most emigrants from the south-west had left Ireland with very little, if any money. Passages to England were often paid for by landlords taking the opportunity to amalgamate holdings. 'The gentry give poor men money, or did give it to them, to send them over here to free the land from its expenses.'[21] Many had been reliant on the support of neigbours for their fare, and many left with the intention of joining contacts already resident in Britain. One young woman, aged eighteen or nineteen, had come via Waterford to Bristol and walked to London, where, her parents now being dead, she lived with an aunt. In the mid-1840s her family had been evicted (from which parish and county she had no idea): 'The thatch of the bit o' home was tuk off above our hids, and we were lift to the wide worruld … the rint wasn't paid, and it couldn't be paid'.[22] Aid from the local community and the parish priest had enabled them to emigrate. The friends of a parentless young labourer from county Wexford raised the money for his passage to Liverpool. From there he had walked to London, where he had relatives.[23]

Not all who left were young and single, though many were. Not all were totally destitute, and not all were evicted. Some smallholders were bought out by landowners. The rights to a normally productive one-acre plot in county Limerick were sold by the tenant, anxious to leave before the Famine took full hold, to the landowner's agent. Mayhew, who has already referred to '[t]he shifts, the devices, the plans, to which numbers of these poor creatures had recourse to raise the means of quitting Ireland',[24] records, without comment, the efforts of one man to raise the fare to England for himself and his wife:

> I filt the famine a-comin'. I saw people a-feedin' on the wild green things, and as I had not got such a bad take, I got Mr.— (he was the head master's agent) to give me 28s. for possission in quietness, and I sold some poulthry I had – their iggs was a blessin' to keep the life in us – I sould them in Limerick for 3s. 3d. – the poor things – four of them. The furnitur' I sould to the nabors, for somehow about 6s … and there's 2s. owin' of it still, and will be a perpitual loss. The wife and me walked to Dublin, though we had betther have gone by the 'long say', but I didn't understand it thin, and we got to Liverpool.[25]

20 Ibid., p. 18. Davis cites Cormac O'Grada's research, which has revealed the importance of seasonal work in Britain in supplementing Irish rural incomes in the middle decades of the nineteenth century.

21 Mayhew, *Morning Chronicle Survey*, vol. 2, Letter XXV, 11 Jan., p. 298.

22 Mayhew, *London Labour and the London Poor*, vol. 1, p. 116.

23 Ibid., vol. 2, p. 337.

24 Ibid., vol. 1, p. 105.

25 Ibid., vol. 1, pp 105–6.

For all his saleable possessions he had acquired the sum of £1 15s. 3d., perhaps the equivalent of two to three weeks wages in the London docks.[26] He could evidently have afforded the fare from Cork (the most convenient port) to London, which in 1848 was about 5s., double the cost from Cork to Newport, in Wales.[27]

For those who could afford the three to four-day sea journey from Cork to London, conditions were often by no means ideal, for deck passengers at least. Though spring and summer were normally the periods of highest demand, with the onset of famine in Ireland, there was a marked increase in autumn and winter crossings.[28] Mayhew records the miserable state in which many emigrants arrived, wet, and soiled with animal excrement through huddling with livestock for warmth. Not uncommonly, for those speaking little English and having no contacts in London, the quality of initial accommodation in the Irish lodging houses in the dock area around Rosemary Lane, Whitechapel, was, for those not destined for America (who were shepherded by the emigration agent) often a matter of luck.[29]

The very poorest did not to travel direct to London, but came by the cheapest route, generally from the south eastern Irish ports to Bristol, from Dublin to Liverpool, or from Cork to Newport. In the latter case, the apparent magnaminity of those captains who seemingly shipped emigrants for minimal rates, saying they would recuperate the cost when the migrants returned, can be partly accounted for by the notorious practice of shipping them as living ballast in coal vessels.[30] It also suggests that these Irish, leaving in dire circumstances, were perceived as temporary migrants rather than as immigrants. On landing, they generally completed their journey by foot, reliant on charity and the workhouse casual wards. Increasingly in the late 1840s, those on the road were families, who, given the expenditure which travelling together entailed, were least likely to find the more convenient passages affordable.[31] An agricultural labourer from county Cork, living rent-free and earning 3s. a week, had needed to raise 2s. 6d. for himself and for each of his family of five in order to leave by the cheapest route. He sold the contents of his subsistence plot, and the local farmers for whom he had worked 'giving their 3d. or 6d. apiece' made up the total of 15s.:

26 See Mayhew, *Morning Chronicle Survey*, vol. 5, Letter LVIII, 27 June 1850, p. 51.

27 See Mayhew, *London Labour and the London Poor*, vol. 1, pp 112–3.

28 Davis, *Irish in Britain*, p. 43.

29 Mayhew, *London Labour and the London Poor*, vol. 1, pp 111–13.

30 Mayhew, *Morning Chronicle Survey*, vol. 3, Letter XXVIII, 22 Jan. 1850, p. 31.

31 Mayhew, *Morning Chronicle Survey*, vol. 2, Letter XXV, 11 Jan. 1850, p. 297; vol. 3, Letter XXVIII, 22 Jan. 1850, pp 25–6; Mayhew, *London Labour and the London Poor*, vol. 1, pp 112–13; see also Lees, *Exiles of Erin*, p. 43.

When I got to Wales I had only 6*d*. lift. I went to the workhouse for a night's lodging, to be sure – what else? I started next day for London with my wife and children, begging as we came, and going from workhouse to workhouse, and very badly we got along. It finished a fortnight to get to London.[32]

Not surprisingly, a high proportion of the inmates in the Asylum for the Houseless Poor in Playhouse Yard, Cripplegate, where this man was interviewed, had their origins in county Cork. Of the total of 14,487 inmates for 1848–9 who were known to have been born in the British Isles or the Channel Islands, 8068 were from Ireland. A more meaningful perspective on migration from Ireland is obtained if inmates born in London and its vicinity (the adjacent counties) are excluded from the figures. Those who came from other areas of Great Britain and the Channel Islands number 4421, and of these, 230 were from Scotland, and 122 from Wales. Over one-quarter of those given shelter between 1834–5 and 1848–9 were Irish-born. The figure rose from 30 in the mid-1830s to 7576 in 1846–7, and reached a peak of 10,756 the following year.[33]

Mayhew found no regret on the part of first-generation costermongers (or, apparently of any other of the Irish poor) at having left their homeland.[34] Given the circumstances that they had left, it is not entirely surprising that despite their evident poverty they considered themselves better-off than in the Ireland of the late 1840s: for many, subsistence farming was no longer an option, and with low rates of pay in Ireland, there was little to return to. Even the individual who had farmed forty acres (though for a prohibitive rent) had been 'comfortable' when earning 10*s*. a week as an agricultural labourer in England, and would have been prepared to labour on the railways for 1*s*. a day ('better than Ireland these times') though he had actually earned considerably more than that.[35] What is more surprising, given the development of a distinctive Irish culture within immigrant communities, is that Mayhew found no evidence of Irish attachment to their homeland. Perhaps, initially at least, the efforts of resettlement and making a living were preoccupations which left little room for nostalgia. Friends in Ireland however, as Mayhew makes clear, were missed.[36] Strenuous efforts were often made to raise the money to bring them, and relatives, over to England:

32 Mayhew, *Morning Chronicle Survey*, vol. 2, Letter XXV, 11 Jan. 1850, p. 297.
33 Ibid., Letter XXV, 11 Jan. 1850, p. 284; Mayhew, *London Labour and the London Poor*, vol. 1, p. 112. There is a discrepancy in the 1848–9 figure for Irish inmates given in the *Morning Chronicle Survey* and in *London Labour and the London Poor*. It is assumed that the original *Chronicle* figure of 8068 is correct, and that the *London Labour and the London Poor* figure of 5068 is a transcribing error.
34 Mayhew, *London Labour and the London Poor*, vol. 1, p. 105.
35 Mayhew, *Morning Chronicle Survey*, vol. 2, Letter XXV, 11 Jan. 1850, p. 298.
36 Mayhew, *London Labour and the London Poor*, vol. 1, p. 105.

As soon as the first settler is thriving in his newly chosen country, a certain portion of his or her earnings are carefully hoarded up, until they are sufficient to pay for the removal of another member of the family to England; then one of the friends left at home is sent for; and thus by degrees the entire family is got over, and once more united.[37]

The highest concentrations of Irish, according to Mayhew, were around Brook-street, Ratcliffe-cross, down both sides of the Commercial-road, and in Rosemary-lane, areas 'peculiarly distinguished, by being peopled almost entirely by visitors from the sister isle'. He also records them as being well-represented in other areas, including Drury Lane and Saffron Hill, described in a London directory of the period as a 'squalid neighbourhood between Holborn and Clerkenwell, densely inhabited by poor people and thieves'.[38] Whitechapel and Holborn had high concentrations of Irish, as did St Giles, where Mayhew found a number of interviewees. Whilst he evidently over-estimates the Irish presence in those areas where they were most populous, his accounts generally correspond with Lynn Lees's findings, based on census enumeration. In London, as in other ports,[39] there was a pattern of scattered settlement in the riverside areas, with concentrations of Irish in the poorer courts and streets, particularly in St Giles and Whitechapel, as well as in St Olaf and Southwark to the south of the river – all areas where, by her census-based estimates, the numbers of Irish exceeded 15% of the population. The south side of Rosemary Lane had a population which in 1851 was 60% Irish, the figure being 74% in two other Whitechapel enclaves.[40] These concentrations were remarkably high. Even in Liverpool, which bore the brunt of Irish immigration, in the areas of densest population it was rare for more than half the households in a street to be Irish.[41]

The Irish population was not static. In London, as in other urban centres with Irish communities, there was some dispersal into the general population, though it was slow. For economic, social and cultural reasons the Irish tended to remain within close proximity to each other; Lees tells us that at mid-century, second-generation Irish commonly lived in the same parish as their parents. Mobility within areas, however, was high.[42] It is clear from Mayhew's accounts that there was also some seasonal migration: it was not only smaller

37 Ibid., p. 109.
38 Ibid., p. 109; Peter Cunningham, *Handbook for London, Past and Present* (London, 1849), vol. 2, p. 721.
39 This was the case in Bristol and Liverpool for instance; see David Large, 'The Irish in Bristol in 1851: a census enumeration', in Swift and Gilley (eds), *Irish in the Victorian City*, p. 41. See W.J. Lowe, *The Irish in Mid-Victorian Lancashire: The Shaping of a Working-Class Community* (New York, 1989), pp 26–7.
40 See Lees, *Exiles of Erin*, ch. 3, particularly pp 67–8.
41 Lowe, *Irish in Mid-Victorian Lancashire*, p. 69.
42 Lees, *Exiles of Erin*, pp 56–8.

centres which provided opportunities to work on the land.[43] Old habits died hard, and rural conservatism, plus the unreliability of casual work in London, ensured that even here the Irish attachment to the rural economy persisted, with workers travelling to those areas which were relatively accessible to take advantage of the economic opportunities afforded by the various harvests. A female inmate of the Cripplegate shelter said of her husband that since coming to London, apart from having briefly sold lemons, 'He never does anything but at the harvest-time, and then he works at raping the corrun. I know nothing else that he does; and I bind the shaves after him. Why, indeed, we get work thin for about a fortnight or three weeks'.[44]

The migratory practice was not confined to recently arrived immigrants. A sixty-six-year-old female crossing-sweeper, resident in the St Giles district for fifty years, customarily went hop-picking each autumn to earn money to provide for the winter months.[45]

WORK, WAGES AND STANDARD OF LIVING

Given that the majority who came to London were amongst the poorest in Ireland, and had little or no capital, and generally little experience of anything other than manual work, economically they were particularly vunerable. Himmelfarb has wrongly interpreted Mayhew's observation that the casual dock workers were 'shut out from the usual means of life by want of character' as disapproval of their general moral and behavioural standards, and as evidence of his inconsistency.[46] Insecure work was undoubtably often all that was available to the more disreputable groups within working-class society. Mayhew, however, is far from suggesting that these are the only types employed. He uses the term 'character' in the sense of confirmation of good character; as when he records that permanent labourers at the London Dock need a recommendation, whereas 'for the casual labourers no character is required'.[47] The immigrant Irish, who figured highly amongst the dock workers, and amongst casual

---

43 Herson speculates that a number of those who came to Stafford in the wake of famine were attracted by the possibility of rural work; see John Herson, 'Irish migration and settlement in Victorian England: a small-town perspective', in Roger Swift and Sheridan Gilley (eds), *The Irish in Britain 1859–1939* (London, 1989), p. 90. Frances Finnegan's study of York indicates that a high number of Irish who arrived at the same period were employed in the rural economy; see Frances Finnegan, 'The Irish in York', in Swift and Gilley, *Irish in the Victorian City*, p. 62.

44 Mayhew, *Morning Chronicle Survey*, vol. 2, Letter XXV, 11 Jan. p. 300.

45 Mayhew, *London Labour and the London Poor*, vol. 2, p. 484.

46 Mayhew, *London Labour and the London Poor*, vol. 3, p. 303. See Himmelfarb, *The Idea of Poverty*, p. 338.

47 Mayhew, *London Labour and the London Poor*, vol. 2, p. 303.

workers generally, not only had very little materially, but lacked contacts who could testify to their capabilities or trustworthiness. This reinforced their tendency to be over-represented in lowly, unskilled occupations such as labouring, rubbish-carting, costering and crossing-sweeping.

Mayhew's account of the general economic position of the Irish is confirmed by recent research. In London specifically, Lynn Lees found that although the Irish were present in almost all occupations, they were considerably over-represented at the lowest levels.[48] This was the case elsewhere too, in both old centres of population and in the expanding industrial areas of the north. In Scotland the picture was somewhat different. In the western lowlands, where most immigration was from relatively prosperous Ulster, although the Irish were at the bottom of the socio-economic ladder, they were fairly easily absorbed into the expanding economy, often in the mines or in the mills.[49] In York, a base for agricultural workers unable to find accommodation outside the city, the percentage of Irish men in work who were labourers of some description rose from 21.8% in 1841 to 52% in 1851.[50] David Large's study of Bristol had shown that in 1851, 36% of Irish-born men were labouring or portering. Although one-tenth of tailors were Irish, of those 121 individuals, only one was a master-tailor, and only nineteen described themselves as journeymen.[51] Furthermore, Lowe found evidence in Lancashire to suggest that those Irish who were skilled were in lowlier situations than equivalently qualified English workers.[52]

In London, when work was slack in one occupation, men would seek work in another, resorting to the lowliest types of street-trading, or crossing-sweeping if all else, or their health, failed. The account of one man interviewed in the Cripplegate Refuge illustrates the casual nature of the work in which many Irish were employed. Resident in England for more than two years, after arriving at Bristol, he initially went to Cardiff:

> At Cardiff I worked on the railway, at 2s. 6d. a day. I did well for a couple of months; ... I worked in Cardiff town with a bricklayer, ... at 12s. a week. I next year had a twelve-month's work, on and off, with a farmer near Bristol, at 10s. a week ... I made for London at the hay harvest. I had a little money to start with, but I got no hay-work, only a trifle of work at the docks. In corn-harvest, near

48 Lees, *Exiles of Erin*, pp 92–3.
49 Tom Gallagher, 'A Tale of Two Cities', in Swift and Gilley (eds), *Irish in the Victorian City*, p. 109.
50 Finnegan, in Swift & Gilley (eds), *Irish in the Victorian City*, p. 60, pp 66–7.
51 Large, in Swift and Gilley (eds), *Irish in the Victorian City*, pp 43–4. Regrettably, Large does not give the equivalent statistic for English labourers and porters.
52 Lowe, *Irish in Mid-Victorian Lancashire*, p. 82. In 1851, almost 22% of Irish male heads of households were recorded as skilled workers, compared to 26% of English.

Brighton, I worked for six weeks ... I got back to London with 40s. I could get no work at all but five days' work at a stoneyard at 1s. a day. I sold a few things in the streets – oranges and apples – so did my wife. It helped to keep us.[53]

Mayhew estimated that seven in twenty street-sellers were Irish, and probably totalled 10,000. Some were costermongers, and others, often the desperately poor, were involved in the humbler types of street-selling, the women frequently combining trading with begging, 'often very eloquently'. Children too, supplemented family incomes by casual street selling. Whereas the sale of more varied produce, including vegetables and fish, was primarily in the hands of men, women predominated in the three-quarters of Irish traders who sold only fruit, principally nuts and oranges.[54] These kept well, so the risk of incurring heavy losses when trade was poor was reduced. Oranges could be bought in relatively small numbers for little outlay.[55] Consequently, of the 4000 individuals Mayhew estimated to be selling oranges at peak season, 3000 were hawking them casually around the streets. Even the stall-holders made no more than a meagre living, though one which must often have provided a buffer against the insecurity of the seasonal manual labour available to men. The income of one woman (apparently a widow) was estimated at 5s. a week in the summer, and 3s. 6d. for the rest of the year, averaging at 4s. 3d., on which she provided for herself and three children.[56] Surprisingly, refuse-sellers, specialising in selling sub-standard fruit and vegetables, made slightly more. Often middle-aged and elderly single women working seven days a week, they earned between 4d. and 1s. a day selling ½d. lots to the poorest, often children, aiming to make 'cent. per cent'.[57]

Mayhew considered the minority of Irish who were reasonably well-established as coster-mongers to 'belong to a better class than the Irish labourers'. This might be expected. Those who had been resident for some time, had not left Ireland in desperation, and who had some small means with which to set up a modest business, or who were simply more resourceful, were likely to be seen as somewhat superior to most of their countrymen. Not surprisingly, given the recent influx of Irish, and the numbers resorting to selling on the streets, there was a degree of hostility towards them on the part of English traders: 'In fact, next to a policeman, a genuine London costermonger hates an Irishman, considering him an intruder'.[58] That the orange season (at its height in late

53 Mayhew, *Morning Chronicle Survey*, vol. 2, Letter XXV, 11 Jan. 1850, p. 298.
54 Mayhew, *London Labour and the London Poor*, vol. 1, pp 104–5; vol. 2, p. 119.
55 Ibid., vol. 1, pp 104–5; Mayhew, *Morning Chronicle Survey*, vol. 2, Letter XIII, 30 Nov. 1849, p. 7. A 'half-hundred' (55 oranges) could be obtained for between 15d. and 18d.: see Mayhew, *London Labour and the London Poor*, vol. 1, p. 88.
56 Mayhew, *Morning Chronicle Survey*, vol. 2, Letter XIII, 30 Nov. 1849, p. 8.
57 Mayhew, *London Labour and the London Poor*, vol. 1, p. 117.
58 Ibid., p. 104.

spring and early summer) was referred to as 'the Irishman's harvest' is indicative of the poor esteem in which the Irish were held. The Irish, traditionally associated with the rural harvests, had little status in society. Increasing urbanisation and changed economic conditions though altering the nature of the 'harvest' in which many Irish were involved, did not alter their position: orange-selling had been for centuries a low occupation.[59]

It appears that those Irish men who resorted to casual street-selling had less success than their women. Prospective buyers responded more readily to women than to Irishmen regarded as capable of work, even when none was available. One respectably dressed woman, who had been a servant in England until she had married, told Mayhew:

> My husband's a labourer; and when he's in full worruk he can earn 12s. or 14s. a week, for he's a good hand and a harrud-worruking man, and we do middlin' thin. He's out of worruk now, and I'm forced to thry and sill a few oranges ... and my husband minds the childer. Bad as I do, I can do 1d or 2d. profit a day betther than him, poor man! for he's tall and big, and people thinks, if he goes round with just a few oranges, it's just from idleniss.[60]

It was evidently true that her husband was no layabout. The next day she had disappeared from her pitch: her husband had found work 'at some distance' and she was looking for new lodgings.

Those fortunate enough to have served apprenticeships, usually in boot and shoe making or in tailoring, almost invariably found themselves involved in equally uncertain work in the slop end of the trade. Irish workers generally were dependent upon contacts within the immigrant community for obtaining work, and for supporting them when none was available: as outsiders, they were not members of the guilds and trade societies which provided some security for English skilled workers.[61] It appears that tannery yard-men, most of whom Mayhew says were Irish,[62] were reasonably paid, though they reported that work was becoming more difficult to obtain, due to the introduction of 'chemicals'. A tanner who had come to England eight or ten years before when his employer's business had failed, had struggled to keep his family on 2s. 6d. a week doing odd jobs, until through a friend he had obtained reasonably reliable work in his trade, paying 18s. a week.[63]

59 Ibid., p. 79, p. 88.
60 Ibid., p. 88.
61 Mayhew, *Morning Chronicle Survey*, vol. 6, Letter LXXVIII, 15 Nov. 1850, pp 174–5. See also Letter XVIII, 18 Dec. 1849 p. 145: a journeyman tailor who had made his way from Bristol to London said he had received no help from the trade on his journey.
62 Lees found in the leather trade as a whole there were few Irish, and those who were employed were involved in the most menial work: see Lees, *Exiles of Erin*, pp 93–4.
63 Mayhew, *Morning Chronicle Survey*, vol. 6, Letter LXXVIII, 15 Nov. 1850, pp 173–4.

Slop workers in the boot and shoe trade working into the night, six days a week, might earn 12s. or 13s. Many, however, had to take what little work was available, and existed on as little as 3s. or 3s. 6d.[64] The conditions in which they worked and lived were often poor:

> I knew a Roman Catholic, who was attentive to his religious duties, but when pronounced on the point of death ... he would not have his priest administer extreme unction, for the room was in such a filthy and revolting state he would not have the priest see it. Five men worked and slept in that room ... Unless a man lodged there he would not be employed. Each man pays 2s. a week ... These men (myself excepted) were all Irish, and all teetotallers, as was the master.[65]

Evidently then, the Irish were as capable as the English of exploiting their countrymen. Those Irish who arrived with no contacts in England were particularly vulnerable. Once trapped in the sweat system, they were, according to one source, unable to raise the money to return home.[66] Mayhew gives an account of the 'street kidnapping system', whereby unwary youths, often Irish, were lured into the employ of sweat-masters, often by women. The wife of one sweater ('an Irishman long notorious for such practices'), persuaded two young men from her native Kerry to come to London, supposedly for wages of 36s. a week. Initially working for 5s. a week, they ultimately found themselves 'apprenticed' to him for £5 a year and decidedly inferior board and lodging.[67] A twenty-one year old from county Limerick told a similar tale. Attracted by the possibility of good earnings, and having a contact in London (who proved to have died), he ultimately found himself working for a Brick Lane sweater:

> He said I must first go a week on trial. I got nothing but my board for that week's work – working six days, long hours. After that he offered me 3s. 6d. a week, board and lodging – not washing. I had no friends, and thought I better take it, as I did ... Bad as I lived in Ireland, it [the food] was wholesomer than this – and I had plenty of it too. My master there gave me a bellyfull; here he never did.[68]

Wages had declined, particularly since the 1830s, forcing many men into employing their families as sweat workers in order to survive. Workers earned as little as 5s. or 6s. a week. Not surprisingly, what appears to have been a

---

The 'chemicals' referred to, types of catechu, or terra japonica, are in fact, like the traditional oak bark, vegetable products.

64 Ibid., vol. 3, Letter XXXVI, 18 Feb. 1850, p. 197.
65 Ibid., p. 200.
66 Ibid., vol. 2, Letter XVIII, 18 Dec. 1849, p. 138.
67 Ibid., pp 143–4.
68 Ibid., pp 145–6. On the lack of tailoring opportunities in Ireland, see Harris, *Nearest Place That Wasn't Ireland*, p. 141.

systematic importation of cheap Irish labour was seen as one cause of low pay, as was the increase in foreign workers, and of women. Most resentment, however, was directed not at these fellow-sufferers, but at the employers commissioning the finished products, who, in an over-stocked labour market and facing hard competition, reduced wages by 'deductions' (paying the rate for children's clothes for smaller adult sizes) and regularly 'fining' outworkers for products not completed in the time allocated.[69]

These were by no means the only devices by which workers wages were reduced to below the nominal rate. On the docks, where many Irish took casual work, those responsible for hiring men were frequently publicans. It was commonly accepted that if a man was not prepared to drink at the employer's establishment, work would not be forthcoming. Consequently, the relatively good wages such arduous work commanded could be rapidly depleted as an indirect consequence of job insecurity. An Irish ballast-heaver told Mayhew:

> I was eight years a teetotaler before I went to ballast-work, and now I am forced to be a drunkard, to my sorrow, to get a job of work. My wife and children have a bit of land in Ireland to keep them, and they're badly off enough, God knows. I can neither help them, nor send money to bring them over to me; nor can I get over to them myself.[70]

Reports given by individuals directly concerned, and by the wives of dockers, tell of men being obliged to drink away half a week's wages: Mayhew details the previous week's full earnings, and the actual amount taken home, by of a group of fifty ballast-heavers he talked with. Of the two who had had 'private' jobs (not obtained through publicans or shop-keepers), one took away a significantly higher proportion of his earnings than the others, and one had the whole amount intact. Mayhew estimated the average earnings over a year to be 10s. a week, with 5s. taken home.[71] The coercion employed by publicans must have done little to dispel the popular view of the Irish as being over-fond of alcohol, and disruptive.

The precarious existence of those involved in dock work was confirmed not only by wages figures but also by other statistical evidence. Numbers of ships at berth at the London Dock in the previous year (evidently 1849) had varied between 29 and 141. The most marked variation in work available had occurred in May 1849.[72] On 4 May, the total number of workers was 2794. By 26 May the figure was 3012, dropping dramatically four days later to 1189. Given that

---

69 Mayhew, *Morning Chronicle Survey*, vol. 2, Letter XVII, 14 Dec. 1850, p. 113, pp 116–17, pp 118–19.
70 Mayhew, *London Labour and the London Poor*, vol. 3, pp 278–9.
71 Ibid., pp 265–91; particularly pp. 275–6.
72 Ibid., p. 303.

these figures include both permanent and casual employees, the effect on the casual market 'of the mere shifting of the wind', preventing ships docking, must have been enormous. Mayhew vehemently opposed men's security being entirely subject to the vagaries of the weather. His extensive statistical information is translated into human terms:

> As the foreman calls from the books the names, some men jump upon the backs of others, so as to... attract the notice of him who hires them. All are shouting. Some cry aloud his surname, some his Christian name, others call out their own names, to remind him they are there. Now the appeal is made in Irish blarney – now in broken English. Indeed, it is a sight to sadden the most callous, to see thousands of men struggling for only one day's hire.[73]

Dock-work not only attracted the resident Irish. One man estimated that there were 200 regular lumpers (workers paid a set amount for an entire unloading job) at Deptford, and, including those at the Deptford, Limehouse, Poplar and Blackwell Docks, probably 500 in total, with 200 seasonal workers brought in on the Cork boats to unload timber imports in the peak period between July and January.[74] Another stated that the rate for experienced hands had dropped by mid-century from the 4*s*. 6*d*. of nine years previously to 3*s*. 6*d*.;[75] yet, by the standards of the time a reasonable wage, and one likely to attract Irish men, on average taller and stronger than their English counterparts.[76] Irish workers were seen as depressing wages not simply because they were present in large numbers, but because unfamiliar with the work, they reduced levels to the rate paid for inexperienced men. It was a common perception that the Irish, accustomed to lower rates of pay, were prepared to work for less than their English counterparts: 'Oft enough he [the foreman] gets the best hands at first, and when a quantity that may be wanted is got off he puts on cheaper hands – new Irish Grecians some people calls them ... They ruin our trade, and are ruining it more and more; they'll work for nothing.'[77]

Such resentment was not entirely without foundation. Nor it seems, was it confined to English workers. Those Irish who were relatively well-established resented being undercut by their fellow countrymen. At Covent Garden, where the ticket-porters were overwhelmingly Irish, one man complained that 'there's lots ready to work for ½*d*. instead of 1*d*. [a turn] in the market, and they're slinking outside for jobs ... It's my counthrymen that's the ruin of me.'[78] Other

73 Ibid., p. 304.
74 Mayhew, *Morning Chronicle Survey*, vol. 2, Letter XXIV, 8 Jan. 1850, p. 272.
75 Ibid., 8 Jan. 1850, p. 277.
76 See Davis, *Irish in Britain*, p. 13, citing investigative work by Joel Mokyr.
77 Mayhew, *Morning Chronicle Survey*, vol. 2, Letter XXIV, 8 Jan. 1850, p. 275.
78 Ibid., vol. 6, Letter LXXXI, 5 Dec. 1850, p. 228. Ticket-porters were those employed officially, paying 1*s*. 6*d*. for the privelege.

factors too were believed to have lowered wages. An old Irishwoman, no doubt remembering the rebuilding of 1830,[79] considered improvements to the market had reduced the need for porters, and consequently her earnings had dropped from 7*s*. 6*d*. in the four or five years following that event to 5*s*. The account of another female Irish porter, aged eighty-seven, confirms the decline in wages over this period. The elderly, with their longer memories, appeared inclined to see the decline in wages and living standards as having come about since the 1830s, a period of relative prosperity, whilst others tended to attribute problems to more recent social changes.[80]

Whether the Irish did reduce wage levels, as many contemporaries believed, is debatable. It was a view in accordance with that challenged by E.H. Hunt, that the developing British economy benefitted from a cheap, flexible pool of Irish labour.[81] More recently, Jeffrey Williamson's highly theoretical revisionist contribution to the ongoing debate has suggested that immigration, rather than lowering urban wages, was a factor in keeping English rural workers on the land and in a low-paid economy; overall, the incoming Irish had the effect of inhibiting wage rises rather than actually reducing income.[82] Much of the debate has focused upon the north, and the impact or otherwise of the Irish upon the developing industrial centres, with which London, with its variety of occupations and (supposed) opportunities, had little in common.

Given that according to Lees, only 14% of the total number of incoming permanent migrants in London between 1841 and 1851 were Irish, this does not suggest excessive additional strain on the job market.[83] However, the picture is more complex than it initially appears. A large proportion of Irish immigrants were young adults, and consequently they were disproportionately represented in the job market: in the 1840s, they accounted for one quarter of the increase in the British workforce.[84] Temporary migration adds to the complexity of the picture. Although, as Mayhew indicates, in London this coincided with the busiest time at the docks, this period stretched well into the winter months, when migrants from the land, unwilling to return to their homeland, were in competition for whatever work was available in the capital. Williamson concedes that the impact of the Irish on labour mobility in Britain was most marked in the 1840s.[85] Even at the time when immigration was at its

79 See Cunningham, *Handbook for London*, vol. 1, p. 240.

80 Mayhew, *Morning Chronicle Survey*, vol. 6, Letter LXXXI, 5 Dec. 1850, pp 228–30.

81 See E.H. Hunt, *British Labour History 1815–1914* (London, 1981), pp 171–8, particularly p. 175.

82 Jeffrey Williamson, 'The impact of the Irish on British labor markets during the Industrial Revolution', in Swift and Gilley (eds), *Irish in Britain*, pp 134–62. For an overview of labour mobility in England see Harris, *Nearest Place That Wasn't Ireland*, pp 105–29.

83 Lees, *Exiles of Erin*, p. 46.

84 Williamson in Swift and Gilley (eds), *Irish in Britain*, p. 147.

85 Ibid., p. 157.

highest, some groups, even amongst the Irish, benefitted financially. Those who set up lodging-houses for incoming migrants clearly made a reasonable living, even out of those who came with little. Given that the impoverished Irish needed to eat (and drink), those Irish who made a living in the streets often relied for at least a large proportion of their trade upon their fellow countrymen.[86]

While the debate surrounding the relationship of the immigrant Irish to the contemporary economic situation remains inconclusive, Mayhew's record of the opinions and social interactions of the poor provides palpable human testimony to the fact that they were perceived as having a negative impact. This fact in itself constitutes an important dimension of historical reality.

SOCIAL CIRCUMSTANCES AND CULTURAL MORES

Given the level of earnings, the particularly precarious nature of casual employment in the 1840s, and the tendency of the Irish, as a consequence of both economic factors and inclination, to form small settlements within the poorer, more densely populated areas of the city, it is self-evident that the social conditions in which they existed were cramped, and conducive to neither cleanliness nor health.

The Irish diet, monotonous, and with the potato the staple food – 'taties and milk and fish and iggs' (Mayhew makes no mention of the Irish pig) – in an age when high intakes of animal (rather than fish) protein were regarded as desirable, was widely considered to be inferior.[87] The taunt that the Irish ate what was 'only meat for pigs' was not entirely without foundation: pre-Famine, one-third of the Irish potato crop was fed to livestock, over half of it to pigs.[88] The fact that this dependence produced workers who were taller and stronger than their English counterparts seemingly did no more than reinforce the view that the Irish were adapted to manual rather than to mental labour. On emigrating, although potatoes and cheap fish, particularly oily fish with a high calorific content (a staple food of the poor generally), continued to be consumed in quantities, the Irish poor began to adopt the diet of the English urban lower classes, and reliance upon bread increased.[89]

86 Mayhew, *London Labour and the London Poor*, vol. 1, p. 109, p. 117: the poorer areas in which the Irish street sellers worked were amongst those with high immigrant populatons.

87 Ibid., p. 118. See also Davis, *Irish in Britain*, p. 87, citing *The Report on the State of the Irish Poor in Great Britain*, Parliamentary Papers (1836) (40) XXX, iv, p. 432: in 1836, Malthus had expressed concern about the likely 'pernicious effect' if dependency on the potato was introduced from Ireland into Britain.

88 Mayhew, *London Labour and the London Poor*, vol. 1, p. 113; Davis, *Irish in Britain*, p. 37.

89 Mayhew, *London Labour and the London Poor*, vol. 1, pp 113–14, p. 118.

There were clearly times when those with the least economic security could not afford this basic diet. The consequences of urban poverty for the Irish, as with the English, must undoubtedly have been most marked amongst the young. Until the mid-1840s many in south west Ireland were poor, but subsistence crops, and the relative stability of potato prices, as accounts in Mayhew suggest, meant they were at least reasonably fed.[90] In London, where money was needed for all of life's necessities, if income was low the health of children particularly suffered. Of the four children of an Irishwoman clearly accustomed to begging, only the two oldest appeared to be in reasonable health:

> In her arms she carried an infant, round which were wound some old woolen rags. As the little thing sucked at its mother's breast it breathed so hard that it needed no words to tell one of its long exposure to the cold … The children were respectively eleven, six, and three years old. The eldest (a good-looking grey-eyed girl …) was covered in a tattered plaid shawl … The next child, a boy, … was clad in all kinds of rags. The youngest child was almost a dwarf. He was three years old, but so stunted that he seemed scarce half that age.[91]

Mayhew, despite evident exasperation at the hapless mother's acceptance of her husband's indifference to his family's welfare, and at her readiness to involve her children in begging, scrupulously records that 'still there was the little bit of clean net inside the old rusty bonnet' – a pathetic testament to her desire to maintain a modicum of self-respect.

Cleanliness, in the overcrowded conditions in which the majority of the poor lived, was difficult to maintain. The reputation which the Irish had for being indifferent to squalor, though undoubtedly reinforced by prejudice, may well have had a basis in fact; from a rural background, and no doubt indifferent to nineteenth-century English ideas of 'respectable' behaviour, many Irish had greater priorities than orderly dress and well-shod children. Mayhew found the one aspect of their poverty which, for all their 'blarney', they were never inclined to exaggerate, but rather the reverse, was the unacceptable nature of their accommodation.[92] If Lynn Lees's estimate that a rent of 4s. per week defined the level of 'respectability', then clearly the Irish, in irregular and often low-paid work, were, as Mayhew confirms, well below this, often paying as little as 1s. 6d., or even 1s. a week.[93] A single room frequently provided accommodation for more than one family. One crossing sweeper who lived in the St Giles area paid 1s. 3d. a week, sharing a room containing three beds with two other families. A man, his wife, mother and child shared one bed: a couple and their

90 See Davis, *Irish in Britain*, p. 12.
91 Mayhew, *Morning Chronicle Survey*, vol. 2, Letter XXV, Fri. 11 Jan. 1850, pp 298–9.
92 Mayhew, *London Labour and the London Poor*, vol. 1, p. 465.
93 Ibid., p. 116; Lees, *Exiles of Erin*, p. 103;

child slept in another. In one Whitechapel lodging house Mayhew found ten recently-arrived immigrants sharing one room which contained, apart from a tea-chest, a single mattress and a makeshift curtain to protect the modesty of the women.[94]

Although poor conditions were common, they were by no means universal. One lodging house described by Mayhew was impeccably clean and cheeerful, the floor 'sprinkled with red sand, while the windows were sound, bright and transparent', and the chimney-mantle 'white and red with the china images ranged upon it'.[95] Although Mayhew clearly considered Irish women to be lacking domestic skills,[96] his scrupulous commitment to recording what he found rather than what he anticipated makes it apparent that theory could not always comfortably accommodate the reality. Dwellings in the courts along Rosemary Lane, although overcrowded and poor, gave the lie to the idea of Irish women as domestically incapable: 'In all the houses that I entered were traces of household care and neatness that I had little expected to have seen ... [and] an air of comfort that strangely disagreed with the reports of the cabins in "ould Ireland".'[97]

Poverty was clearly an important factor underlying overcrowding, but it was not the only one. Close coexistence provided the Irish with a degree of psychological and cultural, as well as economic security. There is a danger, of course, of acquiring an idealised impression of Irish communal solidarity. There is ample evidence, in Mayhew's work and elsewhere, that the Irish were not averse to quarrelling amongst themselves: G.P. Connolly's account of the priest Daniel Hearne's efforts to keep order in his Manchester parish is evidence that it was often regional rather than national loyalties which were significant.[98] As has already been shown, Mayhew's accounts indicate that single Irish men without friends or relatives already established in England had problems, even when they were living with their countrymen. Under stressful conditions, too, family relationships suffered; one elderly woman who declared her daughter-in-law to be 'a very just, clane, sober woman' was on poor terms with her son, a redundant brick-layer, who, having 'no connixion', was under severe financial strain.[99]

Nevertheless, social and family links, as Lynn Lees has shown, were an important stabilising factor, and small communities, consisting of friends and

---

94 Mayhew, *London Labour and the London Poor*, vol. 2, p. 482; vol. I, p. 111.
95 Ibid., vol. 1, p. 111.
96 Ibid., p. 105.
97 Ibid., p. 110.
98 G.P. Connolly 'Little Brother be at Peace: the Priest as Holy Man in the Nineteenth-century Ghetto', in W.J. Sheils (ed.), *The Church and Healing*, Studies in Church History, vol. 19 (Oxford, 1982), p. 198.
99 Mayhew, *London Labour and the London Poor*, vol. 2, p. 484.

families were gradually resettled in Britain, in the hope of a better life.[100] Lees's account of the importance of the Irish extended family, particularly on the paternal side, are borne out by Mayhew's accounts. Where three generations of a family lived together, the oldest member was invariably the mother of the male head of family. That children of siblings, sometimes orphans, were incorporated into the family unit is also evident.[101] Lees makes the point that this was a continuation of the rural tradition. It also made economic sense. Assuming all adults (as well as older children) worked, the more members of a family sharing a home meant a greater income for less outlay on rent. The elderly female crossing-sweeper living with her son and his family (mentioned above) told Mayhew, 'I pay nothing a week, only bring home ivery ha'penny to hilp thim. Sometimes I spind a pinny or tuppence out on mysilf.'[102]

Practical aid – 'the poor help the poor'[103] – reinforced a sense of communal identity. Unlike the English poor, Mayhew reported, the Irish rarely resorted to money-lenders. Interest-free loans were provided by those in work to aid their less fortunate countrymen, sometimes directly, and sometimes with the priest as intermediary, controlling funds.[104] Lowe, in his examination of the Irish in Lancashire, makes the point that the preparedness of the Irish to set aside money for various causes, tended to inhibit their upward social and economic progress.[105] Mayhew implies the same:

> [T]he saving of an Irish street-seller does not arise from any wish to establish himself more prosperously in his business, but for the attainment of some cherished project, such as emigration. Some of the objects, however, for which these struggling men hoard money, are of the most praiseworthy character. They will treasure up halfpenny after halfpenny, and continue to do so for years, in order to send money to enable their wives and children, and even their brothers and sisters, when in the depth of distress in Ireland, to take shipping for England. They will save to be able to remit money for the relief of their aged parents in Ireland.[106]

The Irish Catholic poor placed a higher premium upon the security which their community afforded than upon social advancement. As Lynn Lees writes, 'The

---

100 See Lynn Lees, 'Patterns of Lower-Class Life', in Stephan Thernstrom and Richard Bennett (eds), *Nineteenth-Century Cities: Essays in the New Urban History* (New Haven, 1969), p. 383. See also Mayhew, *London Labour and the London Poor*, vol. 1, p. 109.
101 See Mayhew, *London Labour and the London Poor*, vol. 1, p. 116; vol. 2, p. 482, p. 484. See also Lees in Thernstrom and Bennett, *Nineteenth-Century Cities*, p. 375, p. 380.
102 Mayhew, *London Labour and the London Poor*, vol. 2, p. 484.
103 Mayhew, *Morning Chronicle Survey*, vol. 6, Letter LXXVII, 15 Nov. 1850, p. 174.
104 Mayhew, *London Labour and the London Poor*, vol. 1, p. 115.
105 Lowe, *Irish in Mid-Victorian Lancashire*, p. 95.
106 Mayhew, *London Labour and the London Poor*, vol. 1, p. 115.

signposts of success for labourers ought not to be measured in middle-class terms ... "Getting ahead" signified not [a] rise to fortune, but small achievements that brought a measure of security and help for one's children'.[107]

Although there were undoubtedly exceptions – and Mayhew provides some – it can be surmised from his accounts that the poor Irish, with a different cultural background, did not share those English ideas of 'respectability' which were so bound up with class, and by which, even amongst the poor, large numbers defined their identity. Mayhew found the Irish, always 'eloquent', much more ready than impoverished English (and particularly English men, often, no doubt inhibited by a sense of pride) to reveal the details of their straitened circumstances, particularly if there seemed to be a possibility of money being elicited from a sympathetic hearer.[108] It is perhaps significant that despite the general readiness of the Irish to talk, Mayhew states that he could not make an estimate of the amount which the Irish saved.[109]

Many Irish, it seems, even if they had funds, regarded any opportunity to obtain money or goods, short of personal theft, as one not to be missed. Referring to the street-Irish, Mayhew remarks that amongst other things:

> They will save to defray the expense of their marriage, an expense the English costermonger so frequently dispenses with, – but they will not save to preserve themselves or their children from the degradation of the workhouse; indeed they often, with the means of independence secreted on their persons, apply for parish relief, and that principally to save the expenditure of their own money. Even when detected in such an attempt at extortion an Irishman betrays no passion, and hardly manifests any emotion – he has speculated and failed.[110]

Whereas many impoverished English regarded dependence upon parish relief, and particularly the workhouse, as a humiliation, the Irish resisted strongly the idea that pauperism was a social disgrace. Even by English middle-class standards, this attitude did have positive aspects. Mayhew records with approval that the interests of those sick and elderly for whom the workhouse was the only option were not neglected by those in the community, who 'do not lose sight of him', even to the extent, in the case of a death, of obtaining the body so that it might be waked, and paying funeral expenses.[111]

Graham Davis has suggested that some research, by focussing on examples of the worst conditions and of anti-Irish prejudice, and on the most extreme examples of conflict and hostility, has produced a distorted picture of contemporary attitudes to the Irish in Britain, as well as unintentionally reinforcing

107 Lees, *Exiles of Erin*, p. 121.
108 Mayhew, *Morning Chronicle Survey*, vol. 3, Letter XXIX, 25 Jan. 1850, p. 53.
109 Mayhew, *London Labour and the London Poor*, vol. 1, p. 115.
110 Ibid.
111 Ibid.

stereotypical views of them.[112] Whilst it would be foolish to deny that there were many instances of blatant discrimination – the magistrates' court proceedings in York cited by Frances Finnegan, for instance, leave no room for illusion[113] – mid-nineteenth century contemporary views were by no means universally condemnatory; even the more emphatic assertions of Hibernian inferiority are often qualified. Angus Reach, the *Morning Chronicle's* industrial correspondent, for instance, in his unfavourable account of the Merthyr Irish, attributed the conditions in which the immigrants lived not to any intellectual inferiority, but to their being 'unaccustomed to a better state', and to the fact (not, incidentally, supported by Mayhew's interviews) that they considered themselves to be only temporary residents who would eventually return to their homeland.[114] Roger Swift has noted the observation by Mayhew and Binney in *The Criminal Prisons of London* that the habitual criminals of London were believed to be, in nine cases out of ten, 'Irish Cockneys', persons born of Irish parents in the Metropolis, and that Mayhew attributed much Irish juvenile delinquency to poverty.[115] Thereby, Mayhew challenged popular perceptions of the association between the Irish and crime by concluding that Irish criminality was not the product of innate tendencies:

> This shows, we believe, not that the Irish are more criminal than our own race, but simply that they are poorer, and that their children are, consequently, left to shift for themselves, and sent out to beg more frequently than our people.

And:

> The Irish constitute the poorest section of our people, and the children, therefore, are virtually orphans in this country, left to gambol in the streets and courts… from their very earliest years; the mothers, as well as the fathers, being generally engaged throughout the day in some of the ruder forms of labour or street trade.[116]

There is little evidence in Mayhew's *Morning Chronicle* letters, or in *London Labour and the London Poor*, of any Irish predisposition to crime. In one area of vice, prostitution, the author records that their record is considerably better than that of the English poor, a finding in accordance with most other contemporary

---

112 Graham Davis, 'Little Irelands', in Swift and Gilley (eds), *Irish in Britain*, p. 105.

113 Finnegan, in Swift and Gilley (eds), *Irish in the Victorian City*, p. 78.

114 Angus Reach, 'Merthyr and Dowlais: Public Health, The Irish, Religion in the Ironworks', Letter VII, in Razzell and Wainwright, *Victorian Working Class*, pp 260–2.

115 Roger Swift, 'Crime and the Irish in nineteenth-century Britain', in Swift and Gilley (eds), *Irish in Britain*, p. 163.

116 Henry Mayhew and John Binney, *The Criminal Prisons of London and Scenes of Prison Life* (London, 1862 edn. reprinted 1971), p. 386, p. 403.

evidence.[117] The Irish were apparently rarely involved in common-law liaisons, and took care to supervise their young women.[118] Irish women were popularly regarded as having higher moral standards than the English, and often impressed those who came into contact with them. Although not all informants agreed with the one at the Holborn workhouse who said of Irish young women that he 'never heard an indecent word from any of them, nor an oath', there was general agreement with his opinion of their sexual propriety: 'I have no doubt, not in the least, that they were chaste and modest'.[119]

Mayhew, however, was looking primarily at first-generation immigrants. Lynn Lees, using Catholic Church registers, found illegitimacy rates generally higher amongst the immigrant community in London than in Ireland, rising as more second-generation Irish, who began too adopt the mores of the host community, had children. In 1851, recorded Catholic illegitimacy rates were over 10% in St Giles' parish, with the majority of mothers having been born in England. Interestingly, in 1852 Thomas Beames (who, incidentally, acknowledged a debt to Mayhew's investigations) commented on the loose sexual morality of first generation Irish, both men and women, living in the St Giles rookery, remarking that 'The purity of the female character, which is the boast of Irish historians, here at least, is a fable'.[120] Evidence from a single parish, however, can give a misleading picture. In this, the most notorious of the London slums, with a long-established and unenviable reputation for attracting the disreputable, the social composition of the Irish community may have been atypical.[121]

Roger Swift has calculated that on the evidence from a number of northern and midlands towns, first-generation Irish were three times as likely as the English to appear in the criminal statistics, and suggests that if subsequent generations were included, the proportion would almost certainly be higher. [122] This over-representation is partly attributable to the concentrated policing of poorer areas which had high immigrant populations (no doubt a practice which many residents regarded as provocative), and partly perhaps to the generally less inhibited nature of Irish social life, which Mayhew remarked on.[123] The

---

117 Mayhew, *London Labour and the London Poor*, vol. 1, p. 109. See Swift, in Swift and Gilley (eds), *Irish in Britain*, pp 175–6. See also Lowe, *Irish in Mid-Victorian Lancashire*, pp 102–3.

118 Mayhew, *London Labour and the London Poor*, vol. 1, p. 109.

119 Mayhew, *Morning Chronicle Survey*, vol. 3, Letter XXVIII, 22 Jan. 1850, p. 31.

120 Thomas Beames, *The Rookeries of London* (London, 1852 edn, reprinted 1970), pp 35–6; 38.

121 See M. Dorothy George, *London Life in the Eighteenth Century* (Harmondsworth, 1966), pp 120–9, particularly p. 121. George suggests that St Giles, long a centre for Irish settlement, having had relatively generous poor relief, had perhaps attracted the more disreputable Irish.

122 Swift, in Swift and Gilley (eds), *Irish in Britain*, pp 164–5.

123 Ibid., pp 177–8. Mayhew, *London Labour and the London Poor*, vol. 1, p. 109.

tendency for the Irish to appear regularly on public order and petty theft offences confirmed a widely-held view of the Irish as being generally socially irresponsible and over-fond of alcohol. Needless to say, poverty was a major contributory factor to criminal and public order offences, both directly and indirectly. It is hardly surprising that the wife of an Irish ballast-heaver whose health was broken by drink, on returning from having him admitted into hospital and finding her children evicted in her absence for non-payment of rent, should be provoked into assaulting the bailiffs.[124] In contrast to the popular view, the master of the Wandsworth and Clapham Union, clearly a man of some compassion, found the Irish, almost without exception, well-behaved: if there was trouble, it was invariably because they had been provoked by English inmates.[125]

Although Mayhew did not understimate the distressing social and personal effects of alcohol dependence, his accounts hardly confirm the picture of the Irish as inveterate drinkers. Dock-workers, many of whom were Irish, clearly did drink to excess, but (as already observed) Mayhew was more inclined to attribute blame to the circumstances in which men were hired and paid, and to the insecurity of their way of life than to any inherent weakness. Although he stated that some Irish street-traders 'frequent the beer-shops and are inveterate drinkers, and smokers too', he also remarked on the high levels of abstemiousness amongst the Irish (one informant estimated that twice as many Irish as English street traders were teetotal), something he attributed to their low earnings, to their thrift, to their background, to the influence of Father Mathew's temperance campaign in the early 1840s, and to the continued determination of the priest-hood.[126] He was cautious, however, about estimating the comparative rates of alchohol consumption of the Irish and English. What was clear was that gener-ally the Irish, unlike the English, drank spirits rather than beer, usually gin (they could rarely afford the preferred whisky).

The Irish preference for spirits no doubt meant that if they did drink, they showed the effects fairly quickly. Their reputation, for being troublesome when inebriated, is confirmed by Mayhew. One publican said, 'I had rather have twenty poor Englishmen drunk in my tap-room than a couple of poor Irishmen. They'll quarrel with anybody – the Irish will – and sometimes clear the room by swearing they'll use their knives, by Jasus.'[127] They were however, probably more inclined to quarrel between themselves than with the English. The engaging account given by an interviewee of one such dispute gives in a few lines a wealth of information about immigrant Irish life: the importance of the

124 Mayhew, *London Labour and the London Poor*, vol. 3, p. 280.
125 Mayhew, *Morning Chronicle Survey*, vol. 3, Letter XXVIII, 22 Jan. 1850, p. 26, p. 32.
126 Mayhew, *London Labour and the London Poor*, vol. 1, p. 109, p. 111, p. 114. See also Brian Harrison, *Drink and the Victorians: The Temperance Question in England 1815–1872* (London, 1971), p. 165, p. 168.
127 Mayhew, *London Labour and the London Poor*, vol. 1, p. 114.

street as a communal meeting place; the reliance upon Irish contacts; the menial work and low pay many were prepared to accept; the contempt of the established Irish for the recently arrived immigrant; the readiness of the Irish to resort to physical means to settle an argument; the way in which police involvement could produce an escalation in violence, and not least, the status of the priest:

> Thin I got ingaged by ... a rubbish-carter ... Yis, he was a countryman of mine, but a Cor-rk man – said he's made a bad bargain, for he was bad off and he only clared 4*d*. a load, and he'd divide it wid me. We did six loads in a day and and I got 1*s*. every night for a wake. This was a rise. But one Sunday evening I was standing talking with people as lived in the same coort, and I tould how I was helping Tim. And two Englishmen came to find four men as they wanted for work, and ould Ragin (Regan) tould 'em what I was working for. And one of 'em said I was a 'b— Irish fool', and ould Ragin said so, and words came on, and thin there was a fight, and thin the police came, and the fight was harder ... No, I'm not fond of fightin'. I'm a paceable man, glory be to God, and I think I was put on ... I sarved my month, and it ain't a bad place at all the prison. I tould the gintleman that had charge of us, that I was a Roman Catholic, God be praised, and couldn't go to his prayers. 'O very well, Pat', says he. And next day, the praste came ... and very angry he was, and said our conduc' was a disgrace to religion, and to our counthry, and to him. Do I think he was right, sir? God knows he was, or he wouldn't have said so.[128]

THE PRACTICE AND INFLUENCE OF RELIGION

The priest was a pivotal figure in the Irish community, intimately involved in the practical and social, as well as in the religious lives of his flock.[129] Mayhew himself records the devotion of the Catholic priests in Liverpool at the time of the cholera outbreak, and acknowledges the financial aid which the clergy gave to their poor parishioners.[130] It was the priest, living amongst those he served,

---

128 Ibid., vol. 2, p. 338.
129 Tom Gallagher, writing about the Glasgow area, observes that the priest was the one figure to whom deference was shown by the Irish poor. See Tom Gallagher, *Glasgow, the Uneasy Peace: Religious Tension in Modern Scotland* (Manchester, 1987), p. 12. Gwynn has highlighted the extent to which, in South Wales in the 1840s the priest was involved in the lives of the Irish, to the extent of sharing their very evident poverty. See Denis Gwynn, 'Irish Immigration' in G.A. Beck (ed.), *The English Catholics, 1850– 1950: Essays to Commemorate the Centenary of the Restoration of the Hirarchy of England and Wales* (Glasgow, 1950), p. 277. See also Samuel, in Swift and Gilley (eds), *Irish in the Victorian City*, pp 276–7, and William Sloan, 'Religious Affiliation and the Immigrant Experience: Catholic Irish and Protestant Highlanders in Glasgow, 1830–1850', in T.M. Devine (ed.), *Irish Immigrants and Scottish Society in the Nineteenth and Twentieth Centuries* (Edinburgh, 1991), p. 77.
130 Mayhew, *London Labour and the London Poor*, vol. 1, p. 112, p. 115.

and whose influence rested upon his calling rather than his class, who ultimately called the erring to account, and to whom the poor deferred, often
unquestioningly. Contact with a priest was, Mayhew insisted, the one guarantee
of accurate and unembelished information from his parishioners.[131]

It is typical of Mayhew that in his account of a recently-returned priest on
his round he describes not the man himself, but the community's response to
him: Mayhew's interest was engaged by the attitudes of the poor rather than of
those in positions of authority. Variation in the level of detail lend immediacy
and vitality to the description of the priest's progress. The reader is made
vividly aware not only of the priest's influence, but of the combination of
reverence and affection in which he is held:

> One old crone, as he passed, cried, "You're a good father, Heaven comfort you,"
> and the boys playing about stood still to watch him. A lad, in a man's tail-coat
> and a shirt-collar that nearly covered in his head – like the paper round a bouquet
> – was fortunate enough to be noticed, and his eyes sparkled, as he touched his
> hair at each word he spoke in answer ... Even as the priest walked along the
> street, boys running at full speed would pull up to touch their hair, and the stall-
> women would rise from their baskets; while all the noise – even a quarrel – ceased
> until he had passed by.[132]

The high esteem in which the priest was held is also evident in the account of
another visit. 'Old Norah', literally rescued from the gutter, was persuaded to
renounce alcohol – 'the pledge', as Mayhew reports, being regarded by Irish
Catholics as a religious as much as a social commitment[133] – save her earnings, 'the
father ... keeping her book for her, as he did for the other poor people', and to join
the Association of the Blessed Lady.[134] That in the priest's absence she again
succumbed to temptation, in the form of her brother's persuading, is an indication
of the Church's difficult struggle in the face of adverse social conditions.

The setting up of confraternities and women's organisations such as that
which Mayhew mentions, and help with financial matters, were ways in which
the Catholic Church retained influence whilst inculcating ideas of individual
and communal responsibility (sometimes, as Mayhew's account illustrates, with
limited success). The generally tolerant approach of the priesthood to behavioural lapses which Gilley has remarked upon demonstrated not only the
principle of forgiving the sinner whilst not condoning the sin, but also a healthy
pragmatism on the Church's part.[135] There might be a religious duty to attend

---

131 Ibid., p. 466.
132 Ibid., p. 108.
133 Ibid., p. 114.
134 Ibid., p. 110.
135 Gilley, in Swift and Gilley (eds), *Irish in the Victorian City*, p. 256.

mass, but as one man, a costermonger resident in England for thirty years remarked, 'the priest won't exact too much of a poor man, either about that, or about fasting'.[136] For those existing on a meagre income, religion needed to be affordable. Spiritual and practical needs had to be balanced. An elderly crossing sweeper told Mayhew 'Some people says to me they they would rather I went to church; but I tells 'em I do; and sure sir, afther mass, there's no harrum in a little sweepin' between whiles'. He attended mass every Sunday, and tried to go to confession once a month.[137]

Mayhew clearly regarded the religious attachment of the Irish as a stabilising force, something which was generally, though not entirely, lacking in the lives of the English poor: in rubbish-carting, for instance, Irish Catholics shared the distinction of being the most regular church attenders with English migrants from rural areas (where traditional practices persisted).[138] Where he did find religious indifference amongst the Irish, it was among the few who described themselves as 'Protestant' and among those Catholics who had been in England for a considerable time, and who lived alongside 'the poorest or vagrant class of the English': in matters of religion at least it was the English who were a malign influence.[139] This finding is in line with the broader picture of Irish Catholic devotion. It appears that those Irish who emigrated in the pre-Famine period were more likely to lapse than were those who arrived in the wake of a disaster which could be attributed to divine retribution for earlier profligacy and religious neglect.[140] The Church provided a cultural and religious bulwark in a world beset with insecurity.

As Lowe has observed, 'the priest's concern for for the community's well-being and his intercessions in its behalf were not contingent on good turn-out at Sunday mass'.[141] One second-generation Irish street-trader, who considered that the time taken up by church-going, 'not just while you're there, but in shaving and washing and getting ready' was a deterrent to those in his line of business, would only say that he attended mass 'as often as I can', though he insisted he sometimes went to vespers.[142] Nevertheless, although the church census in 1851 showed Catholic attendance to be lower than amongst other denominations in London, and considerably lower than for the average for all denominations in England as a whole, the figures are somewhat misleading. The low turnout is partly accounted for by a shortage of both priests and

---

136 Mayhew, *London Labour and the London Poor*, vol. 1, p. 107.
137 Ibid., vol. 2, p. 482.
138 Ibid., vol. 1, p. 101, p. 108; vol. 2, p. 295.
139 Ibid., vol. 1, p. 107.
140 See for instance Tom Gallagher, 'The Catholic Irish in Scotland: in search of identity', in Devine, *Irish Immigrants and Scottish Society*, p. 20.
141 Lowe, *Irish in Mid-Victorian Lancashire*, p. 114.
142 Mayhew, *London Labour and the London Poor*, vol. 2, p. 43.

chapels; 20% of the Irish-born in London lived in areas which had no Catholic church. Lynn Lees observes that in areas of high Irish settlement, Catholic churches were filled to capacity.[143] It seems likely that Mayhew's picture of a relatively devout community, contrasting favourably with English groups at an equivalent social level, is not entirely mistaken.

Many of those Irish who were not regular attenders at chapel nevertheless continued to identify with their Church. Some circumspection, however, is necessary when assessing the actual evidence. It should be borne in mind that non-practising Christians of other denominations might well give similarly indignant answers to that of the lapsed Catholic, asked if he if ever attended at other than his own Church ('Av coorse not!'), particularly if they were asked if they were likely to be found worshipping in a Catholic chapel.[144] The real difference lies in the respective attitudes of Catholics and Protestants to religious practice generally. Unlike Irish Catholics (practising or otherwise) a high proportion of the English poor, whatever their fundamental beliefs, were suspicious of overt religious participation, with its connotations of social superiority. In the Catholic Church, the availability of the priest, and the determination to establish the Church's practical as well as spiritual relevance, ensured that it remained an embracing rather than an alienating institution. It is difficult to imagine a non-practising Irish Catholic making the kind of observation about practising adherents which one elderly woman, an English costermonger resident in London for many years, made: 'I never go to church. I used to go when I was a little child at Sevenoaks ... I've forgot what the inside of a church is like. There's no costermongers ever go to church, except the rogues of them, that wants to appear good'.[145]

Irish Catholicism fused cultural and religious elements. The fondness for religious pictures which Mayhew observed is evidence of the importance of representations in Irish popular religion, particularly amongst the illiterate. It was also no doubt in part a counter to the drabness of urban poverty. In one description, of the cheerfully eclectic collection of 'little black-framed pictures, scarcely bigger than pocket-books' in an Irish-run lodging-house, Mayhew nicely captures the balance of secular and religious which enlivened the drab circumstances of slum life:

> Most of these were sacred subjects, with large yellow glories round the heads;
> though between the drawing representing the bleeding heart of Christ and the
> Saviour bearing the Cross, was an illustration of a red-waistcoated sailor smoking

143 Lees, *Exiles of Erin*, pp 181–2. On census Sunday in 1851, 30% of London Catholics attended church. The figure for all denominations in London was 37%, and for all denominations in the whole of England, 41%.
144 Mayhew, *London Labour and the London Poor*, vol. 1, p. 107.
145 Ibid., p. 100.

his pipe. The Adoration of the Shepherds, again, was matched on the other side of the fireplace by a portrait of Daniel O'Connell.[146]

Most Irish Catholics in London were illiterate. The reading of the few who could read (and as Mayhew points out, they had little time for such leisure) was generally confined to such works as lives of the saints. Although among those who had had some education there were exceptions, those at the bottom of the social and economic ladder had little understanding of Church doctrine:

> The blessed saints? ... I – I mane prays to them. O, yis. I pray to them mysilf ivery night for a blissin', and to rise me out of my misery. No, sir, I can't say I know what the mass is about. I don't know what I'm prayin' for thin, only that its right.[147]

Although, as Mayhew himself indicates, traditional hostility towards the Irish was compounded by economic and demographic factors, the part which religious differences continued to play in determining attitudes should not be overlooked. The re-establishment of the Roman Church in 1850, and the high profile of the Church under Wiseman, following in the wake of the Anglican High Church movement (suspected by many of being a back-door route to Rome), offended the sensibilities of many. The Catholic Church's emphasis upon doctrine and upon episcopal authority undoubtedly contributed to the perception of the 'untaught' Irishman as incompetent and unable to reason for himself. One self-educated individual, interviewed at a meeting of ticket-of-leave men which Mayhew called in 1856, remarked on the difference that a replacement prison chaplain, 'a lover of science and literature ... a clergyman whose system was altogether different, having none of these Roman Catholic [High Church] restrictions', had made to his life: 'We were then allowed to think and do as we liked in regard to religion.'[148]

Not surprisingly, those Irish Catholics whose economic circumstances were least secure were the least enthusiastic about Wiseman's high profile and the self-promotion of the Catholic Church, envisaging problems with the English with whom they coexisted. The crossing sweeper whose family survived on 8*d.* a day was apprehensive, believing that he quite literally could not afford any antagonism.[149] Although his fears were not entirely groundless, it appears that anti-Catholic feeling was generally expressed through relatively mild harrassment. A female orange-seller disliked trading in public houses because 'they begins flying out about the Pope and Cardinal Wiseman, as if I had anything to do

146 Ibid., vol. 2, p. 505.
147 Ibid., vol. 1, p. 108.
148 Ibid., vol. 3, p. 434.
149 Ibid., vol. 1, p. 108.

with it'. These religious taunts were one reason for her reluctance to have her unemployed husband, 'a hasty man' who was likely to respond to provocation, selling on the streets.[150] Sentiment was anti-Catholic rather than anti-Irish (for a time the subject of 'papal agression' dominated the repertoire of London street-chaunters, provoking a predictable Irish response[151]) and appears to have been relatively short-lived.[152]

In London there was never the degree of hostility which became evident in those centres of Orangism where antagonism between Catholic and Protestant became almost institutionalised.[153] To see any ill-feeling existing between English and Irish London slum dwellers simply as the product of anti-Irish, or anti-Catholic sentiment is to over simplify the picture; it would be wrong to regard the Irish Catholic communities in London merely as passive victims of anti-Catholic behaviour. Religious distrust was mutual, if relatively low-key. On the part of Catholics it was as much to do with contempt for the irreligion of those English poor who called themselves 'Protistints' as with the conviction that Catholicism alone was the true faith. The degree of segregation of Irish from English was a matter of choice as much as of necessity.

Circumstances might have made them defensive about their religion, but Mayhew's accounts also show that to be a Catholic was also a source of pride, a mark of religious distinction: 'All the worruld may know my riligion, and I wish all the worruld was of my riligion ... I do, indeed. I'm a Roman Catholic, sir ... God be praised for it!'[154] The fact that probably only a minority (if a substantial one) attended Mass regularly is inconsequential: a much higher number considered themselves Catholic. The fact too, that unknown numbers, particularly second and third generation Irish, were absorbed into the host community is immaterial: minority groups in any society lose a proportion of their members in this way. What is significant is that a high enough proportion of Irish Catholics defined their identity through their their faith for 'Irish' to become synonymous with 'Catholic'.

MAYHEW'S IRISH: A MATTER OF DISCRIMINATION

Mayhew, of course, can give no information on those of Irish stock who, being non-Catholic, relatively affluent, or both, were absorbed most easily into the

150 Ibid., p. 88; see also p. 117.
151 Ibid., pp 227–8.
152 Ibid., p. 117. An elderly fruit-seller indicated that her young tormentors had soon tired of the subject.
153 See Lowe, *Irish in Mid-Victorian Lancashire*, pp 154–67; Lees, *Exiles of Erin*, pp 222–3; Graham Walker, 'The Protestant Irish in Scotland', in Devine, *Irish Immigrants and Scottish Society*, pp 50–4, particularly p. 52.
154 Mayhew, *London Labour and the London Poor*, vol. 1, p. 107.

host community. He investigated some of the poorest groups in society (and the Irish, as he recognised, were well-represented among them) but even here, his coverage was by no means comprehensive. There are a good number of London poor, and poor Irish, on whom there is no information simply because Mayhew had no interest in their circumstances, or because he did not consider them appropriate journalistic subjects. Servants, of whom a number were Irish (mainly, he tells us, second-generation or orphaned), although comprising 20% of the London population, are virtually ignored: as inhabitants of the same world (albeit at a different level) as Mayhew's readers, presumably they were of little interest.[155] Mayhew did investigate needlewomen, and there were (as information given to him makes plain),[156] Irish workers amongst them. Nevertheless, he insisted that they were unsuited for such work. The role of Irish women generally, and the contribution which they made to the family economy (which must often have meant the difference between poverty and pauperism) is a field worthy of more examination.

Mayhew, for all his limitations and contradictions, is nevertheless a valuable source of information on the Irish. That his work was produced for commercial reasons does not in any way invalidate it, but rather the contrary. Mayhew's letters for the *Morning Chronicle* had an immense impact. Whatever the evidential merits of his work, the fact that it received widespread acclaim is testimony to its relevance. It has a significance beyond the wealth of factual information it provides. His writing is an indicator not only of how the Irish poor in London lived and felt, and were regarded by their fellow workers, but of how they were seen by those who had relatively little contact with them.

To an extent, Mayhew adopts the generally ambivalent attitude of the professional classes towards the Irish. This is nowhere better indicated than in discussions on the Irishman's aptitude for trade. The 'untaught' Irishman might, through a combination of thrift, abstemiousness and opportunism, succeed in making a living on the lowest rungs of the economic ladder, but for all his fluency and sharp intelligence, says Mayhew, he is better adapted to manual work than to making a profitable living.[157] On the other hand, the author sees this same combination of flair and discipline as giving the Irish costermonger an advantage over his English neigbour:

> A quick-witted Irishman will begin to ponder on his paying 1s. 6d. a week for the
> hire of a barrow worth 20s., and he will save and hoard until a pound is at his
> command to purchase one for himself; while an obtuse English coster (who will

155 Ibid., p. 460: Humpherys, *Travels into the Poor Man's Country*, pp 17–18.
156 Mayhew, London Labour and the London Poor, vol. 1, p. 105; Mayhew, *Morning Chronicle Survey*, vol. 2, Letter XVIII, 18 Dec. 1849, p. 147; see also Large in Swift and Gilley (eds), *Irish in the Victorian City*, p. 45: the 1851 census shows that Bristol had a considerable number of Irish seamstresses.
157 Mayhew, *London Labour and the London Poor*, vol. 1, p. 105.

yet buy cheaper than an Irishman) will probably pride himself on his cleverness
in having got the charge for his barrow reduced, in the third year of its hire, to
1*s*. a week the twelvemonth round![158]

Mayhew does not take, at least not with any conviction or consistency, a view
of the Irish as a generically inferior group. For every example of anti-Irish bias,
if not a counter-view, then at the very least a qualification can be produced.
Discussing a street-seller, a 'modest, and in her way a worthy woman' who had
been a domestic servant, he suggests that a respectable English woman in a
similar position would have struggled to obtain any domestic work. Somewhat
inconsistently, he also recognises the prejudice against Irish servants, and the
fact that they were more likely than the English to be unjustifiably refused a
reference.[159] He disliked the disingenuousness of those Irish women who combined street-trading with begging, yet recognised that the reasons underlying
such behaviour were complex, and would not unreservedly condemn it.[160] He
also commented:

> It may be but proper to remark, in order that one class of poor people may not be
> unduly depreciated, while another class is, perhaps, unduly appreciated, that the
> poor Irishman is much more imaginative, is readier of wit and far readier of
> speech, than an Englishman of a corresponding grade; and were the untaught
> Englishman equally gifted in these respects, who will avouch that his regard for
> the truth would be much more severe?[161]

Such observations hardly support the view of Donald MacRaild, who while
acknowledging that Mayhew's writing is less invested with anti-Irish sentiment
than is Reach's, nevertheless suggests that Mayhew was implicated in the
portrayal of the Irish as 'a kind of sub-species'.[162] Mayhew did see the Irish
poor as part of a wider underclass, and he did make generalisations about their
attitudes and behaviour. But any discrimination in the form of prejudice against
the Irish as an ethnic group was more than balanced by discrimination between
individuals within the group. Unlike other social commentators, he recognised
the particularity of human voices and opinions. Mayhew's talent was to
combine sympathy with detachment. He does not condemn, and nor – unlike
Beames for instance[163] – does he ever subsitute sentimentality for compassion.

158 Ibid., p. 115.
159 Ibid., p. 467, p. 460.
160 Ibid., p. 465.
161 Ibid., p. 466.
162 Donald M. MacRaild, 'Irish immigration and the Condition of England question: the
     Roots of an historiographical tradition', *Immigrants and Minorities*, vol. 14 (March
     1995), p. 80.
163 See Beames' account of the Irish regard for their country in Beames, *Rookeries*, pp 33–4.

The interaction of those various factors, economic, cultural and religious, which were recorded by Mayhew, played a part in perpetuating a distinctive Irish identity. E.P. Thompson famously remarked that 'the Irish were never pressed back into ghettos'.[164] There was undoubtedly a degree of antagonism towards the Irish on the part of the host community, as Mayhew himself makes clear, but their separation was nowhere more than partial. Furthermore, the degree of freedom they had in determining its extent, remains, as M.A.G. Ó Tuathaigh has indicated, a point of debate.[165] The Irish were never, as some have suggested, simply the maligned victims of a hostile society. Prejudice had its foundations in the hard facts of life, as well as in the half-truths of a shared history. As Sheridan Gilley has observed, 'even prejudice can be partly true as a statement about social behaviour and national culture, and can a prejudice be so called when what it alleges is true?'.[166] Whatever the actual effect on the economy as a whole, it remains a fact, and one confirmed by several of Mayhew's Irish interviewees, that immigrants, accustomed to lower wages in Ireland, were prepared to work for less than English workers and live more cheaply. Furthermore, not only their religion, but their tolerance of poor living conditions and their readiness to exploit opportunities for obtaining relief, distanced them from the English 'respectable' poor. Given these facts, it is perhaps less surprising that they were disliked than that their virtues continued to be acknowledged.

What is remarkable about Mayhew is that he does not provide a single perspective, but several. He produces emotive, vivid, superbly-written and often humorous descriptions of immigrant life. He is also at pains to demonstrate a dispassionate approach to his subject, and provides that wealth of statistical evidence which from the 1830s became the obligatory accompaniment to serious research. And most importantly, he recognises the importance of the personal account; Mayhew regarded the experience of poverty not simply as one more fact to be digested and analysed, but as a testament to the humanity of those who felt the full force of its impact. Recent historiography has placed an emphasis upon statistical analysis. Valuable as this is, it should not be forgotten that contemporary perceptions of events and circumstances are as historically significant as their underlying causes. Ultimately, history is about human experience. Mayhew does not allow us to forget this.

164 E.P. Thompson, *The Making of the English Working Class*, 3rd. edn (London, 1980), p. 480.
165 See M.A.G. Ó Tuathaigh, 'The Irish in Ninetenth-Century Britain: Problems of Integration', in Swift and Gilley (eds), *Irish in the Victorian City*, pp 13–36, particularly his references to L.P. Curtis, pp 20–1.
166 Sheridan Gilley, 'English Attitudes to the Irish in England, 1780–1900', in Colin Holmes (ed.), *Immigrants and Minorities in British Society* (London, 1978), p. 99.

Migration, 'community' or integration? Irish families in Victorian Stafford

John Herson

In November 1871 Hugh Woods Gibson was elected mayor of Stafford, a small town in the West Midlands of England.[1] This event reflected the power and influence he had as a member of Stafford's ruling elite in the 1860s and 1870s. It also demonstrated his integration into that elite, for Gibson was an Irish immigrant. By origin he was a shoemaker from a fairly humble Presbyterian background in Bangor, county Down.

Gibson's elevation was an extreme example of integration by an Irish person into Stafford society. In the same week of 1871, by contrast, Thomas Connor from county Galway, a young labourer living in Red Cow Yard, was given two months' imprisonment for violent assault on two of his neighbours.[2] This event conforms more to the stereotypical image of the Irish in nineteenth-century Britain, that of an outcast population, impoverished and degraded. Three months earlier, however, John Walsh and Thomas Kearney, two Irish building workers, had been in court on a rather different charge. They were accused of molesting a building site foreman, and it seems clear they were acting as shop stewards for their fellow workmen and attempting to control the hours worked.[3] At about the same time John Cronin, 'an old Crimea soldier', was retiring from his army post as paymaster's clerk to the 2nd Staffs Militia and starting as rate collector to the Stafford Improvement Commissioners.[4] He and his wife Elizabeth were just beginning to play a more active role in the social life of Stafford's Catholic church. Also in 1871 Mary and James Clewlow were celebrating the birth of their fourth child, Frances, who was unfortunately to die young.[5] Mary was a member of the Corcoran family from Castlerea, county Roscommon. Her mixed marriage, in both ethnic and religious terms, to shoemaker James Clewlow was a stage in the Corcorans' family strategy of integration into Stafford society. By contrast, baby Charles Moore was an unfortunate outcast destined for a shorter and more miserable life than Frances

---

1 *Staffordshire Advertiser* (= *SA*), 11 November 1871.
2 Ibid.
3 Ibid., 12 August 1871.
4 Ibid., 1 May 1889; obituary contained in Birmingham RC Archdiocese Archive, St Austin's Church, Stafford, vol. 11: Mission Book.
5 Census enumeration returns, Borough of Stafford, 1871.

Clewlow. Born around June 1871 to Jane Moore, a widow from county Longford 'at present a servant in Burslem', Charles was lodged with Jane's sister in the Broad Eye part of Stafford. Three months later he was dead from 'inanition or starvation'. He weighed just under six pounds at death.[6]

These incidents in the Stafford of 1871 indicate the diverse experiences of Irish people in a small town in Victorian Britain and suggest the varied roles which they and their families could play in such a town. This essay explores some of the diversity of lifetime and family experiences amongst Irish people in the period from the 1830s to the last decade of the century. It covers part of the period when the Irish perhaps occupied 'a curious middle place' in British life, neither fully integrated nor retaining full Irish identity and loyalty.[7] The essay begins by reviewing the broad history of Irish migration to and from Stafford. It identifies, secondly, the types of families who made up most of Stafford's settled Irish population in the nineteenth century. Thirdly, the responses open to Irish families are reviewed and some family case studies analysed. Finally, some conclusions are drawn on the implications for Irish community identity, migration and assimilation.

All case studies may have some value, but there would be little point in studying a small town like Stafford if both its nineteenth century history and its experience of Irish immigration were totally idiosyncratic. Stafford can in fact be seen as a microcosm of nineteenth century England. It showed many features of the transition from agriculture to industry, and from rural to urban life, which was still incomplete in the nineteenth century. Located in open countryside midway between the Potteries to the north and the Black Country to the south, Stafford's population doubled from 9904 in 1841 to 19,456 in 1891 (table 1).[8] This was much in line with the overall trend for England and Wales. It was not, however, a significant regional metropolis. Charles Dickens described it in 1852 as 'as dull and dead a town as anyone could desire not to see'.[9] This unflattering comment in fact emphasises how *ordinary* Stafford was. It was the county town, it had a small militia barracks and a large gaol, and it was the market and transport centre for its prosperous farming hinterland. It also had one significant manufacturing industry: shoemaking. In 1881 the trade employed

6 *SA*, 30 September 1871; census enumeration returns 1871.

7 David Fitzpatrick, 'A Curious Middle Place: the Irish in Britain 1871–1921' in R. Swift & S. Gilley (eds.), *The Irish in Britain 1815–1939* (London 1989), pp 11–59; the phrase was first used by T.P. O'Connor.

8 These population totals refer to a uniform spatial area of 'Stafford' adopted for this study designed to ensure comparability over time. The census population totals given for Stafford are not comparable due to boundary changes.

9 M.W. Greenslade et al. *A History of Stafford* (contained in vol. VI of the Victoria History of the County of Stafford), (London 1979), p. 201.

15% of the entire population of the town.[10] Shoemaking was still going through the transition from domestic handwork to mechanised factory production and although nominally a skilled occupation there were strong elements of 'sweating'. Shoemakers traditionally had a reputation for heavy drinking and dissolute living,[11] but the growth of factories from the 1860s tightened labour discipline and brought more women into the trade. The parallel between shoemakers and stereotypical views of the Irish are obvious.

If Stafford was a 'typical' English small town, its specific experience of Irish immigration in numerical terms also mirrored quite closely that for England and Wales as a whole (table 1). The proportion of Irish-born in the town was initially below the national average, but the Famine influx and subsequent in-migration boosted Stafford somewhat above the mean. Only after 1871 did the proportion slip back below the national norm. The number of Irish in Stafford at any time was, of course, small by the standards of the big cities, but their relative significance in 1871 was similar to that in cities like London or Birmingham or towns such as Bath or Huddersfield.[12]

Table 1: Population & Irish-born, Stafford, 1841–1891

Year	Stafford population	Irish-born population	% Irish-born Stafford	% Irish-born England & Wales
1841	9,904	128	1.29	1.8
1851	12,328	504	4.09	2.9
1861	12,843	532	4.14	3.0
1871	15,796	403	2.55	2.5
1881	19,110	346	1.81	2.2
1891	19,456	225	1.16	1.6

Source: Census enumeration returns & published census volumes, 1841–91.

A more complete indication of the Irish presence in Stafford needs also to include the English-born children of the Irish, and others in direct household relationship. As table 2 shows, over 9% of the Stafford population could be defined in 1861 as 'Irish-associated' in household terms, the proportion

10 M. Harrison, 'The Development of Boot & Shoe Manufacturing in Stafford, 1850–1880', *J. Staffs Ind. Arch. Soc.*, no. 10, 1981, p. 37. Count of census enumeration returns, 1881.

11 A. Fox, *A History of the National Union of Boot & Shoe Operatives, 1874–1958* (Oxford 1958), pp 20–26.

12 C. Pooley, 'Segregation or integration? The residential experience of the Irish in mid-Victorian Britain', in Swift & Gilley (eds), *The Irish in Britain, 1815–1939*, p. 65.

dropping to 4% by 1891. By then, however, the descendants of the Irish were fanning out in a way more difficult to trace.[13]

Table 2: Household linkages with the Irish, Stafford, 1861–1891

Year	*1* Irish-born	*2* Children	*3* Non-Irish in Irish hhds	*4* Servant & lodger hhds	*5* Total Stafford	*6* % of pop-n
1861	532	294	148	289	1269	9.88
1871	403	351	237	163	1154	7.31
1881	346	414	176	102	1038	5.43
1891	225	336	159	93	813	4.18

Source: Census enumeration returns, 1861–91

Key:
1. Total Irish-born population
2. Total English-born children of Irish-born.ppIncludes those traced living independently in 1881 & 1891
3. Total non-Irish partners and lodgers in households with Irish-born household heads/ wives/relatives
4. Total non-Irish in English households with Irish-born servants or lodgers. Excludes institutions.

It has been widely documented that the immigrant Irish were highly mobile people, and Stafford was no exception.[14] Between the 1830s and 1891 at least 1627 Irish-born people came into the town, and were recorded in the census, whilst 1270 left again in the same period. The true total will, of course, have been considerably higher, and it is estimated that between 1841 and 1891 about 4000 different Irish people may have resided in Stafford for significant periods.[15] It would be wrong, however, to see this large turnover of people as

13 The basic data for this study consists of an ACCESS relational database whose core table consists of household data for the Irish-born and, from 1871 to 1891, their children and household associates. A number of other tables link in non-census data including incidents relating to personalities contained in the core tables. By these means it is possible to build up outline biographies of individuals and families as well as derive general figures for the nature of the Irish population.

14 J.D. Herson, 'Irish migration and settlement in Victorian Britain: a small town perspective' in Swift & Gilley (eds), *The Irish in Britain, 1815–1939*, p. 86.

15 This estimate is based on marriage and death records in which between 40% and 47% of the people recorded also appear in the census returns.

indicating simply that 'once uprooted, many of the victims of the Great Famine spent their lives in search of a place of shelter'.[16] Rather, it represents a purposeful process by which people responded to the varying economic and social opportunities available to them using, where possible, the support of family members, relatives and friends.

The key to understanding the experience of Irish people in Stafford – and probably in most other places – is to focus on families rather than on individuals. An investigation of family structures reveals, for a start, the subtleties of defining 'Irish' people. Whilst the majority of Irish-born people in Stafford were clearly 'Irish' in the 'Celtic Catholic' sense, there were also Anglo-Irish, Ulster Protestants and others from more indefinite ethnic backgrounds. There were, furthermore, people who could be called 'accidental Irish' – those born in Ireland to non-Irish parents. They serve to remind us that, even in the nineteenth century, Irish migration was a two-way flow.

In Stafford the first significant numbers of Irish people seem to have arrived around 1830,[17] and over the next sixty years members of about 134 distinct families settled in Stafford on a long-term basis.[18] Over the whole period from 1841 to 1891 almost 60% of Irish-born people living in the town were members of these families on surname evidence alone,[19] with the proportion peaking at 69% in 1871. There were also other families present in the town at various times who were related to this core group but do not qualify as 'settled'. The settled families are listed in appendices 1 and 2 and classified, where possible, by their provincial and religious origins.[20] Table 3 summarises the overall picture. Irish in-migration to Stafford was dominated by families from Connacht.

16 F.E. Finnegan, *Poverty & Prejudice: a Study of Irish Immigrants in York, 1840–1875*, (Cork 1982), p. 159.

17 J.D. Herson, 'Irish migration and settlement in Victorian Britain: a small town perspective' in Swift & Gilley (eds), *The Irish in Britain, 1815–1939*, p. 88. There was a Catholic family in Stafford called Car(e)less whose members were clearly long-term and established residents by the 1830s. They may have had Irish origins, but this has not been proven. They had no social or marriage links with Irish people arriving in the nineteenth century.

18 A family with 'long-term settlement' was defined as one where at least one Irish-born member of the family, normally a head of household, was present in two census enumerations, i.e. they stayed a minimum of 10 years.

19 A simple surname count was done of all Irish-born males for each census year to avoid the problem of Irish-born women marrying out and losing their family identity. By the later part of the study period the number of core family women who had 'married out', together with *their* children, was significant, although the number has not yet been established.

20 The provincial origin of families was gleaned from census birthplace evidence. Although the majority of people were merely recorded as having 'Ireland' as their birthplace, over successive censuses enough specific placenames could be associated with many families to give reasonable confidence about their origin. Religious allegiance was gleaned from the records of St Austin's Catholic church at the Catholic Archdiocese of

Table 3: Origin of settled Irish families in Stafford, 1830s–1891

Religion	Connacht	Leinster	Munster	Ulster	Unknown	Total
Catholic	52	7	10	5	22	96
Protestant	1	11	2	5	6	25
Unknown	5	0	1	0	7	13
Total	58	18	13	10	35	134

For sources, see text and Appendix 1.

The majority of Connacht families in fact came from a relatively small area of counties Galway, Roscommon and Mayo near the town of Castlerea, county Roscommon.[21] People from this district first came into Stafford in the 1830s, and their numbers increased massively during the Famine exodus. New individuals and family groups from the same locality continued to arrive during the 1850s, 1860s and 1870s, indicating a strong chain migration process. Many of the families were interrelated, and marriages continued between them after their arrival in Stafford. This is not to say, however, that there was a simple bipolar relationship between Stafford and the Castlerea area. Rather, there was almost certainly a multinuclear network of families in the wider region. Some people formed the 'core families' who became resident long-term in Stafford, but there were others who, from the Stafford perspective, formed a 'periphery' of people linked to the core by short-term presence in the town for work and/or marriage.[22] In turn, many of the children who grew up in Stafford did not remain in the town but went elsewhere. Some undoubtedly migrated into the regional family 'periphery'.[23]

Birmingham Archive, Church of England marriage registers at the Staffordshire Record Office (=SRO; microfiches for St Mary's, St Chad's, St Thomas's and Christ Church) and the records of the Congregational and Presbyterian churches in Stafford (SRO D4800/1 Presbyterian Church and D4800/2 Congregational Church).

21 Herson, op. cit., p. 89 and J.D. Herson, 'Why the Irish went to Stafford: a case study of Irish settlement in England, 1830–71', *Liverpool Polytechnic Papers in Social Studies*, no. 1, 1988, pp 28–31.

22 This is seen, for example, in the marriage registers of St Austin's church. Of the 212 marriages between 1835 and 1880 involving an Irish or Irish-descended person, 72 involved members of the Connacht core families, but in 33 of these marriages there is no other record in Stafford of these family members. They were, therefore, either resident only for a short time in the town or lived elsewhere. The sparse occasions when another place of residence is stated points to family connections in the Potteries, Newcastle-under-Lyme and the Black Country.

23 Between 1841 and 1891 nearly 35% of Irish-born males who were only present in Stafford for one census enumeration came from the core families. This total inevitably includes an unknown number of children and older people who in fact died. In other words, at least a third of the apparent 'drifters' were related to families settled in the town.

The same comments would apply to many families from other, or uncertain, backgrounds. The key point is that the superficial picture of mobility and instability derived from a simple head count of individuals in fact hides a substantial core of *family stability*. Although the turnover of Irish people in Stafford was high in the nineteenth century, the proportion of people who were independent drifters or independent family groups, unrelated or unconnected to the settled families, seems consistently to have been in the minority. This minority cannot, of course, be ignored, but the core of this essay concentrates on the settled majority.

People from a Connacht background formed the majority of Irish who lived in Stafford in the nineteenth century, and their numerical dominance was greater than their apparent strength in families. This is because they tended to form larger and more extended families whereas other families were more nuclear. There was, nevertheless, a significant minority of Catholics from other parts of Ireland, and also of Protestants. These groups consistently formed between a fifth and a quarter of the Irish population. Evidence suggests that this minority of people was of higher status and did not generally conform to the 'pauper Catholic Celt' stereotype. Figure 1 shows the marked occupational status differences between Connacht Catholics, Catholics from other provinces and Protestants in 1881.[24] Connacht Catholics largely did semi- and unskilled

Figure 1: Occupational status of occupied Irish-born male & female workers, Stafford, 1881 (%)

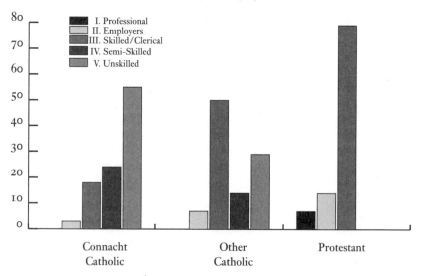

Source: Census enumerations returns, 1881

24 The 'other Catholics' category only includes data from households whose provincial origin is known. The Catholics from unknown provinces have not been included since

work, Catholics from other provinces were a mixture of the skilled[25] and less skilled, whilst Protestants formed an overwhelmingly skilled manual, managerial or professional class of in-migrants.

Table 4: Household location by family type, Stafford Irish,
1851–1891 (%)

a) ALL-IRISH FAMILY HOUSEHOLDS

Location	1851	1861	1871	1881	1891
Adjacent	28.6	49.4	51.1	41.7	21.8
Proximate	38.8	31.3	25.0	25.0	27.3
Isolated	32.7	19.3	23.9	33.3	50.9
n=	49.0	83.0	88.0	72.0	55.0

b) MIXED FAMILY HOUSEHOLDS

Location	1851	1861	1871	1881	1891
Adjacent	6.3	22.2	14.8	9.5	14.1
Proximate	34.4	36.1	26.2	23.8	17.2
Isolated	59.4	41.7	59.0	66.7	68.8
n=	32.0	36.0	61.0	63.0	64.0

Source: Census enumeration returns, 1851–1891

Key:
'Adjacent': Irish household next door to another Irish household.
'Proximate': another Irish household within five doors of an Irish household.
'Isolated': no Irish household within five doors an Irish household.

The general characteristics of Stafford's Irish population were, therefore, similar to those reported in other local studies. Less is known, however, about the responses made by Irish individuals, families and their descendants to the opportunities and threats of the places to which they came, and the rest of this essay discusses this issue in the case of the Irish in Stafford. In doing this two

it is likely that a significant number of these households were in fact from Connacht. The profile of these workers does indeed fall somewhere between the Connacht and Other Catholic characteristics.

25 'Skilled' work includes shoe-making, Stafford's dominant industry. There were in fact many gradations of skill in the shoe trade, and there was, in common with most other trades, a trend to de-skilling with the expansion of factory-based machine work. It is appropriate, however, to define all shoe-workers as 'skilled' for the purpose of this study.

conceptual issues have to be considered. The first is the relationship between individual and family action. Studies of Irish immigration to Britain inevitably draw heavily on census enumeration data and other official sources. The results emphasise either the action of individuals or of the masses. In doing the former they tend to follow implicitly Anderson's perspective that the individual is goal-driven and that the relationship with the family is but one of the mechanisms by which individual goals are attained.[26] The stereotype here is especially of the young, often single, mobile Irish immigrant as an individual actor. There has, nevertheless, been an equal emphasis on the Irish in the mass, perhaps even as a community or communities. The role of the (Catholic) church, politics, ethnic/ national identity and other such factors is emphasised in building – or under-mining – ethnic or class identity.[27] Most of the Irish in Stafford were, however, to be found in family units, even during the Famine influx and its aftermath. The apparent durability of family structures in Stafford suggests the pivotal nature of the family in any analysis of the Irish immigrant experience[28]. It echoes Dupree's perspective that 'documentation of patterns of family relationships suggests the maintenance and importance of [family] relationships in the face of the potentially disruptive forces of industrialisation and urbanisation.'[29] In this study the disruptive force of migration also has to be added. She suggests that there is 'the need to see individuals in families not only as objects but also at the same time as actors or agents constructing and reconstructing their world and "their knowledge of it through interaction with it"'.[30]

There is a need, then, to see the response of individuals within their family context and to assess whether there were consistent responses – perhaps a family strategy – within a particular family unit and between associated families. This raises the second conceptual issue, that of the potential strategies open to Irish individuals and families in nineteenth-century Stafford. The Irish have been portrayed in some writings as a long-term outcast minority whose lives were blighted by prejudice and discrimination, and whose reaction was to maintain Irish identity and the ethnic associational culture. In this view the Irish 'community' was sustained and its values transmitted to succeeding generations; there was no 'ethnic fade'.[31] Steven Fielding has argued more subtly that, for

---

26 M. Anderson, *Family Structure in Nineteenth Century Lancashire* (Cambridge 1971), pp 8–9.

27 S. Fielding, *Class and Identity: Irish Catholics in England, 1880–1939* (Buckingham 1993), e.g. pp 56–61.

28 Pat O'Mara's life story in the very different environment of Liverpool would under-score this point. P. O'Mara, *The Autobiography of a Liverpool Slummy* (orig. pub. 1933; Liverpool 1995).

29 M. Dupree, *Family Structure in the Staffordshire Potteries, 1840–1880* (Oxford 1995), p. 34.

30 Ibid., 35; the quotation within the quotation comes from C. Lloyd, *Explanation in Social History* (Oxford 1986), pp 160–1.

31 See J. Belchem, ''Freedom & Friendship to Ireland': Ribbonism in Early nineteenth-century Liverpool', *Int. Rev. of Soc. Hist.*, 39 (1994), pp 34f for a brief but strong

Irish people in late-nineteenth century Britain, ethnic and class identities were contested concepts.[32] People could adopt differing positions in different situations and at different times in their lives, but his basic premise is that in the long term 'class and ethnic identities were only resolved in a partial and ultimately inconclusive manner.'[33]

It is argued here that, whilst there may have been no *general* resolution of identity problems in the Irish population *as a whole*, at the level of the individual family distinct choices were made which were reflected in the actions of individuals. The choices open to the Irish in nineteenth century Stafford were constrained by the changing economic and social environment within which they lived locally, nationally and internationally. Within this situation the experience of any particular family, and the individuals within it, was likely to be a compromise between countervailing forces, a compromise whose biases would often shift over time. These forces can be summarised as:

- migration
- community
- integration

The Irish people in Stafford continued to receive in-migrant reinforcements from Ireland and from elsewhere in Britain throughout the nineteenth century. Some settled in Stafford long-term, some did not. Irish immigrants and their children in Stafford were, nevertheless, attracted by out-migration to other parts of the country and, more importantly, emigration overseas. By the late nineteenth century such Irish emigrants were distinguished by their *similarity* to native Britons as a tidal wave of emigration occurred.[34] It is clear that there were economic factors at work in Stafford in the second half of the nineteenth century which could make out-migration and emigration an attractive option, and so migration was the first force acting on families and individuals.

The second force was that tending to maintain ethnic identity and 'community' amongst Irish people. The definition of, and forces behind, community identity have been the subject of much debate for which there is no space

statement of this view and the importance of ethnic associational culture. Frances Finnegan emphasises the lack of assimilation of York's Irish population in her study of the 1840–75 period; F. Finnegan, *op. cit.*, esp. Chap 10. The blurb for D. MacRaild, *Culture, Conflict and Migration: The Irish in Victorian Cumbria* (Liverpool 1998) announces that 'by eschewing the "ethnic fade" conception of so many other studies, this book demonstrates that a culture of conflict ... also found expression in what has been a less fashionable region for study.'.

32 S. Fielding, op. cit., pp 10–18 .
33 Ibid., 127.
34 see D.E. Baines, *Migration in a Mature Economy: Emigration and Internal Migration in England & Wales, 1861–1900* (Cambridge 1985), esp. chaps. 3 and 7.

here.[35] It is clear, however, that Irish people in Stafford might potentially have formed ethnic communities[36] promoted by such factors as:

- place of origin kinship links
- territoriality within Stafford
- the churches
- pubs, clubs & associations
- cultural and political activities
- deprived, deviant and criminal sub-cultures, defined and sustained by the host population.

The extent to which Irish people would form communities defined by such factors would be determined by whether it was in their economic, cultural, social and spiritual interests to do so.

The forces leading towards integration and ultimate assimilation potentially offset those towards ethnic community. Again, there are definition problems over what is meant by integration. What could be seen as voluntary and positive strategies to adjust to the values and norms of the host society from one perspective might, from another perspective, be seen as the imposition of cultural hegemony by the dominant culture, backed by sanctions for non-compliance.[37] In the case of the Stafford Irish, it might merely have been prudent for individuals and families to 'lie low' and avoid overt expressions of Irish identity in order to achieve a tolerable life. There might, on the other hand, have been positive benefits in seeking – or accepting – integration through such factors as:

- housing
- children's schooling
- the churches
- workplace situations
- pubs, clubs & associations
- political and cultural life

The factors outlined above to a large extent mirror those listed under the forces towards 'community', and this underlines that the institutions of economic and social life could inherently promote either ethnic identity or integration. The

35 See C.J. Calhoun, 'Community: toward a variable conceptualisation for comparative research', *Soc. Hist.*, 5:1 (Jan 1980), pp 105–29.

36 But not one 'community' for reasons discussed in J. Herson, in Swift & Gilley, op. cit., pp 94–5.

37 In the context of immigration to Britain since 1945, compare, for example, S. Patterson, *Dark Strangers: A Study of West Indians in London* (London 1965), pp 19–26 and A. Rattansi, 'Changing the Subject? Racism, culture and education' in J. Donald & A Rattansi (eds.), *'Race', Culture and Difference* (London 1992), esp. pp 14–16 .

extent to which they did one or other would be determined by the characteristics of the institutions themselves and the responses made by Irish people
to them. This is where the idea of ethnicity as a contested and conditional
concept is important. It is not argued that Irish people would necessarily have
lost all contact with their roots and culture in the face of sweeping pressures of
integration/cultural hegemony. The social significance of such links, and the
trend towards 'community' promotion which they suggest, would nevertheless
have been in tension both with the forces of integration and with those of
renewed migration.

So what were the responses of Irish families in Stafford to these competing
forces ? Fitzpatrick has summarised the problems of the sources available to
historians on migration. On the one hand, reliance on aggregate profiles of
migrants derived from official sources like the census returns results in
generalisations and in intermittent snapshots of individuals, neither of which
tell us anything directly about motivation. Family history, on the other hand,
and the use of family memorabilia, can potentially offer more in terms of
motivation and the richness of experience, but with major problems of lack of
evidence and of generalising from the particular.[38] These problems are very
apparent when trying to explore the Irish families in Stafford. No family
memorabilia has yet been sought from possible descendants of the nineteenth-
century Irish, though potentially this offers some hope of providing a richer
picture. It is, nevertheless, contended that an outline picture can be drawn of
family responses which does fuse the general and particular. This can be done
by reconstructing, as far as possible, family trees of representative Irish in-
migrants and by exploring incidents and possible attitudes of families and
individuals through a synthesis of other documentary sources. Some tentative
generalisations can then be made from the specific experiences.

The Mannion family (appendix 3) conforms in many ways to the classic
stereotype of impoverished Irish immigrants, but their family history demonstrates some of the ambiguity which could occur in the responses of such a
family. The Mannions were Connacht Catholics, probably from the Castlerea
area. Patrick Mannion was the pathfinder. He was a labourer aged forty[39] who
probably emigrated during the Famine due to the death of his wife. By 1851 he
was already settled in Stafford, living with the Rafferty family from county
Galway. During the 1850s he was joined by Patrick junior, one of his three
known children who at that time was unmarried, and by 1861 they were living
in Snow's (or Red Cow) Yard off Foregate Street. This was a slum court of
fourteen cottages which, after 1861, had a strong Irish presence though it was
never an Irish 'ghetto'.

---

38 D. Fitzpatrick, *Oceans of Consolation: Personal Accounts of Irish Migration to Australia*,
    (Cork 1994), pp 3–5.
39 Based on an average of his age as given in census returns. The ages stated by people
    frequently differed between censuses, hence the need to produce best estimates.

The economy of Stafford was fairly buoyant in the late 1850s and 1860s as farming in the region prospered and the shoe trade expanded. This may have been the incentive for further members of the Mannion family to join Patrick and his son. A second son, Martin, his wife Ann, and their young children Michael and Mary, came to Stafford from county Galway between 1859 and 1861. His daughter Mary followed with her labourer husband, John Walsh, and their son Michael between 1861 and 1863. Patrick junior had, meanwhile, got married at St Austin's in Stafford to Catherine Kelly from county Mayo. So, from around 1863, there were three branches of the Mannion family living in Stafford, all of them initially in Snow's Yard. Their integration into wider Stafford society was probably limited but not negligible. The Red Cow pub stood at the entrance to the yard, and that and the Yard itself probably formed the narrow, but often boisterous, focus of social life. In May 1883, for example, the local paper reported on 'a Red Cow Yard disturbance', a classic 'Irish Row' in which, however, members of the Mannion family appear to have been merely bystanders. A feature of the row was that the mayor of the town, who also sat on the magistrates' bench, witnessed the event and gave evidence that it 'was one of the most disgusting scenes he had witnessed in Stafford for many years'.[40] The proximity of classes in a small town like Stafford was probably significant as a force for social control and the linked process of integration.

An earlier example of this proximity and relative integration occurred in 1868 general election, the first to be held under the franchise reform of 1867. This was also the election in which the Liberals under Gladstone made Ireland, and the disestablishment of the Church of Ireland, a key issue. Stafford was historically given to vigorous and sometimes corrupt electioneering,[41] and 1868 was no exception. Party organisers put great effort into registering voters, and this resulted in an electorate which was socially far wider than the artisans assumed normally to have been added in 1867. Many unskilled Irishmen were included, and Martin Mannion (senior.) was one of them. He duly responded by voting Liberal both in the 1868 election and also in the poll of 1869[42] which occurred after the MPs elected in the previous year had been disbarred for intimidation and bribery.[43]

Another force for integration was the workplace, and this is to some extent demonstrated by an incident in 1883 when Martin Mannion (junior.) was working as an apprentice in Elley & Co.'s shoe factory on Foregate St. Martin had been born in Stafford, doubtless had a Stafford accent and probably already occupied 'a curious middle place' in his allegiances. In the company of two English youths, he absconded from the factory with tools, and the three set off

40 *SA*, 5 May 1883.
41 Greenslade (ed.), *A History of Stafford*, op. cit., p. 238.
42 SRO, D5008/2/7/11/1 Borough of Stafford Poll Book: Elections of 1868 & 1869.
43 *SA*, 9 Jan/15 May 1869.

'on tramp' to Leicester, another shoe town 40 miles away. They failed to make it, and came back to Stafford with their tails between their legs, but 'because of their previous good character' the fine was small.[44] Martin had, however, already been before the bench that year in an incident which could be seen as an expression of Martin's Catholic and, possibly, Irish identity. It was Stafford's feeble echo of the sectarian strife of 1883 when, in the spring of that year, Salvationists began to hold processions in the town. Elsewhere these deliberately provocative processions resulted in riots in which Irish Catholics were victimised.[45] Martin Mannion's assault on Daniel Ward is the only known case of trouble in Stafford. Significantly, the magistrate was as concerned to criticise the promoters of the processions for their provocation as he was to censure Martin Mannion, and it seems clear that the town's ruling elite was anxious to avoid religious conflict. This probably reflected the established role of (English) Catholic families and the Catholic church in the town to which reference will be made later. Martin Mannion demonstrated his principled stand in the incident by telling the magistrate 'doggedly' that 'I am not going to pay any money'. He was clearly prepared to go to jail. His mother, Ann, paid the fine, nevertheless.[46]

In the 1880s the Mannion and Walsh families had to make decisions on their future. The children of both families began work in the 1870s and 1880s, and of the twelve children with a recorded occupation, eight worked in the shoe trade. They had thus entered the town's dominant industry and this, it is argued, demonstrated significant upward occupational mobility over their labouring parents, together with an element of social integration.[47] There is also some evidence that economic success could result in a desire to 'escape' from the deprived environment of initial in-migration. By 1881, the Walsh family had moved out of Red Cow Yard into Co-operative Street, an area of solid bye-law housing on the northern edge of town. Bridget Mannion, daughter of Martin and Ann, was now lodging with the Perry family[48] in Broad Street, again a

---

44 *SA*, 12 May 1883.
45 L. Miskell, 'Custom, Conflict & Community: a Study of the Irish in South Wales & Cornwall, 1861–1891', unpub. Ph.D. thesis, Univ. of Wales, Aberystwyth, 1996, Chap 4; J. Reed-Purvis, ' "Black Sunday": Skeleton Army Disturbances in Late Victorian Chester' in R. Swift, ed., *Victorian Chester: Essays in Social History*, 1830–1900 (Liverpool 1996), Chap. 6.
46 *SA*, 10 March 1883.
47 John Denvir noted that the significance of shoe-making for Irish immigrants when he commented that 'A number of our fellow-countrymen in Stafford and Stone are engaged in the staple industries of these places – boot and shoe making. It cannot but be noticed that shoemaking and tailoring are the only trades in which, up to the last few years, you found any considerable number of Irish artizans in this country.' J. Denvir, *The Irish in Britain from the Earliest Times to the Fall and Death of Parnell* (London 1892), p. 426. The comment is clearly true, but the real significance of the industry was as a route for upward social mobility for the *children* of Irish immigrants.

relatively better locality than Red Cow Yard. In 1889 she married James Butler, a paste fitter in the shoe trade. He was a native Staffordian. They then lived on the Marston Road, again a relatively 'solid' neighbourhood. Bridget's brother John and her cousins Patrick and James also stayed in the town and married women from local families. The shoe trade was depressed in the late nineteenth century, however,[49] and it seems clear that the majority view in the Mannion/Walsh family was that prospects would be better elsewhere. The perhaps more aspirant Walsh household left Stafford altogether during the 1880s, while of the six traceable[50] children of the two Mannion families, four[51] had also left the town by 1891. They may have gone to other places in the Midlands – into a family 'periphery' elsewhere – but it is more likely that they emigrated altogether. West Midland industry was generally depressed in the 1880s, and out-migration from Staffordshire strong.[52] The local newspapers had frequent advertisements for emigration to the Americas and Australasia.[53] It has been estimated that an average of 17.4% of males aged 15–24 and 10.6% of females in the same group who were born in Staffordshire emigrated in the decades from 1861 to 1890, and the proportion is likely to have been higher in the 1880s.[54] The Mannion and Walsh children were largely in this age group at the time and, despite their Irish background, they were probably amongst the statistics of this outflow. By 1891 only a minority of the Mannion family remained in Stafford. Two of the original male immigrants, Patrick and Martin (senior), probably died in the 1870s.[55] The others of that generation, Martin's widow Ann, together with Patrick and Catherine Mannion, were drifting into impoverished old age, stuck in their Snow's Yard slum with their remaining children.

The Mannion/Walsh family show evidence, then, of how the forces of

48 An English family apparently unrelated to the Irish Perrys listed in appendix 1.
49 M. Harrison, 'The Development of Boot & Shoe Manufacturing in Stafford, 1850–80', *J. Staffs. Ind. Arch. Soc.*, 10, 1981; Fox, *A History of the National Union of Boot & Shoe Operatives, 1874–1958*, Chaps 9–13; *SA, passim*, 1880s.
50 People not counted here are two known to have died and three daughters who may have married, though there is no record of their marriages at St Austin's church. This perhaps suggests out-migration, though the Mannions' connection with the church appears to have been rather tenuous anyway.
51 James Mannion married Mary Biddulph in 1889 but in 1891 she was living alone in Snow's Yard, "married" but also "head of household". James was absent, and one can only speculate that he was working outside Stafford and/or had deserted his new wife.
52 R. Lawton, 'Population Migration to & from Warwickshire and Staffordshire, 1841–91', unpub. MA thesis, no date (copy of Staffs section in William Salt Library, Stafford, William Salt Library TH48, Chap XII.
53 e.g. *SA*, 30 June 1883, when there were three advertisements for ships to Australia/New Zealand and five for the USA/Canada together with an advertisement by the New South Wales government for assisted passages.
54 Baines, *Migration in a Mature Economy*, table 6.3 & appendix 1.
55 Though evidence has not so far come to light to substantiate this.

migration, integration and community could all find expression in the actions of family members, either in groups or as individuals. Theirs was inevitably a conditional approach – to settlement in Stafford, to involvement in Stafford society and to ethnic solidarity amongst fellow Irish in-migrants. Stafford offered worthwhile security to family members leaving Ireland during the Famine and its aftermath, but over the longer term the town proved to be a staging point from which many in the next generation set off elsewhere.

How typical was the history of the Mannion family? To provide a definite answer to this question it would be necessary to analyse the history of every settled Irish family in Stafford and to develop a more rigorous method of comparing relative mobility, integration and Irish community commitment – a kind of 'integration index' or 'performance index'. Work on this has begun, but its conclusion lies in the future, and only some provisional findings can be reported here. One problem is that it is difficult to assign a numerical measure to many of the experiences of the Mannions and then generalise from them. We can, nevertheless, assess out-migration during the 1880s among the children of Stafford Irish families, and the degree of commitment to the town which this implies. This was done by comparing, for each settled family, the number of male children leaving Stafford in the 1880s with the number still present in 1891. Not all families had children in the relevant age groups, but of the forty six that did twenty one showed more children leaving Stafford than remaining in the town.[56] The results suggest the Mannions typified about half the settled families in Stafford, though they were rather less typical of their fellow Connacht Catholic families. Catholic families from other (and unknown) provinces, and also Protestants, seem to have been less settled in Stafford over the long term than the Connacht Irish. Another indicator of the Mannion family's character was their degree of residential integration with native Staffordians or the lack of it. In 1881 they lived next door to other Irish families in Snow's Yard. The Mannions' lives clearly had an element of territorial 'community', and this seems to have typified about two thirds of the Irish immigrant households in 1881 (table 4).[57] Whilst there was never any Irish 'ghetto' in Stafford, most Irish immigrant households lived close to at least some others until the late nineteenth century. The proportion declined, nevertheless, from a peak in 1861

56 The number of families with an equal number leaving & staying was six and the number with a majority of male children staying was nineteen. Female children were not traced due to the loss of identifiable individuals through marriage.

57 This exercise was done by comparing addresses. Households were defined as 'adjacent' if they lived next door to another household with a predominantly Irish character. They were 'proximate' if they were within five houses of another Irish household, and 'isolated' if they fell outside this range. The system depends on house numbering and there are a significant number of cases where exact location cannot be determined. 'Irish immigrant households' were defined as those containing an Irish-born household head and wife (if present), with or without Irish-born children.

and in 1891 it dipped under half for the first time. By that time Irish immigrant households were themselves a minority. Amongst mixed marriage households a majority lived in independent locations in all census years apart from 1861. Evidence of children's destinations and household location suggests, nevertheless, that perhaps 50% of settled Irish families had the rather conditional stance of the Mannions to life in Stafford.

Evidence of mixed-marriage households leads naturally to a discussion of intermarriage, perhaps the most important long-term factor promoting integration between settled Irish families and Stafford's host society. Between 1859 and 1913 there were six traceable marriages involving members of the Mannion family. Only one was an all-Irish affair, the initial union between Patrick Mannion and Catherine Kelly. All the known Mannion children in the next generation married ethnically English partners, and four out of five compounded the mix by marrying non-Catholics. This is strong evidence that the Mannion descendants who remained in Stafford, albeit a minority, did so as integrated members of Stafford society, not as members of a relict Irish 'community'. The overall pattern of marriages amongst the Irish-born and their descendants confirms that the Mannions were not unique in this respect. Between the 1830s and 1914 there were 356 marriages at Stafford's Catholic churches involving at least one Irish-born partner or a child of at least one Irish parent.[58] Evidence for the ethnic character is clear in 322 marriages and for religion in 335,[59] and the trends are shown in figures 2 and 3. It is striking how the Famine tragedy was followed, in Stafford at least, by a rash of marriages amongst Irish immigrants, a phenomenon which probably reflected some remarriage by those widowed during the Famine, delayed marriage by Famine era children and some new-found security through life in England.[60] Most of

---

58 By the end of the period some marriages of the grand children of Irish immigrants were occurring. Only marriages at the Catholic churches are covered by this discussion since, by definition, these were likely to be more sensitive to the ethnic and religious divide between the Irish and the host society. They are also easier to locate. Irish marriages at Stafford's Protestant churches have only been examined to a limited extent so far, but those traced were all of mixed ethnicity.

59 Catholic priests normally noted mixed marriages in the registers, but some either did not or were inconsistent in their practice. It is almost certain, therefore, that the actual proportion of mixed marriages was higher than is shown on figure 3. Marriage registers for St Austin's church for the period from 1827 to 1880 (volumes 7 & 8) are deposited at the Birmingham Archdiocesan Archive, Cathedral House, St Chad's Queensway, Birmingham. Those for St Austin's from 1880 to 1948 and for St Patrick's from 1894 to 1940 are held by their respective parish priests, and acknowledgement is gratefully given for access to them.

60 The peak of marriages between 1845 and 1854 was not just a reflection of the peak in Irish-born people in Stafford at this time. The crude marriage rate amongst the Irish-born and their children over this decade was 13.2 per 1000. Rates for the succeeding decades were: 1855–64: 8.0, 1865–74: 5.3, 1875–84: 6.3 and 1885–94: 7.4.

these early marriages were all-Irish unions but not all – 16% were ethnically mixed even during the Famine decade (figure 2). The proportion of mixed marriages rose to around half in the period from 1865 to 1884 as the English-born children of the Irish began to marry. By Edwardian times around 90% of the children and grandchildren were intermarrying with the ethnically-English population. The proportion of mixed-religion marriages also rose, although not in such an extreme fashion (figure 3). By the 1900s around half the Irish and Irish-descended Catholics were marrying non-Catholics.

Evidence of behaviour over time in jobs, migration, housing and marriage reveals what is intuitively obvious. In Stafford Irish people and their descendants either left the town or increasingly integrated into its society, albeit at different points in the class hierarchy. The various branches of the Mannion family showed a rather mixed response to these discrete indicators of behaviour, but this was not inevitable. Another Irish family, the Corcorans, showed an altogether more focused approach to life in Stafford. The Corcorans were a Connacht Catholic family from Castlerea who seem to have assiduously sought integration into Stafford's dominant culture (appendix 4). Their precise background is unknown, but it is possible they were artisans whose lives were

Figure 2: Irish marriages, Stafford Catholic churches: ethnic character of partners, 1835–1914

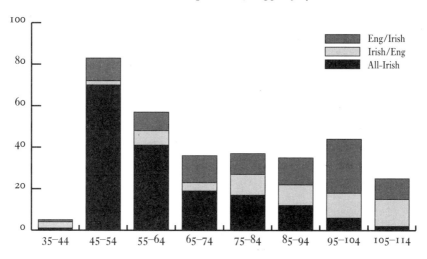

Key:
'Eng/Irish': ethnically English male partner, Irish female partner
'Irish/Eng': ethnically Irish male partner, English female partner
'All-Irish': both parnters ethnically Irish

For sources see text.

Figure 3: Irish marriages, Stafford Catholic churces: religion of marriage partners, 1835–1914

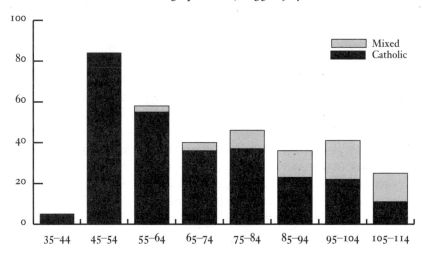

For sources see text.

destroyed in the immediate wake of the Famine.[61] Their early experience in Stafford was superficially similar to the Mannion family but their subsequent history shows how the paths followed by Irish immigrants could diverge. A widowed mother, Catherine Corcoran, arrived in Stafford sometime during the 1850s with three of her children. Where they were before that is not known. In 1861 they were living in Plant's Square, a miserable little court in the North End no better than Snow's Yard.[62] Catherine's son Bartholomew was already working as a plumber, and in the next forty years evidence suggests he strove to integrate himself – some might say ingratiate himself – into Stafford society. In 1863 he married Ann Goodman, a shoe binder[63] from another Connacht Catholic family. It did not look a propitious marriage in social terms,[64] but Ann Goodman seems to have worked hard with her husband to achieve a position of

61 I am indebted to David Noel Doyle for this suggestion. See R.J. Scally, *The End of Hidden Ireland: Rebellion, Famine & Emigration* (New York 1995), chap 6.

62 For a more detailed description of Plant's Square see J. Herson, 'Why the Irish came to Stafford ...', figure 4.3 and pp 65–8.

63 Shoe binding was a relatively low status and predominantly female job to do with the preparation of shoe uppers. It was a largely domestic trade until the 1860s, after which the work was increasingly mechanised and brought into shoe factories. M. Harrison, 'Boot and Shoe Manufacturing in Stafford', appendix 3.

64 The Goodmans were also a single-parent family where the father had presumably died in the Famine. They lived in another slum part of Stafford, the Broad Eye, and Ann Goodman's two brothers were clearly 'teenage tearaways' with a run of convictions for petty crime. One of them was described by a magistrate in 1862 as 'one of the worst characters in the Borough' (*SA*, 30 August 1862) . They left Stafford during the 1860s.

respectability. During the 1860s and 1870s Bartholomew built up his business in Foregate Street,[65] employing a number of men and boys. During the 1880s and 1890s 'B. Corcoran's workpeople' were consistently listed amongst the donors to the annual 'Hospital Saturday' for Infirmary funds. From 1884 we have evidence of Corcoran's increasing involvement in the affairs of the Catholic Church. In that year he was one of the lay notables present at the inauguration of the St Patrick's Young Men's Association, the only Irish immigrant to be listed.[66] The Corcorans were usually amongst those present at the annual Catholic Soirée in the Borough Hall in the later 1880s and the 1890s. These connections are significant in that the Catholic Church in Stafford was well-established, secure and dominated by a network of local families.[67] In 1892 Bartholomew Corcoran was again among the elite at the Requiem Mass in Birmingham for Canon O'Sullivan, vicar-general of the Diocese and former priest at St Austin's.[68] In 1898 he was elected to the Board of Guardians as the Catholic representative from the East Ward of Stafford. His partner from the West Ward was the English Catholic priest, Edward Acton.[69] Bartholomew Corcoran was plainly keen to break into the affairs of the Catholic Church in Stafford. Whilst this demonstrates adherence to his Catholic Irish background, the church environment within which he had to work almost certainly means he had to conform to a 'respectable' English milieu. All the evidence points to the Church in Stafford being a force for the assimilation of the Irish into the dominant English culture, and Bartholomew Corcoran was a leading example of this process. His flexibility was not restricted to church affairs either. It extended to politics. In the 1868–9 elections he voted Liberal each time, but by 1889 he had changed his spots and was on the organising committee for the Grand Conservative Ball held at the Borough Hall, hobnobbing again with the Stafford elite.[70]

Bartholomew Corcoran plainly put a lot of commitment into his chosen role in Stafford society. His children reflected this, staying in the town at least until 1891. The two surviving sons Bernard and John entered the family business and in 1896 Bernard married Annie Catherine Williams. She was the daughter of Frederick Williams, a prosperous cattle dealer with a substantial villa on the edge of town.[71] Bartholemew's daughters, Mary and Agnes, married two

65 Kelly's *Post Office Directory, Staffordshire*, 1876, 1880; census enumeration returns
66 *SA*, 23 February 1884.
67 M.W. Greenslade, *St Austin's, Stafford, 1791–1991*, (Birmingham 1991), pp 3–16.
68 *SA*, 16 January 1892.
69 Catholic Archdiocese Archive, Birmingham, St Austin's Mission Book: poster of Board of Guardians election results for 1898.
70 *SA*, 30 November 1889.
71 In 1891 Frederick Williams was living in Brook House at the beginning of the Eccleshall Road with his second wife, ten children and two servants. He and his family were native Staffordian Catholics.

brothers, William and Peter Westhead, in 1893 and 1900 respectively. They were non-Catholics from Newcastle-upon-Tyne, an intriguing background but one about which nothing more is known. It is equally notable that two of Bartholomew Corcoran's sisters, Mary and Bridget, both married native Staffordians in the shoe trade. In 1866 Mary married James Clewlow, a Protestant from a long-established Stafford family. He also had aspirations for advancement[72] and became a small-time shoe-trade employer before becoming a shoe-factory foreman. Mary was his second wife, and the couple brought up the four surviving children from Clewlow's first marriage and also went on to have seven children of their own. All the five known survivors stayed on in Stafford, the males in skilled artisanal jobs outside the shoe trade. One of them, Frederick, may have worked as a plumber in Bartholomew's business. In 1868 Bartholomew's other sister, Bridget, also married a Staffordian, Henry Follows. Unlike Clewlow, he was from a local Catholic family, and we find references to their involvement in the Church alongside those of the Corcoran family.[73] As with the Clewlows, the male children of this marriage are known to have stayed in Stafford at least until 1891, and, again like the Clewlows, they did not enter the troubled shoe trade. Three went into engineering, a growing industry by the 1890s, and the fourth became a solicitor's clerk, all jobs indicating significant occupational mobility. The second generation's marriages were also strongly integrationist. Of the eight known weddings of children from the Corcoran, Clewlow and Follows families which took place in the 1890s and 1900s, seven involved English[74] partners, and three were to non-Catholics.

The Corcorans, whether by accident or, more likely, by design seem to have had a family strategy of integrating themselves into Stafford society through their work, marriages and social activities. How common was this behaviour amongst Irish immigrants to the town? Testing for this is as problematic as it was for the Mannions, but we have seen already that marriages showed an increasingly strong pattern of integration as the first generation of English born children began to marry. The evidence of social activities is much more sketchy and ambivalent, but a review of workplace incidents, trade union activity, church life and the membership of a burial society[75] produced references to people from nineteen settled Irish families, just 14% of the total. The Connacht Catholics were poorly represented despite the example of the

---

72 Family hearsay; he was the author's great great grandfather.

73 e.g. *SA*, 9 March 1889.

74 Defined as people of English birth and known to be descended from English born ancestors.

75 SRO D4338/E/1/5, Stafford and District Humane Burial Society Register of Members, 1876–1900s. This was burial club which admitted only 'respectable' working class contributors. Ten members at one time or another came from settled Irish families or from families (like the Follows) where the wife was Irish.

Corcorans. Another indicator of relative integration might be voter registration in 1868. Male heads of household from 46 settled Irish families appear, or 34%.[76] On the criterion of what happened to the children of settled families, 41% of families had a majority of their children still resident in the town in 1891. In terms of the housing criterion discussed above, one third of the all-Irish households in 1881 were integrated and two thirds of mixed-family households (table 4). From this disparate evidence we might conclude that a minimum of 15% and a maximum of 50% of Irish families in Stafford by the 1880s were showing a strong degree of integration into the town's society. They were, perhaps, beyond 'the curious middle place'.

At the opposite end of the spectrum, Bridget Kenady's (*sic*) household in 1861 illustrates the minority – but, of course, sizeable minority – of people for whom a stop in Stafford was merely short-term (appendix 5). Her little cottage in Malt Mill Lane was temporary home for ten people, all Irish-born. Bridget herself had arrived in Stafford in during the Famine, and by 1861 she was eking out an existence as a washerwoman and, in practice, running an unlicenced lodging house. All but one of the nine lodgers were agricultural labourers working on the farms at the height of demand for Irish labour between 1852 and 1866.[77] Four were teenage brothers named Grew. None of the people in the household belonged to, or had any obvious connection with, the settled Irish families in Stafford. They truly conformed to the stereotype of transient, young, single, Irish men in the reserve army of labour. After 1871 it becomes increasingly difficult, however, to find similar households in the town. The number of single lodgers dropped from a peak of 108 in 1861 to 40 ten years later and only 16 by 1891 as the demand for farm labour ebbed.

The Kenady household consisted of a number of disparate individuals, not a family group. The Mannions, as we have seen, were a complex family interconnected with other Irish families whilst the Corcorans started off in Stafford as a nuclear family but then forged a marriage link with another Connacht Catholic family, the Goodmans. To talk generally of Irish immigrant 'families' is, therefore, to run the risk of oversimplification. The 134 settled Irish families which form the core of this essay ranged from simple nuclear groups to the complex extended families, and although the pattern which emerges is rather predictable, it carries implications for the extent and especially the timing of integration. The majority of Connacht Catholic families were either complex family groups in themselves or were nuclear families having marriage links with their Connacht kin.[78] Complex and linked families were also to be found

76 Though some settled families were not, at that point, present in the town.
77 Herson in Swift & Gilley, *The Irish in Britain, 1815–1939* pp 90–92.
78 Linkages between families continue to become apparent as more family histories are completed. A provisional conclusion is that thirty seven of the fifty two settled Connacht Catholic families were either complex families or nuclear families linked to others in the kinship group. The real total was probably larger.

amongst the other Catholics, but the proportion was less, and Protestant families were, without exception, nuclear units with no obvious kinship connections.[79] The connections between Connacht Catholic families clearly strengthened a degree of ethnic associational culture, or 'community', in the medium term, but even here the effect did not last and we find a high degree of integrationist behaviour amongst the children born in Stafford. The nuclear families from other backgrounds were inherently likely to respond in an integrationist fashion more or less from the time of their arrival in the town. This is not to say, however, that such families were inevitably 'successful' and soon merged without trace into Stafford society. The experience of the Hamilton family suggests caution in assuming that some families were advantaged merely by their apparently more favourable background (appendix 6).

The Hamiltons' history reflected the continuous ebb and flow of labour in the shoe trade, an industry in which Irish-*born* migrants were under-represented but which offered the children of the Irish a decisive, if modest, rise in occupational status over their parents.[80] Edward Hamilton senior, a Protestant shoemaker from Carrickfergus, county Antrim, came to Stafford with his sons Edward and William in the 1850s. Old Edward was already 60 in 1861, and he seems to have died during the 1860s. William probably left Stafford around the same time. His son Edward, also a shoemaker, married a Staffordshire woman in 1861 and they had four children in the 1860s, two of whom died young. Little Ada was an afterthought in 1878. The second child, Mary, was born in Newcastle-under-Lyme in 1864, so even then it seems the Hamiltons were not fixed in Stafford, although they do appear to have been so after 1865. Judging by their addresses, the Hamiltons made little economic progress during their time in the town but they clearly showed the high degree of residential mobility reported for nineteenth-century working class families. They did manage a move from the mean town centre locality of Clark Street to Mill Street in the second half of the 1860s[81] and then to a rather better address on the Sandon Road around 1876,[82] but in 1881 they were in Browning Street and by 1891

---

79 Seventeen non-Connacht Catholic families were complex or linked nuclear families but twenty-seven appeared to be nuclear. All twenty-five identifiable Protestant families were nuclear and independent of each other.

80 In 1881 15.3% of the total Stafford population worked in the shoe trade. Only 7.8% of the Irish-born did so, but, of the 119 children of the Irish-born with a recorded occupation, 66 or 55.5% worked in the shoe trade. It was a decisive job opening for second generation men and women. Source: census enumeration returns.

81 With a possible intervening period in Newcastle under Lyme during the early 1860s.

82 In 1871 they were at 4 Mill Street but by 1875 they had moved next door to no. 5. William Salt Library, Jones Collection, Accessions 0/00–9/0, sale catalogue, 1875, "valuable freehold house properties … 2 houses, gardens & premises at 5/6 Mill Street in the occupation of Edward Hamilton & Nicholas Maddocks." By 1877 they were living at Victoria Terrace, Sandon Road. SRO D4338/E/1/5 Stafford & District

they had ended up in another small cottage in the same dingy street. This all suggests a decline in their fortunes in later life. That the Hamiltons had aspired to a modest respectability is indicated by their membership of the Burial Society in the 1870s. Edward did perhaps show the colour of his origins and attitudes in the 1868 election when he voted Tory. He would, however, have found no opportunity in Stafford for any stronger demonstration of Orange sympathies. In 1891 he claimed to have been born in Scotland, not Ireland, and although this might be the result of an enumerator's error, it could also suggest a desire in later life to obscure his origins. One can only speculate on the reasons. Hamilton's only surviving son, Albert, seems to have left Stafford in the 1880s, one of the many shoemakers who left the town as the industry ran into problems. His eldest daughter Mary had, however, been forced back into the parental household by 1891. She had been widowed and left with a four year old daughter. All in all, the evidence suggests that the Hamiltons' experience of life in Stafford was mediocre and that their circumstances were as poor, or poorer, than those of many Catholic Irish families in the town. More generally, it suggests the need to investigate seriously the fortunes of that neglected group, the Irish Protestant immigrants to Britain, in order to throw light on their economic and social experiences rather than just on their sectarian proclivities.[83]

The Downing family (appendix 7) illustrates Catholics[84] from a classically mobile group who in fact settled long-term in Stafford. They were an army family. Both Michael Downing and his wife were Irish-born, but the birthplace of their children shows previous postings on Tyneside and in Scotland and Ireland before their arrival in Stafford sometime in the 1860s. Stafford was not a garrison town, but there was a small barracks where the part-time militia was trained. A small squad of regular soldiers was billeted there and some were always Irish like Michael Downing. This reflected the substantial Irish element in the British Army. Downing retired on an Army pension in the 1870s and died in 1884, but his wife stayed on in Stafford and two out of the four surviving children also remained in the town to 1891.

The Downings represent, therefore, a group of Irish immigrants almost totally ignored in the literature. Even in a small town like Stafford there was, throughout the study period, a small but constant throughput of Irish who

Humane Burial Society Register, 1876–1930s. In 1881 they were living at 31 Browning Street but by 1891 they had moved to 18 Browning Street, a small four-roomed cottage.

83 The relationship between geographical location, the economic base and the relative strength of various groups of immigrants will clearly affect the significance of the sectarian issue. See MacRaild, *Culture, Conflict and Migration*, esp. chaps 4, 5 & 6, for an analysis emphasising the sectarian perspective.

84 Both Michael Downing's death and that of his daughter Hannah are recorded in the St Austin's burial register.

were in the military. Others had retired from it or worked in services like the police, the railways and government departments which tended to recruit people from Service backgrounds. Like John Cronin, mentioned at the start of this essay, such people had a relatively secure and favoured position which they could exploit to integrate into local life.

The most obvious example of an Irish person who integrated is Hugh Woods Gibson, also cited earlier. His Northern Presbyterian background was plainly at the opposite end of the spectrum from the numerical majority of 'pauper Catholic Celt' immigrants studied so widely. He was an Irish emigrant nevertheless, and his life history reveals that such an emigrant was no more likely to react stereotypically to a small town like Stafford than either his Catholic compatriots or other Northern Protestants like the Hamiltons. Gibson was a shoemaker from a relatively humble background in county Down. He came directly from Ulster in 1839 with his father. He was then eighteen. On arrival in Stafford he chose to join the local Congregational Church, not the Presbyterian, a perhaps significant act in jettisoning his roots. Gibson's overall behaviour in Stafford prompts the speculation that he came from the liberal wing of Presbyterianism but we must, nevertheless, beware of imputing attitudes and motivation from the evidence of official religious allegiance. He was certainly ambitious. He left Stafford in 1843 and went to London, not returning until 1856.[85] By then he had done well in the shoe trade, and in 1861 he became a partner in one of Stafford's leading shoe firms.[86] In the 1860s he rose quickly to social and political prominence in the town, and was chairman of the local Liberal Party by the time of the 1868 election. He strongly supported Gladstone's policy of disestablishment and had no problem in seeking the support of local Catholics, including the Catholic priest, for the Liberal cause.[87] He rejected Protestant criticism of doing this. No mud seems to have stuck to him as a result of the corrupt 1868 election and he went on to become Mayor in 1871 and again in 1876. Despite the local esteem in which he seems to have been held, he chose, nevertheless, to retire in 1883 to the posh Birmingham suburb of Edgbaston.[88] The reasons are unknown. Overall, however, Gibson was an extreme example of a young Irish immigrant clearly determined to conform to the *mores* of the dominant culture in order to get on. In his public utterances later in life there were no references to his origins. He represents someone apparently prepared to bury his ethnic and cultural background completely.

This brief review of a number of Irish families in Stafford has taken us from the Mannions of Red Cow Yard to the Gibson family in their mansion at

85 SRO, D4800/2/8/1, Stafford Congregational Church, Roll of Members, 1798–1901.
86 A.M. Harrison, 'Elley's of Stafford', *J. Staffs. Ind. Arch. Soc.*, no. 8 (1978), 59.
87 *SA*, 17 October 1868.
88 SRO, D4800/2/8/1, Congregational Church, Stafford, Roll of members, 1798–1901.

Burton Villa. What conclusions are to be drawn? Firstly, that the proportionately average, if numerically small, Irish-born population of Stafford was very typical in its overall characteristics to the Irish who were to be found in the other towns and cities of Britain. Secondly, however, in looking at 100% of a relatively small number of people, a more comprehensive picture of the variety of people and situations can be presented. It is possible to classify the different types and begin to move on from the rather one-dimensional picture of the Irish inherent in the big city locations. Thirdly, the importance of the family unit in understanding peoples' life experiences has been stressed. The Stafford evidence suggests that for the majority of Irish emigrants nuclear and extended family units were the key social institution influencing the courses taken in peoples' lives. The families were subject to the constraints and opportunities of the wider environment, but the range of responses visible from different families, together with the evidence of family cohesion documented in specific incidents,[89] indicates, nevertheless, their historical importance.

Irish in-migrant families in Stafford had, it has been argued, three basic options, summarised as 'migration', 'community' or 'integration'. Contrary to the evidence often cited in the big cities there was little mileage in Irish people asserting or fostering their ethnic identity in a place like Stafford. No instances or allegations of Fenian activity have been found, and the Home Rule issue excited no obvious local debate or political organisation. The town was small, and the Irish population also small, and this meant there were inherent difficulties in sustaining an Irish cultural *milieu*. Even Irish-only pubs would have been unviable. In practice, as we have seen, there was not one Irish 'community' but a number, based on differing geographical origins, religious persuasions, social status and family aspirations. It seems, then, that 'community' was not a realistic long-term option for the Irish in Stafford.

The basic choice was between 'migration' and 'integration' – going away or becoming Staffordians. We have seen that many in-migrants and their children chose the former. Stafford offered limited horizons and opportunities. As farming became depressed and the shoe trade volatile, so many Irish people and their descendants left and they were not replaced by sufficient new people coming in. The inflow did not stop, but the net balance was outward after 1861.[90] For those choosing to stay, the rational family strategy, conscious or otherwise, was to integrate. The evidence suggests that this process was

89 Although space here has precluded most of this type of material, it is striking how much evidence appears of family relationships and cohesion in reports, for example, of petty criminal proceedings.

90 It will, nevertheless, be interesting to see whether the tide turned again during the 1890s as Stafford's economy diversified and revived. The 1901 census will provide evidence. Marriages were found in the 1900s at both St Austin's and St Patrick's churches involving Irish people from families not represented in the 1891 census.

occurring rapidly after 1871 as the first generation in-migrants from the Famine and the subsequent period died off. In this process of integration Irish people and families were supported – or pressurised – by the social and civic environment. Key institutions in Stafford, notably both the Catholic and Protestant churches, clearly performed roles as purveyors of the dominant culture. In civic and political life there were no worthwhile votes in sectarianism, and the political parties appear to have sought mobilisation of their supporters from whatever their background.[91] The local press only very rarely noted ethnic origin in petty criminal proceedings, and offered no obvious channel for the expression of prejudice. Almost no evidence has been found of anti-Irish attitudes by employers, though this is not to say they did not exist.[92]

The evidence suggests, therefore, that the phenomenon of 'ethnic fade' was a reality in the late-nineteenth century history of Irish immigrants in Stafford. The Irish were a significant presence in the town after 1847, and their economic fortunes echoed those of their compatriots in many other towns and cities in Britain. The social and political contrast, however, with the experiences of Irish people in places like Liverpool, Manchester and Glasgow is considerable, and it suggests a need to examine further the experience of Irish people in their 'curious middle place' in nineteenth- and early twentieth-century Britain.

91 Heinrick observed that 'In the town of Stafford, and in the locality known as the Potteries, ... are numerous Irish residents, but so scattered as not to constitute a power relatively.' A. O'Day (ed.), *A Survey of the Irish in England in 1872* (by Hugh Heinrick) (London 1988), p. 59. He was clearly right in relation to Stafford. By 1892 Denvir was more bullish about the 'zeal for the national cause' shown by the Potteries Irish, but the Stafford residents were not included in this assessment. Denvir, *The Irish in Britain*, p. 426.

92 The only incident found so far took place in 1893 when John Martin, an Irish bricklayer, was charged with assaulting and threatening his employer, W.T. Woollams. 'In cross-examination the complainant denied having called the defendant a Fenian or Home Ruler or otherwise provoked him,' an unconvincing statement in the circumstances. Woollams was a native Staffordian Catholic. Martin was fined twenty shillings and bound over for six months. *SA*, 4 February 1893. Employment records do not exist for any of the late nineteenth-century shoe firms. No success has so far been achieved in testing for the specific policies of employers except in the case of certain landed estates in the 1850s and 1860s, reported in J. Herson, 'Why the Irish went to Stafford ...', pp 39–44.

APPENDIX 1

ORIGIN OF SETTLED CATHOLIC IRISH FAMILIES, STAFFORD, 1841–91

Connacht Catholic		Leinster Catholic	Munster Catholic	Ulster Catholic	Unknown Catholic
Blundon	Kelly	Carroll (1)	Carlin	Cavanagh	Beckett
Blyth	Kirwan	Carroll (2)	Collins	Finnigan	Coyne
Bowen	Mahon	Cavanagh	Concannon	Kelly	Cronin
Brennan	Malley/Malieu	Kearney	Duggan	McMahon	Downing
Bryan	Maloney	Kearns	Hingerty	White	Egan
Burke	Mannion	Kernaghan	Moore		Farrell
Caffrey	Martin	Riley	Mulrooney		Feeny
Carney	McCann/Gann		Neild		Giblin
Cassidy	McMahon		O'Brien		Griffin
Caulfield	McTighe		O'Connor		Hand
Coleman	Mitchell				Higgins (1)
Concar	Monaghan				Higgins (2)
Connor (1)	Morris				Keagan
Connor (2)	Murphy				Kenny
Corcoran	Noon				Lyons
Cunningham	O'Shea				McDermott
Devlin	Raftery				McDonald
Dolan	Reddington				Moyers
Durham	Ryan				Mullins
Durkin	Shaughnessy				Murray
Featherstone	Shiel				Perry
Flanagan	Smith				Ruhall
Goodman	Sweeney				
Hagan	Tuohey				
Hart	Walsh				
Jordan	Ward				

For sources see text.

APPENDIX 2

ORIGIN OF SETTLED PROTESTANT FAMILIES AND FAMILIES OF
UNCERTAIN BACKGROUND, STAFFORD, 1841–91
(including 'accidental Irish', marked thus *)

Connacht Prot.	*Leinster Prot.*	*Munster Prot.*	*Ulster Prot.*	*Unknown Prot.*
Hughes	Barnes	Salt*	Clendinnen	Crawford
	Brinson*	Veideman	Crosbie	Durkin
	Clay*		Gibson	Finn
	Disney		Hamilton	McCann
	Gibbs		Radford	Millsafe
	Giltrap			Tomkins
	Livingstone			
	Marshall*			
	McCabe			
	Peach			
	Smith			

Connacht Uncertain	*Leinster Uncertain*	*Munster Uncertain*	*Ulster Uncertain*	*Irish Uncertain*
Farrington		McNeirney		Dyer
Jones				Gavan
King				Larkin
Mann				Lucas
Reddish				Mapp
				Mooney
				Quinn

For sources see text.

APPENDIX 3: THE MANNION/WALSH FAMILIES

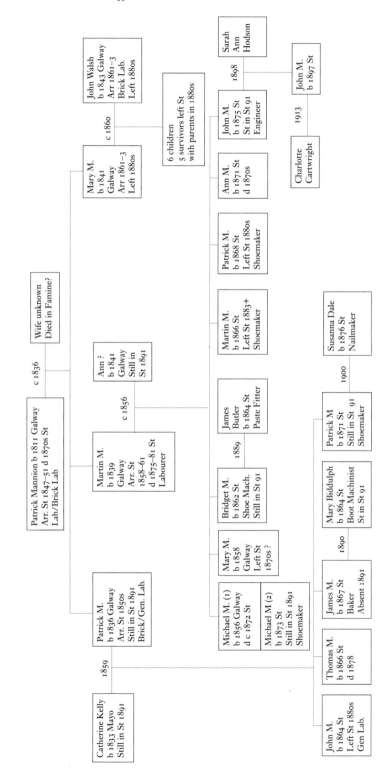

APPENDIX 4: THE CORCORAN/CLEWLOW/FOLLOWS FAMILIES

Patrick Corcoran
Died in Famine ?

Catherine ?
b 1805 Ireland
d 1871 Stafford

c1835

? Goodman
Died in Famine ?

[1]
c 1835

Michael Kernaghan
b 1826 Kildare
Labourer
?Left Stafford 1860s

[2]
1850s

Ann ? Fitzpatrick
b 1806–21 Meath
Arr. St 1847–51
Lodg. Ho. Kpr
St in St '91

Mary C.
b 1838
St in St
91

Bridget C.
b 1845 Ire.
Machinist
St in St 91

Henry Follows
b 1846 Stafford
Clicker
St in St 91

Catherine C.
b 1847 Ire
Bootbinder
d 1875

1868

James C. Clewlow
b 1832 Stafford
Shoe Mfr/Foremn
St in St 91

[2]
1866

[1]
c 1852

Mary Moore
b 1833 Staffs
d c1864

Michael C.
b 1837 Ire.
Cordwainer
Left St '60s

Bartholemew C.
b 1836 Rosc.
Plumber etc.
St in St 98

Ann G.
b 1842 Ire
Binder
St in St 91

Patrick G.
b 1845 Ire.
Cordwainer
Left St '60s

Daniel G.
b 1843 Ire.
Cordwainer
Left St '60s

1863

4 children

Edward C
b 1878 St.
d 1880s ?

Rosa Cl.
b 1878 St
St in St 91

Gertrude F
b 1882 St.
St in St 91

Samuel
Morgan
b 1877
B'ham
Tel. Mesgr

1903

Agnes F.
b 1881 St
St in St
91

Annie
Williams
b 1875 St

1896

Louise
Ann
James

1902

Ernest Cl.
b 1875 St
Mechanic
St in St '91

Wilfred F.
b 1878 St
Turner
St in St 91

Bernard C.
b 1873 St
Plumber
St in St 91

Frederick Cl.
b 1874 St
Plumber
St in St 91

Henry F.
b 1875 St
Solicitor's cl.
St in St 91

Peter
Westhead
Ncle on
Tyne

1900

Agnes C.
b 1870 St
Governess
St in St 91

Frances Cl.
b 1871 St
d 1870s

John
Geoghegan
b 1854
Bridgnorth
Eng. Clerk

1890

John C.
b 1868 St
Painter
St in St 91

Arthur
Shaw

1898

Ruth Cl.
b 1869 St
Shoe Facy.
St in St 91

Rose F.
b 1872 St

William
Westhead
Ncle on
Tyne

Harry Cl.
b 1868 St
Pattern Mkr
St in St 91

John
Vaughan

1899

Catherine F.
b 1871 St

Mary C.
b 1866 St

1893

Cora Cl.
b 1867 St
Died 1880s?

Beatrice F.
b 1869 St
Died
1880s?

APPENDIX 5: THE KENADY HOUSEHOLD, MALT MILL LANE, 1861

Road, Street and no. of House	Name and Surname of each Person	Relation to Head of Family	Condition	Sex	Age	Rank, Profession or Occupation	Where Born
3 Malt Mill Lane	Bridget Kenady	Head	Un.	F	40	Washerwoman	Ireland
	Thomas Moore	Lodger	Un.	M	35	Agricultural Labourer	Ireland
	Patrick Ganley	Lodger	Un.	M	20	Agricultural Labourer	Ireland
	John Ratrick	Lodger	Un.	M	20	Agricultural Labourer	Ireland
	Richard Thornton	Lodger	Un.	M	32	Sailor	Ireland
	John Grew	Lodger	Un.	M	14	Agricultural Labourer	Ireland
	William Grew	Lodger	Un.	M	15	Agricultural Labourer	Ireland
	George Grew	Lodger	Un.	M	12	Agricultural Labourer	Ireland
	Martin Grew	Lodger	Un.	M	18	Agricultural Labourer	Ireland
	Anthony Robins	Lodger	Un.	M	13	Agricultural Labourer	Ireland

APPENDIX 6: THE HAMILTON FAMILY

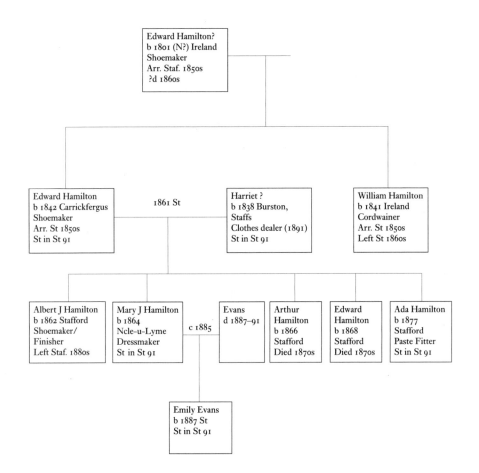

Edward Hamilton?
b 1801 (N?) Ireland
Shoemaker
Arr. Staf. 1850s
?d 1860s

Edward Hamilton
b 1842 Carrickfergus
Shoemaker
Arr. St 1850s
St in St 91

1861 St

Harriet ?
b 1838 Burston,
Staffs
Clothes dealer (1891)
St in St 91

William Hamilton
b 1841 Ireland
Cordwainer
Arr. St 1850s
Left St 1860s

Albert J Hamilton
b 1862 Stafford
Shoemaker/
Finisher
Left Staf. 1880s

Mary J Hamilton
b 1864
Ncle-u-Lyme
Dressmaker
St in St 91

c 1885

Evans
d 1887–91

Arthur
Hamilton
b 1866
Stafford
Died 1870s

Edward
Hamilton
b 1868
Stafford
Died 1870s

Ada Hamilton
b 1877
Stafford
Paste Fitter
St in St 91

Emily Evans
b 1887 St
St in St 91

APPENDIX 7: THE DOWNING FAMILY

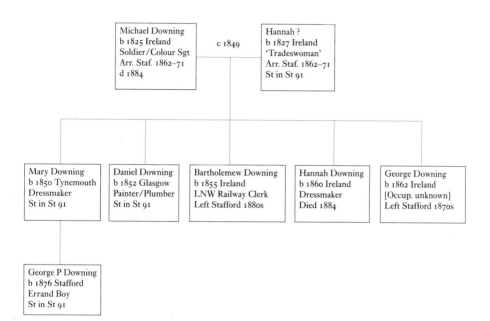

Michael Downing
b 1825 Ireland
Soldier/Colour Sgt
Arr. Staf. 1862–71
d 1884

c 1849

Hannah ?
b 1827 Ireland
'Tradeswoman'
Arr. Staf. 1862–71
St in St 91

Mary Downing
b 1850 Tynemouth
Dressmaker
St in St 91

Daniel Downing
b 1852 Glasgow
Painter/Plumber
St in St 91

Bartholemew Downing
b 1855 Ireland
LNW Railway Clerk
Left Stafford 1880s

Hannah Downing
b 1860 Ireland
Dressmaker
Died 1884

George Downing
b 1862 Ireland
[Occup. unknown]
Left Stafford 1870s

George P Downing
b 1876 Stafford
Errand Boy
St in St 91

Class, creed and country: the Irish middle class in Victorian Liverpool

John Belchem

Coming from a range of backgrounds, Irish migrants were to distribute and integrate themselves throughout mainland Britain, taking up a number of occupational and residential opportunities. One group, however, lies outside this optimistic historiographical re-assessment: those who settled in Liverpool. Cast aside in recent studies, the Liverpool-Irish (of whom Heathcliff, the great other/outsider of Victorian literature, brought starving and houseless from the streets of Liverpool, may well have been one)[1] have always suffered the prejudice and negative reputation which, in the late twentieth century, have come to blight the city itself. Labelled as 'the dregs' by Father Nugent (an Irish-Liverpudlian himself), those who remained in this port of entry have been dismissed in wider (and celebratory) studies of the Irish diaspora as the *caput mortuum*, a kind of under-class, as it were, unable, unwilling or unsuited to take advantage of opportunities elsewhere in Britain or the new world. The proverbial exception which proved the rule, Liverpool is disparaged by historians as a sectarian redoubt, 'marginal to the cultural and political life of the nation'.[2]

Whatever its relationship to national patterns, the large Liverpool-Irish community had a complex cultural and political life of its own which needs to be rescued from historical caricature and stigma. The lowly socio-economic status of the vast majority, anchored at the bottom of the local occupational and social hierarchy, cannot be disputed: factor analysis of the (pre-Famine influx) 1841 census, by which time there were already 49,639 Irish-born in Liverpool, some 17.3% of the population, has highlighted three main clusters of inter-related variables, a three-class model with an Irish/unskilled/lodging/industrial service/court house cluster at the base.[3] However, this paper points to a significant middle-class contribution to Irish Liverpool. Admittedly, some

---

1 Terry Eagleton, *Heathcliff and the Great Hunger* (London, 1995), pp 1–26.
2 For Nugent, see I.C. Taylor, 'Black Spot on the Mersey: a study of environment and society in 18th and 19th century Liverpool' (University of Liverpool PhD thesis, 1976), p. 101. Steven Fielding, *Class and Ethnicity: Irish Catholics in England, 1880–1939* (Buckingham, 1993), p. 5 dismisses Liverpool as a sectarian redoubt.
3 Taylor, pp 114–15, and 213–20. See also Colin Pooley, 'The Irish in Liverpool *circa* 1850–1940' in M. Engman, F.W. Carter, A.C. Hepburn and C.G. Pooley (eds), *Ethnic Identity in Urban Europe* (Aldershot, 1992), pp 71–97.

'Micks on the make' (to use Roy Foster's terminology) favoured 'ethnic fade', distancing themselves from all things Irish to effect the quickest route out of the Liverpool 'ghetto' into economic success and assimilation.[4] A significant number, however, having identified their best interests (or market niche) in servicing the migrant community, chose to accentuate their Irishness. In Irish Liverpool, as in other large migrant 'enclaves', there was considerable internal stratification, but socio-economic success was often legitimized through ethnic leadership, both cultural and political.

Out of place in studies of the Irish in Britain, the Liverpool-Irish 'colony' (the very size of which demands historical attention) is perhaps best approached through comparison with large migrant communities overseas, enclaves within which 'ethnic' culture was not only retained but rewarded. An important difference should be noted at the outset. Language retention, a valuable asset in Hispanic enclaves and among ethnic groups generally, was at a discount among nineteenth-century Irish migrants.[5] 'Irishness' flourished without a specific language, although a later generation of nationalist leaders (outside the scope of this study) tried against the odds to promote a 'Gaelic revival'.[6] But how did 'Irishness' emerge? Looking beyond language, the necessary components of ethnic affiliation – a common proper name; a myth of common ancestry; shared historical memories; elements of common culture; link with a homeland; and a sense of solidarity – were not all in place, ready for instant activation.[7] As local studies of Irish-America have shown, the presence of middle culture-brokers contributed much to the construction of an 'imagined' national identity. An important influence over less fortunate fellow-migrants, they were to superimpose a wider 'invented' affiliation upon traditional and instinctive sub-national loyalties. As role models able to stand above the clan, regional and faction networks of chain migration, middle-class Irish-Americans promoted an inclusive ethnic identity, not least as defence against host stereotyping. Under their guidance, migrants were encouraged to abandon the

4 Roy Foster's essay, 'Marginal Men and Micks on the Make: The Uses of Irish Exile *c*.1840–1922', in his *Paddy and Mr Punch* (London, 1995), pp 281–305. See also J.D. Papworth, 'The Irish in Liverpool, 1835–71: Segregation and Dispersal' (University of Liverpool PhD thesis, 1982).

5 I learnt much from my co-members of the 'Migration, settlement, assimilation and culture' panel at the First European Social Science History Conference, Noordwijkerhout, 9–11 May 1996: Brian Gratton, 'Spanish Culture and Mexican immigrants to the United States'; Walter Kamphoefner, 'Second generation immigrants and the language transition in the United States'; and Leo Lucassen, 'The Chicago School tested once again: assimilation processes in the Netherlands 1850–1960'.

6 On the absence of a 'gaelic' perspective, see Anon., *The Liverpool Irishman, or Annals of the Irish Colony in Liverpool* (Liverpool, 1909).

7 J. Hutchinson and A.D. Smith, *Ethnicity* (Oxford, 1996), pp 6–7 and *passim*, a useful introduction to the sociology of ethnicity.

patterns of itinerancy, intemperance and internecine dispute caricatured and labelled as 'Irish' by their hosts, and to adopt instead a trans-regional national or ethnic 'Irish' pride in themselves. Once implanted, ethnic associational culture provided a means by which successful Irish-Americans could guard against social radicalism while keeping a check on violent inflexions of nationalism.[8] Was there an equivalent leadership cadre in Irish-Liverpool? Comparative research into large migrant communities throughout late nineteenth-century Europe has shown how ethnic associations 'tended to be related to social class, to be bids for group leadership'.[9] Does Irish-Liverpool conform to the pattern?

While a successful cross-class exercise, ethnic mobilization was narrowly sectarian in Irish-Liverpool. Catholic middle class migrants and their descendants took exclusive command of Irish nationalism and 'Irishness'. This appropriation, or 'ethnic absolutism', doubtless accounts for the invisibility of their Protestant counterparts in Liverpool.[10] Denied a role in Irish formations, and in the absence of any equivalent to the American 'Scotch-Irish' alternative, middle-class Irish Protestant migrants merged (even to the point of anonymity) into the host mainstream. While the Ulster-Scots (and their distinct Irish Presbyteries) disappeared quietly from view, some Anglo-Irish migrants were enthusiastic (often demagogic) advocates of Britishness, the populist Protestant identity which secured Tory hegemony in Liverpool until the Second World War and beyond.

Ethnic mobilization took a variety of forms and served a number of functions, ranging from active support for the nationalist cause in Ireland to the welfare needs of the migrant community. Whatever the form, ethnic affiliation among the Irish in Liverpool tended to reflect the social structural characteristics of the migrant community. Irish-born merchants, shipping agents, doctors, other professionals and tradesmen provided leadership and resources. Here, as a subsequent section of this paper will show, there was a division between the charitable and cultural Irish projects sponsored by those at the apex (those whose business interests and commercial practices extended above and beyond

---

8   D.B. Light, Jr, 'The role of Irish-American organisations in assimilation and community formation', in P.J. Drudy (ed.), *The Irish in America: emigration, assimilation and impact* (Cambridge, 1985), pp 113–42. See also T.N. Brown, *Irish-American Nationalism* (Philadelphia and New York, 1966).

9   A.C.Hepburn, 'Ethnic identity and the city', in Engman et al., *Ethnic Identity in Urban Europe*, p. 4. See also J. Rex and B. Drury (eds), *Ethnic Mobilisation in Multi-cultural Europe* (Aldershot, 1994); J. Rex, D. Joly, and C. Wilpert (eds), *Immigrant Associations in Europe* (Aldershot, 1987); and M. Cross (ed.), *Ethnic Minorities and Industrial Change in Europe and North America* (Cambridge, 1992).

10 For a spirited attack on such ethnic absolutism, see D.H. Akenson, *The Irish Diaspora: A Primer* (Belfast, 1996), chapters 1 and 2.

Ireland and the Irish-Liverpool enclave) and the ardent nationalist politics pursued by Catholic merchants in the Irish trade and members of professions in daily contact with poor Irish migrants.

Publicans and shopkeepers, many of whom had risen from the ranks, provided a conduit between the leadership cadre and the wider migrant community. Jack Langan, a former Irish champion boxer, ran the most famous 'Irish' pub, strategically positioned opposite Clarence Dock, the disembarkation point for Irish passenger traffic – it was immediately recognizable by the effigy of St Patrick, shamrock in hand, high on its walls. A strong supporter of 'creed and country', Langan enjoyed considerable fame and fortune in Liverpool – his estate was valued at over £20,000 on his death in 1846 – appearing on the platform when his hero, Daniel O'Connell visited the town.[11] Lacking such celebrity, other Irish publicans sought to attract custom by a variety of 'ethnic' marketing ploys, such as encouraging Irish societies to meet on their premises. Implanted from Ireland with sectarian fervour, the continuum of convivial and bibulous male-based associational culture extended from 'Hibernian' burial and friendly societies, legally approved and sanctioned by the Catholic Church, to secret 'Ribbon' branches linked to networks across the Irish Sea.[12] In his pub in Crosbie Street, John McArdle, an Ulster Catholic by birth, hosted a number of societies, as well as providing popular Sunday night readings from *The Nation*. An accomplished ethnic entrepreneur, McArdle briefly diversified into the grocery and provision trade to cater for the temperance fad in the Irish community following the visit by Father Mathew. Among the 'ethnic' shopkeepers, the most flamboyant was Thade Crowley, a Corkonian who became a successful pork butcher in Liverpool and leader of the local Hibernian society. Surrounded by banners, harps and shamrocks galore, Crowley marched at the head of the lodge on St Patrick's Day in proud display of both his socioeconomic status and his ethnicity, dressed in 'buckskin breeches, top boots, green tabinet double-breasted waistcoat, bottle-green coat with brass buttons, and beaver hat'.[13]

In the absence of significant upward mobility into the skilled working-class and its craft-based Lib-Lab organizations, the popular salience of ethnic associational culture was uncontested. Restricted to 'niche' occupations, Irish labourers remained labourers, protected against adversity by ethno-sectarian networks of collective mutuality. Evidence presented to Cornewall Lewis's 1835 report on the state of the Irish poor in Britain suggested that the Liverpool-Irish, whether in construction, warehousing or the merchant marine, were ill-disposed towards apprenticeship or training in mechanics. Those with ambition, the Revd

---

11 John Denvir, *The Life Story of an Old Rebel* (Dublin, 1910), pp 3–4, and 52.

12 John Belchem, '"Freedom and Friendship to Ireland": Ribbonism in early nineteenth-century Liverpool', *International Review of Social History*, vol. 39 (1994), pp 33–56.

13 Denvir, pp 15–16, and 25.

M. Fisher noted, 'rise to be small-shopkeepers, provision-vendors and public house keepers'.[14] As the Irish 'colony' grew, so such opportunities expanded. For those with enterprise, Irish-Liverpool held out the prospect of upward mobility into the middle class by catering for the migrant community itself, a socio-economic advance topped off by ethnic political leadership.

Despite their importance in ethnic mobilization, little is known about the Irish middle class in Liverpool. Census analysis, restricted in coverage to the Irish-born, has identified some 6.6% of the Irish-born in Liverpool in pro-fessional and intermediate occupations in 1871.[15] Hugh Heinrick, reporting on the Irish in Britain for *The Nation* in 1872, calculated that between one-fifth and one-sixth of the Irish in Liverpool, broadly defined and estimated at 180,000 in total, were 'above the ranks of ordinary toil'. By his 'approximate estimate' there were 300 merchants of the 'first class'; 1500 merchants and factors of the 'second class'; 800 in the professions; 3500 clerks; 3500 shop-keepers; and 2000 commercial assistants. 'Of the Irishmen who have attained to wealth and position in Liverpool', Heinrick asserted, 'there is not one in fifty who has not risen from the ranks of labour – and risen, too, in opposition to prejudices and various hostile circumstances such as no other member of the community has had to encounter and endure'. Heinrick's figures and claims served a nationalist purpose and must be read with caution.[16] A similar caveat must be entered for the cursory and impressionistic study undertaken here. Those who assumed the leadership of the Irish community, the focus of this paper, should not be seen as typical of the migrant middle class. Standing forward as political activists, they are a visible minority within a complex and diverse grouping. Differing considerably in wealth, income and resources, middle-class migrants from across the Irish Sea displayed a bewildering range of political, cultural and 'ethnic' attitudes towards Ireland and Irishness.

Once in Liverpool, some were transients, others took root. Unlike more distant migrant enclaves, Liverpool was generally perceived as stepwise entrepôt, not as place of destination. As the 'second metropolis', Liverpool was

14 *PP.* 1836 (40) XXXIV: *Royal Commission on the Condition of the Poorer Classes in Ireland*: Appendix G, *The State of the Irish Poor in Great Britain*, pp 8–41. Significantly, James Muspratt, father of the British chemical industry, who left Dublin in 1822 to produce soda by the Leblanc process on Merseyside, spoke favourably of the work application of his Irish workforce, as did the soap and sugar manufacturers, also large employers of Irish labour in the kinds of job which native workers preferred not to do. The most disparaging comments came from Irish merchants in linen and other imported goods at Liverpool, commercial men with little workplace contact with their fellow-countrymen.
15 Colin Pooley, 'Segregation or integration? The residential experience of the Irish in mid-Victorian Britain' in R. Swift and S. Gilley (eds), *The Irish in Britain, 1815–1939* (London, 1989), p. 71.
16 Heinrick's letter, dated 24 Sept. 1872, is reprinted in Alan O'Day (ed.), *A Survey of the Irish in England, 1872* (London, 1990), pp 87–95. A Wexford-born journalist, Heinrick's career later included a spell in Liverpool on the *United Irishman*.

an important staging-post in career development for the Irish middle class, a convenient testing-ground for their journalistic, legal, medical, clerical or other talents. When Justin McCarthy came to Liverpool as a 'stepping-stone on my way to London', he found that most of the staff on the *Northern Daily Times* were also Irish.[17] What happened to those whose onward career ambitions were thwarted? How did their embitterment translate into political terms?

Considerable numbers adjusted to permanent residence. Written by a second-generation Irish-Liverpudlian journalist in the 1870s, a satirical survey of the local medical profession, noted for its pursuit of fortune rather than fame, identified a number of long-established Irish practices (replenished by professional chain migration) located both in fashionable areas and in the north end Irish 'ghetto'.[18] The Irish were also well represented in merchant ranks, reflecting the crucial significance of Irish trade in Liverpool's development. Economic historians have focused on the more exotic (and financially less secure) overseas trans-oceanic trade, but Liverpool's prosperity was underwritten by its near-hegemony in the movement of goods and people within and around the 'inland' Irish Sea, trade which attracted and required a significant Irish mercantile presence.[19]

The mainstay of the port, Liverpool's mid-nineteenth-century coasting trade was dominated by the Irish trade, mainly operating on the Liverpool-Dublin axis. Reporting to the Irish Confederation in 1848 on the state of 'Irish trade, with or through, Liverpool, import and export', Ulster-born George Smyth, a successful hat manufacturer in Paradise Street, calculated its value as 'between eleven or twelve millions a year ... greater than that of any other country of the world, the United States of America alone excepted'.[20] The 'western emporium of Albion', Liverpool was Ireland's most convenient point of access to distribution networks in Britain and overseas. Channelled through Dublin, the Irish export economy was overwhelmingly agrarian: Ireland supplied over 75% of the cattle, pigs, oats, oatmeal, butter, eggs, lard and preserved meats imported coastwise at Liverpool.[21] The Anglo-Irish cattle

---

17 L.W. Brady, *T.P. O'Connor and the Liverpool Irish* (London, 1983), p. 37. Irish artisans were similarly mobile: Dublin, Liverpool and Manchester formed an inner triangle within a wider circle from London to Glasgow, Belfast to Cork, Bristol to London. See Fergus D'Arcy, 'Dublin artisan activity, opinion and organization, 1820–50', unpublished MA thesis, National Library of Ireland, p. 9.

18 J.F. McArdle, *A Patient in Search of a Doctor* (Liverpool, 1872). The author was the son of the publican, John McArdle.

19 See the interesting portrayal of 'Liverpool and the Celtic Sea' in Robert Scally, *The End of Hidden Ireland* (New York, 1995), chapter 9.

20 *Nation*, 15 Jan. 1848.

21 Valerie Burton, 'Liverpool's mid-nineteenth century coasting trade' in Burton (ed.), *Liverpool Shipping, Trade and Industry* (Liverpool, National Museums and Galleries on Merseyside, 1989), pp 26–66.

trade was dominated by the Liverpool firm of Cullen and Verdon, comprising Michael and James Cullen – brothers of Cardinal Paul Cullen of Dublin – and their brother-in-law, Peter Verdon. During the Famine the Liverpool-based branch of the Cullen family, noted for their wealth and charity, set up temporary hospital facilities on their premises for Irish immigrants.[22] Although overshadowed by Dublin, Belfast served as outlet for linen and other industries increasingly concentrated in the Lagan valley. By 1839, fierce competition in cross-channel steamship services had effected what the local Chamber of Commerce described as 'an entire change in our foreign commerce, which instead of being carried on as formerly by means of vessels sailing direct from Belfast at long and uncertain intervals is now conducted entirely through Liverpool from whence the valuable manufactures of the North of Ireland are transmitted almost daily to their ports of foreign destination'.[23] There were mutual benefits in this entrepôt arrangement, the basis for subsequent close links between Liverpool shipowners and Belfast shipbuilders.[24] In the 1830s, Liverpool merchants invested heavily in the Ulster Railway (a director was appointed specially to safeguard their interests), and in the new Ulster Bank, 46 of the 56 British shareholders were Liverpool-based, including William Brown.[25]

Brown was a merchant prince in the Atlantic trade, a major figure in flax, linen, cotton, thence in merchant banking. Born near Ballymena to Alexander Brown, a linen merchant of the 'smaller class', William was taken to Baltimore and thence to Liverpool, gaining considerable experience and wealth in the wider family business. W. and J. Brown, however, fell into serious difficulties in 1836–7, from which it was rescued by the co-ordinated support of three Belfast banks. Brown's ancestral links were an important factor (no doubt it was in the banks' self-interest to prevent the collapse of a major Liverpool finance house involved in the Atlantic trade). Thereafter Brown seems to have forsaken his Ulster heritage to secure his position (and a baronetcy) within the Liverpool mercantile elite and the Lancashire establishment. He abandoned Presbyterianism in favour of Anglicanism, and his benefaction was expended, much to the annoyance of Irish nationalists, not on his native Ballymena but on funding the magnificent Liverpool museum, an immortalizing symbol of the culture of commerce in the 'Florence of the north'.

22 Peadar Mac Suibhne, *Paul Cullen and His Contemporaries* (5 vols, Nass, 1967–77), vol. IV, p. 28.

23 Belfast Chamber of Commerce to Morpeth, quoted in L. Kennedy and P. Ollerenshaw (eds), *An Economic History of Ulster* (Manchester, 1985), p. 64. See also, R.C. Sinclair, *Across the Irish Sea. Belfast-Liverpool shipping since 1819* (n.p., 1990).

24 These links were often mediated by G.C. Schwabe, Liverpool merchant and financier, personal friend of Edward Harland and uncle of Harland's assistant, Gustav Wolff, see Kennedy and Ollerenshaw, pp 89–91.

25 E.R.R. Green, *The Lagan Valley 1800–50* (London, 1990), pp 51–4. P. Ollerenshaw, *Banking in Nineteenth-century Ireland: The Belfast Banks, 1825–1914* (Manchester, 1987), pp 48–51.

Commitment to Irish nationalism was found in different quarters, in lower ranks of middle class migrants, essentially among Catholics. As noted above, two groups were particularly prominent: those whose commercial interests still centred on the Irish Sea and took them regularly across to Ireland,[26] and those whose professional practices brought them into everyday contact with the Liverpool-Irish community. In the European revolutionary excitement of 1848, the springtime of the peoples, some of their number abandoned O'Connellite moderation and restraint to prepare for active support of insurrection in Ireland.[27] The leader of the Irish Confederates in Liverpool was Terence Bellew MacManus, a forwarding and commissioning agent prominent in the Irish trade who passed £1.5 million in goods per annum. An Ulster Catholic by birth, he was a friend of Charles Gavan Duffy from early business days together in Monaghan.[28] MacManus was assisted by his second cousin, Dr Patrick Murphy, whose professional duties had brought him into direct contact with the Famine influx. In recognition of his heroic exertions, Murphy was invited to preside at a meeting in February 1848 to raise a memorial to the monks of St Benedict who had given up their lives in the typhus epidemic, the 'Irish fever', of 1847.[29] Significantly, two other members of the medical profession, Francis O'Donnell and Lawrence Reynolds, were among the most militant of the Liverpool Confederates in 1848.[30]

Working through Ribbonite networks, middle-class nationalist leaders reached deep into the migrant community. As the main port of entry, Liverpool played an essential role as the two main Ribbon societies extended their

---

26 Informers such as E. Rorke and P.H. McGloin were also recruited from these two-way commercial travellers, see Belchem, 'Ribbonism', p. 37.

27 I cannot agree with Frank Neal's assertion that the Confederate leaders in 1848 were 'men of no standing in Liverpool, indicative of the lack of political or organizational "weight"': F. Neal, *Sectarian Violence: The Liverpool Experience* (Manchester, 1988), p. 124.

28 T.G. McAllister, *Terence Bellew MacManus 1811(?)–1861* (Maynooth, 1972), draws extensively on the Clark Compendium, Diocese of Clogher Archives, Bishop's House, Monaghan (hereafter Clark Compendium). R. Carleton, a Waterford trader, praised MacManus's 'character for great integrity – so high his character that most of the Irish business was transferred to him', see National Library of Ireland (hereafter NLI), Mss 812, Briefs for the counsel in the trial of T.B. MacManus.

29 T.N. Burke, *Catholic History of Liverpool* (Liverpool, 1910), p.95.

30 For details of the leaders and events of 1848, see John Belchem, 'Liverpool in the year of revolution: the political and associational culture of the Irish immigrant community in 1848' in Belchem (ed.), *Popular Politics, Riot and Labour: Essays in Liverpool History 1790–1940* (Liverpool, 1992), pp 68–97. My conclusions differ significantly from two earlier studies: W.J. Lowe, 'The Chartists and the Irish Confederates: Lancashire 1848', *Irish Historical Studies*, vol. 24 (1984), pp 172–96; and Louis R. Bisceglia, 'The threat of violence: Irish Confederates and Chartists in Liverpool in 1848', *Irish Sword*, vol. 14 (1981), pp 207–15.

coverage to Britain, implanting 'secret' networks of pubs, temperance hotels and private houses. As in Ireland, Ribbonism in Liverpool was multi-functional and morally ambiguous: its secrecy and ritual served *inter alia* to promote republican revolution, organized crime, sectarian protection (the only qual-ification for membership was Catholicism) and collective mutuality (cheap, flexible and mobile 'tramping' benefits for those unable to gain employment). Protected by Ribbonite secrecy (alas, not immune to turn-coats and informers), middle-class nationalist leaders prepared to use para-miltary physical force.

> Every street in Liverpool and every town ought to have its club; every club its president, and other commanding officers; every club ought to take care of defending itself; every officer ought to have his rifle, every committee man his musket, and every member ought to have his pike. (Great cheers)[31]

Alarmed by the rapid spread of armed clubs, the local authorities placed the town under a state of siege. Having petitioned in vain for the Suspension of Habeas Corpus in Ireland to be extended to include Liverpool, they set legal objections aside to raid club premises. By chance, they stumbled across the Confederate minute book, a detailed record of committee membership and meetings. With its leaders in flight and most of its weapons seized, the Confederate conspiracy was rendered powerless on the eve of the Irish rising. MacManus (who had previously chartered three steamers to be on standby ready to sail to Wexford) was unable to provide either the direct assistance or diversionary activity in Liverpool which he had promised Duffy at secret discussions in Dublin in the wake of John Mitchel's trial. Bitterly disappointed, he made personal amends at Ballingarry, proving himself 'the boldest fellow among the entire body of insurgents'.[32]

Several years later, the National Brotherhood of St Patrick, a legal cover for Fenianism, was launched at a fund-raising meeting in Liverpool for the funeral of the exiled MacManus. The funeral in Dublin, a proto-type exercise in Irish political-funereal art, brought the Irish Republican Brotherhood (IRB) to public attention.[33] After the experience of 1848, however, the Liverpool-Irish middle class were reluctant to place themselves at the head of physical-force Fenianism: local leadership was undertaken by a veteran of the cause but a recent arrival in Liverpool, George Archdeacon.[34] John Ryan was the exception who proved the rule: the son of a prosperous Liverpool merchant, he was to

---

31 *Liverpool Mercury*, 13 June 1848.
32 For MacManus's own narrative of events, see Denis Gwynn, *Young Ireland and 1848* (Cork, 1949), appendix 3.
33 J. Newsinger, *Fenianism in Mid-Victorian Britain* (London, 1994), pp 26–7.
34 John Denvir, *The Irish in Britain* (London, 1892), pp 187–88, including details of Archdeacon's arrest in Liverpool on a Dublin police warrant.

devote his life to Fenian military service as 'Captain O'Doherty'.[35] While eschewing active involvement or leadership, the Liverpool-Irish middle class were prepared to offer 'cover', assistance and bail surety to Irish-American officers and other Fenians on military duty, in flight or under detention. Michael Breslin, a leading Fenian, posed as a traveller in the tea trade, having been specially supplied with samples and other credentials by the Liverpool tea merchant James Lysaght Finigan, later MP for Ennis (1879–82).[36] Similar resourcefulness later enabled the Liverpool-Irish middle class to ensure the continued appearance of *United Ireland* following its ban in Ireland: John Denvir made his printing presses available, while packaging and forwarding to Ireland were undertaken in one of the curing-sheds owned by Patrick De Lacy Garton, a wealthy wholesale fish dealer and Irish National councillor for Scotland Ward, 1877–83, and through the trade network of Edward Purcell, a prosperous Liverpool clothier, and Irish National councillor for Scotland ward, 1886–95.[37]

Despite persistent rumours that the highly respectable Liverpool Irish Rifle Corps of Volunteers, commanded by the Catholic Peter Bidwell, a corn importer and Liberal councillor, provided military training for Fenian recruits, police and intelligence reports confirmed the middle-class withdrawal from active leadership of insurrectionary nationalism. Liverpool Fenianism, its historian W.J. Lowe contends, was more important for its open-access pub-based conviviality, briefly shared with Irish-American officers, than for any military planning: 'the social significance of the Liverpool IRB outweighed its military or political importance'. Indeed, with its network of twenty or so pubs and beershops across the city, Fenianism was essentially a social affair which 'furnished a popular organisational foundation that helped to build the constitutional home rule movement'.[38]

The home rule movement brought middle-class nationalists back into the fold of constitutional politics. In so doing, it exposed cultural and political tensions, challenging the patrician ways and means of the elite in Catholic Liverpool. At the top of the scale, the wealthiest Irish Catholic merchants in Liverpool had acculturated themselves to the modern Tridentine norms and political alignment of the small and socially exclusive indigenous Catholic community – high levels of church attendance, and unquestioning support of the rich local Liberal (often Unitarian) merchants, progressive friends of Catholic emancipation. Henceforth their energies were expended on imposing these confessional and political norms on the ever-growing number of their co-

35 Denvir, *Life Story*, pp 74, 77–78 and 111–12.
36 Ibid., p. 124.
37 Ibid., pp 209–18.
38 W. J. Lowe, 'Lancashire Fenianism, 1864–71', *Transactions of the Historic Society of Lancashire and Cheshire*, vol. 126 (1977), pp 156–85.

religionists and fellow-countrymen in Liverpool; as Ireland arguably underwent its 'devotional revolution' only after 1850, many poor migrants were non-practising but not indifferent Catholics. With the advent of home rule, however, the sectarian infrastructure which patrician merchants had helped to construct in poorer parishes was appropriated for nationalist ends. Along with the ethno-sectarian pub-based network, it provided the base to challenge the distant Liberals.

At the time of the Famine influx, the most prominent and influential Irish Catholic merchant was Richard Sheil, cousin of the Irish Liberal MP and orator of the same name. Born in Dublin in 1790, Sheil travelled extensively, particularly in the Caribbean, promoting the Liverpool-based import and export agency of which he was a partner. The principal Catholic layman in Liverpool, and for long the only Catholic member of the council (where he sat as a Liberal), Sheil was a founder member of the Protector Society established in 1839 to register Catholic voters, and of its important successor, the Catholic Club.[39] Intended as a counterweight to Hugh McNeile's Protestant Association in the fierce controversy over the schools issue, the Catholic Club was to extend and solidify the Liberal alliance: prosperous middle-class Catholics, Irish and otherwise, were brought together in continuing support of Liberal candidates drawn from Unitarian and progressive ranks within the mercantile elite.[40]

A pillar of mercantile respectability who had acquired the 'solid and practical character of Englishmen', Sheil did not conceal his 'rich, mellifluous brogue' or his Irishness:

> Ireland has not a son who loves his country better ... He is ever to be found at the head of any movement which, in his opinion, is calculated to promote her political or religious welfare, and his enthusiasm on such occasions shows with what heartiness and zeal he spouses the cause of Ireland.[41]

However, there was a pronounced social conservatism to his political and public life. An intense Catholic, deeply distressed by the spread of 'philosophical unbelief' and social radicalism, Sheil's abiding concern was to prevent leakage from the faith among the ever-growing numbers of Irish in Liverpool. In a private letter written in 1854, in the wake of parliamentary attempts to intervene in the management of Catholic convents, he indicated his outlook and fears:

39 In 1857 he was joined on the Liberal benches in the council chamber by his Catholic business partner, J.C. Corbally.
40 Brady, pp 27–8.
41 H. Shimmin, *Pen-and-Ink Sketches of Liverpool Town Councillors* (Liverpool, 1866), pp 87–91, which observed; 'Some think that the honourable gentleman mistook his profession when he became a merchant, and that he would have achieved great distinction had he been an ecclesiastic'. See also the obituary notice in *Porcupine*, 4 Mar. 1871.

It is almost appalling to hear the lengths to which the bulk of non Catholic young men will go in denying the essential truths of Christianity, and as among the working classes there appears to be a perpetually encreasing (sic) spirit of opposition to the classes above them, I can not help thinking that we are living upon a half concealed volcano which will before many years elapse burst into an eruption as will not be very easily restrained.[42]

A communicant at St Oswald's, Old Swan, the most fashionable of local Catholic churches, Sheil took particular delight, as his letter-book attests, in arranging elite charity functions within the social 'season': in June and July 1853, for example, he organized a fancy dress ball and a soirée in aid of Catholic charity schools.[43] Other aspects of his considerable charitable work were more tiresome.

The cost of building (and maintaining) the Catholic parochial and charitable framework to accommodate the Irish influx was a constant drain on limited resources. 'In most of the other Dioceses (sic) of England', Bishop Brown noted enviously, 'there is a greater number of extensive landed proprietors Catholics than in this Diocess [sic]'.[44] As it outstretched the generosity of the indigenous Catholic community, church provision depended on the goodwill of Irish merchants, prepared to donate money, resources and time. Pending proper premises, warehouses were used as places of worship – this was a variant on earlier practice when the original Edmund Street chapel, destroyed by a Hanoverian mob in 1746, was rebuilt under the disguise of a warehouse by the Irish merchant Henry Pippard.[45] Commercial business skills were put to use in organizing subscription schemes and weekly penny collections for church building, a method pioneered by a group of newly-arrived Irish merchants in the south end where the first mission church, appropriately named St Patrick's, opened for worship in 1824. Thereafter the focus of attention switched to the north end, where most new (Catholic) Irish arrivals were to settle. St Antony's, a small chapel built by French refugees, was rebuilt in the early 1830s through the efforts of a subscription committee assisted by local Hibernian Societies and by a Ladies' Society 'established for the purpose of providing whatever is requisite and becoming for the service of the altar, and the decoration of the

42 NLI, Mss 32,483: Letter-book of Richard H. Sheil, 1850–56, ff. 365–66, letter dated 9 June 1854.

43 Sheil Letter-book, f.318, Sheil to Runge, 15 Apr. 1853, one of many letters on such matters. For the 'elite' at St Oswald's, see Dublin Diocesan Archives: Cullen Papers, 353/2/101, Father McGinity to Dr Cullen, 3 Dec. 1852.

44 Lancashire Record Office: Archdiocese of Liverpool papers, RCLv, Box 40, Bishop Brown 'To the Clergy Only', 23 May 1853.

45 J.A. Klapas, 'Geographical aspects of religious change in Victorian Liverpool, 1837–1901' (University of Liverpool MA thesis, 1977), p. 24.

chapel'.[46] Besides the mounting debt-burden of the mission churches and parish-based schools (regarded as essential after the Tories brought an end in 1841 to the local Liberals' 'crucial experiment' of non-denominational public education on the Irish model),[47] funds were required for extra-parochial institutional and other forms of charity to meet Liverpool's special needs.[48] The poor, a pastoral letter explained, 'are a burden laid by God on the rich; but here it is no customary burden, but swollen out of all proportion by the most helpless classes of a neighbouring country, throwing themselves for support on the richer sister Island'.[49] Through asylums and reformatories, the 'worst' of the Famine poor, reduced to crime and depredation on the streets of Liverpool, were to be rescued for the faith. In the absence of any suitable replacement of equivalent status, Sheil was compelled to continue in office not only as President but also as Treasurer of the Catholic Club, responsible for door-to-door collection of subscriptions for such priority causes.

Sectarian rivalry added to the urgency. Catholic philanthropy sought to negate the bigotry and expose the deficiencies of civic social policy, Protestant sins of commission and omission later to be chronicled by Thomas Burke, a second-generation Irish-Liverpudlian, prosperous poulterer with a stall in St John's market, Irish National councillor for Vauxhall, 1899–1921, and historian of Catholic Liverpool.[50] Above all was the need to counter 'the fearful leakage of Catholic children under Poor Law management', the sorry fate of unfortunate children, often newly-arrived from Ireland, who were taken in care by the Liverpool authorities but denied proper Catholic religious instruction in the workhouse and industrial schools. On behalf of the Catholic Club, Sheil under-wrote an annual contribution of £50 per annum towards the cost of a Catholic chaplain at the Kirkdale industrial schools, on the understanding that a matching sum would be provided by the recently-formed Irish Catholic Club. He was soon complaining that the new society was not fulfilling its share of the obligations:

> The entire task of collecting subscriptions for the maintenance of the Catholic Chaplain to the industrial schools has been allowed to fall upon me and as you will easily conceive this circumstance not only causes very serious inconvenience to me but is also attended with much danger to the charity, for nothing but the great stagnation of business could have enabled me to spare the amount of time which I have already devoted to going about in search of subscriptions.[51]

46 RCLv Box 40, Relation Status Missiorum in Diocesi Liverpolitana, and Box 28 for more material on St Anthony's.
47 Mary Hickman, *Religion, Class and Identity: The State, the Catholic Church and the Education of the Irish in Britain* (Aldershot, 1995), pp 139–48.
48 Sheil Letter-book, ff. 351–52, Sheil to editor of the *Catholic Standard*, 1 Dec. 1853.
49 RCLv Box 40, Pastoral letter, 13 June 1854.
50 T.N. Burke, *Catholic History of Liverpool* (Liverpool, 1910), p. 165 and *passim*.
51 Sheil Letter-book, f. 392 to President of the Irish Catholic Club, 19 Dec. 1854. See also,

The Irish Catholic Club, established amid the controversy surrounding the restoration of the Catholic hierarchy, represented the first tentative step away from the Liberal alliance and mainstream party politics: it aimed to return an independent Catholic MP for the city within twenty years. However, in social composition and political practice it differed little from the Catholic Club. The leading figure was the Wexford-born merchant James Whitty who came to Liverpool in 1848, established business as a woollen draper and entered local politics via membership of the Select Vestry (1853–65), thence as Liberal councillor for Vauxhall (1863–73). He was the cousin of M.J. Whitty, another county Wexford man: originally from farming stock, he progressed through trade and journalism in Dublin and London to enjoy a long and varied career in Liverpool as its first head constable (the appointment of a Catholic to this sensitive post was one of the more imaginative and successful aspects of the Liberals' brief tenure of office in the 1830s), proprietor-editor of the *Liverpool Journal* and founder of the *Daily Post*.[52]

For the most part, the Catholic Club and the Irish Catholic Club worked amicably together as middle-class representatives of the Irish Catholic community. On a fund-raising trip for a Catholic University of Ireland, Father McGinity endeavoured to create some competitive rivalry between the two societies, but the tactic misfired. He was politely informed by the Bishop that he had outstayed his welcome in Liverpool: 'The wants of religion in the town are numerous and pressing indeed I may say greater than can be *adequately* supplied and you know that *Charitas bene ordinata* begins at home'.[53] Confronted by the full force of the Famine influx, the Catholic church redefined its mission: philanthropic and associational provision, along with the recruitment of clerical personnel, underwent a process of 'hibernicization' more rapid and thorough than elsewhere in England (although still stopping short at the upper echelons of the local hierarchy).[54] The overwhelming concern, as Bishop Brown made clear to the local clergy, was not with the

f. 393 to Bishop of Liverpool, 27 Jan. 1855; f. 400 to James Whitty, 15 June 1855; f. 414 to Revd R. Shea, 29 Oct. 1855; and f. 415 to Canon Newsham, 30 Oct. 1855.

52 Brady, p.28. Biographical details can be found in the appendices to C.D. Watkinson, 'The Liberal Party on Merseyside in the Nineteenth Century' (University of Liverpool PhD thesis, 1967, and B. O'Connell, 'The Irish Nationalist Party in Liverpool, 1873–1922' (University of Liverpool MA thesis, 1971).

53 See the correspondence between McGinity and Brown, 12 and 13 Jan. 1853, in Cullen papers 325/8/1.

54 David Fitzpatrick, '"A peculiar tramping people": the Irish in Britain, 1801–70' in W.E. Vaughan (ed.), *A New History of Ireland, V. Ireland under the Union* (Oxford, 1989), pp 650–54. For problems of clerical recruitment, see All Hallows College, Dublin: Correspondence with the Diocese of Liverpool, 1853–68. It includes details of discount fares offered by Liverpool-based Irish shipowners for All Hallows-trained priests bound for America and Australia, see Revd R. McCart, 9 Nov. 1853.

requirements of Ireland, but with the spiritual and material welfare of its migrants, 'the poor of the sister country, who are living among us and under our own eyes. These are a portion of that flock for which I and you have to be answerable to the Divine Lord of the Vineyard'.[55]

As sectarian rivalry intensified, Catholics proudly asserted their supremacy in welfare provision. Cultural style and strategy came to separate what might be termed Protestant 'scientific charity' from Catholic 'alms-giving'.[56] While the Liverpool Domestic Mission, founded by members of the Methodist Chapel on Renshaw Street, saw itself as an agency for moral reform rather than of relief distribution, Catholic charity, such as the Brotherhood of St Vincent de Paul for whom Father Nugent and Richard Sheil were active recruiters, operated as a 'General Purposes Society', granting generous relief in case of need and where there was proof of minimal religious observance.[57] Instead of moral condemnation – such censure was reserved for duplicitous 'begging priests' from across the water[58] – Catholic leaders, clerical and lay, displayed an understanding of material destitution. Brought together in serious discussion of social issues at Nugent's Catholic Institute in Hope Street, leading local Catholics took an inverse pride, as it were, in the destitution of Irish immigrants, 'the thousands of homeless, moneyless, raimentless, foodless creatures that call the Catholic Church their mother in Liverpool'.[59] Indeed, such environmentalism extended to migrants seemingly lost to the faith:

> The best of the labouring classes do not emigrate. Those who do, are not treated on their coming, with kindness and considerateness – very much the reverse. They must descend to the worst work, and accept the worst pay … they are on all sides treated with disrespect, and in many cases, unfortunately, they fail to respect themselves. Their new circumstances suggest brutal habits, and equally brutal enjoyments … Those men of course are not Catholic, but they are not Protestant, and they are Irish.[60]

55 RCLv: Box 40, Brown 'To the Clergy Only', 23 May 1853.

56 For an incisive exploration of this difference, see Martha Kanya-Forstner, 'Gender, ethnicity and the politics of poverty: Irish women in Victorian Liverpool' (University of Liverpool PhD thesis, 1997).

57 Sheil Letter-book, f. 328, Brotherhood of St Vincent de Paul, 7 July 1853. See also, John Davies, 'Parish charity: the work of the Society of St Vincent de Paul, St Mary's, Highfield Street, Liverpool, 1867–68', *North West Catholic History*, vol. XVII (1990), pp 37–46. For an interesting comparison, see Bernard Aspinwall, 'The Welfare State within the State: the Saint Vincent de Paul Society in Glasgow, 1848–1920' in W.J. Sheils and D.Wood, *Studies in Church History: Voluntary Religion* (Oxford, 1986) pp 445–59.

58 There is much condemnation of such 'promiscuous begging' in Brown's pastoral letters, RCLv: Box 40.

59 'Church-Going in Liverpool', *Catholic Institute Magazine*, Nov. 1855. For the Catholic Institute, see Canon Bennett, *Father Nugent of Liverpool* (Liverpool, 1949), ch.2.

60 'Reformatories – their nature, origin and tendency', *Catholic Institute Magazine*, Sept. 1856.

Thenceforth, Catholics claimed the depraved Irish as their particular concern, their special mission for spiritual salvation and welfare protection.

Dialectical developments in other denominations completed the process by which Irishness and Catholicism became synonymous in Victorian Liverpool. Irishness of this order was not simply a matter of 'invented' self-ascription by the Catholics: ethnicity was fluid and relational, part of the socio-historical dialogue (including name-calling and posturing) between dominant and subordinate groups.[61] Presbyterian migrants were cast adrift from their former home: links with Ulster were broken as they were brought within the British synod. The Irish Islington Church in Liverpool, formed in 1843 by Irish Presbyterian migrants, connected itself with the Presbytery of Belfast. A bitter dispute ensued with the Presbytery of Lancaster which was not resolved until the name Irish was deleted, and the General Assembly of the Presbyterian Church in Ireland had disclaimed 'any intention of invading the jurisdiction or territory of the English Synod'.[62] Members of the Reformed Presbyterian Congregation in Liverpool, part of the Eastern Synod of the Reformed Presbyterian Church in Ireland, tried to retain ministerial (and other) links with Belfast, but were finally compelled to transfer allegiance to the Reformed Presbytery of Glasgow in 1857 (under whose auspices a church was built in Shaw Street).[63] On an informal level, however, they continued to provide a reception service at Liverpool for emigrant Ulster Presbyterians en route to America.[64]

As the Catholics claimed the Irish as their own, Anglo-Irish evangelicals in Liverpool stood forward as the standard bearers of British Protestantism, led by the redoubtable Revd Hugh McNeile, 'eloquent even beyond Irish eloquence, Protestant even beyond Irish Protestantism'.[65] Samuel Holme, the Tory culture-broker, applauded their prominence in local Protestant associations:

61 For discussion of the issues involved here, see John Belchem, 'Ethnicity and labour history: with special reference to Irish migration', paper presented at the foundation conference of Labnet on 'The State of Labour and Working-Class History in Europe', Amsterdam, 17–18 February 1997.

62 'The Rise and Progress of Presbyterianism in Liverpool' in *Jubilee Memorial of Canning Street Presbyterian Church* (n.p., n.d), pp 119–20. *Minutes of the General Assembly of the Presbyterian Church in Ireland* (Belfast, 1850), pp 315 and 381.

63 Public Record Office of Northern Ireland (hereafter PRONI): CR5/3, Reformed Presbyterian Church Records: Shaw Street, Liverpool. Presbyterian Historical Society of Ireland, *Minutes of the Annual Meeting of the Eastern Reformed Synod in Ireland at its meeting in Belfast 1857*, p. 20.

64 PRONI: D1835/27/5/3, Letter from Liverpool to James Staveley, 1 Dec. 1860 (on emigration database at Ulster-American Folk Park).

65 'A Celebrated Ulster Divine', *Belfast News-Letter*, 5 April 1924, cutting in Bigger Collection, Belfast City Library.

> We are deeply indebted to the Irish clergy ... Irish energy, and Irish vivacity,
> have assisted to kindle the latent warmth of England, and united, they emit a
> cheerful blaze ... on their fidelity, humanly speaking, the destiny and glory of this
> country mainly depends (hear): and I trust that every pulpit throughout England
> will ring with a sound and scriptural defence of Protestant principles (cheers).66

Fuelled by sensational and lurid stories of the horrors of Catholicism in Ireland, militant Protestantism was to resonate with the wider British public. Although an Irish implant, Protestant sectarianism drew upon an English narrative of libertarian struggle in which 'it is to their qualities, derived from their religion, that Englishmen owe their liberties'. McNeile, a master of populist rhetoric, invoked the patriotic duty to defend 'the glory of England, her open bible, her liberty, her free press, her independence of mind in determining to stand by her law, and not to allow any man, sovereign or subject, to be absolute in the land'.[67] Militant Protestant sectarianism became the very symbol of British patriotism, integral to the 'common sense' of the working man.[68] McNeile's Operative Protestant Association was quickly incorporated within the panoply of local Tory organizations alongside the Operative Conservative Association and other militant Protestant voluntary groups, including the rejuvenated Orange Order which recruited strongly among workers with no Ulster connections. Irish Protestantism was subsumed within a wider British membership and identity, upheld by an interlocking associational network (or 'pillar' to use Dutch terminology) – party, popular and sectarian – which facilitated ready interaction between the classes.[69]

Protestant Liverpool, however, lacked a parish-based 'welfare' support and out-reach structure to match Catholic provision, a deficiency which troubled Abraham Hume, statistician, urban sociologist and from 1847 Anglican vicar of the new district of Vauxhall. Born in county Down into a Presbyterian family, Hume renounced his religious upbringing and heritage on becoming an Anglican. Continued internal dispute with his family developed into strident repudiation of all forms of Nonconformity.[70] A great advocate of the territorial parish system, he condemned the dissenters in Liverpool for deserting the

---

66 *Seventh Annual Report of the Liverpool Protestant Association* (Liverpool, 1842), pp 46–7.

67 Revd Hugh McNeile, *The Gunpowder Plot and the Revolution of 1688* (Liverpool, 1854), p. 12.

68 Joan Smith, 'Class, skill and sectarianism in Glasgow and Liverpool, 1880–1914' in R.J. Morris (ed.), *Class, Power and Social Structure in British Nineteenth-Century Towns* (Leicester, 1986), pp 158–215.

69 John Belchem, 'Introduction: The Peculiarities of Liverpool' in Belchem (ed.), *Popular Politics, Riot and Labour*, pp 10–12.

70 See, for example, Hume to George Hume, 25 Jan. 1845, Letter-book 3, f.137, PRONI: D2765 papers of the Hume Family. There is much similar correspondence in this large archive.

poor: based on the voluntary or congregational principle, Nonconformist churches had followed richer members of the congregation out into the suburbs. To Hume's dismay, the parish system was weak in Anglican Liverpool: much of the town council church building of the eighteenth century had subverted the system; endowments were woefully inadequate, and richer parishes did little to help the poorer.[71] Undeterred, Hume sought to employ middle-class deaconesses to assist in the church's 'home mission to the poor', distinguishing their role from that of either 'Bible-women' or 'District-Nurses': 'From the former indeed our plan is distinguished by its embracing the official employment of women of the higher ranks, and by its organization being parochial, – from the latter by its aiming chiefly at spiritual ends while not forgetting the temporal'.[72]

While high-minded Anglicans sought to reach down to the poor, Irish Catholics in the north end took advantage of the multiplication of parish organizations – 'vereinskatholizismus' to use the German term – designed to meet every need, spiritual, economic and recreational, from cradle to grave.[73] Liverpool's north end evolved as a distinctively Irish community in which new churches with Irish priests became the centre of associational life, not least for women, encouraging the tendency to residential propinquity.[74] In welfare and other functions, the Catholic parish co-existed in complementary rivalry with the local pub where Irishness was given a more masculine expression. Unlike the Liverpool Liberal elite, distant and socially exclusive, Catholic priests (often poor Irish lads themselves) and the new generation of Irish nationalist politicians (often upwardly mobile within the community) displayed a willingness to compromise with the street and the pub.[75] Here was the structural and cultural basis for political independence.

The leading protagonist of home rule was John Denvir, a second-generation, upwardly-mobile Irish-Liverpudlian turned full-time political activist – much to his delight, he could claim Irish birth, having entered the world in county Antrim when his parents briefly returned to the homeland on a work contract. Having followed in his father's footsteps as an apprentice joiner with a Liverpool firm of builders, Denvir established his own business in the trade.

71 L.E. Bosworth, 'Home missionaries to the poor: Abraham Hume and spiritual destitution in Liverpool, 1847–84', *Transactions of the Historic Society of Lancashire and Cheshire*, vol. 143 (1993), pp 57–83.

72 Hume Letter-book 10, f. 220, handbill, 'Female Parochial Agency for Liverpool' (n.d.).

73 H. McLeod, 'Building the "Catholic Ghetto": Catholic Organizations 1870–1914', in Sheils and Wood (eds), *Voluntary Religion*, pp 411–44.

74 Papworth, chapter V. See also, Frank Boyce, 'Irish Catholicism in Liverpool: the 1920s and 1930s' in J. Belchem and P. Buckland (eds), *The Irish in British Labour History* (Liverpool, 1993), pp 86–101.

75 R. Samuel, 'The Roman Catholic Church and the Irish Poor' in R. Swift and S. Gilley (eds), *The Irish in the Victorian City* (Beckenham, 1985), pp 267–300.

Thereafter, Nugent's patronage carried him upward, in recognition perhaps of his prowess as an evening class student at the Catholic Institute and of his enthusiastic adoption of the temperance cause. Denvir was the first to take the pledge at Nugent's League of the Cross. Presumably ignorant of Denvir's Fenian connections, Nugent appointed him Secretary of the Catholic Boys Refuge, the showpiece of Catholic institutional charity, and then put him in charge of the *Catholic Times*. From his new printing and newsagency business in Byrom Street, Denvir turned his talents to full-time promotion of the nationalist cause: as well as his famous 'Irish Library' publications, he was responsible for the *United Irishmen*, organ of the new Home Rule Confederation, of which he was a founder member and later its national agent and organizer. As secretary of the Catholic Club, Denvir hoped to carry its rich merchants and Liberal councillors into the home rule camp. Soon disabused by such 'anti-Irish Irishmen', he devoted his energies to securing the return of independent Irish National councillors.[76]

Efforts were concentrated on the Scotland and Vauxhall wards, where the extensive parish and pub-based ethnic infrastructure facilitated an effective challenge to the traditional Liberal alignment. Aided by some enthusiastic electioneering by a local priest, Father McGrath, Denvir secured Lawrence Connolly's return for the Scotland Ward in 1875. Further electoral successes were to follow: Connolly was the first of 48 Irish Nationalists to sit on the council between 1875 and 1922. Furthermore, the Scotland Division became T.P. O'Connor's parliamentary fiefdom from 1885 to 1929, secured by the same ethnic electoral machinery. O'Connor's contribution to Liverpool Irish politics was minimal, however: a carpet-bag national political figure, he rarely visited the city and was a poor constituency member.[77]

Although a new departure, home rule drew upon the traditional leadership cadre. The mixture of continuity and change is perhaps best exemplified by the fate of the McArdle cousins, prosperous cotton merchants originally from Monaghan. Charles gained a Vauxhall seat for the Irish nationalists in 1876, while his cousin John, standing on the old Liberal Catholic Club platform, was unseated in the Scotland ward by Dr Bligh, the Irish National candidate. Biographical details of the Irish National Party councillors show three major groups, the first two of which had previously been prominent in the Liberal-oriented Catholic Club. First, there were lawyers, doctors (including Bligh and his brother, close friends of Parnell) and other professionals whose practices covered the Irish community. There were no fewer than four INP councillors

---

76 Denvir, *Life Story, passim.*
77 Strictly speaking there was not an Irish National party, but five official home rule organizations which succeeded each other. However, there are good reasons to use the portmanteau term as O'Connell's thesis (indispensable for electoral and biographical detail) shows.

in the office of Irish-born solicitor W. Madden (O'Hare, Lynskey, Flynn and Madden himself who represented the Scotland ward, 1885–87). In the upper professional echelons, the Liberal affiliation tended to persist. Thus, Charles Russell (later Lord Russell of Killowen), the most distinguished Irish barrister on the Liverpool-based Northern circuit, and the first choice of Denvir and Crilly to chair the local home rulers, declined to abandon the Liberals. However, his fellow barrister, the patrician Dr Andrew Commins, a pronounced anti-Fenian, served in his place; a member for the Vauxhall ward (1876–92), he acted as leader of the group on the council.[78] The second major group consisted of traders who prospered and/or diversified as they took responsibility for the Liverpool end of Irish businesses. Connolly, the first to be elected, was a good example. A farmer's son from county Dublin, he came to Liverpool in 1857 in connection with his brother's Dublin-based business. Branching out from the family firm, he established his own business as fruit-broker and commission merchant, and then moved into property speculation, gaining a fortune from resort development at New Brighton (he left £78,000 in his will). Others included the aforementioned Limerick-born Patrick De Lacy Garton, wholesale fish dealer and owner of a large herring fleet at Howth and Kinsale, and O. O'Hara, undisputed 'king' of the Irish egg trade. In typical Irish Liverpudlian fashion, business success carried O'Hara (who came to Liverpool from Ireland in the early 1860s) into politics: a generous donor to party funds (he also made his Scotland Road premises available for party meetings), he was rewarded with a seat in the South Scotland ward (1895–8). The final group, new to political leadership, included shopkeepers and others who attended to the daily needs of the Liverpool-Irish; these included the undertaking service provided at branches throughout the city by Dundalk-born J. Daly, member for North Scotland, 1895–1902. Here there were some genuine 'rags to riches' stories, retail entrepreneurs who made their fortune supplying basic pleasures within the ethnic 'enclave' – for example, J. Clancy (St Anne's, 1904–05; North Scotland, 1911–25) who began as a 'hotel boots' and then developed a lucrative tobacconist business, worth over £25,000 on his death; and 'Dandy' Pat Byrne (Scotland 1883; Vauxhall, 1884–90) who started work as a dock labourer, before acquiring a string of public houses, a remarkable wardrobe and a fortune estimated at £40,000. Only two of the Irish National councillors could be considered working class, the first to serve on Liverpool council: J.G. Taggart (Vauxhall, 1888–1908) who rose from trade union office to become an estate agent (and thenceforth vehemently anti-Labour); and T. Kelly (Vauxhall, 1890–1895) an unsalaried commission agent.

78 Commins anti-Fenianism doubtless accounts for his disparaging (and inaccurate) recollections of MacManus, see Commins to Clark, 12 May 1894, Clark Compendium: Envelope F.

The emergence of this new group reflected a continuing pattern of fissure and radicalization in home rule nationalism in Liverpool. Division over Parnell and Irish policy was accentuated by local concerns: the desire to eradicate all vestige of patrician Liberal dependence, and the determination to protect the interests of the Catholic working-class community against the dominant Tory political machine. As local leadership of the Irish National Party passed steadily into the hands of second-generation (i.e. Liverpool-born) Irish, it displayed less interest in the fate of Ireland than in the immediate needs of the local Catholic community in housing and employment. Even so, the leadership remained distinctly middle class. The new social radicalism owed much to the Harford brothers, Austin and Frank, scions of a prosperous Liverpool-Irish mercantile family in the woollen and cloth trade. Liverpool-born and educated, they successfully combined business and politics (Austin left £76,686 in his will). Having entered the council for South Scotland in 1898 and 1899 respectively, they developed a form of community politics which depended first on a large network of confidants able to produce the goods, and second on the continued estrangement of the Liverpool Irish from other, class-based, political forma-tions. The slow advance of Labour in Liverpool was a tribute to their success.[79] Home rule matured into what Sam Davies has described as 'Nat-labism', a cross-class political formation which proved more resonant and enduring than conventional Lib-Labism elsewhere.[80]

Liverpool stands outside the narrative patterns of modern British history. Its pattern of ethnic-sectarian political affiliation has been ignored or dispar-aged. In calling for historical deconstruction of the complex mechanics of ethnic mobilization, this paper has shown the need to study the interaction between class, creed and country. Particular attention has been accorded to elements within the Catholic middle class, the 'Micks on the make' who were to implant, celebrate and control a distinctive form of Irishness. As promoted by successful migrants, ethnic assertion has tended to be pluralist in purpose, a means of mobilizing resources to gain recognition and inclusion within the wider host society, as in the hyphenated identity secured and enjoyed by Irish-Americans.[81] Across the Atlantic, middle-class promotion of celtic cultural

79 See the articles by A. Shallice, 'Orange and Green and militancy; sectarianism and working-class politics in Liverpool, 1900–1914', and 'Liverpool Labourism and Irish Nationalism in the 1920s and 1930s', *Bulletin of the North West Labour History Society*, vol. 6 (1979–80), pp 15–32, and 8 (1981–2), pp 19–28.
80 Sam Davies, '"A Stormy political Career": P.J. Kelly and Irish Nationalist and Labour Politics in Liverpool, 1891–1936', unpublished paper. See also his *Liverpool Labour: Social and Political Influences on the Development of the Labour Party in Liverpool, 1900–39* (Keele, 1996), pp 69–73.
81 R.A. Kazal, 'Revisiting Assimilation: The Rise, Fall, and Reappraisal of a Concept in American Ethnic History', *American Historical Review*, vol. 100 (1995), pp 437–71.

ethnicity conformed to the norms and values of the host society respecting its foundation myths and unifying civic culture. In Liverpool, Irish nationalism displayed a similar degree of political conformity, hence its blessing by the Catholic Church: as a constitutional project, violence was excluded, socialist radicalism was marginalized, while the poor were instructed in respectability and citizenship. However, in taking such active charge of these tasks, the middle-class culture brokers constructed a self-enclosed, self-sufficient network which, viewed from the host outside, emphasized Irish Catholic apartness. Ironically, the bid for inclusion served to confirm Irish 'difference': they remained the internal 'other' against whom the otherwise 'non-ethnic' English defined themselves.

Nationalists in exile: the National Brotherhood of St Patrick in Lancashire, 1861–5

Gerard Moran

The history of Fenianism in the 1860s has been adequately covered in the biographies and autobiographies of its leading figures and in the work of Leon Ó Bróin and R.V. Comerford.[1] The research of Paul Rose and John Newsinger has broadened our understanding of the movement in Britain.[2] However, major gaps remain in our knowledge of the overall position of Irish nationalism in the 1860s, and nowhere is this more evident than for the National Brotherhood of St Patrick, which has been largely ignored or regarded as peripheral by historians. Not only does the organisation tell us much about Irish nationalism, but a good deal about Irish emigrants and nationalism. Most of these emigrants were poor, and blamed the British government for their exile. Many had been forced out of their small holdings in Ireland and had no alternative but to settle in Britain, a country that they hated and despised. They felt inferior in a society which regarded their language as foreign and their religion as 'a jibe and a reproach'.[3] William Lowe has argued that there was a common image among the Irish of themselves as involuntary emigrants who were forced out of their homes by an uncaring government and an exploitative landlord class and, for those who developed this exile mentality, it was not surprising that they came to support Irish nationalist activities and organisations, blaming British political and economic misrule for their situation.[4] One of the first of these organisations with a radical and militant approach was the National Brotherhood of St Patrick, and nowhere was this more evident than in Lancashire. This essay

1 See Leon Ó Bróin, *Fenian Fever: An Anglo-American Dilemna* (New York, 1971); R.V. Comerford, *The Fenians in Context: Irish Politics and Society, 1848–82* (Dublin and New Jersey, 1985); ibid., 'Conspiring brotherhoods and contending elites, 1857–63', in W.E. Vaughan (ed.), *A New History of Ireland*, vol. V. *Ireland under the Union, 1, 1801–70* (Oxford, 1989), pp 415–30.
2 See Patrick Quinlivan and Paul Rose, *The Fenians in England, 1865–1872* (London and New York, 1982); John Newsinger, *Fenianism in Mid-Victorian Britain* (London and Boulder, Colorado, 1994).
3 *Nation*, 16 Feb. 1856.
4 W.J. Lowe, *The Irish in Mid-Victorian Lancashire: The shaping of a working class community* (New York, 1989), p. 11.

is essentially a study of the local Lancastrian dimension of the movement, which was most important to it, though not without reference to its existence elsewhere.

I

The National Brotherhood of St Patrick was established at the Rotunda in Dublin on 17 March 1861. Its leading personalities were Thomas Neilson Underwood, a barrister from Strabane; Dennis Holland, proprietor of the Dublin-based advanced nationalist newspaper, *The Irishman*; Clinton Hoey, the sub-editor of the *Dublin Review*, and the Dublin Fenian, Thomas Ryan. However, the man most closely associated with the Brotherhood was Father Patrick Lavelle, the radical parish priest of Partry, county Mayo, who became its vice-president in 1862. Among its objectives were the arrangement of nationalist functions, the co-ordination of the efforts of all who advocated nationalist policies, and the celebration of the national feast of St Patrick's Day.[5] The Brotherhood had nine rules, including 'the promotion of cordial union, based on devotion to the independence of our common country, amongst Irishmen of every class and creed'. The sole qualification for membership was 'fidelity to this principle of nationality'. Local branches were allowed make their own by-laws and branch secretaries could communicate with other branches if they so desired, but no attempt was made for this on a regular basis.[6]

The Brotherhood regarded itself as 'simply an organisation of Irishmen, resolved and held together by the resolve to win for Ireland her freedom, and restore a certain equitable title in the soil to the Irish people ... Its rules are legal, its means constitutional, and its objects legitimate'.[7] It set out to raise a constitutional nationalist movement out of the ashes of the Independent Irish Party of the 1850s, but it was merely a loose connection of enthusiasts with little in common except an attachment to the principle of nationality and a desire to gain Irish independence through unity. It also wanted to establish reading rooms where nationalists could congregate and discuss the issues of the day. Initially it had hoped to establish a newspaper to publicise its aims, but the nearest it came to achieving this was an arrangement with the *United Irishman and Galway American* in July 1863.[8]

5 John Moloney, 'The National Brotherhood of St Patrick and the rise of Dublin Fenianism, 1858–1865' (U.C.G. MA thesis, 1976), p. 22; N.L.I. Ms 447 (3257), William Smith O'Brien Papers, Thomas Neilson Underwood to Smith O'Brien, 1 Jan. 1862; N.L.I., Ms 7517, Thomas Larcom Papers, p. 96; Dublin Diocesan Archives (D.D.A.), Paul Cullen Papers (Laity, Jan.–June 1863), dated April 1863; Comerford, 'Conspiring brotherhoods', p. 424.
6 *Irishman*, 13 April 1861.
7 Ibid., 15 Mar. 1862.
8 See Toby Joyce, *The Galway American, 1862–3*, pt. 1: James Roche and the American Civil War', *Journal of the Galway Archaeological and Historical Society*, 47 (1995), pp 108–37.

The spread of the organisation in Britain largely coincided with the pattern of Irish settlement in Britain after the Famine. The main clusters of branches were established in four main centres: London, Yorkshire, greater Glasgow and Lancashire. While branches existed in Birmingham, Wolverhamption and Newcastle-upon-Tyne, they were largely isolated and did not benefit from contact with the larger groups. At its height there were at least thirty branches in Lancashire. Each local committee had twenty-one members, including a president, two vice-presidents, a treasurer and a secretary. The Lancashire branches chose a new committee every three months, probably because of the high turnover of members and because they held on to the old committee structures from the Irish Confederate days of the late 1840s. Their use of the model of the Confederate clubs was not surprising, as many of the Lancashire leadership had been involved in the clubs. New members had to present themselves at the meetings and be proposed by existing members. The chairman then announced the names and asked if there were any objections to them. Members were not bound by any oath or obligations, but paid a weekly subscription, which varied between 1*d*. to 2*d*., which covered the expenses of the branch.[9]

The most important feature of the Brotherhood was that it provided the Irish in Lancashire with a means of unity, as the starting point for all was their love of Ireland. By 1861 the Irish in Liverpool complained that the St Patrick's Day celebrations in the city were being taken over 'by personages who are truly English in birth and principle, and who condescend to take the chair on such occasions, to treat the Irish to a little speechifying'.[10] By the early 1860s the Irish in Lancashire were recognising their strong bonds of national identity. They were the nearest Irish emigrant community to Ireland and political and social influences first appeared in Lancashire.

The Brotherhood attempted to unite Irishmen of all political and religious persuasions into one national organisation. While it hoped to bring the Catholics of the South and the Presbyterians of the North together, in Lancashire the branches were overwhelmingly Catholic. If Irish Protestants in Lancashire entertained any notion of joining the Brotherhood, they were quickly dispelled by its advanced nationalist views. John J. Finigan's lecture at the inauguration of the Stalybridge branch in November spoke of 'England's difficulty being Ireland's opportunity'. In the early stages, the Liverpool leadership was fully aware of the divisions that could arise through the sectarian conflict which was never far below the surface in the city. As a result, most of the meetings in Liverpool highlighted the Protestant contribution to Irish nationalism, and the memories of Grattan, Tone, Plunket, Fitzgerald, Emmet and Davis were constantly toasted and recalled. During 1863–4, many branches were renamed after these patriots and their companions in the United Irishmen and Young

---

9   *Irishman*, 20 July 1861.
10   Ibid., 13 July 1861.

Ireland movements. Many of the smaller Lancashire branches such as Bolton, Preston, Oldham and Blackburn, saw their role as bringing all Irishmen into their ranks, so that they could further the cause of Ireland. The ubiquitous statements emphasised that Irishmen had to unite if they were to achieve anything. Throughout July, August and September 1861, the branches in Lancashire exhorted the Irish in their region to join the Brotherhood. Dennis Holland, of the *Irishman*, in a speech to the Lord Edward Street branch in Liverpool in July 1861, stressed this point: 'I say then to you, Irishmen in England, organise, unite, learn how to work together'.[11]

Initially, the Brotherhood encapsulated Irishmen of all different feelings in Lancashire. The meetings in March 1861 indicated an interest in Irish history, mythology, religion and politics. Compared to the Fenian movement, the Brotherhood had a broader concept of nationalism, not confining itself to the rigid issue of freedom for Ireland. While it helped in the development of the overall philosophical thinking of Irish nationalism, the Brotherhood also appealed to Irish culture, literature and heritage. Providing reading rooms and lectures on Irish themes was an integral part of this program. The Brotherhood wanted to educate the Irish, 'instructing the most illiterate mind', and thereby go on to achieve independence for Ireland.[12]

The branches had an important social role, providing the Irish in Britain with a place to meet and an outlet for expressing their Irish identity. Thus, Thomas O'Neill addressed a full hall on 'The Invasion of Ireland by Strongbow and its consequences' for the Deansgate branch in Manchester. John J. Finigan's lecture on 'Our fatherland, its rights and our responsibilities' to the Oldham Road branch in Manchester in August 1861, was also well attended; similarly a good crowd turned out to hear W. T. Cleary of Manchester speak to the Ashton-under-Lyne branch on 'Ireland's past and future glories, and the duties of Irishmen at home and abroad'.[13] The lectures can be divided into two groups: Ireland's history and its greatness, and Ireland's current plight and poverty, for which the English government was blamed. Many lectures had a purely military theme, such as 'The battle of Benburb', 'The battle of Clontarf' and 'The battle of Aughrim'. These glorified Irish military successes over England and were meant to arouse the military aspects of Irish nationalism. Others were organised to commemorate important historical anniversaries, such as 'the martyrdom of Wolfe Tone', 'The battle of the Yellow Ford, 1598' and 'The siege of Limerick'. When the Liverpool branch held a lecture on 1 September 1863 in the hall of the Grapes Hotel, Milton Street, it was decorated with cards which said 'Remember Limerick and Saxon Tyranny' and 'Sarsfield's

---

11 Ibid., 20 July 1861.
12 Ibid., 24 Aug. 1861.
13 Ibid., 21 Aug. 1861.

Division'.[14] These anniversary lectures created a national spirit among the members and helped attract new ones. Many emigrants attended out of interest in Ireland's past and her heritage, and the lectures were an opportunity to get them actively involved in the organisation. However, they also showed up a fundamental problem of the movement: they appeared to be more interested in Ireland's past than her future, for they spoke little about the type of Ireland that the Brotherhood wanted to see established.

The Brotherhood regarded St Patrick's Day as a day of celebrating and furthering the cause of the organisation. Rule nine stated that 'the several branches shall be bound, in union with the Central Association to make arrangements for the celebration of our national anniversary, St Patrick's Day'. In February 1862 it called on all Irishmen to unite, to put aside their differences and work for the good of the country.[15] Irish unity was the main theme of the address of Henry Malley, president of the Preston branch when he spoke at the St Patrick's Day celebrations in 1863:

> If all the Irishmen in England would unite in one bond of brotherly love, for the independence of the country, they would make the very pillars of that tyranny which has crushed us for so long tremble to its very foundations.[16]

The St Patrick's Day celebrations employed all of the symbolism and iconography of Irish nationalism. Green, white and orange tricolours, along with green flags and harps were displayed, with the ubiquitous images of St Patrick, portraits of prominent Irish nationalists, such as John Mitchel, Thomas Francis Meagher and Terence Bellew MacManus. The branches were told to play only Irish music at their functions. When the Number 2 branch in Manchester held its celebrations at the Markland Arms, Mason Street, 'The Boys of the Irish Brigade' and 'Paddies Everymore' were sung and toasts were drunk to 'The Day we Celebrate' and 'Ireland a Nation', as well as to the leaders of the movement.[17] Other songs regularly sung at the meetings were 'Let Erin Remember the days of old', 'The memory of the dead', 'The exile of Erin', 'Kathleen Mavoureen' and 'An crusheen lán'.

In March 1862 the Brotherhood was the main force behind the St Patrick's Day celebrations in Lancashire. One hundred people attended a tea party at the Angel Arms organised by the Stalybridge branch, while in Manchester a banquet was held at the Mosley Arms, Piccadilly. Although the social aspects of the occasion were important, the principal point was the speeches, with their clear message that Ireland needed to organise her own affairs and be

14 *United Irishman and Galway American*, 12 Sept. 1863.
15 *Irishman*, 22 Feb. 1862.
16 Ibid., 28 Mar. 1863.
17 Ibid., 22 Mar. 1862.

independent of Britain.[18] The St Patrick's Day celebrations brought the energy and enthusiasm of the branches to the fore. Weeks before the event the clubs started organising and many people were involved, including lapsed members. It has been argued by Comerford that many saw their 'patriotism as a pastime',[19] and the upsurge in the membership and activities of the Brotherhood is an indication of this.

One of the most important functions of the branches was the establishment and maintenance of reading rooms, an aspect of the Irish Confederate Clubs of the late 1840s. Most reading rooms were open at least once a week for two hours, and articles were read from the more extreme nationalist newspapers such as the *Irishman*, the *United Irishman and Galway American*, the *Connaught Patriot*, and the *Universal News*. In the early stages *The Nation* was available, but virtually all reading rooms refused to purchase it after A.M. Sullivan of the *Nation* pursued a successful libel action against Dennis Holland of the *Irishman*.[20] In May 1862 the Oldham branch stopped buying *The Nation* for its reading room because 'of its anti-nationalist policy and its hostility to the Brotherhood'. Similar attitudes were taken by other Lancashire branches such as in Manchester.[21] No English newspapers were provided, not even those which carried articles relating to Ireland. Articles were read from the newspapers about Irish issues at home and abroad. A member would read from the newspapers or books to an assembled audience, indicating that many members were illiterate and from the labouring and artisans classes. In this way, members who would have been ignorant about Irish events gained information about Ireland. Members thus became aware of the approaching subsistence crisis in the early 1860s and set up relief committees to help ward off the threatened famine. They were also cognizant of the exploits of people like Father Patrick Lavelle in Partry.[22] Consequently, they came to his aid when he sought money for food for his parishioners and for his legal fees in his fight against landlords.

The success of the reading rooms meant that many had to move to larger accommodation on a number of occasions because of the big numbers that they attracted. This created its own problems, as many of the reading rooms were

18 Ibid., 29 Mar., 1862; 5 April 1862.
19 R.V. Comerford, 'Patriotism as a pastime: the appeal of fenianism in the mid 1860s', *Irish Historical Studies*, vol. XXII, no. 87 (Mar. 1981), pp 239–50.
20 In 1862 the *Irishman* had published a letter from the Fenian, Jeremiah O'Donovan Rossa, stating that A.M. Sullivan was an informant, for he had provided information about the Phoenix Society to the government. As a result Sullivan sought £1,000 in damages against Denis Holland and the *Irishman*. See Richard Pigott, *Recollections of an Irish National Journalist* (rep. Cork, 1979), p. 139; N.L.I., Thomas Larcom Papers, Ms 7793, newspaper clippings from the *Dublin Evening Mail*, 20 June 1862.
21 *Irishman*, 10 May 1862; 31 May 1862.
22 See Gerard Moran, *A Radical Priest in Mayo: Fr Patrick Lavelle. The rise and fall of an Irish nationalist, 1825–1886* (Dublin, 1994) pp 15–44.

situated in public houses and taverns, including the Hyburn Inn in Accrington; the Concert Tavern, Oldham Road, Manchester; the Stanley Arms, Manchester Street, Liverpool; the Harp and Crown, Blackburn; and the Harp and Shamrock, Rochdale Road, Manchester. Such locations were unsuitable for a people notorious for drunkenness. Branches that existed over time tended to move frequently, like the Liverpool branch, which moved three times in 1862 before settling at 50 St Anne Street. Individuals often donated their own books and reading materials to get the reading rooms established, as with the Number 1 branch in Birkenhead.[23] The Oldham branch reading library had 106 books which included, besides Irish books, the complete works of Byron, Burns and Milton. It also had a number of maps of Ireland which a member presented to the library. It was open each day from 8 a.m. to 10 p.m. and copies of the *Irishman*, the *United Irishman and Galway American* and the *Connaught Patriot* were available.[24] The Spennymore branch lent books to its members and charged 1*d*. a week.[25]

The Brotherhood also launched a number of other clubs and societies to promote an Irish sense of identity and culture. These included Irish language classes and a successful debating society in Liverpool. Another project in Liverpool was the Emmet Literary Club, established in September 1863, whose president, John V. Ryan was a leading member of the Brotherhood in the city. Individuals were assigned particular aspects of Irish history and literature to study and the club was open every day except Sunday.[26]

From the outset, the organisation feared the use of alcohol in its activities: in April 1861 the *Irishman* stated that while it was slow to pronounce water as a qualification for membership, 'certainly sobriety is a virtue'.[27] That the Brotherhood held many of its activities in public houses only added to its difficulties. The Liverpool central branch promoted an athletics and games program which 'would draw men from public houses' and 'render young men more healthy'.[28] Some branches went so far as to expel members who arrived at the meetings drunk. The problem of alcohol was reinforced by one of the founding members of the Brotherhood in Warrington, John Farley, who spoke about the evils of drink and warned members not to imbibe. Still, the Warrington branch continued to hold its meetings at the Bear's Paw Inn.[29] Other branches that held their meetings in public houses included the Emmet branch in Bolton which met at the Stork Tavern on Old Hall Street, the Blackburn branch in the Harp

23 *Irishman*, 20 Dec. 1862.
24 *United Irishman and Galway American*, 3 Oct. 1863.
25 Ibid., 24 Oct. 1863.
26 Ibid., 19 Sept. 1863.
27 Ibid., 6 April 1861.
28 *United Irishman and Galway American*, 19 Sept. 1863.
29 Ibid., 13 Feb. 1864.

and Crown, and the Liverpool Number 1 branch in the Shamrock, Standish Street. The venues for meetings changed regularly for a number of reasons, including opposition to the use of public houses, the inconvenient times and places of the assemblies and the increased surveillance by the local constabulary. In December 1863, the Emmet branch in Bolton was forced at short notice to leave its premises by the Irish landlord, who had been forced to this action by the police. This led the corresponding secretary, Patrick Kelly, to state of his fellow Irishmen, 'some of the class I speak of have no conscience nor country; their fate is to court the smile of the Saxon'.[30]

Membership was not cheap, and this deterred some people from joining. The entrance membership fee of the Number 2 Liverpool branch, which met at Hunter Street, was 6*d.*, with an additional weekly subscription of 2*d.*[31] The Emmet branch in Bolton also charged 6d. membership and a weekly rate of 1*d.* If a member was in arrears for six weeks he lost all of the Brotherhood's privileges.[32] There was little conformity among the branches. Different subscription rates were set, but members were entitled to use other branch reading rooms once they produced their membership cards. There appears to have been a large turnover of members, partly because of the relatively high membership charges and partly because of the opposition of the Catholic Church in Lancashire described below. Unemployment was high in Lancashire in the early 1860s because of the depression in the cotton industry, and many members were unable to make regular contributions, and they allowed their membership to lapse.

Women played a more active role in the organisation's activities than in most other nationalist groups in the nineteenth century. They were included in most of the Brotherhood's social activities, like the historical lectures and the celebrations for St Patrick's Day. However, they did not make speeches or take an active role in the proceedings, though they often sang nationalist songs and recited poetry. In November 1862, the Salford branch passed a resolution expressing gratitude to Irishwomen:

> We feel proud of their patriotism, for in no place is it more pure then in the breasts of our ladies. Who else can inspire their husbands, and sons, and friends with true courage?[33]

Once the Brotherhood had established itself in Lancashire, it was understandable that it should turn its attention to social and political issues in Ireland.

30 Ibid., 28 Dec. 1863.
31 *Irishman*, 4 May, 1861; 15 May 1862.
32 *United Irishman and Galway American*, 14 Nov. 1863.
33 *Irishman*, 23 Nov. 1861. In the Autumn of 1863 an attempt was made to organise women into a nationalist organisation. This was the Sisterhood of St Bridget which was established by women in County Clare, but which appears to have made no impact among Irish women in Britain. See *United Irishman and Galway American*, 10 Oct. 1863.

While the branches in Manchester, Liverpool and Preston were involved in the preparation for the Terence Bellew MacManus funeral, they also helped Dennis Holland of the *Irishman*, a leading figure in the Brotherhood, when his newspaper ws found guilty of libel. The Oldham Road branch in Manchester set up an Indemnity Fund.[34] The Brotherhood also came to the aid of other leading members of the organisation thoughout the early 1860s. One of the Brotherhood's most important activities was the establishment of the Patrick's Pence fund in the Autumn of 1861, which was used to combat poverty and oppression. Father Patrick Lavelle and his parishioners in Partry, where the local landlord, Bishop Thomas Plunket, was attempting to proselytise the tenants and where there was widespread destitution, was the first recipient of this collection.[35] The Lancashire branches subscribed heavily to this fund. Many members of the Brotherhood had endured the poverty and oppression of the Partry tenants and were only too happy to contribute towards their fight against landlordism and destitution. This allowed the Irish in Lancashire to give practical expression to their feelings about Ireland and to assist their fellow countrymen against the stresses and pressures of destitution and starvation, at a time when the Irish in Lancashire were facing their own economic problems.

II

The Brotherhood quickly took hold in those cities and towns with large Irish populations. Manchester and Liverpool were the main centres in Lancashire, for by 1861, 18.9% of the population of Liverpool and 11.3% of the population of Manchester were Irish-born.[36] The first branch to be located in Lancashire was in the Irishman's Reading and News Room, Goulden Street, Oldham Road, Manchester, on 17 March 1861, the day that the movement was being founded in Dublin. The first Liverpool branch was established on 29 April after a meeting at the The Shamrock, Standish Street; its leading personalities were Henry Fildes and Patrick Galligan. By September the Brotherhood had spread to Oldham, Blackburn, Ashton-under Lyne, Salford and Preston, while additional branches were in place in Manchester at Hulme, Deansgate and Oxford Road, and in Liverpool at Lord Nelson Street. Outside of London, Manchester was the most vibrant and active centre. By late 1861,

34 *Irishman*, 14 Sept. 1861.
35 For the fight against Plunket and the poverty in Partry and the Patrick's Pence collection, see Moran, *Radical Priest in Mayo*, pp 15–44; idem, 'The radical priest of Partry: Fr Patrick Lavelle, 1825–1886' in Gerard Moran (ed.), *Radical Irish Priests, 1660–1970* (Dublin, 1998), pp 114–17.
36 Frank Neal, *Sectarian Violence: The Liverpool Experience, 1819–1914: An aspect of Anglo-Irish History* (Manchester, 1988), p. 9.

there were six active branches, and they helped in extending the movement into outlying towns such as Accrington and Stalybridge. In September 1861, it was found necessary to establish the Central Council of the Brotherhood in Manchester to co-ordinate the different branches. This aimed to provide guidance for the various branches in the city, to help in the promotion and advise in the formation of new branches, and to cut down on the level of duplication in the individual groups. Each branch was to send two representatives to the Central Council, which would meet once a fortnight and adjudicate on diffences between local branches. The Central Council was, however, a short-lived body.[37]

Outside factors also helped in the development of the branch network in Lancashire. The role of the *Irishman*, and in particular that of its proprietor, Dennis Holland, was important, especially among the Irish exiles in Britain. Each week the newspaper provided extensive coverage of the Brotherhood's activities in Britain, stimulating interest in the branches and the objectives of the organisation and helping in its expansion. Many members felt that the establishment of their own newspaper was necessary for the furtherance of the organisation.[38] However, nothing ever materialised and the Brotherhood had to rely on the *Irishman*, the *United Irishman and Galway American*, and the *Irish Liberator* to express its opinions.

The growth of the Brotherhood in Lancashire occurred in two stages: between March and December 1861, and from late 1862 to March 1864. Two factors were responsible for its advancement in 1861: the enthusiasm in the immediate months after the movement was established in Dublin and during the demonstrations attending the reburial of Terence Bellew MacManus in November 1861. On both occasions a strong sense of Irish identity manifested itself, indicating that the Irish in Lancashire were poorly organised: up to this point there was not even a committee to help organise the St Patrick's Day celebrations.[39] The MacManus funeral helped to rally the Irish to the Brotherhood, as can be seen in the great demonstration at St George's Hall, Brook Street, Manchester on 19 November 1861, when over 4000 Irishmen met to honour the patriot's reburial. Branches made clear their other objective: 'To bring the National Brotherhood of St Patrick more prominently before the Irish in Manchester, so that a union of some sort may exist between us in exile; that by union we may learn how to win back our liberty'.[40]

---

37 The branches involved were Deansgate, Oldham Road (Gouden Street), no. 1; Oldham Road (German St) no. 2; Hulme, Salford, and Oxford Road.

38 See speech of Peter Gill of the *Tipperary Advocate* to the National Brotherhood of St Patrick on St Patrick's Day, *Irishman*, 22 Mar. 1862.

39 See letter of J.L. in the *Irishman*, 9 Mar. 1861, who stated that there was no body of Irishmen who were prepared to organise a celebration for the feast day, although moves were afoot to remedy this.

40 *Irishman*, 14 Dec. 1861.

MacManus was the ideal symbol for the Brotherhood in Lancashire, as he represented the sacrifices of Irish exiles in the past for their country. In July 1861 the central branch in Liverpool agreed to contribute towards his reburial costs. The branch in the north of the city contributed 27s., and this was used to publicise the Brotherhood's existence so that more members could be recruited. It was agreed to organise a lecture, the proceeds of which would be used for the reinternment. It was not surprising that the Brotherhood in Liverpool played such as active role, for MacManus had lived in the city for many years, before returning to Ireland to take part in the Young Ireland rebellion in 1848.[41] Contributions were also received from branches in Oldham, Preston, and Oldham Road, Manchester. By November 1861, the Brotherhood was at its peak, primarily because the MacManus funeral helped to increase the sense of nationalism among the Irish exiles. New members were enrolled and new branches were established at Birkenhead, New Mount Street, Manchester and Blackburn (no.3). Existing branches also became more vibrant. Comerford describes the MacManus funeral as a lost opportunity, for it might have advanced the Brotherhood and brought together the various strains of Irish nationalism.[42] The failure must be largely attributed to the condemnations and criticisms of the Catholic hierarchy in Britain and Ireland.

It is difficult to estimate the membership of the organisation in Lancashire at this time. There were 5000 members in Ireland and the organisation was making major progress in all of the major cities in Britain. As the branches had only a loose affiliation to the central organisation in Dublin in the early days, it is impossible gauge its strength. We have an indication of the membership of some of the individual branches in Manchester and Liverpool, between six and eight hundred members, but it is impossible to know how many were active. At least twenty were active branches, but others also existed. The only way of determining the extent of the branch network is through the columns of the *Irishman* in Dublin, but some did not submit weekly reports. Other, such as Oldham and Salford, corresponded when they were established, but there is little information about them after this. Consequently it is difficult to determine how lively they were. The erratic nature of membership meant that the smaller branches tottered on the edge of extinction. While the Stalybridge branch was founded in the Spring of 1861, it was disbanded in early 1863 and re-established in August 1863. In August 1863, it had 43 members, but within six weeks this increased to 100.[43] Patrick Geraghty, secretary of the Preston branch, appealed to the Irishmen of Preston to join the organisation, as

41 See *Irishman*, 6 July 1861. For information on MacManus's life especially in Liverpool, see Thomas G. McAllister, *Terence Bellew MacManus* (Maynooth, 1972).
42 Comerford, 'Conspiring brotherhoods and conspiring elites', pp 424–5.
43 *United Irishman and Galway American*, 22 Aug. 1863.

otherwise their apathy would lead to its demise.[44] This indicates the transient character of the membership: while many Irish people attended particular functions and joined up, they were not active members. As a result some branches were inactive. By the end of 1861, just after the impact of the MacManus reburial had worn off, some branches complained that there had been a major decline in attendances.

Lowe, in his work on the Irish in mid-Victorian Lancashire, minimises the impact of the Brotherhood on the cities and towns of the region. He underestimates the extent of the organisation in stating that its activities were confined to Preston, Oldham, Manchester, Oldham and Liverpool.[45] This fails to recognise that the movement made its way in the smaller towns of Lancashire which had Irish settlements, such as Ashton-under-Lyne, Accrington and Warrington. A branch of the Brotherhood was only established in Warrington in October 1863, largely because of the assistance provided by the branches in Liverpool and Manchester.[46] The Brotherhood also continued in existence in the major centres of Irish settlement between 1861 and 1865, when most of the branches were taken over by the Fenians. Lowe also dismisses the branches as only being involved in sponsoring teas and balls for fund-raising. This fails to take into account their role in the development of an Irish cultural, historical and social identity in the region.

Events in Ireland in 1861–2 also aided in the development of the Brotherhood. Two major evictions, in Partry, co. Mayo in November, 1860, and at Derryveagh, co. Donegal in April 1861, highlighted the merciless conduct of Irish landlords.[47] At the same time, another major subsistence crisis threatened western Ireland.[48] This was the first important crisis since the Great Famine of 1845–52, and resurrected the memories of the want and starvation of that era. Thus the Brotherhood became a centre for Irish discontent and helped to unify the Irish in Lancashire and Britain. When Fr Patrick Lavelle visited Manchester on 6 October 1862, the occasion was marked by a celebration by the Irish in the city. A committee, mainly composed of members of the Brotherhood, organised the occasion, in recognition of the heroism of his attempts to save his parishioners from starvation and stop the evictions in Partry.

44 Ibid., 22 Aug. 1863.
45 Lowe, *Irish in Mid-Victorian Lancashire*, p. 192.
46 *Irishman*, 14 Dec. 1861.
47 Gerard Moran, *The Mayo Evictions of 1860: Fr Patrick Lavelle and the 'war' in Partry* (Westport, 1986); W.E. Vaughan, *Sin, Sheep and Scotsmen: John George Adair and the Derryveagh evictions, 1861* (Belfast, 1983); Liam Dolan, *Land War and Evictons in Derryveagh, 1840–65* (Dundalk, 1980).
48 See J.S. Donnelly, 'The Irish agricultural depression of 1859–64', *Irish Economic and Social History*, vol. III (1976), pp 33–54; Timothy P. O'Neill, ' Minor famines and relief in county Galway, 1815–1925' in Gerard Moran and Raymond Gillespie (eds), *Galway: History and Society* (Dublin, 1996), pp 461–5.

The peak of the Brotherhood's popularity was around St Patrick's Day 1862, just before it was condemned by the Catholic Church. By this stage the constabulary in Ireland and Britain were paying increased attention to its activities, and detectives and constables regularly attended them. In July 1863, the constabulary in Manchester tried to stop W.J. Finnigan delivering a lecture on Poland and Ireland, but were prevented from doing so by the crowd.[49] The demise of the Brotherhood came in early 1862 and can be seen by the amalgamation of the No. 1 and No. 2 branches in Manchester. While officially for the better development of the movement, in reality the problem was falling membership brought on by clerical opposition.[50] The four branches in Blackburn amalgamated under the presidency of James Kennedy in April 1862.[51] While new branches were established during 1862, the organisation did not have the same commitment or liveliness as in 1861. An examination of the branch reports for Lancashire indicates that little of importance was being debated. This highlights the fundamental problem which the movement was encountering – lack of direction, how to keep interest going for the majority of the members and what strategy to put in place for the future. Resolutions were passed about unity and Irish independence, but the leadership seemed unsure how this would be achieved. This was a national and not a local problem for the Brotherhood, as similar problems were being encountered in Ireland.[52]

III

The Brotherhood's greatest obstacle was its condemnation by the Catholic Church, which claimed it was a secret society. This accusation was first made in 1861 and became more serious by 1862. It was the main issue for the Lancashire leadership and one which it was unable to overcome. The condemnation meant that moderate Catholic Irishmen who sympathised with the Brotherhood never joined because of the clergy's denunciations. By March 1862 the moderates had left the Brotherhood.[53] Bishops like Goss of Liverpool

---

49 *Irishman*, 1 Aug. 1863. The proprietor of the Markland Arms on Mason Street had been visited by the local constabulary and told not to allow the lecture to go ahead: see *United Irishman and Galway American*, 25 July 1863.
50 *Irishman*, 31 May 1861.
51 Ibid., 19 April 1861.
52 Report of Daniel Ryan, dated 29 Jan. 1862 (National Archives, Dublin, Chief Secretary's Office, Registered Papers, 1861/124086). In 1862 the Brotherhood was in total disarray in Dublin with the younger members leaving and the central committee unable to pay the rent on their offices at 2 Marlborough Street, Dublin.
53 See Oliver P. Rafferty, 'The Church, the state and the Fenian threat, 1861–75' (University of Oxford D.Phil thesis, 1996), pp 54–5. The point is best exemplified by the case of The O'Donoghue, MP, who was advised by some Dublin clerics not to be

and Turner in Salford were worried that the organisation was lay-controlled and that the Catholic clergy had no part in. As it was, the Catholic clergy in most of Lancashire had little in common with the Irish exiles. Most of the priests in Preston, St Helens, Liverpool and Widness were English-born and, while they had made an important contribution to their flock in ministering to the Irish Famine victims in the late 1840s, they had little feeling for Irish political and social matters and were not sympathetic to Irish political aspirations. Bitterness was also evident among English Catholics in Lancashire who did little to help the new settlers.[54] Thus the emergence of the Brotherhood in the early 1860s only added further to the pressures on the Catholic Church in Lancashire to keep the Irish in check. Many clerics in England felt that the Brotherhood was competing with the Catholic Church for the affections and support of the Irish working class. The Church did not want to be diverted from its task of church-building and providing the most basic of spiritual resources for the burgeoning Catholic population: it was imperative that it had control of its flock.

Goss did not know how to deal with the Brotherhood and sought advice from Archbishop Paul Cullen of Dublin in March 1862 as to whether the organisation should be condemned as a secret society.[55] Cullen was having similar problems in Dublin, and his advice formed the overall Church attitude towards the organisation in Lancashire and Ireland. In the spring of 1862, Cullen made membership of the Brotherhood a reserved sin and the Lancashire bishops followed this line. Thus the Church's attitude to the Brotherhood evolved from the stand of the Irish bishops. This is significant because the Brotherhood had more branches and members in Lancashire than in Ireland and had different functions. The Cullen papers indicate that the bishops and clergy in Lancashire and Britain were worried by the Brotherhood's growth; Archbishop McDonald summed up this attitude:

> We here, feel convinced that it is just a new cloak, or rather a new name for Ribbonism, but without something more than mere suspicion, it is difficult for us to act in the matter.[56]

associated with the Brotherhood or their St Patrick's Day celebrations, if he wanted to retain his friendship with Archbishop Cullen.

54 David Fitzpatrick, ' "A peculiar tramping people": The Irish in Britain, 1801–70' in W.E. Vaughan (ed.), *A New History of Ireland*, vol. V, *Ireland under the Union, 1801–70* (Oxford, 1989), p. 652; Tom Gallagher, 'A tale of two cities: Communal strife in Liverpool and Glasgow before 1914', in Roger Swift and Sheridan Gilley (eds), *The Irish in the Victorian City* (London, 1989), p. 108.

55 Alexander Goss to Cullen, dated 8 Mar. 1862 (Dublin Diocesan Archives, Cullen Papers: Foreign Bishops, 1862). It is also interesting to note that Goss was also seeking advice as to whether Fr Patrick Lavelle of Partry should be allowed to say mass in the diocese for Goss felt 'his presence bodes no good in Liverpool'.

56 Archbishop McDonald to Cullen, dated 15 Feb. 1862 (D.D.A., Cullen Papers; Foreign Bishops, 1861). Part of this fear was that in the early stages the leading members were

This attitude was adopted despite the continuous assurances to the bishops from the Brotherhood that it administered no oath to its members and that it was not a secret organisation. In May 1862 the hierarchy in Britain issued a letter warning their flocks against those who administered unlawful oaths and encouraged people into secret associations which were dangerous to religion.[57] Bishop Goss made his position clear in a pastoral in February 1862:

> Beware of a watchword inserted by the agents and fomentors of revolution, who under the guise of patriotism, endeavour to sow anarchy and confusion amongst people living together under a common Soverign.[58]

He called on the people to be led by the priests, not by outside agencies who did not have the best interests of the people at heart. At the same time, a priest in Manchester denounced the Brotherhood 'as the phase of Ribbonism' and added that its members were bad Catholics and were excommunicated.[59] Members would not be allowed to receive the sacraments.

The clergy's intervention resulted in the decline of the Brotherhood in Liverpool and other towns. The Cullen Papers indicate that the bishops were eager to hear of the movement's demise, as when P.B. O'Brien reported that the secretary of the Council for Great Britain had written that the Brotherhood was disappearing rapidly in Liverpool.[60] Nevertheless, the bishops and clergy were not complacent, and were especially worried by Father Patrick Lavelle's presence in the region. While many priests denounced the Brotherhood in Lancashire and warned their flocks not to become involved, Lavelle's attendance at meetings in Manchester, Preston and Liverpool gave the organisation a status among the Irish emigrant population. While Lavelle was working and suffering for Ireland, and more importantly living in one of the poorest areas of Ireland, where the ravages of landlordism were only all too evident, the English clergy appeared unmoved towards him. The Lancashire bishops were adamant that Lavelle had helped to generate support for the Brotherhood. They cited Lavelle's letter from Liverpool as evidence of this:

> Once more, young men of Ireland, you have your choice. Love and serve your country and your God together, and join the Brotherhood, or deny your country and join the Young Men's Society, who will exclude you from their association.[61]

classified as Ribbonmen, an all embracing term which the clergy used in the late 1850s and early 1860s for those who opposed them.
57 Rafferty, 'Church, state and Fenian threat', p. 64.
58 Goss to Cullen, dated 17 Oct. 1862 (D.D.A., Cullen Papers; Foreign Bishops, 1862).
59 *Irishman*, 2 April 1862.
60 P.B. O'Brien to Cullen, dated 16 Apr. 1862 (D.D.A., Cullen Papers, Priests, 1862). It would appear that these reports were exaggerated.
61 *Irishman*, 22 Mar. 1862.

Such comments, as well as his continuous conflict with Archbishop Paul Cullen and the manner in which he denounced prelates like Goss and Ullathorne of Birmingham, made the Lancashire clergy fearful of Lavelle.[62]

During the early months of 1863, there were reports that the membership of the Brotherhood in Britain was increasing, causing the bishops concern.[63] This led to conflict between the clergy and the Brotherhood, as in Liverpool during the summer of 1863 when the priests attempted to destroy the movement in the city. The number 2 branch in Toxteth Park, which met in Parliament Street, was told that the local clergy would join if the organisation changed its name. The president, Peter Monaghan, and the treasurer, Mr Farrell, were prepared to dissolve the branch and reconstitute it as a new society, Erin-go-bragh. However, other branch members and the leading officers of the Brotherhood in the city, George Archdeacon and Henry Fildes, blocked this move. In July the branch was reformed and renamed the Wolfe Tone (First Division) branch.[64] This incident indicates the level of opposition to the Brotherhood from the clergy in Liverpool. It was a dangerous strategy for the clergy, however, for in their attempt to control the people they risked driving the more radical members into the arms of the more militant nationalist groups such as the Fenians.

The bishops' condemnations incensed the Brotherhood, and in March 1862 Thomas Neilson Underwood wrote to Cullen rebutting the accusation that it was a secret society.[65] He added that its meetings were open and that its members were not bound by oaths or declarations: 'its objects are not against the doctrines of the Catholic religion, any more than the Repeal Association was'.[66] Despite their continuous protestations, the Brotherhood found it difficult to refute the charges of the Catholic Church. This had its impact on the organisation's morale. What horrified the leadership was that the bishops looked at one area of the Brotherhood's policies, that of Irish independence, and refused to recognise its other objectives – those of raising the moral, social and intellectual horizons of the Irish people. The point was forcefully made by the O'Connell branch at Stalybridge:

62 Goss to Cullen, dated 17 Oct. 1862 (D.D.A., Cullen Papers, Foreign Bishops). For Lavelle's conflict with Cullen, see Moran, *Radical Priest in Mayo*, pp 47–87; for his conflict with English bishops, see ibid., pp 90–1.

63 Unknown to Cullen, dated 20 Apr. 1863 (D.D.A., Cullen Papers, Foreign Bishops, 1863).

64 *United Irishman and Galway American*, 1 Aug. 1863; 22 Aug. 1863. The Erin-go-bragh club was established and carried out much of the same functions as the Brotherhood branches with lectures and reading rooms. Its president was Revd H.H. O'Bryan and it held its meetings in the Hall of the Catholic Institute, Hope Street. However, it failed in its efforts to attract the large number of Irishman into its ranks that it had hoped.

65 Rafferty, 'Church, state and Fenian threat', p. 63.

66 *Irishman*, 22 Mar. 1862; Thomas Neilson Underwood to Cullen, dated 10 Mar. 1862 (D.D.A., Cullen Papers, Laity, 1862).

> We are resolved to encourage Irish manufactures in every material that may be
> within their capacity; and must we be condemned for this blessed work and every
> defence of it?[67]

Had the bishops done anything towards the material advancement of the
people, it asked, except generate statements that the Irish were persecuted?

Why did the bishops condemn the Brotherhood, especially as it had simi-
larities with the Confederate Clubs of the late 1840s and many of its ideals and
much of its organisation were based on that movement? The Catholic Church had
never condemned the Confederate Clubs. The reason was that the Brotherhood
was the public and only identifiable face of radical Irish nationalism. Even
though the Fenians had been active in the MacManus funeral arrangements
and had infiltrated most of the Lancashire branches, they were not to become
an easily recognisable group until 1864. In August 1863 the Brotherhood was
condemned by name by the Irish bishops, providing the hierarchy in
Lancashire with further ammunition to attack it. The censure mainly centred
on the administration of an oath of support for an Irish republic.[68] The correspondence from the branches during the summer of 1863 indicates that the
Lancashire clergy were becoming more hostile, but the Brotherhood was
determined to withstand this for 'the cause the Brotherhood has in hand is the
cause of Ireland's independence'.[69]

Matters were also not helped by the seditious tone of some of the speakers at
the Brotherhood's meetings. In the declaration of 9 April 1862, signed by the
leadership (including Underwood, Doran, Hoey and John 'Amnesty' Nolan), the
Brotherhood argued that the Irish people had a right to possess arms and to
know the discipline of arms because parliament had refused to listen to Irish
grievances, even though the people of Ireland had petitioned them on a number
of occasions.[70] The letters and addresses of the Lancashire leadership also
created difficulties. Henry F. Fildes, the corresponding secretary of the
Liverpool branch, in an address to the Irish in the city in September 1862 wrote:

> If you are of the race of Emmet, you will not fear to die for your native land. If
> there is any of the blood of the Grattans, Floods, Sheils or O'Connells in your
> veins, you will not fear to speak for her? ... The opportunity so long prophesied
> will arrive – when every man must either join the enemy of 'Strike for freedom'.[71]

67 *United Irishman and Galway American*, 3 Oct. 1863.
68 Comerford, 'Conspiring brotherhoods and contending elites', p. 424.
69 *United Irishman and Galway American*, 25 July 1863.
70 *Irishman*, 12 April 1862. The declaration went on to say: 'The National Brotherhood of
    St Patrick believes no Irishman is worthy of the name nationalist until he is master in
    the use of some weapon of defence'. Their reference to petitions was no doubt to the
    National Petition of The O'Donoghue, MP.
71 *Irishman*, 6 Sept. 1862.

Similar sentiments were expressed by the Preston branch in February 1864, when it called upon the members not to come to the meetings to hear newspapers being read, but to 'gird themselves for the coming struggle, and if no foreign opportunity comes they must make an opportunity themselves'.[72]

Tensions were exacerbated by the conflict between the Brotherhood and the Catholic Young Men's Society (C.Y.M.S.), an organisation established by Dean Richard B. O'Brien of Newcastle West, county Limerick, to extend the spirit of religion and brotherly love through 'public lectures, private classes, a library and a reading room'. It wished to unify and solidify Catholic organisations and competed with the Brotherhood for the minds and souls of young Irishmen.[73] It made rapid strides among the Irish in Lancashire and it was only a matter of time before the two organisations came into open conflict with each other. The tensions became apparent in late 1861 when the Brotherhood in Liverpool invited Father Patrick Lavelle to deliver a public lecture on behalf of the suffering poor of Ireland and, in particular, his parishioners in Partry. While the C.Y.M.S. had agreed to distribute the tickets through its branches, the secretary published a letter disclaiming any involvement with the lecture a few days before it was due to take place.[74] Control over the youth of Liverpool was more important than charitable work for the poor of Partry.[75] An attempt was made to reconcile the two organisations when the Oxford Road, Manchester, branch of the Brotherhood organised a lecture, 'The Brotherhood of St Patrick v Secret Societies', by J.J. Finnigan. While the C.Y.M.S. was invited, it seems that few members attended, thus continuing the feud.[76] The Brotherhood feared the formation of other organisations as it would have had an impact on its activities.

The Catholic Church's condemnation of the Brotherhood meant that many of the smaller branches disappeared or failed to make any worthwhile contribution to the development of the organisation. This reason was given for the demise of the Birkenhead branch in the spring of 1862. It was not re-established until October 1862, when it appears that most of its members were Fenians. Similar

72 *United Irishman and Galway American*, 27 Feb. 1864.

73 Lowe, *Irish in Mid-Victorian Lancashire*, pp 130–1; Moran, *Radical Priest in Mayo*, p. 56.

74 *Irishman*, 22 Mar. 1862. This was to be the origin of a major conflict between O'Brien and Lavelle; see Moran, *Radical Priest in Mayo*, pp 56–7.

75 Throughout this period O'Brien made various attempts to have the Brotherhood condemned because it was competing with his organisation. See Richard B. O'Brien to Cullen, dated 27 Jan. 1863 (D.D.A., Cullen Papers; Secular Priests, 1863). Dean O'Brien had written to Martin Rankin, secretary of the C.Y.M.S. in Liverpool in 1862 condemning the Brotherhood and forbidding members of the C.Y.M.S. to join it. Rankin was also General Secretary of the C.Y.M.S. in Britain. O'Brien said the Brotherhood was a cover for a secret society whose members were excommunicated: See *Tablet*, 15 Mar. 1862; 22 Mar. 1862. O'Brien to Cullen, 31 Mar. 1862, 11 April 1862 (D.D.A., Cullen Papers, Secular Priests, 1862). I am indebted to Dr Oliver Rafferty for this information.

76 *Irishman*, 12 April 1862.

problems existed in Oldham, where many of the Irish believed that the Brotherhood was a dangerous organisation.[77]

In late 1863, the Catholic Church launched another major attack on the Brotherhood. Many of the Lancashire branches repudiated the criticisms of the Catholic bishops. The Emmet branch in Bolton issued a statement in September 1863 condemning the bishops' censures, and the Brian Boroimhe branch in Manchester passed a resolution which condemned 'the attempt to suppress by spiritual authority the right of opinion in matters purely temporal'.[78] These incidents indicate that sections of the Irish community were increasingly frustrated with the clergy's intervention in what they regarded as a political issue. The leadership was also mystified because the Papacy and the Catholic Church appeared to condone revolution by the Poles against their Russian masters, but attacked Irish nationalists for suggesting or even speaking about military action to free Ireland.[79] It seemed that there was a different set of criteria for dealing with the two issues. The Brotherhood did, however, support Polish independence, for the Lancashire branches held meetings, made collections and passed resolutions in support of the Polish cause. Some members of the Brotherhood felt that Catholicism was an important part of their Irish background. At some functions toasts were drunk to the Pope and the Catholic religion, and some lecturers spoke of the signifance of the Reformation and the Penal Laws for Catholic Ireland.[80] Some realised that the role of the priests was important for securing national self-determination.[81]

IV

In late 1862 a revival took place in the fortunes of the Brotherhood in Lancashire, and the impetus came from the Liverpool Central District branch. It was the most active and enterprising of the branches in Britain and Ireland, largely due to the exertions of its president, George Archdeacon and, to a lesser extent, Henry E. Fildes. The activities ranged from lectures and debates to readings from Irish nationalist newspapers. Its progressive approach can be seen in the special organisation committee, which issued a report dividing the city for the establishment of new branches and promoting the formation of new branches

77 Ibid., 18 Oct. 1862.
78 *United Irishman and Galway American*, 26 Sept.1863; 31 Oct. 1863.
79 See *Irishman*, 28 Feb. 1863.
80 See speech at meeting of the Ashton-under-Lyne branch in December 1863, *United Irishman and Galway American*, 5 Dec. 1863.
81 One correspondent to the *United Irishman and Galway American* said that the role of the clergy was important in bringing about Irish independence: *United Irishman and Galway American*, 14 Nov. 1863.

in neighbouring towns.[82] A new branch was in place in Toxteth Park by April 1863. By now the Liverpool branches had been infiltrated by the Fenians and a more radical approach was in evidence. At a meeting of the Central District branch on 18 April 1863, a stirring letter was read from the secretary of the Fenian Brotherhood and was received with loud cheering.[83] By this stage the Liverpool central district branch had helped in the formation or re-establishment of branches in Birkenhead, St Helens, Little Bolton and Everton. The Brotherhood's importance can be noted by the glowing reports sent by Charles G. Doran and Clinton Hoey about the organisation. The central association in Dublin in 1863 regarded Liverpool as the strongest centre of the association.[84] Other English branches looked to Liverpool for guidance and inspiration, including the Preston branch, which decided to affiliate with the district branch in Liverpool, and which also advised the Bradford and Glasgow branches on how they could be strengthened.[85]

The leadership of the Liverpool resurgence was George Archdeacon, who was elected president of the Central District branch in spring 1863. He was well-respected by all sections of the Irish community in Lancashire, and was a link with the Confederate Clubs of 1848, as he had been secretary of the Manchester branch.[86] After the failure of the 1848 Young Ireland rebellion, he had worked in the United States as a private detective before settling in Liverpool.[87] By the 1860s, all nationalist activity in Liverpool revolved around Archdeacon, who helped to establish new branches and ensured that the organisation was not taken over by the Catholic clergy. He attended nearly all of the Brotherhood's events in the Liverpool area, and his contribution to the movement was constantly cited.[88] His speeches were radical and in October 1863 he called for a:

> Close alliance with our transatlantic brethren and total independence. For those things we will contest, they are worth the struggle, and I believe the issue is at hand.[89]

82 *Irishman*, 18 April 1863.
83 Ibid., 25 April 1863.
84 *United Irishman and Galway American*, 29 Aug. 1863; 17 Oct. 1863.
85 *Irishman*, 5 Sept. 1863.
86 Lowe, *Irish in Mid-Victorian Lancashire*, p. 192. The strong connection with the 1848 Confederates can also be seen with the president of the Preston branch, Henry Malley, who had also been a confederate.
87 *United Irishman and Galway American*, 22 Aug. 1863.
88 See ibid., 12 Sept. 1863, on report of the anniversary of the Siege of Limerick in Liverpool.
89 *United Irishman and Galway American*, 10 Oct. 1863. This is undoubtedly a reference to the Fenian Brotherhood in the United States.

Radicalism was also evident in the more militant attitude adopted by the membership of the Brotherhood and the changes in name of the branches. They dispensed with the names of the districts where they were based and called the branches after Irish nationalists, such as Brian Boroimhe, Thomas Francis Meagher, Father Patrick Lavelle, Robert Emmet, Wolfe Tone, John MacHale and others. The Blackburn branch became the Great MacHale branch; the central branch in Manchester changed to Brian Boroimhe; Preston became the O'Mahony branch; and Bootle became the Father Lavelle branch. The aim was to instil a greater sense of nationalism among the Irish in Britain and to commemorate the great Irish patriots. At the same time, there was an increasingly militant tone in the speeches. Mr Mooney told the branch in Bolton in October 1863 that its members should realise that they had been robbed of their liberties and should do something about it. The Preston branch in February 1864 stated: 'The members should be instructed that coming to the meetings to hear newspapers read is not sufficient – they should gird them-selves for the coming struggle, and if no foreign opportunity comes they must make an opportunity themselves'.[90]

The establishment of district councils and better co-operation helped achieve a closer relationship between the regional groups, especially in Liverpool and Manchester. The General Secretary of the Central Association, C.G. Doran, visited Liverpool in August 1863 and spoke in glowing terms about the Liverpool organisation. The Central Council in Dublin suggested that district councils should be established in Manchester, Leeds, Birmingham, London, Glasgow and Edinburgh, based on the Liverpool model.[91] In November 1863, the Brian Boroimhe branch in Manchester became the central branch for the Manchester district. It was hoped that this would redress the Brotherhood's declining fortunes in a city which had had seven branches in 1861, but had fallen to two because of the opposition by the Catholic Church. A further aim of the district council was to assist in the development of the movement in the neighbouring small towns.[92] However, this failed to invigorate the Manchester movement because it lacked an organisational leader like Archdeacon.

In 1863 the Brotherhood in Lancashire made major advances in branch activity. On 6 September 1863, a conference was held in Warrington to achieve greater co-operation between the branches and to establish guidelines for a conference of the Lancashire branches to take place on the first Sunday of each quarter to discuss points of mutual benefit. Seventeen branches from thirteen

90 Ibid., 24 Oct. 1863; 27 Feb. 1864.
91 Ibid., 22 Aug. 1863. The visit of Doran and Hoey was an attempt to strengthen the branches and give them some recognition for their work. Many of the smaller branches felt isolated and unable to contribute to the overall development of the organisation.
92 Ibid., 7 Nov. 1863.

towns were represented.[93] This had immediate benefits, for in October 1863 the Ashton-under-Lyne, Oldham and Stalybridge branches helped in the formation of a new branch at Hyde, Cheshire, which had twenty-one members, and in the re-establishment of the Deansgate branch.[94]

In the autumn of 1863, George Archdeacon stated that the Brotherhood was making major progress in England and Scotland, although he provided no concrete information as to its exact membership.[95] Other reports in the *United Irishman and Galway American* from the same period support this claim and reveal that there were seventeen active branches in Lancashire. Still, some areas remained relatively weak, notably Manchester, where only two branches were active in late 1863. They sent only one delegate to a conference of the Manchester district on 6 December, while each of the other six branches sent three. There was also evidence of frustration in the first resolution of the conference which recognised Manchester as the centre of the region, but only if Manchester performed its duty: 'if not we do not recognise it as our centre'.[96] Many felt that Manchester was not leading, and should be replaced as the centre for the region.

The organisation was becoming much more forceful and critical of clerical condemnation. While the 1862 censure had led to the more moderate members leaving the organisation, there was no major exodus when the bishops attacked the Brotherhood in the autumn of 1863. Indeed the leadership asked what the bishops had done for Irish nationalism, when compared with the bishops and priests of Poland. Evidence suggests that new branches were being established in Lancashire after the bishops' condemnation.[97]

In December 1863 and early 1864 the movement was making plans for its future. By February 1864 there were twenty active branches in Lancashire. The Liverpool Central District branch felt that the organisation needed to get away from its local structure, and advocated the establishment of a General Council for England, which would meet periodically to discuss issues which would benefit the organisation. Archdeacon was to the fore in proposing this and he hoped to put the financial affairs of the Brotherhood on a firmer footing.[98]

While plans were being made for the future, the Brotherhood suddenly ceased to exist in March 1864. Matters were brought to a head at a meeting in the Rotunda, Dublin, in February 1864 to protest against the proposed erection of a statue to Prince Albert on a site earmarked for a memorial to Daniel O'Connell. While the leaders of the National Brotherhood of St Patrick

---

93 Ibid., 29 Aug. 1863.
94 Ibid., 17 Oct. 1863.
95 Ibid., 28 Nov. 1863.
96 Ibid., 19 Dec. 1863.
97 Ibid., 6 Feb. 1864. One gets the impression that such statements were made to boost morale at a time of increasing pressure from the clergy.
98 Ibid., 9 Jan. 1864; *Irishman*, 5 Dec. 1863, 16 Jan. 1864.

attended along with The O'Donoghue and A.M. Sullivan, the meeting was broken up on the expressed orders of the Fenian leader, James Stephens, who feared that the resurgence of constitutional nationalism would weaken the Fenians. Branches of the Brotherhood no longer supported the leadership, and they came under total Fenian control.

V

By March 1864 the Brotherhood in Lancashire had effectively ceased to exist, especially in its former strongholds around Liverpool where it had been taken over by the Fenians. Branch reports no longer appeared in the newspapers and there is no indication that they communiciated with one another. The structures which the Liverpool Central District Branch had installed had disappeared. Reports from Manchester, Blackburn and Warrington indicate that meetings were still being held, but there was little other activity. James Stephens, the Fenian leader, had never been a great admirer of the Brotherhood, fearing that its social and cultural activities were diverting Irish people away from the main goal of advanced nationalists – that of securing Irish independence. It was thus important that the Fenians control the Brotherhood. It was not difficult to terminate the Liverpool branches once they were Fenian-controlled. The Fenian withdrawal took away the most active and hard-working members of the organisation. The demise of the Brotherhood in Lancashire coincided with the Fenian movement's emergence in Lancashire and especially around Liverpool. The situation was different in Manchester, Blackburn and other towns, and these branches continued to function until early 1865, although they achieved little.

Despite its short existence the Brotherhood had an important function for the Irish in Lancashire. It was the first organisation after the Famine to organise the Irish into a movement focusing on Irish problems, not confining itself exclusively to political issues. It also encouraged the social and cultural aspects of the Irish tradition. This was at a time when these were in decline in Ireland. It also reveals the problems that such organisations would encounter from militant nationalist groups: infiltration and take-over. Cultural organisations such as the Gaelic League and the Gaelic Athletic Association experienced a similar subversion at the end of the century. The greatest obstacles which the Brotherhood never overcame were the opposition of the Catholic Church and the criticism of other nationalist groups. The Fenians were suspicious because the Brotherhood threatened to steal away many of the young recruits whom the militant organisation hoped to attract. Constitutional nationalists such as George Henry Moore and The O'Donoghue stayed clear because of the bishops' condemnations. Even moderate Irish nationalists such as John Martin did not support it, largely because its principles were not clearly defined. The

Brotherhood did not help itself because it devoted its activities to so many other issues, lectures, fund-raising activities and Patrick's Pence, rather than give itself a realistic long-term objective. Branches were also dependent on the goodwill and energy of their members for promotion. It had no paid officials to carry out its work. With the economic downturn in the early 1860s and thousands in the cotton industry unemployed, many members were unable to give the same commitment as they had in the past. The most important short-term achievement of the Brotherhood was as an instrument for unifying the Irish in Lancashire, after the fragmentation of Irish nationalism in the late 1850s. It thereby helped to organise the Irish in Lancashire into a reasonably effective movement, and laid the basis for the Home Rule movement of the 1870s.

Alternative historiographies of the Irish in Britain: a critique of the segregation/assimilation model

Mary J. Hickman

The aim of this essay is to argue the merits of an alternative historiography of the Irish in Britain to that of the segregation/assimilation model which characterises much of the available literature. The silent discourse in much of the work of segregation/assimilation historians is that of the nation state. The dominant culture and institutions of the nation state in which migrants have settled is not usually problematised; in fact it is mostly taken for granted. As a consequence, the ethnicity of the migrant population is assessed in incremental terms, viewed as relatively strong or weak according to the degree to which they are seen to support an autonomous sub-culture. In addition, the segregation/assimilation model ignores that many displaced populations are part of wider diasporic communities and that this is a significant determinant of communal identities.

The first volume co-edited by Roger Swift and Sheridan Gilley, *The Irish in the Victorian City* (1985) reflected a consensus view about the Irish in nineteenth-century Britain.[1] This was that the majority experience was of large urban concentrations of unskilled labourers, showing evidence of Catholic and Irish nationalist activity, who experienced social, political and religious segregation and who by the end of the century had achieved a distinctive place in British life while maintaining a definite apartness. The sequel to this volume, *The Irish in Britain, 1815–1939* (1989) was to show where this general outline might require qualification and revision.[2] Consequently it stressed the heterogeneity of Irish experiences in Britain and suggested that evidence of patchy mobil-isation as an ethnic group and an absence of segregation into ghettos meant that insofar as the Irish Catholic community came into existence and survived, it was essentially as a Catholic church-based one. Many of the chapters in this volume stressed relative assimilation or integration.

The two volumes were a fair representation of the state of the historical debate about the Irish in nineteenth-century Britain as it was conducted in the 1980s; with the first volume broadly of a segregation perspective and the second volume

1 London, 1985.
2 London, 1989.

much more to the assimilation end of the spectrum. Where did this debate get us? On the one hand a wealth of complexly structured data and interpretation about the historical experiences of the Irish in Britain has been made available in these and other volumes.[3] On the other hand one was left with a distinct sense of only knowing half the story. This absence is not one that can be filled solely by advocating more local studies or making sure that the Irish middle-class, Irish Protestants or most importantly Irish women are adequately addressed. All of these are useful additions to the historical literature but just adding them to the existing body of knowledge about the Irish in Britain is not sufficient.

Many historians seem to assume that an accumulative approach to historical investigation is sufficient; only when we have exhausted every archive will we be in a position to make any substantive claims. It is a process of generating knowledge which seems to thrive on the practice of exceptionalism. As Raphael Samuel pointed out, one of the chief criticisms to be made of most historiography is its inherent empiricism.[4] He argued that many historians have remained wedded to the single instance, accumulating endless examples and finding exceptions to every rule. In his view knowledge of the sources was often the profession's substitute for thought. Unfortunately the paradigm of segregation/assimilation that dominates the historiography of the Irish in Britain seems to lend itself to many of these tendencies. This is because it sets up a debate which is ultimately sterile, as one instance of relative assimilation in Stafford can always be set against another of relative segregation in London and so on. The prime activity becomes dissection of the minority group itself and the constant comparison of a multiplicity of factors (for example, class, religion, politics, ethnicity) with little attempt to intermesh them to produce an analysis of how they together structured Irish experiences.

Another problem with the segregation/assimilation model is the sort of questions it poses. Examples of frequently asked questions are: were the Irish a distinctive ethnic group? did the Irish develop an ethnic consciousness? did the Irish live in residentially segregated areas? did the Irish act as a cohesive force politically? These questions transpose the analysis of the Chicago school (whose project was unproblematically about the desirability of Americanization) to a British context with no examination of their appropriateness. Now to one extent or another it is possible to argue that given the exigencies of a nation state concerning all of its resident population or citizens these questions will always yield valuable knowledge about the experiences of a particular migrant group. However, they will never deliver a full picture because the focus remains irremediably on the minority group itself. In a critique of British geographers, Jackson has observed:

3 See, for example, Graham Davis, *The Irish in Britain* (Dublin, 1991).
4 Raphael Samuel, *London Review of Books*, 14 June 1990.

many geographers have continued to use the outdated and problematic concept of ethnic 'assimilation' despite fundamental criticisms of the concept on political and theoretical grounds. 'Assimilation' is simplistically defined as the socially desirable converse of 'segregation', an historically inevitable outcome of a unilinear process of ethnic competition and upward social mobility. The advocates of minority group 'assimilation' rarely pause to consider precisely whose interests such a process would serve, casually assuming it to be a universally desirable goal of social policy.[5]

An identical critique can be made of many historians of the Irish in Britain. The assimilationists do not dispute the historical evidence that many Irish people in the nineteenth century were disadvantaged, often subject to discrimination and hostility. What is important for the assimilationists is to establish the parallel existence of other experiences, which already presage the gradual access of all Irish migrants and their descendants to acceptance within British society. To this end, historians of the Irish in Britain are impelled to examine key criteria of assimilation: for example, patterns of residence, voting behaviour and social mobility, in order to identify the processes of and journeys towards assimilation.

Usually an important part of the analysis undertaken by those working within an assimilation framework is to engage in a process of disconnecting ethnicity/national identity from structural factors such as social class and employment opportunities.[6] If a particular ethnic/national grouping is predominantly of one class, which the Irish were in the nineteenth century, then the logic of the argument goes, that given British society at the time, the incoming migrants would have been differentiated on the basis of social class and subject to the extant patterns of class segregation in Britain. Residential segregation and evidence of cultural homogeneity, for example, in voting behaviour, would then be weighted as significant evidence that factors other than social class were at work, when explaining Irish experience in Britain.

The assumption in these historical accounts is that 'race' or ethnicity plays no part in class formation. Although 'race' and class are analytically distinct concepts, they cannot be treated as two distinct sets of relations.[7] Most writing about the Irish in nineteenth-century Britain fails to place the experience being analysed within the context of the formation of class relations of the period; it ignores the significance of the Irish presence in Britain for the establishment of a cross-class racist British nationalism; it fails to render an adequate account of the dynamic intersection of class, religion and national identity as the context of the experience of the Irish in Britain; it ignores the role of the British State

5   P. Jackson (ed.), *Race and Racism: Essays in Social Geography* (London, 1987).
6   R. Lawton, 'Irish Immigration into England and Wales in the Mid-Nineteenth Century', *Irish Geography*, vol. 4, no. 1 (1959), pp 35–64; Davis, *The Irish in Britain* (1991).
7   For a discussion of this point, see F. Anthias and N. Yuval-Davis, *Racialized Boundaries: Race, Nation, Gender, Colour and Class and the Anti-racist Struggle* (London, 1992).

except in the context of responding to the political activities of the Irish in Britain; and it unproblematically assigns to the Catholic Church either the main responsibility, or the chief credit, for forging anything resembling an Irish community in Britain.

The teleology of the segregation/assimilation model is that all migrants pass in a series of adaptive processes from emigration to ultimate absorption into the 'host' population. The 'segregationists' differ from the 'assimilationists' primarily on the timing and the range and complexity of the processes involved in assimilation. An alternative approach would not assume ultimate assimilation (nor for that matter ultimate segregation) but would aim to analyse the complex of issues of settlement for a migrant group in the context of the social relations of the specific nation state to which they had migrated. Thus, just as most class analysis has been about national economies, when analysing the experience of a migrant group it is necessary to address the different and distinctive institutional and cultural contexts which charaterise the nation state in which they settle.

The other half of the story, therefore, can only be supplied by adopting a different framework, one which problematises the nation state. Firstly, by locating the experiences of Irish migrants and their descendants in the context of the social relations of British society. Secondly, by acknowledging that even in the nineteenth century, before the advent of modern global telecommunications, Irish communities were in contact with and had as an alternative reference point a wider Irish diaspora. In this essay I am going to concentrate on the former, as space does not allow consideration of both aspects.

The present volume of essays focuses on local studies of the Irish in nineteenth-century Britain. In the segregation/assimilation model local studies are either utilised in order to demonstrate the heterogeneity of the ethnic population, with the resulting deduction that the prime conditions of ethnic identity or community are missing; or they are used to show the vibrancy and multi-dimensional character of the ethnic community. An alternative approach is to assert the value of local studies, as long as they are placed in the context of the wider national set of social relations. Explicating the relationship between the local, the national and the diasporic should be our aim, and in this essay I am concentrating on the relationship between the local and the national, with occasional references to the wider diasporic context.

I want, therefore, to do three things. First, to examine some of the writings about the Irish in Britain which are within the segregation/assimilation perspective. My intention is to explore in more detail how some of these writings close down understanding about Irish experiences whereas others can help us towards a full account. Second, I want to outline one aspect of an approach which can deliver 'the other half of the story', that is, locating Irish experiences in the context of the social relations of British society. This includes a discussion about the education of Irish Catholics in Britain, a vital realm for understanding the articulation of religion, class and national identity for a large proportion of the migrants. Third, I want to briefly examine how this different approach would treat some of the main themes of the segregation/assimilation perspective, in particular the debate about whether the Irish population in Britain were a community.

THE SEGREGATION/ASSIMILATION MODEL

One of the most unproblematic applications of the segregation/assimilation model is found in the work of David Fitzpatrick.[8] He argues that the Irish were not segregated in nineteenth-century Britain and concludes from this that the Irish did not form a community. Thus the alienation the Irish experienced in British culture was not cushioned by the creation of an immigrant community with an autonomous sub-culture. The evidence advanced for this interpretation is that Irish immigrants to Britain adopted different strategies. Some tried to replant their Irish culture in Britain, others created a hybrid culture, yet others did their best to forget that they were Irish.

The heterogeneous nature of their responses is taken by Fitzpatrick to rule out community. Despite their persistently low social status, Irish settlers, he argues, adopted patterns of residence, religious practice, political participation and criminality which do not suggest a segregated population locked in defensive ethnicity. He implies that integration, at least to 'a curious middle place', came for those of Irish descent. Fitzpatrick gives no explanation of how he defines community nor does he make explicit what framework should be adopted in understandng a migrant population. His argument implies, however, that community is characterised by homogeneity, defensive ethnicity, distinctive social practices and segregation, all of which he argues are largely absent in the case of the Irish.

Fitzpatrick's notion of community derives from one that was influential in British sociology up until the 1970s. This concept of community was very much tied up with the geographical concept of locality, especially working class areas. Fitzpatrick's study of the Irish in Britain is really about how the Irish, despite in the early part of this century occupying a 'curious middle place', assimilated to a working class community that was homogenous, white and British, if not actually English. He assumes, as did many of the community studies of the 1950s, that 'community' if it exists must be a direct reflection of an observable reality. There is no place in this analysis for creative consciousness; what people are is what they think, in a straightforward relationship. There is no space to explore the systems of representation of the imagined community

8   D. Fitzpatrick, 'A Curious Middle Place: the Irish in Britain, 1871–1921', in Swift and Gilley (eds), *The Irish in Britain 1815–1939*, pp 10–59.

of the Irish in Britain. Thus evidence of Irish and English people living in the same streets is taken as literal proof that there was no segregation; this is a very restricted definition of the complexities which may inform the relations of neighbours.

Another example of historical interpretation which is positioned within the segregation/assimilation perspective is that of Alan O'Day writing about the political representation of the Irish in Great Britain.[9] He also disparages the notion that the Irish in Britain formed a community, arguing that there is some doubt as to whether the Irish warrant the description of a fully fledged 'ethnic' group due to their diversity of experience and absence of pre-existing ethnic cohesion. Again the assumption permeating O'Day's account is that heterogeneity negates community. He sees the crucial question as: how and to what degree could a sense of common identity be activated?

O'Day argues that Irish ethnic politics in the late-nineteenth century always formed part of a wider matrix of Catholic and Liberal politics. Thus in most circumstances local success depended on an Irish candidate being acceptable in some measure to British interests. Consequently, a high point of Irish ethnic politics came after Gladstone adopted Home Rule, when Cardinal Manning was also an advocate of the policy, and the Irish middle class supported Home Rule to a greater degree as it became more respectable. After this, O'Day argues that in the early twentieth century the Church and the Labour party were critical for absorbing the Irish population into mainstream British institutions and thus a specifically ethnic politics, always a limited option was on the wane. The inability of the Irish to construct and maintain effective communal political institutions reflected Irish indifference to their fate and this was a vital factor in the failure to preserve a flourishing ethnic identity among descendants of the exiles. Catholicism in contrast fared much better.

There are three immediate problems with O'Day's approach. First, there is a constant slippage between the notion of an ethnic conciousness and an ethnic politics. There seems to be an assumption that the former would lead automatically to mobilisation within the latter. Second, basing any suppositions of the period on the exercise of the franchise is shaky as by default those who had the vote were quite a minority of the Irish population. Third, there is little consideration of the extent to which Irish ethnic identities were contested and in particular were subject to an active strategy of incorporation. The absorption of the Irish into mainstream British national institutions is naturalised (there is no questioning of whose interests such a process served) and only a successful cross-class homogenous ethnicity is deemed likely to have prevented this happening. Thus any failure to achieve an ethnic politics becomes a failure of the group, enabling their easy disparagement.

9 Alan O'Day, 'The Political Representation of the Irish in Great Britain, 1850–1914, in G. Alderman (ed.), *Governments, Ethnic Groups and Political Representation* (New York, 1993).

Thus both Fitzpatrick's and O'Day's frameworks of interpretation close down understandings of Irish experiences because they utilize an unproblematic notion of the trajectory from segregation to assimilation and they tend to disaggregate causative factors in this process. I want to turn to two other examples of writing within this perspective which come to very different conclusions. In both cases, the analysis is predicated on an implicit segregation/assimilation model, but the authors are arguing that a viable Irish Catholic subculture or community did exist. Fielding's study of the Irish in Manchester and Salford leads him to conclude that the Irish population in Britain were neither simply Irish, Catholic nor working class, but an amalgam of all three.[10] He makes these points in the course of a critique of the view that Irish workers had been fully absorbed into the English working class by 1914. This latter notion is based on a belief in the ability of trade unions to foster the integration of minority groups into the working class. Fielding makes the point that only a minority of the Irish migrants were members of trade unions by the twentieth century and that occupation cannot be taken as determining each and every aspect of a person's identity.

Fielding's case is that Irish Catholics in England did construct for themselves a separate and viable way of life, and the evidence for this can be traced down to 1945 and beyond. He argues that the 'problem' with Irish Catholic immigrants is that they neither wanted full assimilation nor complete separation from English society. For them class (assimilation) and ethnicity (segregation) formed a continuum, not mutually exclusive poles of attraction. The consequence was the development of a strong but heterogeneous Irish Catholic subculture within the working class. What Fielding's exemplary local study opens up for further exploration is that heterogeneity does not necessarily negate community; it is also an attempt to trace the inter-relationship between various facets of Irish communal identities and is not based on an assumption that disaggregation of causative factors is the appropriate method to understand identity formation.

To the extent that Fitzpatrick or O'Day think there was any sub-culture in Irish areas they see it as the creation of the Catholic Church. Sheridan Gilley, who has written extensively about the Irish in nineteenth-century Britain, agrees that a church-related culture was dominant in Irish areas but he differs in that he sees Irish Catholics maintaining a separate culture and identity and describes the Irish in Britain as part of an international community of the Irish emigrant in which religion, nationalism, and ethnic identity came together – priests and politicians were in his view the instigators of this international consciousness.[11] What Gilley's work opens up is the possibility of considering diaspora as a formative context for Irish communities abroad. The concept of

10 Steven Fielding, *Class and Ethnicity: Irish Catholics in England, 1880–1939* (Buckingham, 1993).
11 Sheridan Gilley, 'The Irish', *History Today* (June, 1985).

diaspora' provides the opportunity to make 'connections' in many directions across and between different communities of the Irish abroad.

For Gilley and other writers, religion and Home Rule/nationalist politics were the cornerstone of the Irish community.[12] But it is on the basis of these same criteria, religion and politics, that Fitzpatrick and O'Day pour scorn upon the idea that an Irish community existed. These differing interpretations are all the more puzzling as they all operate with the notion that 'community' is created by institutions, primarily the Church. This apparent paradox can only be explained by drawing back from the dissection of the Irish community and engaging in an analysis that locates Irish experiences in the social relations of the society in which they have settled.

BRITAIN IN THE NINETEENTH CENTURY: RELIGION, CLASS
AND NATIONAL IDENTITY

The historical experience of the Irish in nineteenth-century Britain affords us the opportunity to trace over two centuries the trajectory of what today we would call an ethnic minority. In the United States this type of investigation can be undertaken for a number of European immigrant groups. In Britain only the Irish provide the example of a significant labour migrant group whose experiences can be studied over a similar timescale. For such an analysis it is vital that the specificity of the society into which the Irish were migrating be delineated and in this context an estimate made of the relevant conceptual framework to adopt.

The nineteenth century was a time in which global space began to be systematically divided into bounded political entities known as nation states. Thus as Massey points out 'places' came to be seen as bounded, with their own internally generated authenticities, as defined by their difference from other places which lay outside, beyond their borders.[13] She argues that this process embodies an imagination of defensible places, of the rights of 'local people' to their own 'local places', of a world divided by difference and firm boundaries. Massey sees space/society as the sphere of juxtoposition, or co-existence, of distinct narratives, as the product of power-filled social relations. Within that context, 'places' may be imagined as particular articulations of these social relations, including local relations 'within' the place and those many connections which stretch way beyond it. This is place as meeting place.

12 For example, W.J. Lowe, *The Irish in Mid-Victorian Lancashire: The Shaping of a Working-class Community* (New York, 1989).

13 D. Massey, 'Imagining Globalisation: power-geometries of time-space', in A. Brah, M.J. Hickman, and M. Mac an Ghaill (eds), *Global Futures: Migration, Environment and Globalization* (London, 1999, forthcoming).

This is a notion of space where specificity (local uniqueness, a sense of place) derives not from some mythical primordial inheritance nor from relative segregation but precisely from the absolute particularity of the mixture of influences found together there. Thus hybridity is related to a particular space be it a local community or nation state. Heterogeneous experiences and strategies are not necessarily the negation of community or a common identity. The specificity of working class areas of British cities in the nineteenth century in part derived from the mixtures of influences to be found there. In particular, despite erroneous notions that plurality originated in the 1950s, the fast-growing urban areas of the last century were ethnically mixed from the outset, and this occured in a period when the political subjectivity of the working class was subject to sustained contestation. These ethnic differences were sometimes combined in solidarity, but at other times they were firmly segregated and hostilely engaged.

It has been a main function of national cultures to represent what is in fact the ethnic mix of modern nationality as the primordial unity of 'one people'. This has been achieved by centralised nation-states with their incorporating cultures and national identities, implanted and secured by strong cultural institutions, which tend to subsume all differences and diversity into themselves.[14] The nineteenth century was the period in which the social construction of the 'national-racial unit' which came to underpin Englishness/ Britishness was underway. In this process the role of the state, both centrally and locally, was crucial in shaping the 'national-racial unit' or the unity of 'one people'. Britishness as a national identity developed as the appropriate identity for a state constructed on the basis of a series of either forced or negotiated unions of different societies. The point of interest for us is that the Irish first came in very large numbers to Britain during the period which was most critical for the successful securing of a national identity and culture in Britain (and by that means a class alliance) i.e. the nineteenth century. In that period the Irish were both the most sizeable and most visible minority element in the population. The consequences have been profound for the subsequent history and experiences of the Irish in Britain.

Between 1801 and 1922 the Irish migrating to Britain travelled within the same state. However, all the evidence suggests that although citizens of the same state, on arrival in England, Scotland or Wales, Irish Catholic peasants, who mostly became part of the urban working class, were treated as Other by the institutions and agencies who were involved in the formation of and contestations over the political and moral character of the working class. Historically, being a citizen of the state has not been the key to acceptability

14 S. Hall, 'Our Mongrel Selves', *New Stateman and Society* (Borderlands Supplement), 19 June 1992.

within the nation in Britain, unlike in France. The experiences of the Irish Catholic working class in nineteenth-century Britain demonstrate this just as did the later experiences of migrants from the Caribbean and Asian sub-continent in mid-twentieth century Britain.

The processes by which Britain was becoming transformed into the first industrial capitalist nation, and dominant colonial power, were well underway in the nineteenth century and they raised key questions about the appropriate ways of imagining the nation (and its empire) and constructing forms of belonging. The presence of large numbers of Irish migrants and their children is a relevant part of the story of how the state in the form of central government actively intervened to construct political subjects and foster national conscious-ness. The ultimate acceptance of the superiority of being English/British by the indigenous working class was not only generated in contrast to the peoples of the Empire, beyond Europe, but also involved the Othering of those within the domestic sphere who shared not only a European 'ethnic' heritage but were citizens of the same state. Thus another aspect of the social relations of Britain in which Irish experiences have to be set is the construction of certain people, events or behaviours both inside and outside the polity as alien and as social problems.

The state, particularly at a local level, and other institutions utilised the presence of Irish immigrants as a means both of reinforcing a British, Protestant identity amongst the 'indigenous' working class and of defining 'respectable' working class habits and morals (Irish Catholics were by definition taken as representing the Other of such a morality). We can see this very clearly in examining the work of James Phillips Kay, Secretary to the Manchester Board of Health in the early 1830s, becoming an Assistant Poor Law Commissioner in 1835 and later to become head of the Committee of the Privy Council on Education, the first central state agency of education. As Poovery argues:

> In Kay's treatment of the Irish, we see a particularly complex example of the way that a proponent of one set of issues – in this case social reform at the national level – mobilized prejudices against a particular group of people by constructing an image of the nation that excluded this group.[15]

For Kay the ills of the social body, the nation, were linked into the presence of the Irish who had a demoralising effect on English, Welsh and Scottish workers. The sentiments being expressed at national level by Kay, and also by Engels, Carlyle and others chimed with those being manifested at local level where anti-Irish prejudice was also an influence on policy formation and implementation. As Finnegan in her study of the Irish in York, comments:

15 M. Poovery, *Making a Social Body: British Cultural Formation 1830–64* (Chicago, 1995), p. 65.

There was a marked degree of anti-Irish prejudice in the city, stemming mainly from the middle classes and apparent in the attitudes and utterances of the Poor Law Guardians, Sanitary Inspectors and magistrates, and particularly evident in newspaper editorials and the coverage of local news. If these attitudes were not merely reflections of the public's views, but were also instrumental in forming them, then their influence could have been considerable. Those in authority, English, middle-class, respectable Protestants, were prejudiced against the immigrants, and prejudice led them to make stereotyped, misleading judgements about the Irish.[16]

What was the case in York was also true of other cities.[17] Father Kelly, an Irish priest in the Westminster diocese, wrote to Cardinal Wiseman in 1854 saying that Catholics applying for poor relief

are generally told in the most insulting way to go to their priests. They seldom meet with Sympathy from any member of the various boards of Guardians, the Relieving Officer is frequently a ribald bully ... The threat of being sent back to Ireland, even where they have legal rights to relief but no friend to indicate it for them, sends the poor applicant back broken hearted to his or her friends. The consequence of all this is that the Catholic working classes have a heavy burden thrown upon them in relieving their poorer brethren, whilst this duty is taken off the shoulders of the Protestant working classes, by falling back in cases of distress, upon rates levied on Catholics and Protestants alike.[18]

This type of differentiation between sections of the working classes was constantly made; everyone understood that the Catholic working classes were Irish. They were a very visible minority, identified as unwelcome immigrants and subject to discriminatory practices.

In the critical period of 1830–70, the Irish, despite being members of the same polity, were differentiated as an immigrant labour force, a social problem and a political threat. In particular, the reaction of the intermediate and petty bourgeois classes was to advocate segregation in order to prevent contamination. It was the magistrates, Poor Law guardians, health inspectors and police who at local level constructed a segregationist rationale focusing on the Irish. This explains why paying attention to local conditions and variations is important. However, each local scenario was part of a wider national set of social relations in which the articulation of religion, class and national identity

16 Frances Finnegan, 'The Irish in York', in Swift and Gilley, *The Irish in the Victorian City*, p. 77.

17 On London, see especially S. Gilley, 'Protestant London, No-Popery and the Irish Poor, 1830–60', *Recusant History*, vol. X (1970), pp 210–30; on Liverpool, see T. Burke, *Catholic History of Liverpool* (Liverpool, 1910).

18 K.G.T. McDonnell, 'Roman Catholics in London, 1850–65', in A.E.G. Hollaender and W. Kellaway (eds), *Studies in London History* (London, 1969), p. 434.

formed the crucial framework for Irish experiences. Understanding the relationship between the local and the national is essential; it is important not to assume
that every local instance necessarily negates a wider national coherence.

Considering such local studies within the broader context of national strategies
facilitates mapping some of the continuities and discontinuities in the structure
of power and inequality and their connections to the making of welfare policies
and practices in Britain. It also allows us to consider arguments about the ways
in which the categories of class, gender, 'race' and ethnicity have patterned the
structure of social relations in Britain in the last 200 years. The visibility of the
Irish in nineteenth-century Britain lay in that a conjunction of migrant labour,
poverty and Catholicism was recognised as 'Irish' and as 'immigrant'. This
explains why Irish migrants were seen, categorized and subject to the attention
of magistrates and Poor Law guardians to a greater degree than, for example,
Scottish migrants. The latter were poor too, but they were part of a longer-
established and more acceptable union, and they were Protestants. How the
socially constructed attributes of different populations were articulated together
is the task for analysis rather than attempts to disaggregate the separate 'causative
factors' to establish whether it was class or ethnicity or religion which was
determinate.

The strong cultural institutions created in the nineteenth century – police
forces, schools, mass media – engaged in a process of nationalizing the national
identity: Britishness. For example, in the case of schools far from simply aiming
to repress or neutralize the political activities of certain classes or social groups
in society, educational reform sought to reconstruct political rule by reconstructing
the political subjectivity of the population, specifically the working class. This
was achieved by developing and heightening consciousness within newly
constructed state forms. Thus educational reform sought to build the political
subject and in so doing constructed the state.

EDUCATION AS A MEANS OF INCORPORATING AND DENATIONALIZING THE IRISH CATHOLIC WORKING CLASS

Central to an alternative approach to the segregation/assimilation model is
therefore a conception of the social relations of a particular society as made up
of a set of contestations. The State intervened to regulate the expression and
development of separate and distinctive identities by potentially oppositional
groups in order to create a single nation-state; this process is captured by the
concept of incorporation. The Catholic Church became the agency of this
process as regards the Irish Catholic working class in Britain. The strategies of
incorporation which the Church developed, in particular Catholic education,
aimed to regulate the expression and development of Irish identity. The
particular focus of incorporation was changing the identity of Irish pupils in

Catholic schools. It is in the arena of education that a link between socio-political objectives of the state and the aims of the Catholic Church was established.

After the experience of the Reformation and the persecution of Catholics which followed, and with continuing political suppression, it became paramount for many English Catholics to prove themselves 'an ultra-loyal minority'. Proving their loyalty to the State remained a priority for English Catholics after the attainment of Catholic Emancipation in 1829. It was to be a decisive factor in their relations with the Irish migrants already swelling the ranks of Catholics in England by the end of the eighteenth century. This background about the differences between the clergy and lay congregations in England, and to a certain extent in Scotland, and Irish migrants needs to be borne in mind when considering the the policies and system of elementary schools which the Catholic church developed in Britain. Catholic state elementary schools were primarily developed to school the Irish. Most important from the perspective of the British State, on national and class grounds, the Catholic Church could be 'trusted' with the task of incorporating and denationalizing the Irish.

In the changed political circumstances of the 1830s and 1840s the State, in the form of various Whig and Peelite administrations, wanted a national system of education to include all working class children; their aim was to produce the appropriate work force and political subjects of the future. Education was the means by which the long term regulation and transformation of the working class was to be achieved. In this context it is important to note that a separate Catholic elementary schools system did not develop as a result of any sectarian tendencies of the Catholic Church and Irish Catholics in Britain. Despite internal differences on the issue, the Catholic authorities, including Cardinal Wiseman would have accepted interdenominational schools as long as the church retained full control of the religious instruction of Catholic children.

Objections to the children of Irish Catholic migrants being schooled with other working class children came from other denominations, especially the Church of England, and from certain political forces, in particular the Conservative party. These objections were forcibly expressed at local level. Their objections centred on the fear of contamination from the Irish Catholic working class. These fears were articulated by the Protestant Association and by the local and national press through the discourse of anti-Catholicism and opposition to the 'Irish System' (of education). In the end, the State successfully introduced grant aid for separate Catholic schools in 1847, against still significant opposition to the funding of any Catholic enterprise.

The Catholic Church created the Catholic Poor School Committee (CPSC) in 1847 in order to receive government grant-in-aid. The bishops' intention was not only to provide the organisational framework for the transfer of government monies to schools, but, to ensure the existence of a body under their supervsion to deal with educational questions. The Catholic bishops of

England and Wales charged the CPSC with being responsible for the general interests of the education of the poor. The presentation of the interests of the State, the Church and the Catholic poor as being mutually reinforcing was to be an insistent theme of Catholic educational policy.

The long-term aim of the Catholic authorities therefore was not just to produce good Catholics but also to produce a body of loyal, respectable working-class English and Scottish Catholics of limited social mobility out of the Irish masses. As the number of Catholic elementary schools increased, what developed was a hierarchically organised system which united the Catholic body in Britain as did no other enterprise. The clergy and many of the Catholic laity in England, Wales and Scotland were convinced of the charitable necessity of educating the Catholic poor. The clergy were able to elicit the participation of Irish Catholics in the parish on the issue of the education of their children, if not on any other issue. The whole enterprise was overseen by the bishops through the agency of the CPSC.

The strengthening of Catholic identity became the principal objective of Catholic elementary schools. This was a strategy designed not only to arrest lapsation but also to weaken Irish national identity. From the beginning of the Catholic elementary system the content of the secular education of Irish working-class children in Britain contained little reference to Ireland. What mention was made of Ireland in the new Catholic readers, which replaced the Irish lesson-books later in the nineteenth century, primarily praised the Catholicity of the Irish as their outstanding feature and otherwise contained lessons on the political economy of Ireland. These characteristics of Catholic schools curriculum were little changed over a century later. The identity of Irish working-class children as Catholics was implanted and constantly reinforced in the schools by the priority placed on religious instruction, in the effort which went into religious instruction, and in the manner in which the religious pervaded all the rituals of school life. This was a strategy of incorporation. There was a corresponding silence in the curriculum content of Catholic schools about Ireland. This was a strategy of denationalization.[19]

19 For a fuller development of the argument in this section see M.J. Hickman, *Religion, Class and Identity: The State, the Catholic Church and the Education of the Irish in Britain* (Aldershot, 1995). One area of published work has to a considerable extent involved placing research about the Irish in the context of wider social relations, that is the literature about the policing of the Irish in nineteenth-century British cities. See, for example, D. Philips, 'Riots and Public Order in the Black Country, 1835–1860' in J. Stevenson and R. Quinault (eds), *Popular Protest and Public Order* (London, 1974), pp 141–80; Roger Swift, 'Another Stafford Street Row: Law, Order and the Irish Presence in Mid-Victorian Wolverhampton' in Swift and Gilley (eds), *The Irish in the Victorian City* (1985), pp 179–206; J. Davis, 'From "Rookeries" to "Communities": Race, Poverty and Policing in London, 1850–1985', *History Workshop Journal*, no. 27 (Spring, 1989), pp 66–85.

THE CONTESTATION OF IRISH IDENTITIES

By the end of the nineteenth century the local school had become a central institution of every Catholic parish. The school was an integral part of the ecclesiastical system and the most careful statistics were kept of Roman Catholic children attending elsewhere and of the number of first communions, confessions and confirmations from amongst the children. As Alan Bartlett has observed:

> The sense of responsibility for the schools was spread throughout the Roman Catholic community by means of the out-door collection, which in turn was an essential tool in retaining the sense of identity and loyalty in the wider Roman Catholic constituency.[20]

These activities ensured that the priest knew his parishioners well even if they did not visit the church very often other than to mark key rites of passage: birth, marriage and death. The closeness of these ties (whatever antagonisms lay beneath the surface), the network of community organizations based on the church and the assiduous training of the young in the primacy of Catholic identity ensured that in this period the differentiation of Irish Catholics and their descendants, from their neighbours and often from their workmates, was regenerated across many decades.

This highlights why assessing Irish communality or degree of assimilation through measuring mass attendance or voting habits is not an adequate way of gauging the complexity of Irish experiences. It is clear that the Catholic Church has been, on the one hand, the agency of incorporation and denationalization and, on the other hand, one of the main means by which the Irish Catholic working class established a viable community life within British society, a community life which has always included more than their religious identity, reflecting class allegiances, gender priorities and national aspirations as well as supporting the local Catholic church and school.

Thus many Irish Catholics in Britain acknowledged the power and role of the Church in the community, while at the same time maintaining spheres which were protected from the interference of the Church. In this way Irish working class Catholics established an 'ethnic space' for themselves in which a variety of forms of belonging were possible. While institutions, and in particular the Church, were very influential they never exercised that influence in an uncontested arena. Thus the mask of Catholicism, the public profile afforded the Church by their congregation, hid from view multiple forms of ethnic space. These spaces were gendered and also marked by class, regional and generational differences.

20 A. Bartlett, 'From Strength to Strength: Roman Catholicism in Bermondsey up to 1939', in *Catholics and their Church in Britain 1880–1939* (Warwick Working Papers in Social History, University of Warwick, Coventry, 1988), p. 35.

As stated earlier, incorporation is distinct from assimilation in that it assumes state and institutional intervention in the regulation of the experience and identity of significant labour migrant groups. In the nineteenth century, the Church was the only national institution in Britain to win the identification of Irish working-class migrants, and herein lay much of its subsequent influence. The long-term success of the Church lay not in the eradication of all Irish identities (although denationalization was successful in specific conjunctures) but in gaining acquiescence to the necessity of a low public profile for Irish Catholic communities and individuals.

It is important to note that the extent of the Church's influence was always contingent on its negotiation of the complex scenario in which figured not only the national and class identities of Irish communities, and the institutions representing these identities, but the continuing generation of anti-Catholic and anti-Irish discourses and practices. The unskilled Irish had not been politicized in the main by trade unionism but by the struggle for Home Rule. This had meant in the second half of the nineteenth century that they were arguably the most politicized part of the unskilled and semi-skilled stratum of the working class.

The support for Home Rule caused internal tensions within Irish Catholic communities, as did increasing support for the Labour party, but this did not cause those communities necessarily either to disintegrate or assimilate or become strangled by the grip of the Church to the point where an Irish dimension was lost altogether. More accurately, the situation should be characterized as one in which the Church had to accommodate the politics of its Irish working-class congregation (although the extent of this accommodation varied between dioceses and parishes and between levels of the hierarchy), as its institutional embrace of these communities increased.

Some historians have argued that the Church preferred to encourage moderate Irish nationalism rather than adherence to socialism.[21] This may have been true in some areas, particularly at parish level, and especially amongst Irish priests, but for the hierarchy this was not the case. Incorporation to national institutions in Britain was encouraged even when by the early part of the twentieth century this involved supporting the Labour Party: an institution which in this period (in England) was considerably more ambivalent about separate Catholic schools than it was about Irish independence. The Church therefore continued to develop a dual strategy: the construction of relatively insular parish-based community structures, ensuring the institutional survival of the Church; and, as had been the case since the middle of the nineteenth century, incorporating Irish Catholics within national institutions: be it the education system or the political system. This contradictory process was

21 For example, W.M. Walker, 'Irish Immigrants in Scotland: their Priests, Politics and Parochial Life', *Historical Journal*, vol. XV, no. 4 (1972), pp 649–67.

implicit in all relations between the British Catholic Churches and Irish communities.

Within the segregation/assimilation model the fact that British institutions should aim to absorb the Irish population is naturalised instead of being examined for elements of their specific role in the contestation of Irish identity. The Irish may have been subject to conflicting loyalties, but multiplicity is the condition of all diasporic communities. What is of interest is how the seemingly inherent contradictions of their class position, religious affiliation and national identity were juggled and resolved or not. These same characteristics ensured that they were subject to active attempts by the State and other institutions to neutralise their national identity; these processes were successful in some cases but resisted by many. This is the context which needs exploration.

The quiescence of Irish Catholics lay in the acceptance of a public mask of Catholicism as its communal identity. This in turn had an impact on the way in which Irish Catholics intervened and raised issues in various public arenas. No other institution was as well placed as the Church to exercise this influence and no other institution had both the class and national profile to be entrusted and funded by the State, despite massive opposition, to this end. As the features of institutional life determine the forms that protest takes, one consequence of the dominant position of Catholic institutions in Irish areas was that many Irish people maintained a low profile (outside Irish areas) about being Irish and about Irish national issues. Irish people, especially if in any way socially mobile, were more likely to participate in public arenas as Catholics first, and as Irish men or women second.[22]

CONCLUSION

This essay has argued for a different approach to the historiography of the Irish in Britain – one that in placing analysis of Irish experiences in the context of a wider study of British social relations engages more directly with debates pertinent to British social and political history in general. The constant circularity of the debates about the Irish in Britain generated by the segregation/assimilation model have contributed directly to the marginalisation and silencing of Irish issues in these wider debates. The chapter has also argued for placing Irish experiences in Britain within a wider diasporic context, as yet a still relatively uncharted territory.

The chapter sought to demonstrate the advantages of this alternative approach by considering relations between the British Catholic churches and the Irish Catholic working class within the context of British social relations. It

22 See Fielding, *Class and Ethnicity* (1993), for an account of the participation of Irish Catholics in the Labour party in the inter-war period.

was argued that the low public profile, or invisibility, of the Irish in Britain is the main achievement of the state and institutional response to the Irish presence in nineteenth-century Britain. The success of the incorporatist strategy of the Church lay in its being the agency of a low public profile for the Irish in Britain. The production of this low public profile is frequently misrecognized as a process of assimilation. A low profile is not evidence of assimilation but of a specific response by Irish people to the various anti-Irish and anti-Catholic discourses and practices, which have been encountered and negotiated within the context of specific communal institutions. In contrast, issues which were sanctified by the Church, for example, education, did not have a low profile, because these issues not only had the backing, but the exhortation, of a powerful institution.

However, it must in conclusion be stressed that many Irish Catholics in Britain acknowledged the power and role of the Church in the community, while at the same time maintaining spheres which were protected from its interference. Many other Irish people were beyond the influence of the Catholic Church altogether, for example, Irish Protestant migrants. It is necessary to recognise these differences and explore their implication further. When considering 'community', as well as many points of similarity, there are also critical points of deep and significant difference which constitute 'what we really are' or 'what we have become'. None of this negates that an 'ethnic space' to be Irish was established. If that 'ethnic space' was relatively narrowly defined in the past (primarily as an expression of the Irish Catholic working classes) that was in part the consequence of the fact that the imagined communal identity of being Irish in Britain was constructed in resisistance to the regimes of representation of 'the Irish' within a racist British nationalism.

A discussion of community as constituted by diversity and hybridity, recognises that the symbols that represent the differences and boundaries of the Irish community do not necessarily have the same meaning for all Irish people or those of Irish descent. This differentiation is a strength rather than a weakness (this is why Fitzpatrick and O'Day are so wrong to imply homogeneity is a necessary element of 'community'). The diaspora experience must necessarily recognise heterogeneity and diversity, because identity lives with and through difference. In this way we may approach the 'full story' of the Irish in Britain.

The Gaelic revival in London, 1900–22: limits of ethnic identity[1]

John Hutchinson and Alan O'Day

There are probably a quarter of a million of people resident in London of Irish birth and parentage, and these more nearly represent the nation at home than do the Irish residents of any other town or city on earth.

Here we have the very extremes of Irish society mixing and commingling in the rush and roar of life that rolls for ever in the haunts of fashion, the busy marts, and the crowded thoroughfares of this all absorbing centre of life.[2]

INTRODUCTION

Between 1890 and 1922 Irish nationalism entered a new phase with the emergence of a Gaelic revival which infused into it an intense ethnic and separatist strain. Although initially formulated in cultural terms, this revival was transformed by a group of modernising journalists, including Arthur Griffith, D.P. Moran and W.P. Ryan, into a significant, if loosely-knit, social movement that sought Ireland's economic, social and political regeneration as a distinctive civilisation. Until 1916 this movement of a frustrated intelligentsia appealed only to a minority of Irish people at home and abroad. However, as a consequence of events between 1916 and 1921 its programme was adopted as the core cultural aspiration of the part of Ireland that separated from the Union. To the extent that Ireland experienced a revolution at all, it was the ideology of the Gaelic revival based on the notion of the Gaeltacht that set the agenda.

1   We wish to thank the research committee of the University of North London for financial assistance. Also, we want to acknowledge the help of Geoffrey Alderman, Peter Alter, John Broad, George Boyce, Miles Bradbury, David Feldman, Barbara Gauntt, Donald and Shirley Ginter, Sheridan Gilley, Terry Gourvish, David Howell, Michael Hurst, Donal Kerr, the late John Leslie, Johathan Moore, Margaret Mullally, Roland Quinault, Roger Swift, Charles Thomas, F.M.L. Thompson, Gabrielle Ward-Smith, and the members of group four under the leadership of Kevin B. Nowlan in the project, 'Governments and Non-Dominant Ethnic Groups in Europe, 1850–1940', sponsored by the European Science Foundation. From the Foundation, Christoph Mülberg, now in Bonn, and Genèvieve Schauinger are owed special thanks.
2   Hugh Heinrick, *A Survey of the Irish in England* (1872) edited by Alan O'Day (London, 1990), p. 2.

The Irish in Great Britain, especially those residing in London, played an important role in the unfolding of this new mode of nationalism. The rise of cultural nationalism among the 'exiles' followed a parallel course to that in the homeland and arose from many of the same motivations. Confronted by a British State that was increasingly ready to intervene in the field of education and welfare, the Irish in Britain, like their counterparts in Ireland, were preoccupied with questions of communal identity. Chief among these was a debate over whether they ought to accept or resist incorporation into the dominant metropolitan culture.

As a diaspora and minority community dispersed into random pockets in Great Britain, the 'exile' Irish differed in important respects from their compatriots at home. They were part of a predominantly industrial society, and even at the turn of the century they were concentrated disproportionately in the working class. Many had an affinity for the labour movement that competed with nationalism for their adherence. With the exception of the United Irish League of Great Britain and a plethora of small ephemeral institutions and clubs, they had no major native institution that could act as a focus for Irish identity. The Catholic Church and particularly Catholic schools served not to bolster Irish distinctiveness but to incorporate the group into the host community while preserving its religious character. Also, the Irish in Great Britain did not lay claim to a territory for themselves, nor did they demand concessions outside the religious/education sphere such as those that typically were demanded by ethnic communities in central, eastern and south-eastern Europe. The Irish did not seek separate political representation, special ethnic voting lists, control over occupations restricted to themselves, language rights, distinctive social recognition or dispensations. Finally, the problem of identity of a disapora group is always more intensely felt on a day-to-day basis. Only in very limited enclaves did they form localised pluralities; they had to share living space and the work place with the non-Irish.

Cultural enthusiasm was not new. Its various small institutional expressions had existed for decades; nearly all these groups eschewed politics and were the preserve of cadres of intellectuals. Communal political aspirations were channelled through associations devoted to the interests of Ireland; from the 1870s these could be found in a succession of bodies such as the Home Rule Confederation of Great Britain, the Irish National League of Great Britain and the United Irish League of Great Britain.[3] The latter was founded in 1900, and like its predecessors was controlled by Irish parliamentarians, directing its

3 For a fuller discussion of these groups see, Alan O'Day, 'The Political Representation of the Irish in Great Britain, 1850–1940' in Geoffrey Alderman, John Leslie and Klaus Erich Pollmann (eds), *Governments, Ethnic Groups and Political Representation* (Aldershot and New York, 1993), pp 31–83.

labours towards marshalling the ethnic vote for Home Rule. Religious, educational and social life was filtered through different institutions, the Catholic
Church being by far the most important. Although the Church did not foster,
indeed generally attempted to submerge a specific Irish national identity into
the wider British entity, political and other groups on the whole were not in
competition with one another but tended (within limits) to be complementary.
This working relationship was eased by the Liberal party's adoption of Home
Rule. Yet educational questions strained the political dynamics of the Liberal
alliance, and there was a certain amount of criticism that Irishmen and
Catholics received too few of the rewards from that alliance at local level. In
November 1888 the *Catholic Herald* grumbled:

> There is a great deal of fuss being made over the London Vestry elections.
> Irishmen are being called on to support Radicals and Reformers. Very good. But
> have we got anything in return? We don't see the names of any Irishmen or
> Catholics selected as representatives. Our contention is that if we are to vote for
> a certain set of men all over London, we should have a share of the represen-
> tation in return. If we are good enough to return candidates by our votes there
> are surely some of our people good enough to be selected to sit on the Boards.[4]

Liberal secularism, especially on education, presented a continuing problem. A
compromise was worked out in practice along the lines suggested in May 1888
by the *Catholic Herald*:

> Our contention is that in Parliamentary elections we should go for Home Rule
> and support Home Rulers; in School Board elections we should support the
> friends of our schools and of all voluntary schools; for Boards of Guardians we
> should vote for those who will do justice to our Catholic poor; and for Town
> Councils we should, if no vital issue is at stake, go for a Home Ruler; but if there
> is any Catholic interest to which our Home Rule friend is opposed then we
> should oppose him.[5]

Despite an element of friction over where the Irish fitted into the political and
social spectrum, the main bodies purporting to speak for the Irish as Irish or
Catholics in Great Britain used their weight for Home Rule or to secure minor
concessions tending towards incorporation in the dominant society. The formula
proposed by the *Catholic Herald* did not require an elaborate institutional
framework to ensure compliance; it reflected the proclivities of the ethnic
community. A new movement like the Gaelic revival, with a different and
potentially competing vision based on a distinctive Irish nationality, had to face
obstacles and would have a mountain to climb before its ideas would be accepted

4 *Catholic Herald*, 9 Nov. 1888.
5 Ibid., 18 May 1888.

even in Ireland. The problems were even larger in Great Britain, particularly in London, because among other things its implementation would impel the 'exiles' to separate themselves in ordinary affairs from their non-Irish neighbours.

The Gaelic revival took place at a time when the Irish community itself was undergoing demographic shifts and the economy of Great Britain was in a critical stage of structural transition.[6] After 1871 the numbers of Irish coming to Great Britain declined. Some 566,540 Irish-born were recorded as living in England and Wales in 1871, a number which fell to 426,565 in 1901 and to 375,325 in 1911. As a proportion of the total population, the Irish-born dipped from 3% in 1861 to merely 1% in 1911; this was a minority that was tending to get older as the young were not replenishing the earlier arrivals at sufficient levels to maintain a generational balance.[7] By the twentieth century the vast majority, probably something like a 3:1 ratio of the so-called potential ethnic body, were born in Great Britain. Intermarriage and upward mobility, as Hugh Heinrick predicted in 1872, ate away at communal affiliation.[8] Some of the British-born upheld Ireland's right to self-government but few had any real intention to return 'home' permanently or to establish a virtually self-segregating community in exile. These were not obvious recruits to the ideals of a revival emphasising language and cultural differentiation, not to mention the bucolic values of the movement. Earlier male migrants outstripped females but between 1891 and 1921 the position was reversed. Also, the economic character of migration changed. Although the largest number of males entered the working-class, the number of professional and commercial men emigrating from Ireland to Britain rose significantly after the late 1870s. While it is impossible to give a precise account of the change, it is known that the numbers leaving Ireland in this category more than doubled between the 1870s and the second decade of the twentieth century. The rise was less sharp for women who continued to be heavily over-represented in domestic work, but there was a notable increase in the numbers migrating to be teach in Catholic primary schools. In 1871 16.1% of the Irish living in England and Wales were situated in London. The attractiveness of the metropolis continued, especially for an aspiring educated class of migrant. This trend combined with the substantial embourgeoisement of a section of the community born in Great Britain to make the lives of a section of the Irish during the Edwardian era qualitatively different from those of 1850s and 1860s.[9] A caveat must be entered at this

---

6 The basic information cited is derived from John Archer Jackson, *The Irish in Britain* (London, 1963), pp 186–201; Donald Harman Akenson, *The Irish Diaspora: A Primer* (Toronto and Belfast, 1996), pp 189–215.

7 David Fitzpatrick, 'The Irish in Britain, 1871–1921', in W.E.Vaughan (ed.), *A New History of Ireland*, vol. VII, *Ireland under the Union, II, 1870–1921* (Oxford, 1996), p. 655.

8 Heinrick, *Survey*, pp 127–8.

9 Fitzpatrick's contention that the Irish in Britain were the residue of those leaving Ireland is perhaps a shade overly influenced by his Australian origins: 'Irish in Britain', p. 655.

point: many of the educated and professionally qualified Irish were Protestant, and its is probable that appropriately 20 to 30% of the Irish-born total were Protestants. Still, if those who identified themselves as 'Irish' were over-represented in the working-classes, they were now dispersed more generally through the occupational pyramid. The economic slow-down in the traditional industries encouraged the drift to London. As the Gaelic revival was a movement of the intelligentsia, it had much to gain from the structural alteration, particularly in London.

HISTORIOGRAPHY

Neither the Gaelic revival in Britain nor the Irish communities in London have been studied extensively. The first has been a preserve of literary scholars whose interests are not primarily in theoretical formulations of national revivals; the latter is neglected because of the immense technical problems of researching a group so geographically and socially dispersed. It is not even appropriate to speak of the London Irish as a single entity because there were, in fact, a multiplicity of ethnic communities spread around the capital often at such distance from one another that intra-communal contact was intermittent. Individual communities had differing structures and its members followed a range of distinct occupations. These enclaves drew a substantial part of their residents from a particular county or area of Ireland.[10] The Gaelic revivalists, however, differed from previous settlers in crucial ways. Though its elements were to an extent scattered, the revival generally attracted the same or similar followings of people who unlike their working-class counterparts were accustomed to ranging more extensively for social intercourse and employment opportunities. London's place in the revival was central not merely in Great Britain, but was an important adjunct to the movement in Ireland. Additionally, its position as the political and administrative heart of the empire, as the site of Parliament, with the key figures of Irish politics regularly in residence there, gave the metropolis an incontestable importance.

Irish nationalism is a dynamic ideological movement for attaining and maintaining the autonomy, unity and identity of Ireland and her people; it is a means to activate people and create solidarity among them in the common quest for a cherished goal. Three ideas are fused – the collective self-determination of the people; the expression of national character and individuality; and the vertical division of the world into unique nations, each contributing its special genius to the common fund of humanity. It rests on what Elie Kedourie terms the assumption that a nation must have a past, and no less fundamentally,

10 Ibid., p. 661.

a future.[11] Cultural revivalists were part of this wider movement, falling into two categories – romantic scholars and artists on the one hand and on the other modernising journalists.[12] Each rejected the British model of national development implicitly promoted by the Irish parliamentary party, but while the former believed the regeneration of Ireland's ancient Gaelic ways would inspire a heroic civilisation of small-scale rural communities, the latter saw revitalised indigenous *mores* as a means to build an autonomous modern nation capable of competing in the international economic and political order. Political and cultural nationalism were apt to be different species with sometimes incompatible objectives. Of the London intellectuals, W.B. Yeats, Eleanor Hull and Sophie Bryant belong to the category of romantic scholars; Moran and Ryan were modernising journalists. Many of the individuals active in London circles were Irish-born 'exiles' who subsequently returned to Ireland to inaugurate or participate in the revival there. Yeats went back in 1899, Moran in 1900 and Ryan in 1905. They left behind in the capital important institutions like the Irish Literary Society, the Gaelic League of London and the Gaelic Athletic Association.

An influential literature assigns a special importance to the leading role of the intelligentsia in the spread of national revivals.[13] Among those who emphasise its place in the vanguard are Kedourie, Ernest Gellner, Anthony Smith, Eric Hobsbawm, Benedict Anderson and Miroslav Hroch. Collectively they stress the modern invented origins of nationalism and explain how the intelligentsia spread its message. Hroch developed a typology of stateless nations in which cultural revival is the crucial first stage. He makes two further observations relevant to the current discussion: that national agitation receives the support of the masses when social and economic conflicts or tensions coincide with linguistic or religious differences; and that educated members of the non-dominant ethnic group had the dilemma of attempting to establish their authority while at the same time maintaining the way of life and value system of the established ruling classes.[14] As well, the observations of Milton Esman

---

11 See, John Hutchinson and Anthony Smith, *Nationalism* (Oxford, 1994), p. 211.

12 These points are developed more fully in John Hutchinson, *The Dynamics of Cultural Nationalism: The Gaelic Revival and the Creation of the Irish Nation State* (London, 1987).

13 Short extracts from many of these figures can be found in Hutchinson and Smith, *Nationalism*.

14 Miroslav Hroch, *Social Preconditions of National Revival in Europe* (Cambridge, 1985), p. 197; as a shortened form this can be found 'Social and Territorial Characteristics in the Composition of the Leading Groups of National Movements' in Andreas Kappler, Fikret Adanir and Alan O'Day (eds), *The Formation of National Elites* (Aldershot and New York, 1992), pp 257–75 and reprised in an amended form in 'National Self-Determination from a Historical Perspective', in Sukumar Periwal (ed.), *Notions of Nationalism* (Budapest, London and New York, 1995), pp 65–82. See also Hroch,

and Don Handleman are pertinent.[15] The first draws attention to the triangular relationship of diaspora people, host community and homeland, noting that the ability of diasporas to influence the course of events is conditioned by their access to resources, the opportunities offered by the host society and their degree of solidarity. This diaspora usually experiences fewer tensions over expressing a dual allegiance than is true of their compatriots at home. Handleman usefully categorises four stages of development: an ethnic category (a loose level of incorporation, where there is a perceived cultural difference between the group and outsiders); an ethnic network (where there is regular interaction between group members, allowing the network to distribute resources among its members); ethnic association (where members develop political organisations to express common goals); and an ethnic community (which possess a permanent, physical or more appropriately in this case a mentally bounded territory, over and above its political organisations). John Hutchinson argues for the recurring basis of cultural revivals alternation with political nationalism, observing that the movement growing up in the 1890s was the third Irish cultural revival. A weakness of the various political leagues and associations in Britain before the revival was their working-class membership and orientation; the respectable middle-class Irish were reluctant to be associated with these organisations. Earlier bodies had some strength in places like Glasgow and Liverpool but scarcely functioned in London. Thus the revivalists' middle-class base and exceptional concentration in London offered an opportunity for an alternative Irish national vision, while at the same time providing a means to test some of the important propositions in the theoretical literature on national revivals.

Examination of this movement also illuminates a key debate among investigators of the Irish in Great Britain: why this group disappeared or became invisible as an ethnic community. Older writings from the pens of members of the diaspora emphasised the heroic self-sacrifice of an Irish community faced with native hostility, in order to preserve the faith and advance the aspirations of the fatherland. This perspective appears for the Irish whether they settled in America, Australia or Great Britain.[16] Hugh Heinrick's *Survey* and John Denvir's *The Irish in Britain* (1892) are notable examples of this outlook. A

'Nationalism and National Movements: Comparing the Past and the Present of Central and Eastern Europe', *Nations and Nationalism*, 2 (1996), pp 40–1.

15 For Esman, see Milton J. Esman, 'Diasporas and International Relations', in John Hutchinson and Anthony D. Smith (eds), *Ethnicity* (Oxford, 1996), pp 316–20; For Handleman, see ibid., p. 6.

16 Much of this comment is based on Alan O'Day, 'Revising the Diaspora' in D. George Boyce and Alan O'Day (eds), *The Making of Modern Irish History: Revisionism and the Revisionist Controversy* (London and New York, 1996), pp 188–215.

refinement can be found in the methodology pioneered by an American, Oscar Handlin, and extended in the 1960s by Stephan Thernstrom. This sees the Irish as disadvantaged outsiders cast between two worlds, the old one of Ireland and the new adopted home. Never quite escaping this dilemma, they remain permanently disadvantaged. Handlin's *The Uprooted* (1951) is the guide book of this school. The theme is associated with Harvard University where Handlin taught. The one full-length academic investigation of the Irish in London by Lynn Hollen Lees, *Exiles of Erin* (1979) undertaken as a Harvard Ph.D. thesis, is influenced by the Handlin school. Her account of the experience of the Irish in London looks remarkably similar to the Handlin-Thernstrom account of Boston. Recent scholarship casts doubt on such pessimistic assessments, instead finding that the diaspora had a myriad of experiences. Since the mid-1980s a number of writers have viewed the Irish as willing victims of assimilation or integration. In 1990, for example, referring to post-1945 immigrants to Great Britain, one authority comments:

> Irish assimilation into British society is among the fastest that occurs among immigrant groups anywhere in the world. Assimilation is practically complete in a single generation. The children of Irish immigrants, sometimes to the distress of their parents, grow up seeing themselves as English or Scots; they may acknowledge their Irish ancestry and exhibit a few inherited traits, but for all practical purposes they are indistinguishable from their British peers whether in respect of dress or in social, cultural, or religious behaviour.[17]

A bevy of historians, looking back at Irish migration over the past 150 years, adopt a broadly similar stance. Their view is implicitly criticised by Steven Fielding who finds in Manchester at any rate, a more lingering sense of Irish identity though the weight of his account is in the direction of immigrant integration albeit on a lengthened time scale and perhaps to a less comprehensive degree.[18] Recently, Mary Hickman has argued that the concept of assimilation masks a process of racialisation and racism.[19] She prefers the term 'incorporation' to 'assimilation', and on balance this seems a more satisfactory means of expressing the process. Her tendentious style and political purpose obscure a conclusion essentially consistent with scholars who are impressed by the rate at which Irish Catholics have disappeared into British society. The main value of this analysis is to show that the process was more complex and sometimes involuntary, for Dr Hickman attributes incorporation to the

---

17 Quoted in Akenson, *The Irish Diaspora*, p. 211.
18 Steven Fielding, *Class and Ethnicity: Irish Catholics in England, 1880–1939* (Buckingham and Philadelphia, 1993).
19 Mary J. Hickman, *Religion, Class and Identity: The State, The Catholic Church and the Education of the Irish in Britain* (Aldershot, 1995), see, pp 2–19, 252, passim.

collusive machinations of the British State and Catholic Church. Cultural revivalism in London affords a useful further opportunity to explore the place of the Irish in British society along with the Irish tendency to merge into the wider community.

With its large Irish population and its cultural, economic and political importance, London was bound to be a major centre in the larger revival, as a recruiting ground, for providing financial support and as a sympathetic audience for the Gaelic and Anglo-Irish movements. There was a regular interplay between London and Dublin on the part of figures like Griffith and Yeats. For this reason, although on the whole London leaders and institutions were very much of the second rank, initiatives in the metropolis made a substantial contribution to the political-cultural revival over the years between 1890 and 1922. Diaspora cultural nationalism was not simply derivative from the homeland. Inspired by rising anti-Irish sentiment in London and disillusionment with an increasingly oligarchic Home Rule organisation, revivalists had a *raison d'être* of their own, namely the formation of a self-reliant Irish community through permeating all aspects of disapora life with a sense of nationality. This is much the same message as Henrick conveyed in 1872.[20]

Beginnings of the London revival date from the establishment in 1883 by Frank Fahy, an Irish-born civil servant, of the Southwark Irish Literary Club. This took place contemporaneously with developments in Ireland such as the founding of the Gaelic Athletic Association (1884) and the *Dublin University Review* (1885). Like its Irish counterparts, the Southwark Club was intended to be an integrative centre for Irish men and women of all creeds and politics, inspired by the anti-Irish feeling resulting from the Land War and growing sectarian divisions in Ireland. Like them as well, though ostensibly non-political, it attracted the active involvement of Fenians. The club soon became the meeting place of Irish intellectuals – Yeats, Moran and Ryan – and provided the platform and personnel for later revivalist activities. But like so many similar communal organisations, it made relatively little wider impact on London Irish life.

The major wave of revivalism came in the wake of the religious-political schisms and anti-English revulsion arising from the Parnell divorce scandal in November 1890 and his death the following October. Reacting against these divisions, cultural revivalists were moved to re-create an alternative moral basis for the national community, one that departed in fundamental respects from that promoted by an Anglicised and factionalised parliamentary party. For the

20 Henrick, *Survey*, pp 128–31.

revivalists the route was to discover and publicise the heroic myths and culture of Ireland's ancient Gaelic civilisation. In this spirit Yeats and his circle in 1891 transformed the Southwark Club into the Irish Literary Society. In its new guise the Society became a busy centre, organising lectures, concerts and sponsoring the theatrical productions of Yeats along with those of his dramatic collaborators before and after the creation of the Irish Literary Theatre in 1899.[21] The hub of the revival in London, as in Ireland, was to be the Gaelic League which was founded in 1893 in Dublin, and opened a London branch in 1896. Along with the Gaelic Athletic Association first established in London in 1896, the revivalists worked to regenerate the ideal of a Gaelic nation with its distinctive language, literature, music, dances and games.[22]

The Gaelic League intended to set in train a moral revolution. Its journal set out the vision of the 'new man' who would emerge:

> The first duty of the Gaelic Leaguer is to make himself an efficient individual. Not only must be speak Irish, but his heart and soul must be Irish ... he must live temperately and think honourably of women and treat them according. It is only if we have a population of men and women striving to be perfect that we shall ever establish a new and beneficial civilisation in Ireland.[23]

With this missionary zeal, the League, under the leadership of Fahy and Art O'Brian, set out to influence London Irish life, forming language classes in Catholic schools, establishing a monthly journal, *Inis Fail* in 1904, annual industrial exhibitions of Irish manufactures (Aonachs), religious celebrations in the Irish tongue on St Patrick's Day and an employment centre.[24] Supported strongly by a section of the Irish lower clergy, it spearheaded a host of related patriotic movements. As this case illustrates, the role of the Church was not uniformly directed towards eradicating Irish identity.

If the intellectuals inspired the formation of the London Irish-Ireland movement, the driving force underpinning it came from the Irish-born Catholic lower intelligentsia, comprising minor civil servants, teachers and postal officials. This group grew rapidly in the late nineteenth century. It was a stratum that only emerged in Europe from the eighteenth century and gained an identity and purpose by virtue of education and professional qualifications, aspirations to social and political mobility and a sense of vocation to the community. Hroch and others note that this group is essential to the formation of national revivals, as it has been in the development of all modern ideological movements. In the

21 See R.F. Foster, *W.B. Yeats: A Life*, vol. I, *The Apprentice Mage 1865–1914* (Oxford, 1996).
22 Mark Ryan, *Fenian Memories* (Dublin, 1945), p. 162.
23 *Inis Fail*, Oct. 1907.
24 See, M.J. Walters, 'W.P. Ryan and the Irish Ireland Movement' (University of Connecticut PhD thesis, 1970), chapter 5.

late nineteenth century the Catholic intelligentsia migrating to London were the shock troops of the cultural revival, diffusing its ideals among the wider population and tentatively challenging the established political leadership for prestige and power in the Irish community.

The preconditions for its emergence were the expansion of opportunities in the bureaucracy, coupled to rapidly growing access for Catholics to appropriate training through education. Recruitment in the civil service by open competitive examination, especially that favouring literary attainment, triggered an immediate response from the Catholic Irish even before the introduction of the intermediate education system under legislation passed in 1878 and of the Royal University created by an Act of Parliament the following year. Special classes preparing youth for the examinations were opened by the Christian Brothers. In the 1880s the Irish party under Parnell's leadership routinely exposed alleged bias in the examinations favouring English candidates.[25] By that time there was a steady increase in the number of educated lower middle-class Catholics who were imbued with aspirations to social and political mobility. But Ireland's limp economy, based on agriculture and a declining national population, limited the prospects for a career at home. Demand for professional and civil service positions outstripped supply. Large numbers of Irish men and some women looked to the lower and middle ranks of the British Home Civil Service as an outlet for their ambitions. Postal clerks, sorters and telegraphists appointments were available in profusion, and managers of the urban centres often observed that the Irish 'swamped' these grades.[26] In 1914 a leading Irish figure in a London claimed that 'the civil services swarm today with bright, keen, intelligent youths. We could run a branch of the United Irish League in some of the London Post Offices'.[27] Irish schoolteachers similarly went to London in search of a career. By the 1880s there were no fewer than seven training colleges in Ireland funded by the state, but the number of positions available at home was practically static. In London, as well, wages were generally higher and conditions better.

If a rising proportion of educated Irish men and women were rejecting the traditional order in Ireland for a career open to talents in Great Britain, not all would find a comfortable niche either in society there or in the London Irish community. Many, it seems, took up positions in Great Britain in the hope of subsequent transfer home. But, as Post Office managers reported, such transfers were not always feasible and there was sometimes considerable frustration for disappointed aspirants.[28] Apart from this, many Irish arrivals perceived an anti-

---

25 Alan O'Day, *The English Face of Irish Nationalism: Parnellite Involvement in British Politics, 1880–86* (Dublin, 1977), p. 169.
26 Post Office Archives, Post 33/1041/Minute 7219/1923.
27 *Catholic Herald*, 25 April 1914.
28 Post Office Archives, Post 33/1041 Minute 7219/1923, files 1 and 3.

Irish hostility that had been inflamed by the two Home Rule episodes and further exacerbated by nationalist criticism of the Boer War. The rising mood of imperialism contained an anti-Irish dimension. From one direction this intelligentsia recoiled against Anglo-Saxon jingoism; from another it was appalled at the squalor of Irish working-class life and the ossified leadership of 'their' people in London. One young civil servant gave vent to this sentiment when writing, 'I may say that one of the things that first struck my colleagues and myself on coming to England was the humble, and almost degraded, position held by our fellow countrymen in Great Britain'.[29] As in Ireland, this displaced intelligentsia discovered an alternative politics in the regenerative programme of the Gaelic revival that, rejecting both British Imperial hegemony and the machine politics of parliamentary nationalism, sought to mobilise grass roots Irish organisations, religious, temperance, educational and social welfare, to create a dynamic cohesive self-assured 'native' community. The Irish-Ireland movement that they sponsored was never very large. But, like the movement at home, it achieved 'take-off' between 1900 and 1908, the year in which Home Rule nationalism suffered a number of body-blows. Even in 1906, however, the Gaelic League membership in London was no more than 3000 out of an ethnic population estimated at 375,000.[30] When the prospects of Home Rule improved, the Irish Party's standing rose, causing the Gaelic League's slide into decline. Cultural nationalism had, nevertheless, acted as a powerful socialising agent, forming a dedicated self-conscious patriotic elite. After 1918 this elite assumed the leadership of a major quasi-revolutionary organisation, the Irish Self-Determination League, that mustered broad-based support in London. Thus, the story is not one of unlimited false-starts and is relevant to the wider discussion of the Irish in London.

REGENERATIVE POLITICS, 1900–14

The years between 1900 and 1908 were the halcyon days of the Gaelic revival in London. During this time the Gaelic League enjoyed the support of liberal priests anxious to align a Church threatened by 'leakage' with the constructive national movement. The League experienced a rapid expansion in membership. Language classes were established in Fulham, Kennington, Islington, Tower Hill, Wandsworth, Clapham, Hampstead, Vauxhall and Camberwell. Other activities included industrial exhibitions (Aonachs), Irish language services on St Patrick's Day along with offshoots such as the Irish School of Learning, the Irish Folk Song Society, Cumann na bPiobain for the Irish bagpipe, and social clubs.[31] The movement revitalised the Gaelic Athletic Association and founded *Inis Fail*.

29 *Catholic Herald*, 2 May 1914.
30 *The Universe*, 16 Mar. 1906; but reported as only 2500 by *Inis Fail*, Sept. 1905.
31 *Inis Fail*, Oct. 1904.

Newspaper reports reveal that the organisers of these activities were primarily young men and women who recently had migrated from Ireland to take up positions in the civil service and schools. In 1902 the Irish columnist of the *Catholic Herald* observed that Irish women working in the Post Office were practically all enthusiastic supporters of the Gaelic League. Nearly two years later a similar claim was made; a priest in Bermondsey commented upon the numbers of educated Irish flooding into London and their tendency to associate with one or more of the revivalist organs.[32] This enthusiasm had political nuances. By 1900 the London Irish were increasingly disillusioned with the Home Rule party, which showed little concern for its local needs. Up to the turn of the century discontent manifested itself in independent groups like the Catholic League of South London, founded in 1895 to promote denominational rights in education and campaigns in the *Catholic Herald* and *The Universe* on these and other issues.[33] The Unionist triumph at the general election in 1900 postponed any possibility of Home Rule in the foreseeable future, undermining the status of the Irish party and setting the stage for the emergence of a new ethnic communitarian movement. This new phase, cultural nationalism, took several forms. Among its most interesting manifestations was the Irish National Society, a breakaway from the United Irish League of Great Britain in 1902; it exemplified the enthusiasm of the migrant intelligentsia for democratic politics oriented to the aspirations of the London Irish communities.

Although the Irish National Society emerged from a conflict between sections of the United Irish League branches in London, its origins can be traced to 1896 when Thomas Martin, a London architect, angered at the oligarchic dictation over the movement by Irish MPs, unsuccessfully proposed internal reforms. By 1901 Martin, a member of the Southwark branch of the League, formulated a plan drawing upon the more democratic structure which existed in Ireland. He wanted to decentralise the organisation in Britain, and to create provincial directories along with the replacement of MPs on the central executive by elected representatives in order to allow the Irish in Great Britain a genuine voice.[34] His democratising zeal was coloured by Gaelic revivalism. Among Martin's prominent supporters was William McCarthy, a Councillor in Peckham and Treasurer of the Gaelic Athletic Association in London. In 1905 he became President of the Irish National Society.

By 1901 Martin won over the London branches to his reforms. His proposals attracted considerable backing but were rejected by the old guard. In June 1901 Martin and his allies regrouped to call a South London Branch conference with the specific aim of creating a council of the whole of London.[35] In September

32 *Catholic Herald*, 25 July 1902, 15 and 22 Jan. 1904.
33 Ibid., 2 Aug. 1902.
34 *The Universe*, 12 Jan. 1901.
35 Ibid., 22 June 1901.

they attempted to form a London Central Committee and despite opposition from the executive of the United Irish League of Great Britain, they attracted to the first meeting in February 1902 the support of the President or Secretary of eleven London branches augmented by representatives from three others (Camberwell, Clapham, Dulwich, Forest Gate, Fulham, Hoxton, Peckham, Southwark, Stratford, Walworth, Wandsworth, West End, Whitechapel and Woolwich).[36] The Central Committee immediately sprang into action. Alarmed at this insubordination, the League executive moved against it. The dissidents coalesced in June 1902 under the banner of the Irish National Society, adopting an ethnic communalist self-help platform that espoused the revival of the Irish language and culture, along with the need for representation of Irishmen on local councils and poor law boards in their adopted country.[37]

From the start the Society attracted restless young Irish-born teachers, solicitors, civil servants, journalists and clerks who were keen to harness revivalist ideas to further the social and political needs of the 'exiles'. Denounced by the leaders of the United Irish League of Great Britain as 'young men in a hurry' and 'brand new reformers', they wasted no time in complaining that the traditionalists were a 'mere handful of people' who made 'politics a profession' but had little to show for themselves.[38] In contrast to the use of paid organisers by the League, the Irish National Society pledged to carry out its work by voluntary effort and to advance the cause of the Irish community.[39] In many respects the Irish National Society resembled the emergent Sinn Féin movement in Ireland and both sent forth the message of economic self-help in the local community. In 1905 the Society amalgamated with Griffith's movement.[40] It was distinctive from Sinn Féin, however, by its ardent identification of Catholic with national interests which accorded with the situation on the ground in London.

The activities of the Society are not well-documented. Some information can be found in sympathetic reports in *The Universe*. In January 1903 the Forest Gate branch, soon followed by that in Hoxton, formed subcommittees to promote the Irish language, sponsored recreations held on Saturdays for children and fostered the sale of Irish goods in local Irish-owned shops.[41] Getting even shops owned by the Irish to carry good manufactured in Ireland was never straightforward. When secretary of the United Irish League of Great Britain J.F.X. O'Brien was made aware of the limits of patriot fervour when it

---

36 Ibid., 14 Sept. 1901, 15 Feb. 1902.
37 Ibid., 12 April 1902.
38 Ibid., 1 June 1902.
39 Ibid., 5 July 1902.
40 The relationship between the two can be traced in Richard P. Davis, *Arthur Griffith and Non-Violent Sinn Féin* (Dublin, 1974), pp 22–3, 28–9.
41 *The Universe*, 3 Jan. 1903.

conflicted with commercial prospects. On one occasion he pointed out, 'some years ago I did try to get our branches to join in for Irish manufactures – there are many difficulties on this side of the water. And I am sure that shop-keepers & even the Irish Industries Ass[ociation] have some imposed on me – passing off on me English goods. Irish shopkeepers, it appears, can make a larger profit on English goods'.[42] In February 1903 the Gaelic League advocated the establishment of an employment bureau, something that eventually took place under the auspices of the Gaelic League.[43] In January 1904 the Society published a pamphlet 'Irish Freedom and How to Win it', publicising its programme with the subtext of castigating the Irish party.[44] It is not easy to assess the level of activity. In 1903 and 1904 the Society was considered sufficiently important by some Irish local councillors, poor law guardians and professional men to ensure their attendance at meetings. Though still small, the Society entertained grandiose ambitions. In anticipation of a general election it advised the Irish in London in July 1905 to vote for Labour candidates, countermanding the policy of the United Irish League of Great Britain which, as usual, threw its weight behind the Liberals.[45]

From an early date the Society enlisted support from notable proponents of the Gaelic revival. In 1902, the leading Gaelic Leaguer, William Gibson, acted as a patron of the Irish National Society, inviting its members and those from the St George's Catholic Club in Southwark, to visit his country seat near Dorking.[46] W.P. Ryan addressed the Society's meetings.[47] More importantly, the work of the Society crystallised the growing discontent within the Irish communities in London over the Irish party's neglect of their interests, especially on religious questions and social welfare. By exploiting these issues the Irish National Society sought to channel the energies of Irish groups into the task of forming a self-conscious community in London. Its formal success was limited but it served to warn old nationalism that it had to pull up its socks, acting as a rallying point for an intelligentsia largely excluded from the upper echelons of the United Irish League of Great Britain.

Revivalism intersected with wider communal interests. Three developments by 1900 are significant to the story. Irish activism was the creation of municipal councils whose first elections were held in 1900. These bodies exercised extensive powers over education, housing and social welfare. Second, the Conservative government, though hostile to Home Rule, was receptive to

42 J.F.X. O'Brien to Alfred Webb, 7 Nov. 1900, J.F.X. O'Brien Papers, National Library of Ireland, Ms 13,456.
43 *The Universe.*, 14 Feb. 1903.
44 Ibid., 9 Jan. 1904.
45 Ibid., 15 July 1905.
46 Ibid., 19 July 1902.
47 Ibid., 13 Dec. 1902.

Catholic claims on funding for education. Third, the growth of trade unions and the emergence of a political labour movement posed a distinct challenge to the leadership of the United Irish League of Great Britain with its commitment to the Liberal alliance. This was accompanied by questioning within the London Irish community about its place in British society. Traditional Irish politics had not addressed these matters.

Leaders of the Irish in London, to be sure, had not been wholly oblivious to their local situation; their problem was that the existing institutions meant to look after ethnic needs had higher priorities. Already by 1900 a number of attempts had been made to infiltrate local elective bodies. Arthur O'Neill was a significant participant. He embodied the search for corporate identity and political leadership by the rising Catholic professional strata. O'Neill, a prominent organiser, helped found the National Union of Catholic Teachers and took a leading part in the (Catholic) Metropolitan Teachers Association.[48] He was only one of many teachers and civil servants active in Irish communal life. Of the fourteen Irish Catholic councillors profiled in the London *Catholic Herald* in later 1903, four were civil servants (three in the post office and the fourth a customs officer), three were schoolteachers, and one a physician. Association with the Catholic League was soon an essential condition for those standing for local bodies.

Even before the conflict over the Education bill of 1902, a number of lower clergy and the Catholic press tried to differentiate their flock from the materialistic Saxon. In the Dockhead area of Bermondsey, Father Moloney led the way in creating a self-reliant Catholic laity.[49] He was an active member of the Gaelic League and responsible for inaugurating the St Patrick's Day Irish language service in 1901. Enthusiasm for the Irish language spread to the Catholic League of South London. In 1901 it presented a memorial to the London School Board requesting that Irish be taught in an evening school in Greenwich.[50] In the early years of the new century there was a convergence between the goal of the Irish National Society/Gaelic revivalism, the creation of an Irish community politically independent of British parties, and those of Catholic pressure groups incensed by the Irish party's adherence to the Liberals. *The Universe* gave coverage to revivalist groups at the expense of the United Irish League and vigorously promoted slates of independent candidates to represent Catholic interests in local elections. These and other actions helped advance the Gaelic League.

In 1902 the Gaelic League had 1000 paid up members; two years later it had continued to expand, particularly in the East End, thanks to a dedicated

48 *Catholic Herald*, 13 Nov. 1903.
49 *Inis Fail*, June 1905 (his obituary).
50 *The Universe*, 23 Nov. 1901.

priesthood; and by early 1906 it could claim 3000 members.[51] In a mood of growing confidence the League established *Inis Fail* in 1904 to serve and extend the Irish-Ireland message. One of its objects was to form an Irish Association as a forum for Irish activities in London. This was only achieved in 1911 with the formation of the Union of Four Provinces, an organisation which survived into the 1920s and possibly beyond.[52] Most revivalist and radical nationalist societies worked out of the same quarters, 55 Chancery Lane, the headquarters of the Fenian movement.[53] This address was the office of the Gaelic League, the Gaelic Athletic Association, the O'Donovan Rossa Reception Committee, the Irish National Club, and Cumann na nGaedheal and other organisations.[54] Mark Ryan was included in all but one of the various bodies. A plethora of societies for folk singing, pipe music, dancing, debating (Dalcassian Society), the Aonachs, seasonal festivals (Beltaine and Samhain), sporting meetings and outings to the Gaeltacht worked to animate a self-conscious Irish-Ireland community in London. This spirit, however, was centred on Ireland rather than London. The effect, ironically, was to undermine the revival in London. Convinced of their duty to Ireland and of its grand destiny, many of the most enthusiastic members of the Gaelic League in London went home.[55]

To become a permanent force the revival had to permeate the dominant London institutions. It had no more than mixed success. The League secured the agreement of the London County Council in 1906 to place Irish on the same footing as French and German in evening classes but this, and similar concessions, were minor and in some instances short-lived.[56] A major failure was the absence of support from the Catholic Church. In Ireland the revival won important support from the Church. Early on in London the lower clergy had given the movement assistance. In 1905 Cardinal Bourne allowed the transfer of the Gaelic language service on St Patrick's Day to Westminster Cathedral, but this was revoked by the end of 1908.[57] Cultural revivals made limited headway against the established national organisations. The Irish National Society was unsuccessful in bringing Catholics together as an independent force. The slate of independent Catholic candidates who stood in 1903 for councils and poor law boards polled poorly. Moreover, the Irish party and its allied organisations recovered after December 1909 when the prospects of Home Rule rose. Perhaps more important was the growth of the Ancient Order

51 Ibid., 29 March 1902, 16 Jan. 1904. Fitzpatrick accepts the Gaelic League's own higher total of 1,500 in 1902, 'The Irish in Britain', pp 676–7.
52 *The Irishman*, March, December 1911.
53 Ryan, *Fenian Memories*, p. 172.
54 Fitzpatrick, 'Irish in Britain', p. 676.
55 *Inis Fail*, September 1905.
56 Ibid., July 1906.
57 See Cardinal Bourne Papers, B65/83g, 1904–1908.

of Hibernians among the Irish Catholic working class.[58] It offered concrete benefits whereas the revivalists, representing a mainly middle-class vision, proffered what proved to be in practice, a form of psychological reassurance.

RESURGENCE OF CULTURAL NATIONALISM, 1916–22

Support for the war had begun to fade even before the Easter Rebellion; the revolutionary movement in London had begun to crystallise by July 1916. It found expression in 'front' organisations like the O'Donovan Rossa Club and the Irish National Relief Fund (transformed in March 1918 into the Irish Self-Determination League).[59] Many of the leading figures in the resurgence were or had been Gaelic revivalists and several, including Art O'Brian, C.B. Dutton, J.J. Fintan Murphy, William McCarthy and J.H. MacDonnell, nephew of Sir Anthony MacDonnell, the prominent former civil servant in India and then in Dublin Castle, went on to play a key part in the Irish Self-Determination League.

The Irish Self-Determination League was established by Eamon de Valera in March 1918. At first its purposes were limited and vague, largely confined to advocacy of an Irish Republic and the cause of the political prisoners. In November 1920 it took on more substance, promoting the language, history, literature, sports and pastimes of Ireland. It was restricted to those of 'Irish birth or descent resident in Great Britain' and members were to eschew involvement 'in English politics, either local government or parliamentary' without the authority of the Sinn Féin directorate in Dublin.[60] Soon this movement was accompanied by a revitalisation of the Gaelic League and Gaelic Athletic Association in London. Between 1919 and 1921 the membership of the League doubled, reaching a peak of 1100 in 1920; in 1921 the London County Board of the Gaelic Athletic Association re-emerged to supervise four hurling and four football teams.[61] The Irish Self-Determination League expanded well beyond the cultural forum and had ambitions to make the transition from Handleman's typology, considered above, of an *ethnic category* to an *ethnic network*, to an *ethnic association* and even possibly though more hesitantly to an *ethnic community*. By 1921 it had gained a popular following, smaller but perhaps more committed than the pre-war membership of the United Irish League of Great Britain.

---

58 Fitzpatrick, 'The Irish in Britain', p.674; see the useful consideration of the Ancient Order of Hibernians in Belfast and Glasgow in A.C. Hepburn, *A Past Apart: Studies in the History of Catholic Belfast 1850–1950* (Belfast, 1996), pp 203–17.
59 *Catholic Herald*, 8, 22, 29 July 1916.
60 Quoted in Fitzpatrick, 'The Irish in Britain', p.868; *Irish Exile*, April 1921.
61 Fitzpatrick, ibid.; *Irish Exile*, June 1921.

The Irish Self-Determination League differed from the old United Irish League of Great Britain in vital respects and was not just a re-constituted version of it under new management. Although attracting membership across the country, it was very much London-oriented. The United Irish League of Great Britain had never functioned well in London. The effective leader, Art O'Brian (the 'official' representative in Britain of the Republican government) and J.H. MacDonnell lived in the capital. A disproportionate number of seats on the central executive were reserved for London representatives and the League's journal, *The Irish Exile*, first published in March 1921, was during its short existence only distributed in London and the south of England.[62]

The League operated on two levels. It raised funds for relief schemes and organising propaganda work like public meetings for political figures, working with British sympathisers and holding demonstrations. It also sponsored social events appealing to the larger Irish community, using these to infiltrate other communal groups. At the same time the League, or a section of it to be accurate, gave aid and material assistance to the Irish Republican Army campaign in Great Britain. The Secretary of the League, Sean McGrath, was jailed for six months in 1919 for arms smuggling.[63]

Prominent leaders had been active in the pre-war London Gaelic League, the Gaelic Athletic Association and the Irish National Society. Under this leadership the Irish Self-Determination League was the centre of a set of overlapping clubs and societies promoting an Irish-Ireland revival. Pre-1914 activists included O'Brian, Button, Murphy, McCarthy and O'Hart. Like the earlier revival, the League recruited its support from an Irish-born minor intelligentsia of school teachers, post office officials and excise clerks who acted as lecturers, branch secretaries and the like.[64] A remarkable number were younger women teachers. Margaret Leonard, President of the Cumann na nBan, the female arm of the Irish Republican Army, was a former teacher. The Secretary of the Gaelic League and her counterpart in the Roger Casement Sinn Féin Club were teachers. Where the new League differed from its revivalist predecessors is that it drew substantial support from the mainstream Irish community, including from the former United Irish League of Great Britain, councillors, professionals, businessmen and trade union organisers.

Sources for a partly underground organisation like the Irish Self-Determination League are often unrevealing. However, some of its labours can be teased out of *The Irish Exile*, the *Woolwich Pioneer and Labour Journal* and most usefully of all, Special Branch records. Its development can be broken into five phases, which correspond with events in the struggle in Ireland:

62 *Irish Exile*, Jan. 1922.
63 *Times*, 7 Feb. 1919.
64 Irish Deportees Compensation Tribunal, Public Record Office T80/10.

1. March 1919–March 1920: a quiescent time that saw a quickening of interest in early 1920 when the Better Government of Ireland bill was introduced;
2. April 1920–December 1920: the 'take-off' when intensification of the Anglo -Irish war spurred the League to mobilise the Irish community and also to seek the support of the English Trade Unions;
3. December 1920–June 1921: spread of the armed struggle to Great Britain in retaliation for the military campaign in Ireland;
4. July 1921–December 1921: decline during the peace negotiations, punctuated at the close of these months by a bitter internal wrangle over the Treaty;
5. December 1921–March 1922: the reformation of the League into a radical London-based rump.

Although the first phase was unremarkable in most respects, two events were important – the local council elections in October 1919 and the announced intention in December to introduce a further Home Rule bill. The council elections, the first held since 1912, were conducted under the new franchise. A number of Irish Self-Determination League organisers and other Irish sympathisers were elected on the Labour party ticket.[65] In Battersea, where the largest contingent of Irish councillors had been returned before the war, seven Irishmen triumphed, including two officers of the League. No fewer than five branches could boast its president as a serving councillor (Blackheath, Charlton and Greenwich, Limehouse, Poplar, Stepney and Woolwich). This helped establish the credentials of the League while also giving it a forum to preach republican goals. In November 1919 the Battersea Labour group forced through a motion demanding the withdrawal of British troops from Ireland.[66] Additionally, these electoral successes helped open up public rooms for meetings, a vital resource in an environment where so many places, especially, Catholic premises, were closed to the League.[67] Second, the prospect of a new Home Rule measure intensified interest and coincided with an upsurge of violence in Ireland. In January 1920 London membership was appropriately 2000 spread among twenty branches; women formed a large proportion of activists in some branches.

From March 1920, despite a succession of police raids on its offices and the deportation of key officials, the League began to grow into a large-scale movement. In April the total membership may have risen to 9000. Intelligence reports indicated that League and Gaelic League meetings were well attended.[68] During this time the League sought to unite the Irish in Great

65 'Irish Self-Determination League', Public Record Office, CAB24/89, CT8400 (23/10/1919).
66 *Catholic Herald*, 22 Nov. 1919.
67 *Irish Exile*, Mar. 1921.
68 CAB24/96, CP458 (15/1/1920).

Britain and to enlist the adherence of the Catholic clergy by emphasising the violence of the Black and Tans in Ireland and the legitimacy of the home country's cause. The leadership of the League intended to use the current troubles in Ireland to create an Irish-Ireland sentiment. Art O'Brian, speaking in Woolwich, insisted that the London Irish must strive for political, economic and cultural freedom.[69] He placed stress on the role of the language in the quest for a truly independent Ireland. Other revivalist lecturers advanced this theme. Republican politics and the Gaelic revival went hand-in-hand, with the latter meant to heighten the London Irish sense of distinctiveness.[70] Branch meetings included time for singing Gaelic songs, Irish pipe music and dancing, and offered a haven for many immigrants from the current swirl of anti-Hibernian abuse. The round of violence in Ireland, hunger strikers at Wormwood Scrubs and the death while on hunger-strike of Terence MacSwiney, increased the appeal of the League; a number of clergy began attending branch meetings. Bourne's Lenten pastoral in 1921 denounced 'self-determination' as a 'foolish catchword',[71] yet individual priests became active in League affairs. In January 1921 membership across the country reached 27,000,[72] though many of its members were only nominal.[73] By early 1921 the Irish Self-Determination League undoubtedly served as the chief vehicle of the ethnic community. In March national membership climbed to its highest peak, 38,726, some 6481 being in London.[74] The journal of the League claimed a monthly circulation of 12,000 in the capital.[75]

The third phase – retaliation for violence in Ireland by attacks in Great Britain – saw a drop in support for the League. Increasing violence and its extension into Great Britain coupled with the detention of League officials soon led to a decline in the organisation.[76] In March the police arrested dozens of Irish Self-Determination League officials. In May 1921 a series of incendiary attacks on the houses of relatives of members of the Royal Irish Constabulary brought the conflict to the doorsteps of Catford, Shepherds Bush, Battersea, Tooting and West Kensington. In June there was acts of sabotage on the railway in London.[77] Further deterioration in the League's fortunes came during the fourth phase, commencing with the peace negotia-

69 *Woolwich Pioneer and Labour Journal*, 23 Jan. 1920.
70 Ibid., 6 Feb., 5 Mar. 1920.
71 'Pastoral Letter of Cardinal Bourne', Bourne Papers, B.O.5/87 (Ireland).
72 CAB24/134, CP3854 (16/3/1922).
73 Bourne Papers, B.O.5/36A (Ireland).
74 *Catholic Herald*, 11 Mar. 1921.
75 *Irish Exile*, Sept. 1921; Fitzpatrick cites the figure as 10,000, 'Irish in Britain', p. 687.
76 CAB24/120, CP3154 (21/7/1921).
77 *Times*, 2 Dec. 1920, 22 April, 16, 21 May, 18 June 1921.

tions from July to December 1921. Police reports noted a rapid drop in membership and even the closure of some London branches.[78]

Acceptance of the Treaty by Dail Eireann in January 1922 induced the final phase, which witnessed the end of an era of communal mobilisation. O'Brien notably tried to revitalise the Gaelic movement in an effort to keep the community cohesive. The Treaty split reverberated through the League. Northern branches tended to support it; opponents were mainly based in London. By March 1922 total membership had dwindled to 19,104 (3699 in London).[79] As the Irish Self-Determination League withered, the London republicans seized the organisation and aided de Valera's forces in the Irish civil war. In March 1923 the British government deported many of the main leaders to Ireland. The short, not unimpressive, life-span of revivalism was for all practical purposes over.

CONCLUSION

The course of Gaelic revivalism in London affords a test case for several hypotheses. This stage came late and except for brief moments commanded the enthusiasm of only a tiny section of the ethnic body. The revival appealed mainly to an educated Irish-born minor intelligentsia; its programme, centred on acquiring skills, offered few attractions to the traditional working-class base of the Irish community. Moreover, the message conveyed was discordant with the realities and needs of the Irish in London, though perhaps no more so than that of the United Irish League of Great Britain. Yet much the same point can be made, if on a lesser scale, about the movement in Ireland. For a moment, it appeared that the Irish Self-Determination League might become the political organ of the Irish in Britain, and be a better such organ than its predecessors. It was more democratic and also better-led at local level than earlier organisations. But the instant passed. Events in Ireland, violence in Britain, and the ambivalence of the leadership quickly rebounded on the League.

Hroch's typology is limited to that of stateless nations and certainly was not fashioned to take account of diaspora groups. The experience of the Irish in London suggests that political mobilisation may precede a cultural revivalist social movement, and that the two may operate in a contrapuntal manner. Again the literature on the leading role of the intelligentsia is shaped by reference to the core group not the diaspora community. The current investigation suggests that timing, size, and the nature of the activism of the intelligentsia is relevant to the form of 'exile' communal development. Without a significant educated middle class able to imagine a national community (an

---

78 PRO, CAB24/129, CP3408 (14/10/1921).
79 *Catholic Herald*, 11 Mar. 1922.

extensive print culture), finance, co-ordinate and mobilise a national group from separated populations, a cohesive disaporic movement will be hard to sustain. The Irish-born, Ireland-focussed character of the revivalists limited the appeal of the movement. Some indirect light is thrown on the general issue on the degree of Irish incorporation into British society. The attitudes of established leaders, that is the clergy and politicians, was not so unified or effective as is recently alleged. The Gaelic revival offered the ethnic community an avenue to escape incorporation but unable to effectively 'colonise' the social institutions most germane to the life of the Irish population – the Catholic Church and trade unions – any revival was likely to be short lived. This largely conforms to the propositions advanced by Esman and Handleman. The impact of the Irish Self-Determination League during the Anglo-Irish war shows that there was still something to play for in the contest for the hearts and minds of the ethnic community. That window, perhaps no more than a narrow one in any event, was swiftly closed. The unsympathetic attitude of the English Catholic hierarchy and the indifference and at times hostility of the bulk of the labour movement was decisive. It is vital at this stage to look back at Hroch's insistence that widespread endorsement of 'national' agitation only takes place when social and political conflicts or tensions are channelled into ethnic grievances. In Great Britain, as well as in London, these were instead successfully marshalled along class and economic lines. He notes as well the dilemma facing a would-be new elite which is especially relevant in the diaspora context: The aspirant elite has to maintain the way of life and the value system of the established ruling class or in this instance of the leaders of the working classes. To speak of forcible 'incorporation' of the Irish in England is misleading and ignores the dispersed character of the population and the voluntary, even enthusiastic, accommodations of many of their leaders who advocated a union of hearts with the radical wing of British democracy. Reviving flows of immigration together with the re-ignition of conflict in Ireland would ensure the revival of ethnic activism in England. But as a largely proletarian diaspora without autonomous institutions, the Irish trod a predictable path towards a willing incorporation into the host society never advancing, or at least seldom interested in developing beyond an *ethnic category* or at most an *ethnic network*.

From Victorian 'Little Ireland' to heritage trail: catholicism, community and change in Liverpool's docklands

Frank Boyce

John Walton and Alastair Wilcox, in an introduction to their selections from the work of Hugh Shimmin, a nineteenth-century Liverpool journalist, claim that in none of the recent studies of Liverpool's history 'has a sustained attempt been made to present the Liverpool working class, or a significant fragment of it, in all the phases of its existence: at work at play, at prayer, and in its relations with its betters'.[1] This essay is a partial and tentative response to the challenge implicit in Walton and Wilcox's claim. The focus of my discussion is a clearly defined area of working-class Liverpool, that area of the northern docklands which consists of the Vauxhall, Scotland, Everton and Exchange political wards. I use 'Vauxhall' in the text as an umbrella term which includes the other wards. In the title, 'Little Ireland' is intended to acknowledge the popular perception of the area which emerged during the nineteenth century. By the end of that period the area had become densely populated with Irish immigrants. 'Heritage' is intended to encapsulate the gradual transformation of the area, socially and culturally, since the 1970s: the decline of population; closures and mergers of Catholic parishes and Catholic schools; closures of major industries which once dominated the landscape and provided employment, and the demolition of nineteenth-century slum housing and 1930s tenement blocks. It is also an acknowledgement of the range of environmental improvements which are still taking place. 'Canalside Park', a section of the Leeds and Liverpool Canal, threads its way through the Vauxhall area and is shortly to become a link in Liverpool's designated Heritage Trail. Improved housing projects such as the Eldonians and the Athol Village, together with educational initiatives and community focused projects, have emerged through the determination of local people to preserve a sense of community and identity, which is rooted in the collective memory of traditional parochial life.

---

1 J.K.Walton and A.Wilcox (eds), *Low Life and Moral Improvement in Mid-Victorian England: Liverpool through the Journalism of Hugh Shimmin* (Leicester, 1991), pp 1–2.

I

On the 3 October 1997, a packed congregation, led by Archbishop Patrick Kelly, gathered at the church of St Anthony, Scotland Road, to commemorate the 150th anniversary of 'Black '47', the most tragic year of the Irish Famine. It was an appropriate setting, for St Anthony's has long been regarded as the 'mother parish' of the northern docklands and was the first of Liverpool's Catholic parishes to be administered by secular clergy.

There is a touch of irony in the circumstances which led to the founding of the parish in 1804, and its subsequent history. Founded by two French refugees escaping from political turmoil in their own country, the church eventually became the centre of a large population of Irish refugees fleeing from famine and destitution. The Frenchmen, Father Antoine Gerardot, and an unnamed layman, raised sufficient money to build a modest brick chapel at the corner of Dryden Street and Scotland Road, at that time a district noted for its walled gardens, fruit trees and snug cottages, a popular weeked retreat for some of the town's busy tradesmen.[2] By 1833, eight years after the death of Father Gerardot, the chapel had closed and been replaced with the spacious neo-Gothic church which still stands in Scotland Road. This was necessary to accommodate the increasing numbers of Irish Catholics who were populating the area from the beginning of the 1830s. Paradoxically, as Liverpool blossomed during the middle decades of the nineteenth century as 'The Gateway of Empire'[3] it also festered as 'The Black Spot on the Mersey'. Many Irish immigrants must have hoped they had left poverty and hunger behind in their own country. Instead, they came to a town in which problems of poverty, housing, public health, and education were already at crisis point.

Between 1847 and 1853, 1,500,000 Irish landed at Liverpool's docks. Of these, 586,000 were designated as paupers.[4] Between January and November 1847, 278,000 arrived, of whom 123,000 remained in the town, where they 'occupied every nook and corner of the already over-crowded lodging houses, and forced their way into the cellars (about 3000 in number), which had been closed under the Health Act of 1842'.[5] Those who stayed increased the populations of existing Irish communities:in the south end area of Park Road, Park Lane and St James's Street and in the north end area of Vauxhall, Scotland, Everton and Exchange. The north end of Liverpool became the most densely populated area of Irish immigrants in mainland Britain, so much so that the St Paul's ward of Vauxhall was openly spoken of as 'Little Ireland'. As table 1

2   J.A. Picton, *Memorials of Liverpool* (Liverpool, 1903), p. 326.
3   T. Lane, *Liverpool: Gateway of Empire* (London, 1987).
4   Frank Neal, *Sectarian Violence: The Liverpool Experience, 1819–1914* (Manchester, 1988), p. 33.
5   T. Burke, *Catholic History of Liverpool* (Liverpool, 1910), p. 84.

illustrates, census returns for the years 1841 and 1851 show the increase of population of the north end areas, with the Irish-born as a percentage of these totals:

Table 1: Irish settlement in Liverpool's North End, 1841–1851

		1841			*1851*	
Ward	*Total*	*Irish*	*% Irish*	*Total*	*Irish*	*% Irish*
Scotland	35,290	6,095	17.3	60,065	18,275	30.4
Vauxhall	25,330	8,529	33.7	25,663	12,115	47.2
Exchange	17,652	6,115	34.3	16,935	7,965	47.0

Source: Census returns, 1841–51.

By 1851, Dryden Street had become notorious for its court dwellings, a cheap method of house-building condemned as early as 1804.[6] Census returns for 1851 show that out of a total of 583 people living in the street's six courts, 202 were born in Ireland.

Before the middle of the nineteenth century the Irish were widely regarded as the major social problem in the town, and the cause of alarming increases in mortality rates. They were perceived as carriers of epidemic disease, especially fever, a view justified by the recurring outbreaks in the districts where they settled.[7] Dr W.H. Duncan, Liverpool's Medical Officer of Health, reporting on an outbreak of typhus in 1847, observed:

> In one densely peopled district between Scotland Road and Vauxhall Road ... in which are situated most of the lodging houses resorted to by the migratory Irish, fever has become more than usually prevalent, that one half of the deaths from fever, since the first of January, had taken place in the Irish district in question ... that the disease affected almost exclusively, the Irish.[8]

The situation became a matter of national concern:

> Liverpool, created in haste by commerce by men too intent upon immediate gain; seared without any very tender regard for flesh or blood; and flourishing while her working population was rotting in cellars – has been taught severely the lesson, that a part of the population – whether in cellars or on distant shores –

6 M. Simey, *Charity Rediscovered* (Liverpool, 1951, revised 1992), pp 10–11.
7 R. Robins, *The Miasma: Epidemic and Panic in Nineteenth Century Ireland* (Dublin, 1996), p. 193.
8 Dr W.H. Duncan, *Report of Medical Officer of Health* (Liverpool, 1847).

cannot suffer without involving the whole community in calamity. In itself one of the unhealthiest towns of the Kingdom, Liverpool has for a year been the hospital and cemetery of Ireland.[9]

The clergy at the time showed remarkable heroism in caring for the victims of fever. Between March and September 1847, twelve Catholic priests died of typhus contacted while ministering to their parishioners. But deaths were not confined to the Irish Catholic community. The Revd John Johns, who led the Unitarian-sponsored Domestic Mission in Liverpool between 1836 until his death from typhus in 1847, often exceeded the conventional bounds of his ministry by advocating the need for urgent and drastic social reforms. Material conditions must be improved, he argued, if the spiritual and moral lives of the poor were to flourish. Indeed, Johns called for the cellars to be closed, while his plea for the gradual extension of facilties for education to the whole population went so far as to visualise state responsibility.[10]

October's Commemoration service at St Anthony's was a grim reminder of the extent of suffering and destitution caused by the epidemics of 1847. In the vaults of the church are the remains of 2303 victims of typhus and related diseases. In addition, 7129 victims, mainly inmates of the Brownlow Hill Workhouse, were buried in pauper graveyards in the Vauxhall and Abercomby districts. Further epidemics occured in 1848 and 1854; in consequence, life expectancy in the docklands areas of Liverpool became the lowest in the country. In 1866, Liverpool Corporation set up a sub-committee to enquire into the causes of mortality in the town. Monsignor James Nugent, in his evidence to the sub-committee, expressed the view that typhus arises,

> from the want of pure air, owing to the overcrowding of houses ... where typhus rages the most, there are so many people living in the houses that they have not pure air to breathe.[11]

But the sub-committee's final Report argued that the quality of housing, sewage, and drainage had been improved, concluding:

> The result of the enquiry is the conviction, suggested by most of the evidence, that the proximate causes of the increased death rate are intemperance, indigence, and overcrowding; these two latter being generally found in the train of intemperance, although all three act and react on each other as cause and effect.[12]

9 Quarterly Return of Registrar General, 30 Sept. 1847.
10 Simey, p. 39.
11 Mortality Sub-Committee: Report and Evidence (1866), p. 196.
12 Ibid., p. ix.

By implication, the Irish had only themselves to blame for their plight. They had brought their fever and diseases over with them, together with a culture of poverty and fecklessness, which had led Liverpool to be denigrated as the 'Black Spot on the Mersey'.

In the year the Report was published, the combined populations of the Vauxhall, Scotland and Exchange wards was 135,122, almost a third of the entire population of Liverpool. In the same year, 4805 deaths were recorded in those wards, mainly from typhus and diarrhoea.[13] Vauxhall and its surrounding areas became stereotyped as disease ridden and poverty-stricken, populated by the feckless Irish who were prone to drunkenness and violence. These images persisted well into the twentieth century. The English novelist and dramatist, J.B. Priestley, during a short visit to Liverpool in 1933, recorded his impressions of 'Paddy's Market' off Scotland Road, which he described as being, 'surrounded by slum streets, dirty little pubs, and the Irish'. Priestley held the Irish responsible for creating and sustaining the slums and 'the dirty little pubs', and he advocated their deportation back to Ireland where, he felt, 'a seductive call or two from De Valera, across the Irish Sea, might help'. 'Liverpool', he concluded, 'would be glad to be rid of them … what a fine exit of ignorance and dirt and drunkenness and disease'.[14]

Priestley's verdict on the Irish in Liverpool echoed the views of an Anglican priest, Canon Charles Raven, who, in May 1931, had published an article ominously entitled 'The Irish Problem' in the *Liverpool Review*. In this, he warned of the implications a revival of Irish immigration would have:

> Liverpool would never recover prosperity … the religious and racial bitterness for which our city has been unpleasantly notorious is undoubtedly increasing … there is a very widespread belief that our social progress is hampered and our financial stringency increased (by the Irish).[15]

Raven was concerned about the number of Irish who began to filter into the city after the setting up of the Irish Free State in 1922. Liverpool, as in the nineteenth century, seemed to offer the Irish the prospect of employment. The Irish, again, as in the nineteenth century, were seen as the cause of the city's social and economic problems. Like Priestley, Raven proposed a programme of repatriation, but with an added incentive. He argued that a reduction in the number of Irish in the city made good economic sense in that there would be huge savings in the amount of money spent on public assistance.

The assertion that the Irish were a financial liability on the public funds of the city was repeated in April 1937 in an interview with the Anglican bishop of

13 Ibid., Appendix l.
14 J.B. Priestley, *English Journey* (London, 1936, revised 1994), pp 248–9.
15 Charles Raven, 'The Irish Problem', *Liverpool Review*, vol. vi., no. 5 (May 1931).

Liverpool, Albert Augustus David, published in the *Manchester Guardian*. Bishop
David claimed that there were a quarter of a million Irish in Liverpool and that

> they continue to come every year for the higher dole. Ireland has discovered a
> way to make England support her surplus population. Their chief effect on
> Church life is to drive our conservative evangelicals into extremism. The most
> serious effect is political. They may give control to the Labour Party, which in
> turn may gain control of local government. In this event, Liverpool will be
> dominated by Roman Catholics.[16]

However, D. Caradog Jones' *Social Survey of Merseyside*, published in 1934,
shows that the number of Irish-born residents in Liverpool in 1921 was 28,700,
increasing to 30,000 by 1931, not a significant increase over a period of ten
years, and an insignificant percentage of the total population of 856,070, in
1931.[17] Bishop David was referring to the percentage of Catholics in the city,
using 'Catholic' and 'Irish' as synonymous terms. Religious mischief-making
had become a way of life in Liverpool since the 1830s. By the 1930s, sectarian
street violence had almost disappeared, but sectarianism still cast a shadow over
local politics, in the Council Chamber, and in the pages of respectable mag-
azines and newspapers.

II

By 1851, over 22% of Liverpool's population were Irish-born.[18] In 1850, the
Anglican Canon Abraham Hume estimated that 31% of the city's population
were Catholic, the majority living in the Vauxhall-Scotland area in which,
according to Hume, the number of Protestant families had been reduced by
16%. He warned that if that trend continued, the Vauxhall-Scotland district
would consist only of Catholics.[19] By the end of the century that forecast had
almost been fulfilled.

   A measure of the growth of Catholicism in Liverpool was the building
throughout the nineteenth century of a system of closely-knit parishes within
the city boundaries. At the start of the century, Liverpool had only two
Catholic parish churches, St Mary's and St Peter's, both near the town centre
and administered by the Benedictines. There was also a small chapel in Sir
Thomas Street which closed after the death of its priest in 1813. By 1886 the

16 *Manchester Guardian*, April 1937.
17 D. Caradog Jones (ed.), *Social Survey of Merseyside* (Liverpool, 1934), vol. 1.
18 Neal, p. 8.
19 Revd Canon A. Hume, *Missions at Home: or A Clergyman's Account of a Portion of the
    Town of Liverpool* (Liverpool, 1850), pp 8–12.

number of parishes had increased to twenty one, and by 1914 to twenty-four, sixteen of which were clustered in the Scotland, Vauxhall and Everton areas.

Although the development of the parochial system in Liverpool is associated with the administrations of Bishop Goss (1856–72) and Bishop O'Reilly (1873–94), the initiative for founding new parishes and building schools was sometimes taken by lay people. In February 1848, for example, a committee formed by a Dr Murphy and a Mr J. Neale Lomax considered the effects of overcrowding at St Mary's church, Edmund Street, where

> The Benedictines ... were absolutely unable to cope with the tens of thousands living in hovels in the district east and north of their church ... the 'poorest Irish congregation in the town'.[20]

The committee subsequently agreed that a new parish be founded, and to that end

> A warehouse was bought at the corner of Great Howard Street and Chadwick Street, and at a meeting presided over by Father Wilkinson OSB., the decision was ratified to commemorate 'the late lamented priests of St Mary's.[21]

The initiative of lay people also led to the building of St Francis Xavier's Jesuit church in Salisbury Street. The movement which led to this began in January 1840, when the first of a series of meetings was held in the 'Rose and Crown', Cheapside, leading to the formation of a Church Building Committee consisting entirely of lay people calling themselves 'The Society of St Francis Xavier'. According to Thomas Burke, 'the great bulk' of the committee had Irish surnames, fourteen of them living in the Vauxhall Road district. Meetings were always held in taverns and inns, leading Burke to comment:

> The social habits of Liverpudlians of the forties is well illustrated by this quaint list of taverns in which the meetings of a church building committee was held.[22]

But the committee met with strong opposition, and several attempts were made from within the Catholic community to frustrate their plan. The clergy at St Anthony's argued that there was no need for a new church. There was further criticism because the committee had not sought the approval of either the bishop of the Vicariate of the District or the provincial of the Jesuit order before making their plans public. There were heated objections from non-Catholics which led to extended correspondence in the Protestant journal *Protector*. The committee sent their case to the Vatican and in April 1842

20 Burke, p. 94.
21 Ibid., pp 95–6.
22 Ibid., p. 61.

received permission, under certain conditions, to proceed with the building of St Francis Xavier's, but the church was not given parochial status until 1848.[23]

Parish churches were built to accommodate large congregations and were furnished with Italian marble altars and pulpits, gold sanctuary lamps, monstrances and chalices embellished with jewels. They provided a powerful symbol of the authority of the Church and represented a world difficult to reconcile with the poverty of parishioners, and the squalor of their daily surroundings. By 1914 there were twenty-four parishes throughout the city area, and during the 1920s and 1930s an additional eighteen were founded to keep pace with the development of council housing estates in Norris Green, Fazackerley and Huyton. New parishes were also opened in the residential areas of Crosby, Broadgreen and Mossley Hill. This rate of building seems remarkable considering the social deprivation and poverty experienced by the majority of Liverpool's Irish-Catholics.

III

By the interwar years, each dockland parish had come to resemble the social structure of a pre-industrial English village, with the church, presbytery, and elementary school all in close proximity to each other, evidence of the centrality of Catholicism within the community. There was a parish church within five minutes walking distance from the majority of parishioner's homes. This became a bonus for some of the devout:

> We used to enjoy doing the Seven Churches on Holy Thursday. After going to Mass we were expected to say special prayers for the dead in seven different parish churches. So we would go off together and take it in turns to read out the prayers. Looking back, the churches were always quiet and peaceful on Holy Thursday, but, yet, full of people, with the altar in a side chapel set out like Our Lord's tomb – a white veil over the tabernacle and lots of candles. It was easy to walk from one church to another. It was a straightforward walk down Stanley Road and Scotland Road. It would take us about an hour at the most.[24]

Children's attendances at Sunday Mass, Confession and reception of Communion were overseen by teachers. There were special 'Children's Masses' each Sunday with teachers present, registering through various means the childrens' attendance. Regular Confession was timetabled during normal school hours. Schools and parishes prided themselves on the high quality of their boys' choirs,

23 Revd N. Ryan, *St Francis Xavier's Church Centenary: 1848–1948* (Liverpool, 1948), pp 17–23.
24 Taped Interview: J.G., M.K.

performing plainsong and motets during the weekly High Mass and Sunday Benediction. The choir at the parish of St Sylvester was oustanding. They broadcast a Benediction service from the church, and a St Patrick's Night Concert from Liverpool's Grafton Rooms, in 1936. This was no mean achievement in the early days of BBC radio. Devotions such as Benediction, the Forty Hours and Stations of the Cross remained popular features of parish life and were often the source of sensory pleasure:

> The parish churches were like peoples' palaces ... The smell of the flowers and the incense stick in your memory. In another way it was like going to the big picture houses in town, with their deep carpets and chandeliers, and the usherettes in their nice dresses. Going to church and going to the pictures took you out of yourself. In church you could do a bit of thinking. In the picture house you could escape.[25]

For one parishioner, reflecting on the late 1930s, the presbytery symbolised the difference between the life-style of the clergy and the people:

> We were never admitted into the presbytery. We were kept at the door, or allowed into a small waiting room just inside the house. Between the door and the hallway of the house, was a vestibule door, very beautifully decorated with stained-glass. On one occasion I was allowed in through the house to gain access to the church and I just glanced into the dining-room. The dining table was laid out for dinner. It was like a set from a Hollywood high-society film.[26]

Throughout the 1920s and 1930s, the combined Catholic population of the northern docklands parishes averaged about 100,000. The number of priests serving the parishes varied between seventy and seventy-five.[27] The priests came from contrasting social backgrounds and educational experiences. The Jesuit community at St Francis Xavier's and the Benedictines at St Mary's and St Augustine's, for example, included some who had been educated at public schools and universities. Holy Cross parish, nicknamed locally 'the Famine church', was staffed by members of the Irish missionary order, the Oblates of Mary Immaculate. Some of these had a reputation for toughness and straight talking through their involvement in industrial disputes in support of Liverpool dockers and transport workers. During local and national election campaigns, they actively campaigned on behalf of candidates who supported Catholic schools, irrespective of political party (excluding the Communist Party, of course!). As we shall see, they also became involved in the politics of

25 Taped Interview: M. O'C, June 1991. Terence Davies in his film, *The Long Day Closes*, dwells on a similar theme.
26 Taped Interview: J. McK, August 1995.
27 Quarant Ore Guides, Archdiocese of Liverpool, 1929–30.

Corporation housing policy during the 1930s. Among the secular clergy were some from the small towns and rural districts of Lancashire. But the majority were Irish-born, and the tradition of recruiting priests from Ireland continued until the 1950s.[28]

Irish priests received their training and education in diocesan seminaries. Some came for a short term to serve on the 'English Mission', returning after a five-year stay to their own diocese. Many came from rural areas of Ireland and without any practical experience of life in an industrial city. In 1936 a newly ordained priest arrived in Liverpool from Galway via Dublin:

> On arrival I had to report to the archdiocesan offices to meet the Vicar – General. Without any preliminaries, he ordered me to kneel in front of him to take the oath against Modernism. I had to recite this in Latin. Then he told me he had 'a nice little parish' for me to go to in the Scotland Road area. I had just enough money in my pocket for my tram fare and a small suitcase with a clean shirt, underclothes and socks. All my worldly belongings![29]

His parish was divided into districts with a priest in charge of each. An annual census kept an update on parishioners, including details of age, employment and marital status. Within a few minutes of arriving in the presbytery:

> Even before I was asked to sit down, the parish priest produced a notebook with a black cover and said, as he handed it to me, 'This is your district'. When I started to look through the book later, I was amazed to find so many people with the letters 'B.A.' after their names. I assumed this stood for Bachelor of Arts! I felt very uneasy. After all, I was a country boy from Galway. I was relieved later to find out that 'B.A.' meant British-American Tobacco Company. It was the place where they worked![30]

Sunday Mass attendance, abstaining from meat on Fridays, frequent Communion, and Confession were expected and priests were quick to visit families whose attendance at Mass was thought to be lax:

> My parents used to tell me about this parish priest in St Anthony's who used to go around the parish on a Sunday morning knocking people up to go to Mass. He would carry a long walking stick, and just bang on doors and windows until someone answered. Then he would storm into the house and demand that the people inside get ready to go to church. My parents said they were more frightened of him than they were of going to Hell![31]

28 J. Plumb, *Found Worthy: A Biographical Dictionary of the Secular Clergy of the Archdiocese of Liverpool since 1850* (Liverpool, 1985).
29 Taped Interview: Fr G.C., Nov. 1990.
30 Taped Interview: Fr G.C., Mar. 1991.
31 Taped Interview: S.C., Aug. 1995.

Some priests are remembered for their eccentricities. While at St Gerard's, from 1923–1928, Father Hoey was the cause of much amusement in the parish when, occasionally, he rode through the streets on a chestnut-coloured pony belonging to the late Mr Henry Schumacher, of 8 Nursery Street, Liverpool. Father Hoey was in his element, fondly imagining, it is thought, that he was back in Ireland in a country parish.[32] Others were remembered for their brusque manners:

> In our parish it wasn't unusual to be sitting in the house and suddenly the front door would be pushed open and one of the priests walk in. They usually wanted something. My Dad was in the Catholic Young Men's Society, and he would do anything for the priests. But, as I got older, I used to resent the idea that they could walk into your house like that, and boss you around.[33]

Parishes developed their individual identities and traditions. The parochial system with which the majority of people identified, was on occasion a divisive factor between parishes within the Vauxhall area. This was attributed to the influence of priests and schoolteachers. Competiveness between parishes was especially strong in sport: football, boxing and swimming in particular; outdoor processions and the raising of money for approved causes, such as the 'Good Shepherd Fund'. Within parishes, employment, levels of poverty and quality of housing contributed to patterns of social differentiation:

> In my parish, the poorest district – my district – was on the south side. Housing was very bad, children played truant and got into trouble with the police. Women could be as aggressive as men. Sunday mass attendance was lower … people showed less respect to the priest. The other district was called 'The Vatican' because the people there were the backbone of parish societies. They dressed quite smartly. Some of them had their own little shops and businesses. They were generous to the priests. There was one small street we called 'The Milky Way' because we were always offered a glass of milk at each house when we did our visitations.[34]

The social structure of some of the parishes began to change during the inter-war years. St Francis Xavier's, for example, when first founded in 1848, was situated in an area 'with only a few but fashionable houses … in which some Catholics had taken up residence', mainly in the Everton district. The rapid increase of population through Irish immigration during the 1840s and 1850s led to 'a feverish activity of house building … many jerry-built … and rented before they were completed'. While residence in the Everton district came to

---

32 *The Fortieth Jewel: St Gerard's, 1915–1949* (Liverpool, 1949), p. 20.
33 Taped Interview: W.M., Sept. 1995.
34 Taped Interview: Fr G.C., Nov. 1991.

confer a 'distinction on its dwellers', the Liverpool side of the parish, the district which housed the Irish, became identified with the 'real poor, for whose good the Free Dinners and Free Dispensary were undertaken'. From the beginning of the 1920s, the 'bettter-off Catholics began to migrate to the suburbs', leaving the more fashionable residences to become centres of trade and business, 'often controlled by Jews'. By then, the parish consisted almost entirely of 'working-class people, dependent on labour conditions and especially the dock trade'.[35]

Such social variations within parishes were not unusual and frequently influenced attitudes towards people living in particular neighbourhoods:

> I lived in Latimer Street when I was at school. Although there was poverty and poor housing on our side of the parish, I always felt nervous when I had to cross over to the other side, say Hornby Street or Tatlock Street. Once I passed the Gem (picture house), I used to feel that people were weighing me up wondering what I wanted. It seems silly now that I look back on it. We all lived in the same parish, but in those days, people who lived on that side of the parish were poorer and they were thought to be tougher.[36]

In the late 1920s the Jesuits set up a Council for Catholic Action at St Francis Xavier's, the purpose of which was to coordinate the work of existing parochial societies. One outcome was an Enquiry Bureau, 'to give advice ... on the various difficulties and problems which arise on Employment Benefit, Public Assistance, Landlord and Tenant rights, etc'. A club for girls and young women was opened in Shaw Street to provide facilities for sewing, choral training and amateur dramatics. The Association of the Ladies of Charity (defunct since 1878) was reconvened 'to bring relief to the poor of the parish'.[37] But such welfare work was not confined to the Catholic church in the area. Salisbury Street Council School, which was within the boundaries of St Francis Xavier's parish, pioneered parent-teacher associations during the 1930s, through the influence of the headmistress, Miss Jessie Crosbie. Miss Crosbie took a particular interest in the welfare and health of all the children of the area irrespective of their religion. She provided a bathroom in her school for mothers to bath their children. She also introduced a neighbourhood curfew 'as a way of preventing juvenile delinquency ... and to keep children indoors after a certain hour'.[38] This experiment was imitated by the Jesuits, who introduced a curfew for the children of their parish. The curfew was sounded by the ringing of the church bell every evening at 8.00 p.m., after which the children were called to

35 Ryan, pp 68–9.
36 Taped Interviews: T.B. and J.B., Oct. 1995.
37 Ryan, p. 70.
38 Private correspondence re: Miss Crosbie, 1996.

assemble in the church for prayers and hymn singing, before being despatched home to bed. The scheme was reported widely in the national press, but after less than a year, during which the numbers of children responding to the curfew had dwindled from 3000 to a mere 10, the curfew was dropped.

Perhaps more than any other parish in the dockland area, Holy Cross managed to retain its distinctive Irish identity, due perhaps to the strong personalities of the Irish Oblates and the tightly-organised parish societies. Nicknamed the 'Famine Church', Holy Cross was founded in 1848 to 'cope with the new masses of Catholic population which crowded the area'. Included in the parish was the site between Marybone and Hatton Garden, enshrined in a local legend as the place where St Patrick had preached before embarking for Ireland! The priests showed a political nous which was used effectively in their efforts to safeguard the future of the parish during a period of slum clearance and rehousing projects. In 1933 the number of parishioners totalled 4878, almost all of them living in dwelling houses which had been condemned under the 1930 Housing Act. This Act enabled the City Council to clear slum areas and to rehouse people in new suburban housing estates. The parish priest, Father James O'Shea, protested that, if implemented, this clearance would devastate his parish and the church would be 'left in the midst of a wilderness'.[39] With organised support from local Catholic councillors, the City Council were persuaded to rehouse people within the parish boundaries, and in November 1935, a block of modern tenements, Fontenoy Gardens, opened with accommodation for sixty-three families. This proved to be merely a partial victory for Father O'Shea; by April 1938 the population of the parish had fallen to 2497, due to the movement of parishioners to the new estates in the suburbs.

Although the vast majority of Catholics in the docklands community were descendants of Irish immigrants, there were also minority groups of Catholics of Italian, German and Polish descent. There were also streets where Catholics co-existed with Christians of other traditions. One such street was Wrexham Street, which lay between Stanley and Kirkdale Roads. Of the fifteen families living there, twelve attended the High Anglican church of St James-the-Less, which was situated next to the Catholic church of St Gerard in Cranmer Street.

The folklore of the area included many stories of religious sectarianism. Catholic children were warned by their elders not to cast their eyes on an Orange Lodge parade for fear of being struck blind! The Protestants strung up a line of rotting kippers across China Street (near the 'sectarian divide') on St Patrick's Day, with the caption 'Cured at Lourdes'. Out of such experiences grew a strong sense of place, a feeling of belonging to a neighbourhood where people knew each other well and instinctively acknowledged their adherence to the same cultural and religious roots. With few exceptions people had received

39 Revd J. Murray, OMI, *A History of Holy Cross Parish* (Liverpool, 1954), p. 61.

their formal education at their parochial elementary school and, through the powerful combination of church and school, Catholicism sustained its dominance as the major cultural influence – a fixed point in the life of the community and a badge of identity. So much so, that if people were asked where it was they lived, they were more likely to name their parish, rather than their street.

IV

The 1950s saw the beginning of the transformation of the Vauxhall and Scotland districts, a process which gathered momentum during the 1980s and 1990s, mainly through the community organisations the Vauxhall Neighbourhood Council and the Eldonians. Both organisations came into being during the 1970s as a result of peoples' reaction against the social changes taking place within the community.

At the start of the 1970s, Scotland Road, the traditional focal point of the docklands' neighbourhood was designated to become the main service road for the new Mersey Tunnel, linking Liverpool with Wallasey. This decision meant the closure of dozens of well-established neighbourhood shops, banks, post offices and a public library. It also meant the demolition of houses, including some built within the previous ten years. The Council planned to rehouse displaced families in new housing estates outside the city boundaries. The consequent reduction in population became another matter of concern to the people of Vauxhall. Since the post war period, City Council slum clearance policies had led to the exodus of thousands of families from the inner city areas to the new town of Kirkby. By 1971, the population of the Scotland and Vauxhall wards had fallen to 17,743. By 1981, this had been reduced further to 12,021.[40]

The origin of the Vauxhall Neighbourhood Council was a grass roots group who initiated a protest campaign against the City Council's decision about the siting of the Mersey Tunnel. The protests went unheeded and the tunnel was built. With suppport from members of Liverpool University's Sociology Department, the City Council agreed to fund a research project to identify the specific social and educational needs of the people of the area. The results led to the establishment of a permanent Vauxhall Neighbourhood Council, situated in the premises of a former elementary school. The Council began by offering a range of services: tenant associations, care groups, playschemes, sports projects, welfare rights, a law centre, and a youth service. A community newspaper, the *Scotty Press*, was started in 1972 and a docklands' history project consisting of documentary and photographic material followed. Education classes in basic subjects, trade unionism, speaking with confidence and creative writing were added to the facilities and continue successfully today.

40 *Liverpool Community Atlas* (John Moores University, Liverpool, 1991). p. 8.

In 1989, the Neighbourhood Council established the Vauxhall Housing Cooperative and received funding through Housing Agencies to launch a house building project on the west side of the Leeds and Liverpool Canal, north of the Eldonian Village. This project has provided good quality rented houses for people from the Scotland and Vauxhall areas. Thus far, about 100 houses have been built, with twice that number planned for completion over the next five years. Currently under construction is a new Neighbourhood Council Centre at a cost of £3.4 millions, with all but £369,000 coming from Objective One Status funding. This will enable the Council to extend its activities to include community business and technology training, a new library, and a bowling green. The Centre staff are all local people under contract to the City Council.

In 1978, the City Council announced its intention to build a new ring road through the Vauxhall and Scotland districts. This meant the further demolition of houses and no guarantee that people would be rehoused in their own neighbourhood. These were the events which led to the formation of the Eldonian Community Association in that year. It took its name from Eldon Street, one of the oldest streets in the district, and the street associated with their parish church, Our Lady of Reconciliation. The aim of the Eldonians was to campaign to keep their parish community together. A house-to-house survey disclosed 80% support for this aim. In 1980, the community became part of a protest campaign against the closure of the Tate and Lyle sugar refinery in Vauxhall Road. Because of the closure, more than 1700 people became redundant, most of them living in the vicinity of the factory. Subsequent developments helped to consolidate the ambitions of the Eldonians. The City's Liberal Council encouraged a partnership between Merseyside Improved Housing Association, thus creating the Eldonian Housing Cooperative. In the aftermath of the Toxteth riots in 1981, the Conservative government set up a Task Force to coordinate government strategy in the city. In 1984, the Task Force funded a comprehensive investigation into the viability of using the former Tate and Lyle factory site for housing development.

In the meantime, the Eldonians had formed a second cooperative with the assistance of local architects and the City Council. Their first task was the conversion of a tenement block into bungalow accommodation for elderly people. Plans were also drawn up to build houses and bungalows on neighbouring sites. In 1982, plans for developing the 'Eldonian village' on the Tate and Lyle site received the support of English Estates. In 1983, the newly elected Militant Labour Council refused to support this proposal and announced an alternative plan for extensive municipal housing projects in the inner city areas. An application from the Eldonians for permission to change the Tate and Lyle site from industrial to residential use, was refused by the Council, but when the application went to a public enquiry, the Eldonians won their case.

The success of the Eldonians started with that victory. In 1986, tenants moved into the converted tenement blocks; the government awarded a £2.1 million grant towards bringing the Tate and Lyle site up to green field standard; the Task Force funded £4.5 millions to the Cooperative for the building of 145 new houses on the site. In May 1989 Phase 1 of the Eldonian Village was officially opened by Prince Charles. Since then, Phase 2 has been completed with the building of 150 additional houses on land adjacent to the first development. The Eldonians have become a successful model of urban regeneration, a success which has been recognised both nationally and internationally. Throughout their campaigning they were supported by the Conservative government, with Mrs Thatcher and several of her senior ministers making official visits at different stages in the progress of the building programme. Politicians from European countries, the United States and Japan are among recent visitors. The chairman of the Trust has made a lecture tour of United States and been awarded an M.B.E., as well as an honorary M.A., in recognition of his services to the community. Recently he has been designated 'Ambassador of Merseyside' by the Merseyside (Business) Partnership.

Archbishop Worlock and Bishop David Sheppard became involved at an early stage. They laid the foundation stone of the Village before construction work began, and in recognition of their support, their names are permanently enshrined in street names. At the time of the official opening, Bishop Sheppard wrote:

> The God we believe in is concerned about the quality of life of all people. He cares about good housing and good opportunities for school and jobs. The Eldonians' motto, 'Better Together' sums up that spirit and that provided the Archbishop and me with the perfect title for our joint book about our Liverpool experience.[41]

And, at the same time, Archbishop Worlock wrote:

> For my part I would want to single out their remarkable community solidarity. This has combined well with their faith and in their recognition that in many matters they may turn in friendship to those able to offer them the professional advice needed in the complex tasks they have tackled.[42]

The Eldonians' success continues. They are now a Community Based Housing Association, which means they build houses for sale and rent to non-Vauxhall residents. Consequently they have formed a partnership with Wimpey Homes in providing 130 houses for sale. There are further plans to build 250–300 new 'executive homes' on a vacant site known locally as 'The Land to

41 'The Eldonians', 3 May 1989.
42 Ibid.

the North'. In so doing, they have moved away from their own 'parish' area into other districts of Vauxhall. On the site of a demolished Catholic church stands 'St Gerard Majella Close', a fifteen-unit scheme completed in 1989 for tenents of pensionable age. The Eldonians have established a Community Trust, a registered charity which arranges a variety of activities for local people, ranging from day trips to Knowsley Safari Park to trips to Lourdes. In a colourful and attractively produced brochure, the Trust is described as fulfilling 'a vital role in the Eldonian culture that encourages people to socialise and help one another. No one is forgotten or left on their own'.[43] Some examples of the range of facilities are listed: regular visits from a chiropodist, an optician and a dentist, while a hairdresser pays a weekly call. The Village has its own Hall, Day Nursery, Community Centre, Outdoor Sports Facilities and a Multi-use indoor sports centre. These have all been completed with funding from private sources, and from the Merseyside Development Corporation. Like the Vauxhall Neighbourhood Council, all the staff of the Eldonians are recruited locally, although there are specialist workers, including some of the medical and care staff, who are outsiders.

Since the recent demise of Liverpool's Irish Centre, Irish cultural activities, such as dancing and music tuition, take place at weekends in the Village Hall. There is a possibility that in due course an Irish-Liverpool Heritage Centre will be set up there. The Leeds and Liverpool canal has been cleaned and two brightly painted canal barges – one called 'The Eldonian' – are ready for service during the tourist season. Vauxhall Road itself is currently being improved with extra pedestrian crossings, safety islands and speed restrictions. The Eldonian Village Hall and Administrative Centre are the centre pieces of the first phases of development. To these have been added a new link road which crosses the canal, giving access to the housing estates and into 'Eldonian Quay', the site currently under development for building an estate of executive houses. The Eldonian Community Trust has partnerships with Merseyside business employers such as Littlewoods, Carlsberg, the City Council and various Housing Trusts. Through these contacts, training and educational facilites are made available, and there is a recent proposal to establish a purpose-built Information Technology centre for community use, on the basis of a 'drop-in' facility. The overall management of the Eldonians is structured around six committees. Some members are elected by residents, others because of particular areas of expertise. The parish priest of St Anthony's parish is a member of the Trust and Management Committees.

Community developments pioneered by the Vauxhall Neighbourhood Council and the Eldonians will continue well beyond the millennium. From their inception, both organisations had different priorities: the Vauxhall

---

43 'The Eldonians: An Insight', 1996, p. 12.

Council's first task was to provide welfare, education and related services. For the Eldonians, the priority was to provide houses, with the aim of maintaining the remnant of what had once been a densely populated neighbourhood. The extent of the Eldonians' achievement can be seen in the impressive housing and community developments which dominate Vauxhall Road and adjacent areas. The achievements of the Vauxhall Community are not so evident in terms of bricks and mortar (apart from the Athol Village estate and the forthcoming Centre, now under construction), but in the range of services available daily throughout the neighbourhood and the commitment of the community workers.

Although there is no evidence of hostility between the management of the two organisations, neither is there much evidence of cooperation. The reason may be rooted in different political ideologies. The Neighbourhood Council has retained strong financial and political links with Liverpool's Labour Council and has used those links to obtain financial support from European sources. The Eldonians, on the other hand, took control of their own destiny after a series of confrontations with Militant Labour at City Council level, and in local municipal wards. The leadership, consisting mainly of former dockers and factory workers from Tate and Lyle, was quick to adapt to the entrepreneurial climate generated by Mrs Thatcher's government. This spirit of entrepreneurship is still a motivating force. For example, plans are currently under discussion to restore traditional-style shopping facilities. This will mean to a considerable extent that residents could become self-sufficient, with a range of facilities available to them within the urban village district, which, by the millennium, may have come to resemble a working-class commune.

Although this essay has been confined to the activities of the Eldonian and Vauxhall Neighbourhood communities, other housing developments have also been proceeding. Some of these were sponsored by the City Council in the early 1980s, others have been built by Housing Associations. Of good quality, they were built mainly to replace the high rise and walk-up tenement flats which dominated the area from the early 1960s. The achievements of the Eldonians, the Vauxhall Neighbourhood Council and other agencies have been remarkable, considering the base lines from which they started. However, high levels of unemployment continue, as Table 2 illustrates:

Table 2: Unemployment [%] in Vauxhall, 1971–91

	Vauxhall	*City*
1971	16.0%	10.7%
1981	36.6%	20.4%
1991	45.1%	21.6%

Source: *Liverpool Community Atlas* (1991).

Moreover, many of the social problems associated with unemployment persist in the district. 22% of residents suffer from long-term illness, whilst 81% of households have no car.[44] There are two Catholic High Schools, with 664 on roll in the boys' school, and 1065 on roll in the girls'. This imbalance can be explained. The girls' school was formerly a grammar school under the auspices of the Sisters of Notre Dame. It continues to enjoy a good reputation and is in demand from parents living outside the usual catchment area of Vauxhall. There are six Catholic primary schools with a total pupil roll of 1192 children. One primary school, Bishop Goss, closed in 1997 due to rationalization. An update on the 1991 Census Returns shows that 10.20% of pupils of the Vauxhall area currently in secondary education live in lone parent households.[45] In March 1998 the Liverpool City Council, through its Education Directorate, made a bid for Education Action Zone status. Part of the area designated for this was Vauxhall, which was described in the Bid as 'arguably, the most economically disadvantaged urban area of Europe'. The Bid, which would have brought extra resources and funding into schools, was unsuccessful.

V

At the beginning of the twentieth century, the Catholic Church in Liverpool faced the new century with confidence. Sixty years of extraordinary growth during the previous century were followed by thirty years of consolidation. In 1911, the Vatican showed its confidence in the Catholic community of Liverpool by raising the diocese to the status of an archdiocese, elevating its bishop to the rank of archbishop, and extending diocesan geographical boundaries. The September 1929 celebrations to commemorate the centenary of Catholic Emancipation, held at Thingwall Park and attended by 300,000 people, provided the impetus to build a cathedral in the city. It was Liverpool's first Archbishop, Thomas Whiteside (1894–1921), who established the principle of building a cathedral, but it was Richard Downey, archbishop from 1928 to 1953, who decided in 1930 to proceed with one of the most ambitious and original religious projects of the twentieth century: the building of the Cathedral of Christ the King, on the site of the former workhouse in Brownlow Hill.

By the turn of the century, progress had also been made in education. Twelve Catholic high schools were providing secondary education, all under the jurisdiction of religious teaching orders. There were a sufficient number of Catholic undergraduates at the city's university to establish a Catholic Society in 1913, the purpose of which was 'to create a bond of union amongst its

44 *Liverpool Community Atlas*, p. 8.
45 Data supplied by Liverpool City Council, Directorate of Education, April 1998.

members, to promote lectures on religious topics, and to organize social functions'.[46] A permanent Catholic Chaplaincy was founded at the university in 1941, with financial help from the Jesuits.

While the arrival of the twentieth century promised the further expansion of Catholicism in Liverpool, the arrival of the twenty-first century, at least in the docklands areas, is likely to herald a period of further contraction. Demographic changes have led to an extended process of rationalisation. Between 1968 and 1996, five docklands' parishes have closed and the vacant sites sold for redevelopment. The church of St Alban, closed in 1991, is in the process of renovation and conversion to an outdoor pursuits centre. Three parishes have merged and another, St Mary's, Highfield Street, has become a centre of ecumenical ministry in the city. Further closures and mergers are likely in the near future. The profile of the eleven priests still serving the area shows a significant weighting towards the 60+ age group. Given the current shortage of priests in the archdiocese it is unlikely that they will be easily replaced as they become eligible for retirement. Some organisational changes introduced by the archdiocese in recent years seem to have by-passed the docklands parishes. Of the eighty-one permanent deacons throughout the archdiocese, none serve in the docklands. The Archdiocesan Youth Service has active centres in Norris Green, Toxteth and Speke, but none exist in Vauxhall. The Vauxhall Deanery is one of only three deaneries without a marriage-contact group (the other two being Kirkby and Old Swan). Local priests claim that about 10% of Catholics living in Vauxhall attend Sunday mass regularly, although baptisms and first Communions are joyfully celebrated by extended families and at considerable expense. Contact between some of the priests and their parishioners seems minimal. Sodalities and parish organisations which were part of the old parish structures, no longer exist. Gone also, are the social aspects of parochial life.[47] Churches are open only at mass times. A recent meeting of the Catholic Mothers Union, at St Anthony's consisted of five elderly women playing bingo! On a more positive side, the Jesuits at St Francis Xavier parish (now merged with the former Franciscan parish of St Mary of the Angels) have participated in effective community work across Everton's traditional religious divide, since the mid-1980s. An order of nuns have a convent in a high-rise block of flats in the Holy Cross parish, from which they combine parish visiting with full time nursing and welfare work.

Catholics in the Vauxhall areas have, in the past, identified very closely with their parishes, and have looked with respect upon their priests and sought guidance from them. With very few exceptions this tradition has died. People

46 J. Brothers, *Church and School* (Liverpool, 1964), p. 106.
47 Pat Ayers, *The Liverpool Docklands: Life and Work in Athol Street* (Docklands History Project, University of Liverpool, n.d.).

now identify more closely with the Eldonians and the Vauxhall Neighbourhood Community Centre. Out of the process of regeneration have emerged individuals of vision, determination and strong leadership, with a deep commitment towards improving the quality of life for residents of the area. This level of involvement and commitment has not, so far, been matched by the Catholic Church. The influence of local clergy in this process has been marginal. While the 'secular' organisations are facing the millennium with confidence, with well-researched and well-resourced programmes charting progress towards the completion of 'Utopia' in Vauxhall, Catholicism seems to be drifting. For more than a century the people of Vauxhall provided the numerical strength of the Catholic Church in Liverpool. Through their parishes, they helped to establish a vibrant devotional and social tradition which now exists only in the memories of an older generation. That Catholicism will survive in the regenerated urban villages of Vauxhall is highly probable. But questions on the structures and forms of ministry which may be appropriate for the people living there, have yet to be faced.

Select Bibliography

PRIMARY SOURCES

Anon., 'The London Irish', *Blackwood's Edinburgh Magazine*, vol. 170 (July 1901), 124–34.

Barclay, T., *Memories and Medleys: The Autobiography of a Bottlewasher* (Leicester, 1934).

Booth, C., *Life and Labour of the People of London*, series 1, *Poverty*, 4 vols; series 2, *Industry*, 5 vols; series 3, *Religious Influences*, 7 vols (London, 1902–3).

Carlyle, T., *Chartism* (London, 1839).

Denvir, J., *The Irish in Britain* (London, 1892).

Denvir, J., *Life Story of an Old Rebel* (Dublin, 1910).

Devoy, J., *Recollections of an Irish Rebel* (New York, 1929).

Engels, F., *The Condition of the Working Class in England* (1845, trans. & ed. Henderson, W.O. and Chaloner, W.H., Oxford, 1958).

Gainsforce, R.J., 'English and Irish Crime', *Dublin Review*, vol. 42 (March 1857), 142–56.

Gallagher, P., *My Story. By Paddy the Cope* (London, 1939).

Garratt, S., 'The Irish in London', in *Motives for Missions* (London, 1852).

Heinrick, H., *A Survey of the Irish in England in 1872* (Dublin, 1872; edited by Alan O'Day, London, 1990).

Kay, J.P., *The Moral and Physical Condition of the Working Classes employed in the Cotton Manufacture in Manchester* (Manchester, 1832).

MacGill, P., *Children of the Dead End: The Autobiography of a Navvy* (London, 1914).

Mayhew, H., *The Morning Chronicle Survey of Labour and the Poor: The Metropolitan Districts* (6 vols, London, 1849–50; reprinted, with an introduction by Peter Razzell, Firle, 1980).

Mayhew, H., *London Labour and the London Poor* (4 vols, London, 1861–2, reprinted New York, 1968).

Mayhew H., and Binney, J., *The Criminal Prisons of London* (London, 1862).

O'Connor, T.P., *Memoirs of an Old Parliamentarian* (2 vols, London, 1929).

O'Neill, J., 'Fifty Years Experience as an Irish Shoemaker in London', *St Crispin*, nos 1 and 2 (1869).

O'Mara, P., *The Autobiography of a Liverpool Irish Slummy* (London, 1934)

Roberts, R., *The Classic Slum* (London, 1983).

Royal Commission on the Conditions of the Poorer Classes in Ireland. Appendix G, The State of the Irish Poor in Great Britain, Parliamentary Papers (1836), XXXIV.

Sexton, J., *Sir James Sexton. The Life Story of an Agitator* (London, 1936).

Thackeray, W.M., *The Irish Sketchbook* (1843).

Thompson, F., *Lark Rise to Candleford* (London, 1930).

Tillett, B., *Memories and Reflections* (London, 1931).

Todd, W.G., 'The Irish in England', *Dublin Review*, vol. 41 (September 1856), pp 470–521.

Waugh, N., *These, My Little Ones* (London, 1911).

SECONDARY SOURCES

A. Books and Contributions to Books

Akenson, D.H, *The Irish Diaspora: A Primer* (Belfast, 1996), chapter 8, 'Great Britain: The Place Nearest Home', pp 189–216.

Arnstein, W.L., *Protestant versus Catholic in Mid-Victorian England: Mr Newdegate and the Nuns* (Columbia and London, 1982).

Aspinwall, B. and McCaffrey, J., 'A Comparative View of the Irish in Edinburgh in the Nineteenth Century', in Swift, R. and Gilley, S. (eds), *The Irish in the Victorian City* (London, 1985), pp 130–57.

—— 'The Catholic Irish and Wealth in Glasgow', in Devine, T.M., *Irish Immigrants and Scottish Society in the Nineteenth and Twentieth Centuries* (Edinburgh, 1991), 91–115.

—— 'A Long Journey: The Irish in Scotland', in O'Sullivan. P. (ed.), *The Irish World Wide*, vol. 5, *Religion and Identity* (Leicester, 1996), pp 146–82.

Devine, T.M., 'The Welfare State within the Welfare State: The Saint Vincent de Paul Society in Glasgow, 1848–1920', in Shiels, W.J. and Wood, D. (eds), *Voluntary Religion*, Studies in Church History, 23 (Oxford, 1986).

Bartlett, A., 'From Strength to Strength: Roman Catholicism in Bermondsey up to 1939', in Fielding, S.J. (ed.), *The Church and the People: Catholics and their Church in Britain, 1880–1939* (University of Warwick, 1988), pp 29–47

Beck, G.A., (ed.), *The English Catholics* (London, 1951).

Bermant, C., *London's East End: Point of Arrival* (New York, 1975).

Belchem, J.C., '1848: Feargus O'Connor and the Collapse of the Mass Platform', in Epstein, J. and Thompson, D. (eds), *The Chartist Experience* (London, 1982).

—— 'English Working-Class Radicalism and the Irish, 1815–50', in Swift and Gilley, *The Irish in the Victorian City* (1985), pp 85–97.

—— *Industrialization and the Working Class: The English Experience, 1750–1900*, (Aldershot, 1990).

—— (ed.), *Popular Politics, Riot and Labour: Essays in Liverpool History, 1790–1940* (Liverpool, 1992).

Belchem, J.C., 'Liverpool in the Year of Revolution: The Political and Associational Culture of the Irish Immigrant Community in 1848', in Belchem, J., *Popular Politics, Riot and Labour* (1992), pp 68–97.

—— 'The Irish in Britain, United States and Australia: Some Comparative Reflections on Labour History', in Buckland, P. and Belchem, J. (eds), *The Irish in British Labour History* (1993), pp 19–28.

—— 'The Immigrant Alternative: Ethnic and Sectarian Mutuality among the Liverpool Irish during the Nineteenth Century', in Ashton, O., Fyson, R., and Roberts. S. (eds), *The Duty of Discontent: Essays for Dorothy Thompson* (London, 1995), pp 231–50.

Best, G.F.A., 'Popular Protestantism in Victorian Britain', in Robson, R.(ed.), *Ideas and Institutions of Victorian Britain* (London, 1967), pp 115–42.

Bohstedt, J., 'More than One Working Class: Protestant and Catholic Riots in Edwardian Liverpool', in Belchem, J., *Popular Politics, Riot and Labour* (1992), pp 173–216.

Boyce, D.G., *Englishmen and Irish Troubles* (London, 1972).

Bossy, J., *The English Catholic Community, 1570–1850* (London, 1975).

Brady, L.W., *T.P. O'Connor and the Liverpool Irish* (London, 1983).

Brooke, D., *The Railway Navvy* (Newton Abbot, 1983).

Bryson, A., 'Riotous Liverpool, 1815–60', in Belchem, J., *Popular Politics, Riot and Labour* (1992), pp 98–134.

Buckland. P. and Belchem, J.C. (eds), *The Irish in British Labour History* (Conference Proceedings in Irish Studies, University of Liverpool, 1993).

Busteed, M.A., Hodgson, R.I., and Kennedy, T.F., 'The myth and reality of Irish migrants in mid-nineteenth century Manchester: a preliminary study', in O'Sullivan, P. (ed.), *The Irish World Wide*, vol. 2, *The Irish in the New Communities* (1992), pp 26–51.

Butt, J., 'Belfast and Glasgow: Connections and Comparisons, 1790–1850', in Devine, T.M. and Dickson, D., *Ireland and Scotland, 1600–1850* (Edinburgh, 1983).

Canavan, B., 'Story-tellers and Writers: Irish Identity in Emigrant Labourers' Autobiographies, 1870–1970', in O'Sullivan, P. (ed.), *The Irish World Wide*, vol. 3, *The Creative Migrant* (Leicester, 1994), pp 154–169.

Champ, J., 'The Demographic Impact of Irish Immigration on Birmingham Catholicism, 1800–1850', in Sheils, W.J. and Wood, D. (eds.), *The Churches, Ireland and the Irish*, Studies in Church History, 25 (Oxford, 1989).

Chase, M., ' The Teeside Irish in the Nineteenth Century', in Buckland and Belchem, *The Irish in British Labour History* (1993), pp 47–58.

Collins, B., 'The Irish in Britain, 1780–1921', in Graham, B.J. and Proudfoot, L.J. (eds), *An Historical Geography of Ireland* (London,1993), pp 366–98.

Coleman, T., *The Railway Navvies* (London, 1965).

—— *Passage to America* (London, 1972).

Curtin, C., O'Dwyer, R., and O'Tuathaigh, G., 'Emigration and Exile' in Bartlett, T., Curtin, C., O'Dwyer, R., and O'Tuathaigh, G. (eds), *Irish Studies: A General Introduction* (Dublin, 1988), pp 60–86.

Curtis, L.P., *Anglo-Saxons and Celts* (Bridgeport, Connecticut, 1968).

—— *Apes and Angels: The Irishman in Victorian Caricature* (Newton Abbot, 1971).

Collins, B., 'Irish Emigration to Dundee and Paisley during the first half of the Nineteenth Century', in Goldstrom, J.M. and Clark, L.A. (eds.), *Irish Population, Economy and Society* (Oxford, 1981).

—— 'The Origins of Irish Immigration to Scotland in the Nineteenth and Twentieth Centuries', in Devine, *Irish Immigrants and Scottish Society* (1991), pp 1–18.

Connolly, G., 'Irish and Catholic: Myth or Reality ? Another Sort of Irish and the Renewal of the Clerical Profession among Catholics in England, 1791–1918', in Swift and Gilley (eds), *The Irish in the Victorian City* (1985), pp 225–54.

—— '"Little Brother be at Peace": The Priest as Holy Man in the Nineteenth-Century Ghetto', in Shiels, W.J. (ed.), *Studies in Church History: The Churches and Healing* (Oxford, 1982), pp 191–205.

Daly, M., *The Famine in Ireland* (Dublin, 1987).

Darragh, J., 'The Catholic Population of Scotland, 1878–1977', in D. McRoberts (ed.), *Modern Scottish Catholicism* (Glasgow, 1979), pp 211–47.

Davis, G., 'Little Irelands', in Swift and Gilley (eds), *The Irish in Britain, 1815–1939* (London, 1989), pp 104–133.

—— *The Irish in Britain, 1815–1914* (Dublin, 1991).

—— 'The Historiography of the Irish Famine', in P. O'Sullivan (ed.), *The Irish World Wide*, vol. 6., *The Meaning of the Famine* (Leicester, 1997), pp 15–39.

Devoy, J., *Recollections of an Irish Rebel* (New York, 1929).

Devine, T.M. (ed.), *Irish Immigrants and Scottish Society in the Nineteenth and Twentieth Centuries* (Edinburgh, 1991).

Doyle, P., 'The Catholic Federation, 1906–29', in Shiels & Wood, *Voluntary Religion* (1986).

Edwards, R. and Williams, T.D. (eds), *The Great Famine: Studies in Irish History, 1845–52* (Dublin, 1956).

Edwards, O.D., 'The Irish in Scotland', in Daiches, D. (ed.), *A Companion to Scottish Culture* (London, 1982), pp 182–6.

—— 'The Catholic Press in Scotland since the Restoration of the Hierarchy', in McRoberts, D., *Modern Scottish Catholicism 1878–1978* (1979), pp 156–82.

—— *The Mind of an Activist: James Connolly* (Dublin, 1971).

—— (ed., with Ransom. B.), *James Connolly: Selected Political Writings* (London, 1973).

—— *Burke and Hare* (Edinburgh, 1980).

—— *The Quest for Sherlock Holmes* (Totowa, New Jersey, 1983).

—— (with Storey, P.J.), 'The Irish Press in Victorian Britain', in Swift and Gilley (eds), *The Irish in the Victorian City* (1985), pp 158–78.

Epstein, J., *The Lion of Freedom: Feargus O'Connor and the Chartist Movement, 1832–42* (London, 1982).

Fielding, S.J. (ed.), *The Church and the People: Catholics and their Church in Britain, 1880–1939* (Warwick University Working Papers in Social History, 1988).

—— 'A Separate Culture? Irish Catholics in working-class Manchester and Salford, c.1890–1939', in Davies, A. and Fielding, S.J. (eds), *Workers' Worlds: Cultures and Communities in Manchester and Salford, 1880–1939* (Manchester, 1992), pp 23–48.

—— *Class and Ethnicity: Irish Catholics in England, 1880–1939* (Buckingham, 1993).

Finnegan, F., *Poverty and Prejudice: Irish Immigrants in York, 1840–75* (Cork, 1982).

—— 'The Irish in York', in Swift and Gilley (eds), *The Irish in the Victorian City* (1985), pp 59–84.

Fitzpatrick, D., *Irish Emigration, 1801–1921* (Dublin, 1984).

—— 'A curious middle place: the Irish in Britain, 1871–1921', in Swift and Gilley (eds), *The Irish in Britain, 1815–1939* (1989), pp 10–59.

David Fitzpatrick, '"A Peculiar Tramping People": The Irish in Britain, 1801–70', in W.E.Vaughan (ed.), *A New History of Ireland*, vol. 5, *Ireland under the Union*, I, *1801–70* (Oxford, 1989), pp 623–660.

Fitzpatrick, D., 'The Irish in Britain: Settlers or Transients?', in Buckland and Belchem, *The Irish in British Labour History* (1993), pp 1–10.

—— *Oceans of Consolation: Personal Accounts of Irish Migration to Australia* (Cork, 1994).

Foster, J., *Class Struggle and the Industrial Revolution* (London, 1974).

Foster, R.F., 'Marginal Men and Micks on the Make: The Uses of Irish Exile, 1840–1922', in Foster, R.F., *Paddy and Mr. Punch* (London, 1993).

Gallagher, T., *Paddy's Lament: Ireland 1846–7, Prelude to Hatred* (Dublin, 1985)

—— *Glasgow: The Uneasy Peace – Religious Tension in Modern Scotland, 1819–1940* (Manchester, 1987).

—— 'A Tale of Two Cities: Communal Strife in Glasgow and Liverpool before 1914', in Swift and Gilley (eds), *The Irish in the Victorian City* (1985), pp 106–129.

—— *Edinburgh Divided* (Edinburgh, 1987).

—— 'The Catholic Irish in Scotland: In Search of Identity', in Devine, *Irish Immigrants and Scottish Society* (1991), pp 19–43.

Garrard, J.A., *The English and Immigration, 1880–1910* (London, 1971).

George, M.D., *London Life in the Eighteenth Century* (London, 1925, rep. 1979).

Gillespie, W., *The Christian Brothers in England* (Bristol, 1975).

Gilley, S., 'Papists, Protestants and the Irish in London', in Cumming, G.J. and Baker, D. (eds), *Popular Belief and Practice*, Studies in Church History, 8 (Cambridge, 1972).

—— 'The Catholic Faith of the Irish Slums: London, 1840–70', in Dyos, H.J. and Wolff, M. (eds), *The Victorian City: Images and Reality*, 2 vols (London, 1973), vol. 2, pp 837–53.

Gilley, S., 'English Attitudes to the Irish in England, 1780–1900', in Holmes, C. (ed.), *Immigrants and Minorities in British Society* (London, 1978), pp 81–110.

—— 'Catholics and Socialists in Glasgow, 1906–12', in Lunn, K. (ed.), *Hosts, Immigrants and Minorities: Historical Responses to Newcomers in British Society, 1870–1914* (New York, 1980), pp 160–200.

—— 'Vulgar Piety and the Brompton Oratory, 1850–1860', in Swift and Gilley (eds), *The Irish in the Victorian City* (1985), pp 255–66.

—— 'Irish Catholicism in Britain, 1880–1939', in Fielding, S.J. (ed), *The Church and the People* (1988), pp 1–28.

—— 'Catholics and Socialists in Scotland, 1900–30', in Swift & Gilley (eds), *The Irish in Britain, 1815–1939* (1989), pp 212–238.

Goodway, D., *London Chartism, 1838–48* (Cambridge, 1982), pp 61–7, 'The Irish'.

Gwynn, D., 'The Irish Immigration' in Beck, G.A. (ed.), *The English Catholics, 1850–1950* (London, 1950), pp 265–90.

Greaves, C.D., *The Life and Times of James Connolly* (London, 1961).

Handley, J.E., *The Irish in Scotland, 1789–1845* (Cork, 1943).

—— *The Irish in Modern Scotland* (Cork, 1947).

—— *The Celtic Story: A History of the Celtic Football Club* (1960).

—— *The Navvy in Scotland* (Cork, 1970).

Hanham, H., 'Religion and Nationality in the Mid-Victorian Army', in Foot, M.R.D. (ed.), *War and Society: Essays in Honour of J.R. Western* (London, 1973).

Hannon, J., *The Life of John Wheatley* (Nottingham, 1988).

Harmon, M. (ed.), *Fenians and Fenianism* (Dublin, 1968).

Hartigan, M., O'Day, A., and Quinault, R., 'Irish Terrorism in Britain: A comparison between the activities of Fenians in the 1860's and those of Republican Groups since 1872', in Alexander, Y. and O'Day, A. (eds), *Ireland's Terrorist Dilemma* (Dordecht, Netherlands, 1986).

Harris, R.A., *The Nearest Place That Wasn't Ireland: Early Nineteenth-Century Irish Labour Migration* (Ames, Iowa, 1994).

Herson, J., 'Irish migration and settlement in Victorian England: a small-town perspective', in Swift & Gilley (eds), *The Irish in Britain, 1815–1939* (1989), pp 84–103.

Hickey, J., *Urban Catholics: Urban Catholicism in England and Wales from 1829 to the Present Day* (London, 1967).

Hickman, M. and Hartigan, M., *The History of the Irish in Britain: A Bibliography* (London, 1986).

—— *Religion, Class and Identity: The State, the Catholic Church and the Education of the Irish in Britain* (Aldershot, 1995).

—— 'Incorporating and Denationalizing the Irish in England: the Role of the Catholic Church', in O'Sullivan, P. (ed.), *The Irish World Wide*, vol. 5, *Religion and Identity* (Leicester, 1996), pp 196–216.

Holmes, C., *John Bull's Island: Immigration and British Society, 1871–1971* (London, 1988).

Holmes, J.D., *More Roman than Rome: English Catholicism in the Nineteenth Century* (London, 1978).

Hunt, E.H., *British Labour History, 1815–1914* (London, 1981).

Inglis, K.S., *Churches and the Working Classes in Victorian England* (London, 1963).

Jackson, J., *The Irish in Britain* (London, 1963).

Jeffes, K.T., 'The Irish in Early Victorian Chester: An Outcast Community ?', in Swift, Roger (ed.), *Victorian Chester: Essays in Social History, 1830–1900* (Liverpool, 1996), pp 85–118.

Jones, C., *Immigration and Social Policy in Britain* (London, 1977).

Joyce, P., *Work, Society and Politics: The Culture of the Factory in Later Victorian England* (London, 1980).

Kee, R., *The Green Flag* (London, 1972).

Kennedy, R.E., *The Irish: Emigration, Marriage, Fertility* (Berkley, 1973).

Killen, J. (ed.), *The Famine Decade: Contemporary Accounts, 1841–51* (Belfast, 1995).

Kinealy, C., *This Great Calamity: The Irish Famine 1845–52* (Dublin, 1994).

Kirby, R.J., and Musson, A.E., *The Voice of the People: A Biography of John Doherty, 1798–1854* (Manchester, 1975).

Kirk, N., 'Ethnicity, Class and Popular Toryism, 1850–70', in Lunn, *Hosts, Immigrants and Minorities* (1980), pp 64–106.

Large, D., 'The Irish in Bristol in 1851: A Census Enumeration', in Swift and Gilley (eds), *The Irish in the Victorian City* (1985), pp 37–58.

Lavery, F., *Irish Heroes in the War* (London, 1917).

Lennon, M., McAdam, M., and O'Brien, J., *Across the Water: Irish Women's Lives in Britain* (London, 1988).

Lees, L.H., 'Patterns of Lower-Class Life: Irish Slum Communities in Nineteenth-Century London', in Thernstrom, S. and Sennett, R. (eds), *Nineteenth-Century Cities* (New Haven, 1969), pp 359–85.

Lees, L.H., *Exiles of Erin: Irish Migrants in Victorian London* (Manchester, 1979).

Leetham, C., *Luigi Gentili: A Sower for the Second Spring* (London, 1965).

Lesourd, J.A., *Sociologie du Catholicisme Anglais, 1767–1851*, 2 vols (Nancy, 1981).

Letford, L. and Pooley, C., 'Geographies of Migration and Religion: Irish Women in mid-Nineteenth Century Liverpool', in O'Sullivan, P. (ed.), *The Irish World Wide*, vol. 4, *Irish Women and Irish Migration* (Leicester, 1995), pp 89–112.

Lowe, W.J., *The Irish in Mid-Victorian Lancashire: The Shaping of a Working Class Community* (New York, 1989).

MacDermott, T.P., 'Irish Workers on Tyneside in the Nineteenth Century', in McCord, N. (ed.), *Essays in Tyneside Labour History* (Newcastle, 1977), pp 154–77.

Machin, G.I.T., *Politics and the Churches in Great Britain, 1832–68* (Oxford, 1977).

MacRaild, D.M., 'William Murphy, the Orange Order and Communal Violence: the Irish in West Cumberland, 1871–84', in Panayi, P. (ed.), *Racial Violence in Britain, 1840–1950* (Leicester, 1993), pp 44–64.

Macraild, D.M., ' "Principle, party and protest": the language of Victorian Orangeism in the north of England', in West, S. (ed.), *The Victorians and Race* (Aldershot, 1996), pp 128–140.

MacRaild, D.M., *Culture, Conflict and Migration: The Irish in Victorian Cumbria* (Liverpool, 1998).

McAuley, J.W., 'Under an Orange Banner: Reflections on the Northern Protestant experiences of Emigration', in O'Sullivan, P. (ed.), *The Irish World Wide*, vol. 5, *Religion and Identity* (Leicester, 1996), pp 43–69.

McCaffrey, J.F., 'Politics and the Catholic Community since 1878', in McRoberts, *Modern Scottish Catholicism* (1979), pp 140–55.

—— 'Irish Issues in the Nineteenth and Twentieth Century: Radicalism in a Scottish Context', in Devine, *Irish Immigrants and Scottish Society* (1991), pp 116–137.

McClelland, V.A., *Cardinal Manning: His Public Life and Influence, 1865–92* (London, 1962).

McDonnell, K.G.T., 'Roman Catholics in London, 1850–65', in Hollaender, A. and Kellaway, W. (eds), *Studies in London History presented to Philip Edmund Jones* (London, 1969), pp 429–46.

McFarland, E., *Protestants First: Orangeism in Nineteenth Century Scotland* (Edinburgh, 1990).

McLeod, H., *Class and Religion in the Late Victorian City* (London, 1974).

—— 'Building the "Catholic Ghetto": Catholic Organisations, 1870–1914', in Sheils and Wood, *Voluntary Religion* (1986), pp 411–44.

McRoberts, D. (ed.), *Modern Scottish Catholicism* (Glasgow, 1979).

Messinger, G.S., *Manchester in the Victorian Age: The Half-Known City* (Manchester, 1985).

Milburn, G.E., *Church and Chapel in Sunderland, 1780–1914* (Sunderland Polytechnic Occasional Paper, 4, 1988).

Miller, K., *Emigrants and Exiles: Ireland and the Irish Exodus to North America* (Oxford, 1985).

Millward, P., 'The Stockport Riots of 1852: A Study of Anti-Catholic and Anti-Irish Sentiment', in Swift and Gilley (eds), *The Irish in the Victorian City* (1985), pp 207–24.

Morgan, D., *Harvesters and Harvesting, 1840–1900* (London, 1982).

Moore, K., '"This Whig and Tory Ridden Town": Popular Politics in Liverpool in the Chartist Era', in Belchem, *Popular Politics, Riot and Labour* (1992), pp 38–67.

Mokyr, J., *Why Ireland Starved* (London, 1983).

Mokyr, J. and O'Grada, C., 'Across the Briny Ocean: some thoughts on Irish Emigration to America, 1800–50', in Devine, T. and Dickson, D. (eds), *Ireland and Scotland: Essays in Comparative Economic and Social History* (Edinburgh, 1983).

Murdoch, N.H., 'From Militancy to Social Mission: The Salvation Army and Street Disturbances in Liverpool, 1879–87', in Belchem, *Popular Politics, Riot and Labour* (1992), pp 160–172.

Murray, B., *The Old Firm: Sectarianism, Sport and Society in Scotland* (Edinburgh, 1984).

Neal, F., *Sectarian Violence: The Liverpool Experience, 1819–1914* (Manchester, 1987).

—— English-Irish Conflict in the North-East of England', in Buckland and Belchem, *The Irish in British Labour History* (1993), pp 59–85.

—— 'The Famine Irish in England and Wales', in O'Sullivan, P. (ed), *The Irish World Wide*, vol. 6, *The Meaning of the Famine* (Leicester, 1997), pp 56–80.

—— *Black 47: The Famine Irish in Britain* (London, 1997).

Newsinger, J., *Fenianism in Mid-Victorian Britain* (London, 1994).

Norman, E.R., *Anti-Catholicism in Victorian England* (London, 1968).

—— *The English Catholic Church in the Nineteenth Century* (Oxford, 1984).

O'Connor Eccles, C., 'Scottish, Irish and Welsh London', in Sims, G.R. (ed.), *Living London* (London, 1903), reprinted as *Edwardian London*, 4 vols (London, 1990), vol. 3, pp 98–104.

O'Connor, K., *The Irish in Britain* (London, 1972).

O'Day, A., *The English Face of Irish Nationalism: Parnellite Involvement in British Politics, 1880–86* (Dublin, 1977).

—— *Parnell and the First Home Rule Episode, 1884–87* (Dublin,1985).

—— 'Irish Home Rule and Liberalism', in O'Day, A. (ed), *The Edwardian Age: Conflict and Stability, 1900–14* (London and Connecticut, 1979), pp 113–32.

—— 'The Irish Problem', in Gourvish, T.R. and O'Day, A. (eds), *Later Victorian Britain, 1867–1900* (London, 1988).

—— 'The political organization of the Irish in Britain, 1867–90', in Swift and Gilley (eds), *The Irish in Britain, 1815–1939* (1989), pp 183–211.

—— 'Varieties of Anti-Irish Behaviour in Britain, 1846–1922', in Panayi, *Racial Violence in Britain* (1993), pp 26–43.

O'Day, A. and Stevenson, J. (eds), *Irish Historical Documents since 1800* (Dublin, 1992).

O'Day, A., 'Revising the Diaspora', in Boyce, D.G. and O'Day, A. (eds), *The Making of Modern Irish History: Revisionism and the Revisionist Controversy* (London, 1996), pp 188–215.

O'Dowd, A., *Spalpeens and Tattie Hokers: History and Folklore of the Irish Migratory Agricultural Worker in Ireland and Britain* (Dublin, 1991).

Ó'Gràda, C., 'Some Aspects of Nineteenth-Century Irish Emigration', in Cullen, L.M. and Smout, T.C. (eds.), *Comparative Aspects of Scottish and Irish Economic and Social History, 1600–1900* (Edinburgh, 1977), pp 65–73.

O'Leary, P., 'Irish Immigration and the Catholic Welsh District, 1840–50', in Jenkins, H. (ed.), *Politics and Society in Wales, 1840–1922* (Cardiff, 1988).

—— 'From the Cradle to the Grave: Popular Catholicism among the Irish in Wales', in O'Sullivan, P. (ed.), *The Irish World Wide*, vol. 5, *Religion and Identity* (Leicester, 1996), pp 183–195.

O'Poitoir, C. (ed.), *The Great Irish Famine* (Dublin, 1995).

O'Sullivan, P., 'A literary difficulty in explaining Ireland: Tom Moore and Captain Rock, 1824', in Swift and Gilley (eds), *The Irish in Britain, 1815–1939* (1989), pp 239–74.

—— (ed.), *The Irish World Wide: History, Heritage, Identity* (6 vols, Leicester, 1992).

Poirteir, C. (ed.), *The Great Irish Famine* (Dublin, 1995).

Pooley, C., 'Segregation or integration ? The residential experience of the Irish in mid-Victorian Britain', in Swift and Gilley (eds), *The Irish in Britain, 1815–1939* (1989), pp 60–83.

Price, R.T., *Little Ireland: Aspects of the Irish and Greenhill, Swansea* (Swansea, 1992).

Proctor, M., *The Irish Community in North West England: a guide to local archive sources* (Liverpool, 1993).

Quinlivan, P. and Rose, P., *The Fenians in England, 1865–72* (London, 1962).

—— 'Hunting the Fenians: Problems in the Historiography of a Secret Organisation', in O'Sullivan, P. (ed.), *The Irish World Wide*, vol. 3, *The Creative Migrant* (Leicester, 1994), pp 133–53.

Read, D., and Glasgow, E., *Feargus O'Connor: Irishman and Chartist* (London, 1961).

Redford, A., *Labour Migration in England, 1800–50* (London, 1926, revised ed. Manchester, 1964).

Richter, D., *Riotous Victorians* (London, 1970).

Rose, P., *The Manchester Martyrs* (London, 1970).

Ryan, M.F., *Fenian Memories* (Dublin, 1945).

Samuel, R., 'The Roman Catholic Church and the Irish Poor', in Swift and Gilley (eds), *The Irish in the Victorian City* (1985), 267–300.

—— 'An Irish Religion', in Samuel, R. (ed.), *Patriotism* (London, 1992), vol. 2, pp 94–120.

Saville, J., *1848: The British State and the Chartist Movement* (Cambridge, 1987).

Senior, H., *Orangeism in Ireland and Britain, 1795–1836* (London, 1966).

Short, K.R.M., *The Dynamite War: Irish-American Bombers in Victorian Britain* (Dublin, 1979).

Spencer, A.E.C.W., 'The Demography and Sociography of the Roman Catholic Church of England and Wales', in Bright, L. and Clements, S. (eds), *The Committed Church* (London, 1966).

Skinnider, M., 'Catholic Education in Glasgow, 1818–1918', in Bone, T.R. (ed.), *Studies in Scottish Education 1872–1939* (London, 1967), pp 13–70.

Sloan, W., 'Religious Affiliation and the Immigrant Experience: Catholic Irish and Protestant Highlanders in Glasgow, 1830–50', in Devine, *Irish Immigrants and Scottish Society* (1991), pp 67–90.

Stevenson, J., *Popular Disturbances in England, 1700–1870* (London, 1979).

Strauss, E., *Irish Nationalism and British Democracy* (London, 1951).

Swift, R. and Gilley, S. (eds), *The Irish in the Victorian City* (London, 1985).

—— (eds), *The Irish in Britain, 1815–1939* (London, 1989).

Swift, R., 'Crime and the Irish in Nineteenth-Century Britain', in Swift and Gilley (eds), *The Irish in Britain, 1815–1914* (1989), pp 163–182.

—— *The Irish in Britain 1815–1914: Perspectives and Sources* (Historical Association, London, 1990).

—— 'The Historiography of the Irish in Nineteenth-Century Britain', in O'Sullivan, P. (ed.), *The Irish World Wide*, vol. 2., *The Irish in the New Communities* (1992), pp 52–81.

—— 'The Historiography of the Irish in Nineteenth Century Britain: Some Perspectives', in Buckland and Belchem, *The Irish in British Labour History* (1993), pp 11–18.

Taplin, E., 'False Dawn of New Unionism ? Labour Unrest in Liverpool, 1871–73', in Belchem, J., *Popular Politics, Riot and Labour* (1992), pp 135–59.

Thompson, D., 'Ireland and the Irish in English Radicalism before 1850', in Epstein, J. and Thompson, D. (eds.), *The Chartist Experience* (London, 1982).

Thompson, E.P., *The Making of the English Working Class* (London, 1963).

Treble, J.H., 'The Irish Agitation', in Ward, J.T. (ed.), *Popular Movements, 1830–50* (London, 1970).

—— 'Liverpool Working Class Housing, 1800–51', in Chapman, S. (ed.), *The History of Working Class Housing: A Symposium* (Newton Abbot, 1971), pp 165–220.

—— 'O'Connor, O'Connell and the Attitudes of Irish Immigrants towards Chartism in the North of England, 1838–48', in Butt, J. and Clarke, I.F. (eds), *The Victorians and Social Protest* (Newton Abbot, 1973).

—— 'The Development of Roman Catholic Education in Scotland, 1878–1978', in McRoberts, D. (ed.), *Modern Scottish Catholicism* (1979), pp 111–39.

Vincent, J.R., *Pollbooks: How Victorians Voted* (London, 1967).

Waller, P.J., *Democracy and Sectarianism: A Political and Social History of Liverpool, 1868–1939* (Liverpool, 1981).

Walker, G., 'The Protestant Irish in Scotland', in Devine, *Irish Immigrants and Scottish Society* (1991), pp 44–66.

Walker, W.A., *Juteopolis: Dundee and its Textile Workers, 1885–1923* (Edinburgh, 1979).

Walton, J., and Wilcox, A. (eds), *Low Life and Moral Improvement in Mid-Victorian England: Liverpool through the Journalism of Hugh Shimmin* (Leicester, 1991).

—— *Passage to Britain: Immigration in British History and Politics* (London, 1984).

Williams, A.M., 'Migration and Residential Patterns in Mid-Nineteenth Century Cardiff', *Cambria*, vi, 2 (1979), pp 1–27.

Williamson, J., 'The impact of the Irish on British labor markets during the Industrial Revolution', in Swift and Gilley (eds), *The Irish in Britain, 1815–1939* (1989), pp 134–162.

Wolffe, J.R., *The Protestant Crusade in Great Britain, 1829–60* (Oxford, 1991).

Wood, I.S., 'Irish Immigrants and Scottish Radicalism', in McDougall, I. (ed.), *Essays in Scottish Labour History* (Edinburgh, 1979), pp 64–89.

Wood, I.S., *John Wheatley* (Manchester, 1990).

Woodham-Smith, C., *The Great Hunger* (London, 1962).

B. Journal Articles

Arnstein, W.L., 'Victorian Prejudice Re-examined', *Victorian Studies*, vol. XI (1968–9), pp 452–7.

—— 'The Murphy Riots: A Victorian Dilemma', *Victorian Studies*, vol. XIX (1975), pp 55–71.

Aspinwall, B., 'The Formation of the Catholic Community in the West of Scotland', *Innes Review*, vol. 33 (1982), pp 44–57.

—— 'Popery in Scotland: Image and Reality, 1820–1920', *Records of the Scottish Church History Society*, vol. 22 (1986), pp 235–57.

Aspinwall, B., 'The Irish Abroad: Michael Condon in Scotland, 1845–78', *Studies in Church History*, vol. 25 (1989), pp 279–97.

Belchem, J., 'English Working-Class Radicalism and the Irish, 1815–50', *North-West Labour History Society Bulletin*, vol. 8 (1982–3), pp 5–18.

Best, G.F.A., 'The Protestant Constitution and its Supporters, 1800–1829', *Transactions of the Royal Historical Society*, vol. 8 (1958).

Bhreathnach-Lynch, S., 'Framing the Irish: Victorian paintings of the Irish peasant', *Journal of Victorian Culture*, vol. 2, 2 (Autumn 1997), pp 245–63.

Boyle, J.W., 'Ireland and the First International', *Journal of British Studies*, vol. XI (May, 1972), pp 44–62.

Brooke, D., 'Railway Navvies on the Pennines, 1841–71', *Journal of Transport History*, vol. 3 (1975–6), pp 41–53.

Busteed. M., & Hodgson, R., 'Irish migration and settlement in nineteenth-century Manchester, with special reference to the Angel Meadow district', *Irish Geography*, vol. 27, 1 (1994), pp 1–13.

Cahill, G.A., 'Irish Catholicism and English Toryism', *Review of Politics*, vol. 19 (1957), pp 62–76.

Chase, M., 'Dangerous People? : The Teeside Irish in the nineteenth century', *North-East Labour History Journal*, vol. 28 (1994), pp 27–41.

Clapham, J.H., 'Irish Immigration into Great Britain in the Nineteenth Century', *Bulletin of the International Committee of Historical Sciences*, vol. V (June, 1933), pp 596–604.

Collins, B., 'Proto-industrialisation and pre-Famine Emigration', *Social History*, vol. 7, 2 (1982), pp 127–46.

Collette, C., 'So Utterly Forgotten: Irish Prisoners and the 1924 Labour Government', *North West Labour History Journal*, vol. 16 (1991–2), pp 73–7.

Coney, A.P., 'Mid-Nineteenth Century Ormskirk: Disease, Overcrowding and the Irish in a Lancashire Market Town', *Transactions of the Historic Society of Lancashire and Cheshire*, vol. 139 (1990), pp 33–111.

Connolly, G.P., 'The Transubstantiation of Myth: Towards a New Popular History of Nineteenth-Century Catholicism in England', *Journal of Ecclesiastical History*, vol. 35 (1984), pp 78–104.

—— 'The Revd Mr. Peter Kaye: Maverick or Englishman?', *North West Catholic History*, vol. 11 (1984), pp 8–21.

—— '"With more than ordinary devotion to God": The Secular Missioner of the North in the Evangelical Age of the English Mission', *North West Catholic History*, vol. 10 (1983), pp 8–31.

—— 'The Catholic Church and the first Manchester and Salford Trade Unions in the Age of the Industrial Revolution', *Transactions of the Lancashire and Cheshire Antiquarian Society*, vol. 135 (1985).

Cooter, R.J., 'Lady Londonderry and the Irish Catholics of Seaham Harbour: "No Popery" out of context', *Recusant History*, vol. 13 (1975–6), pp 288–98.

—— 'On Calculating the Nineteenth Century Catholic Population of Durham and Newcastle', *Northern Catholic History*, vol. 2 (1975).

Cousens, S.H., 'Emigration and Demographic Change in Ireland, 1851–61', *Economic History Review*, vol. 14 (1961–2), pp 275–88.

—— 'The Regional Pattern of Emigration during the Great Irish Famine', *Transactions and Papers of the Institute of British Geographers*, vol. 28 (1960), pp 119–34.

Davis, J., 'From "rookeries" to "communities": Race, Poverty and Policing in London, 1850–1985', *History Workshop Journal*, vol. 27 (1989).

Dillon, T., 'The Irish in Leeds, 1851–61', *Thoresby Miscellany*, vol. XVI (1979), pp 1–29.

Doyle, P., 'The Education and Training of Roman Catholic Priests in the Nineteenth Century', *Journal of Ecclesiastical History*, vol. 35, 2 (1984), pp 208–19.

Doyle, P., 'Accommodation or Confrontation: Catholic Responses to the Formation of the Labour Party', *North West Labour History Journal*, vol. 16 (1991–2), pp 64–72.

Duffy, P., 'Carrying the Hod: Irish Immigrant Labour in the Manchester Building Trades', *North West Labour History Journal*, vol. 16 (1991–2), pp 36–41.

Dunleavy, J., 'The Manchester Irish National Convention, 1918', *North West Labour History Journal*, vol. 16 (1991–2), pp 56–60.

Feldman, D., 'There was an Englishman, an Irishman and a Jew … Immigrants and Minorities in Britain', *Historical Journal*, vol. 26 (1983).

Feheney, J.M., 'Delinquency among Irish Catholic children in Victorian London', *Irish Historical Studies*, vol. XXIII, 92 (1983), pp 319–29.

Fielding, S.J., 'Irish Politics in Manchester, 1890–1914', *International Review of Social History*, vol. XXXIII (1988), pp 261–84.

—— 'The Catholic Whit-Walk in Manchester and Salford, 1890–1939, *Manchester Regional History Review*, vol. 1, 1 (1987), pp 3–10.

Fitzpatrick, D., 'Irish Emigration in the Later Nineteenth Century', *Irish Historical Studies*, vol. XXII, 86 (1980), pp 126–43.

Frow, R., and E., 'Biographies of Irish Chartists', *North West Labour History Journal*, vol. 16 (1991–2), pp 86–93.

Gilley, S., 'The Roman Catholic Mission to the Irish in London, 1840–60', *Recusant History*, vol. 10 (1969–70), pp 123–45.

—— 'Protestant London, No Popery and the Irish Poor, 1830–70', *Recusant History*, vol. 10 (1969–70), pp 210–30; vol. 11 (1971), pp 21–46.

—— 'Heretic London, Holy Poverty and the Irish Poor, 1830–70', *Downside Review*, vol. 89 (1971), pp 64–89.

—— 'The Garibaldi Riots of 1862', *Historical Journal*, vol. 16 (1973), pp 697–732.

—— 'The Roman Catholic Church and the Nineteenth-Century Irish Diaspora', *Journal of Ecclesiastical History*, vol. 35 (1984), pp 188–207.

—— 'Irish Immigration to Britain, 1911–51: Patterns and Policy', *Irish Economic and Social History*, vol. 8 (1981).

Hamer, D.A., 'The Irish Question and Liberal Politics, 1886–1894', *Historical Journal*, vol. 12 (1969).

Harris, R., 'The Failure of Republicanism among Irish Migrants to Britain, 1800–40', *Eire-Ireland*, vol. 21 (1986), pp 122–36.

Haslett, J. and Lowe, W.J., 'Household structure and overcrowding among the Lancashire Irish, 1851–71', *Histoire Sociale*, vol. 10 (1977).

Hunter, J., 'The Gaelic Connection: the Highlands, Ireland and Nationalism 1873–1922', *Scottish Historical Review*, vol. 54 (1975), pp 179–204.

Hyland, B., 'Eva Gore-Booth: An Irishwoman in Manchester', *North West Labour History Journal*, vol. 16 (1991–2), pp 52–5.

Jackson, J., 'The Irish in East London', *East London Papers*, vol. 6 (1963).

Kemnitz, T.M., 'Approaches to the Chartist Movement: Feargus O'Connor and Chartist Strategy', *Albion*, vol. V (1973), pp 67–73.

Kerr, B.M., 'Irish Seasonal Migration to Great Britain, 1800–1838', *Irish Historical Studies*, vol. II (1942–3), pp 365–380.

Koseki, T., 'Patrick O'Higgins and Irish Chartism', *Ireland-Japan Papers*, 2 [Hosei University] (1988).

—— 'The Liverpool Irish and the Threat of Physical Force', *Ireland-Japan Papers*, 3 [Hosei University] (1989).

Larkin, E., 'The Devotional Revolution in Ireland, 1850–75', *American Historical Review*, vol. XXVII (1972), pp 625–52.

Lawton, R., 'Irish Immigration to England and Wales in the Mid-Nineteenth Century', *Irish Geography*, vol. IV (1959–63), pp 35–54.

Lees, L.H., 'Mid-Victorian Migration and the Irish Family Economy', *Victorian Studies*, vol. XX (1976), pp 25–43.

Lewis, C.R., 'The Irish in Cardiff in the Mid-Nineteenth Century', *Cambria*, vol. VII (1980), pp 13–41.

Lobban, R.D., 'The Irish Community in Greenock in the Nineteenth Century', *Irish Geography*, vol. VI (1971), pp 270–81.

Lovell, J., 'The Irish and the London Dockers', *Bulletin of the Society for the Study of Labour History*, vol. II (1975), pp 63–5.

Lowe, W.J., 'The Irish in Lancashire, 1846–71: A Social History', *Irish Economic and Social History*, vol. II (1975).

—— 'The Lancashire Irish and the Catholic Church, 1846–71', *Irish Historical Studies*, vol. XX (1976), pp 129–55.

—— 'Social Agencies among the Irish in Lancashire during the Mid-Nineteenth Century', *Saothar*, vol. 3 (1977), pp 15–20.

—— 'Lancashire Fenianism, 1846–71', *Transactions of the Historic Society of Lancashire and Cheshire*, vol. 126 (1977), pp 156–85.

—— 'The Chartists and the Irish Confederates: Lancashire, 1848', *Irish Historical Studies*, vol. XXIV, 94 (1984), pp 172–96.

MacRaild, D.M., 'Irish Immigration and the 'Condition of England' Question: The Roots of an Historiographical Tradition', *Immigrants and Minorities*, vol. 14, 1 (March 1995), pp 67–85.

—— 'A Case of Undercutting Wages?: Sectarian Tension and the Barrow Anti-Irish Riot of 1864', *Transactions of the Cumberland and Westmorland Antiquarian & Archaeological Society*, vol. XCVI (1996), pp 215–22.

—— 'Culture, Conflict and Labour Migration: Victorian Cumbria's Ulster Dimension', *Saothar*, vol. 21 (1996), pp 23–38.

Mason, F.M., 'The newer Eve: The Catholic Women's Suffrage Society in England, 1911–23', *Catholic Historical Review*, vol. 52 (1986).

McCaffrey, J.F., 'The Irish Vote in Glasgow in the Later Nineteenth Century', *Innes Review*, vol. 21 (1970), pp 30–6.

McCaffrey, J.F., 'Roman Catholics in Scotland in the 19th and 20th centuries', *Records of the Scottish Church History Society*, vol. 21 (1983).

—— 'The Stewardship of Resources: Financial Strategies of Roman Catholics in the Glasgow District, 1800–70', *Studies in Church History*, vol. 24 (1987), pp 359–70.

—— 'Irish Immigrants and Radical Movements in the West of Scotland in the Early Nineteenth Century', *Innes Review*, vol. XXXIX, 1 (1988), pp 52–4.

McGill, J., and Redmond, T., 'The Story of the Manchester Martyrs', *North West Labour History Journal*, vol. 16 (1991–2), pp 42–51.

Miller, D., 'Irish Catholicism and the Great Famine', *Journal of Social History*, vol. IX (1975–6), pp 81–98.

Mokyr, J., and O'Grada, C., 'Emigration and Poverty in Pre-Famine Ireland', *Explorations in Economic History*, vol. 19 (1982), pp 360–84.

Moody, T.W., 'Michael Davitt and the British Labour Movement, 1882–1906', *Transactions of the Royal Historical Society*, vol. 4 (1953), pp 53–76.

Morris, K.L., 'John Bull and the Scarlet Woman: Charles Kingsley and Anti-Catholicism in Victorian Literature', *Recusant History*, vol. 23, 2 (Oct. 1996), pp 190–218.

Mulkern, P., 'Irish Immigrants and Public Disorder in Coventry, 1845–75', *Midland History*, vol. XXI (1996), pp 119–35.

Murphy, P., 'Irish settlement in Nottingham in the early nineteenth century', *Transactions of the Thornton Society*, vol. 98 (1994), pp 82–91.

Neal, F., 'The Birkenhead Garibaldi Riots of 1862', *Transactions of the Historic Society of Lancashire and Cheshire*, vol. 131 (1982), pp 87–111.

—— 'Liverpool, the Famine Irish and the Steamship Companies', *Immigrants and Minorities*, vol. 5, 1 (1985), pp 28–61.

—— 'Manchester Origins of the English Orange Order', *Manchester Region History Review* (Autumn 1990), pp 12–24.

—— 'A Criminal Profile of the Liverpool Irish', *Transactions of the Historic Society of Lancashire and Cheshire*, vol. 140 (1991), pp 161–99.

—— 'English-Irish Conflict in the North West of England: Economics, Racism, Anti-Catholicism or Simple Xenophobia?', *North West Labour History Journal*, vol. 16 (1991–2), pp 14–25.

—— 'Lancashire, the Famine Crisis and the Poor Law: A Study in Crisis Management', *Irish Economic and Social History*, vol. 22 (1995), pp 26–46.

O'Connell, B., 'Irish Nationalism in Liverpool, 1873–1923', *Eire-Ireland*, vol. 10 (1975), pp 24–37.

Ó'Gràda, C., 'A Note on Nineteenth-Century Irish Emigration Statistics', *Population Studies*, vol. 29 (1975), pp 145–48.

O'Higgins, R., 'The Irish Influence in the Chartist Movement', *Past and Present*, vol. 20 (1961), pp 83–96.

O'Leary, P., 'Anti-Irish Riots in Wales, 1826–82', *Llafur*, vol. V, 4 (1991–2), pp 27–36.

Ó'Tuathaigh, M.A, 'The Irish in Nineteenth-Century Britain: Problems of Integration', *Transactions of the Royal Historical Society*, vol. 31 (1981), pp 149–74.

Parry, J., 'The Tredegar Anti-Irish Riots of 1882', *Llafur*, vol. III (1983), pp 20–3.

Pooley, C.G., 'The residential segregation of migrant communities in Mid-Victorian Liverpool', *Transactions of the Institute of British Geographers*, vol. II, 3 (1977), pp 369–72.

—— 'Irish Settlement in North West England in the Mid-Nineteenth Century: A Geographical Critique', *North West Labour History Journal*, vol. 16 (1991–2), pp 26–35.

Reid, T.D.W., and N., 'The 1842 "Plug Plot" in Stockport', *International Review of Social History*, vol. XXIV (1979).

Richardson, C., 'Irish Settlement in Mid-Nineteenth Century Bradford', *Yorkshire Bulletin of Economic and Social Research*, vol. XX (1975), pp 40–57.

—— 'The Irish in Victorian Bradford', *Bradford Antiquary*, vol. 9 (1976), pp 294–316.

Shallice, A., 'Orange and Green and Militancy: Sectarianism and Working-Class Politics in Liverpool, 1910–14', *North West Labour History Journal*, vol. 6 (1979–80), pp 15–22.

Smith, A.W., 'Irish Rebels and English Radicals, 1798–1829', *Past and Present*, vol. 7 (1955), pp 78–85.

Smith, J., 'Labour Tradition in Glasgow and Liverpool', *History Workshop*, vol. 17 (Spring, 1974).

Stack, J.A., 'The Catholics, the Irish Delinquent and the origins of Reformatory Schools in nineteenth-century England and Scotland', *Recusant History*, vol. 23, 3 (May 1997), pp 372–88.

Steele, E.D., 'The Irish Presence in the North of England, 1850–1914', *Northern History*, vol. XII (1976), pp 220–41.

Swift, R., 'Crime and Ethnicity: The Irish in Early Victorian Wolverhampton', *West Midlands Studies*, vol. 13 (1980), pp 1–5.

Swift, R., 'Anti-Catholicism and Irish Disturbances: Public Order in Mid-Victorian Wolverhampton', *Midland History*, vol. IX (1984), pp 87–108.

—— '"Another Stafford Street Row": Law, Order and the Irish Presence in Mid-Victorian Wolverhampton', *Immigrants and Minorities*, vol. 3 (1984), pp 5–29.

—— 'The Outcast Irish in the British Victorian City: Problems and Perspectives', *Irish Historical Studies*, vol. XXV (1987), pp 264–76.

—— 'Anti-Irish Violence in Victorian England: Some Perspectives', *Criminal Justice History*, vol. 15 (1994), pp 1227–141.

—— 'Heroes or Villains?: The Irish, Crime and Disorder in Victorian England', *Albion*, vol. 29, 3 (1998), pp 399–421.

Treble, J.H., 'The Attitude of the Roman Catholic Church towards Trade Unionism in the North of England, 1833–42', *Northern History*, vol. 5 (1970), pp 93–113.

—— 'The Navvies', *Scottish Labour History Society Journal*, vol. V (1972).

—— 'Irish Navvies in the North of England, 1833–42', *Transport History*, vol. 6 (1973), pp 227–47.

—— 'The Development of Roman Catholic Education in Scotland, 1878–1978', *Innes Review*, vol. 29, 2 (1978).

Turley, F., 'Centenary of the Fenian Raid', *Cheshire Sheaf* (Oct. 1967), pp 45–6.

Walker, R.B., 'Religious Changes in Liverpool in the Nineteenth Century', *Journal of Ecclesiastical History*, vol. 19, 2 (Oct. 1968), pp 195–211.

Walker, W.M., 'Irish Immigrants in Scotland: their Priests, Politics and Parochial Life', *Historical Journal*, vol. 15 (1972), pp 649–67.

Werly, J.M., 'The Irish in Manchester, 1832–49', *Irish Historical Studies*, vol. XVIII (1973), pp 345–58.

Williams, F.J., 'The Irish in the East Cheshire Silk Industry, 1851–61', *Transactions of the Historic Society of Lancashire and Cheshire*, vol. 136 (1986), pp 99–126.

Williamson, J.G., 'The Impact of the Irish on British Labour Markets during the Industrial Revolution', *Journal of Economic History*, vol. XLVI (Sept.1986), pp 693–721.

Wood, I.S., 'John Wheatley, the Irish and the Labour Movement in Scotland', *Innes Review*, vol. XXXI (1980), pp 71–85.

Yeo, E., 'Christianity in Chartist Struggle, 1838–42', *Past and Present*, vol. 91 (1981), pp 83–94.

C.   Theses

Bartlett, A., 'The Churches in Bermondsey, 1880–1939' (University of Birmingham PhD thesis, 1987).

Benjamin, H.W., 'The London Irish: A Study in Political Activism, 1870–1910' (University of London PhD thesis, 1971).

Betney, N.R., 'An Irish Tale? Emigration or Immigration: A Study of Irish Migration' (University of York MA thesis, 1987).

Bryson, A., 'Riot and its control in Liverpool, 1815–60' (Open University MPhil thesis, 1990).

Cassirer, R., 'The Irish Influence on the Liberal Movement in England, 1798–1832' (University of London PhD thesis, 1940).

Champ, J., 'Assimilation and Separation: The Catholic Revival in Birmingham, 1650–1850' (University of Birmingham PhD thesis, 1989).

Collins, B., 'Aspects of Irish Immigration into Two Scottish Towns' (Dundee and Paisley) in the Mid-Nineteenth Century (University of Edinburgh MPhil thesis, 1978).

Connolly, G.P., 'Catholicism in Manchester and Salford' (University of Manchester PhD thesis, 1980).

Cooter, R.J., 'The Irish in County Durham and Newcastle, 1840–1880' (University of Durham MA thesis, 1973).

Fielding, S.J., 'The Irish Catholics of Manchester and Salford: Aspects of their Religious and Political History 1890–1939' (University of Warwick PhD thesis, 1988).

Gilbert, P.J., 'In the midst of a Protestant people: the development of the Catholic community in Bristol in the nineteenth century' (Brunel University PhD thesis, 1996).

Hall, R., 'Irish music and dance in London, 1890–1970: a socio-cultural history' (University of Sussex PhD thesis, 1994).

Herson, J., 'Why the Irish went to Stafford: A Case Study of Irish Settlement in England, 1830–71' (London School of Economics MSc thesis, 1986).

Hickey, J.V., 'The Origin and Growth of the Irish Community in Cardiff' (University of Wales MA thesis, 1959).

Horgan, D.T., 'The Irish Catholic Whigs in Parliament 1847–74' (University of Minnesota PhD thesis, 1975).

Hutchinson, I.G.C., 'Politics and Society in Mid-Victorian Glasgow, 1846–86' (University of Edinburgh PhD thesis, 1974).

Ingram, P., 'Sectarianism in the North West of England, with special reference to class relationships in the City of Liverpool, 1846–1914' (Lancashire Polytechnic PhD thesis, 1988).

Ives, E.J., 'The Irish in Liverpool. A Study of Ethnic Identification and Social Participation' (University of Liverpool MPhil thesis, 1988).

Jackson, J.A., 'The Irish in London: A Study of Migration and Settlement in the past hundred years' (University of London MA thesis, 1958).

Kanya-Forstner, M., 'Irish women in Victorian Liverpool' (University of Liverpool PhD thesis, 1997).

Koseki, T., 'Chartism and Irish Nationalism, 1829–48: Bronterre O'Brien, the London Irish and Attempts at a Chartist-Irish Alliance' (University of Birmingham MPhil thesis, 1988).

Lees, L.H., 'Social Change and Social Stability among the London Irish' (University of Harvard PhD thesis, 1969).

Lowe, W.J., 'The Irish in Lancashire, 1846–71' (Trinity College Dublin MA thesis, 1975).

MacDermott, M., 'Irish Catholics and the British Labour Movement: a study with special reference to London, 1918–70' (University of Kent MA thesis, 1979).

MacRaild, D.M., 'The Irish in North Lancashire and West Cumberland, 1850–1906: Aspects of the social history of Barrow-in-Furness and Cleator Moor and their hinterlands' (University of Sheffield PhD thesis, 1993).

Maguire, M.G.P., 'A Community at War: the Irish in Britain and the War of Independence' (University of Surrey PhD thesis, 1983).

Masson, U., 'The Development of the Irish and Roman Catholic Communities of Merthyr Tydfil and Dowlais in the Nineteenth Century' (University of Keele MA thesis, 1975).

McClelland, M., 'Early Educational Endeavour: A Study of the Work of the Hull Mercy Nuns, 1855–1930' (University of Hull MPhil thesis, 1993).

McFarland, E., 'The Loyal Orange Institution in Scotland, 1799–1900' (University of Glasgow PhD thesis, 1986).

Miskell, L., 'Custom, conflict and community: a study of the Irish in South Wales and Cornwall, 1861–91' (University of Wales PhD thesis, 1996).

Moore, K., '"This Whig and Tory-Ridden Town": Popular Politics in Liverpool, 1815–50' (University of Liverpool MPhil thesis, 1988).

O'Connor, B.J., 'The Irish Nationalist Party in Liverpool, 1873–1922' (University of Liverpool MA thesis, 1971).

O'Day, A., 'The Irish Parliamentary Party in British Politics, 1880–86' (University of London PhD thesis, 1971).

O'Leary, P., 'Immigration and Integration. A Study of the Irish in Wales, 1798–1922' (University of Wales PhD thesis, 1989).

Papworth, J.D., 'The Irish in Liverpool, 1835–71: Family Structure and Residential Mobility' (University of Liverpool PhD thesis, 1982).

Pooley, C.G., 'Migration, mobility and residential areas in nineteenth-century Liverpool' (University of Liverpool PhD thesis, 1978).

Quinn, J., 'The Mission of the Churches to the Irish in Dundee, 1846–86' (University of Stirling MLitt thesis, 1994).

Quirke, J., 'The Development of the Roman Catholic Community in Wolverhampton, 1828–67' (Wolverhampton Polytechnic MA thesis, 1983).

Rafferty, O.P., 'The Church, the State, and the Fenian threat, 1861–75' (University of Oxford PhD thesis, 1996).

Reid, C.A.N., 'The Chartist Movement in Stockport' (University of Hull MA thesis, 1974).

Schofield, R.A., 'A Peculiar Tramping People ? Irish and long-distance British migrants in a northern English manufacturing town: Keighley, 1841–81' (Open University PhD thesis, 1990).

Scott, C.L., 'A Comparative Re-examination of Anglo-Irish Relations in Nineteenth-Century Manchester, Liverpool and Newcastle-upon-Tyne' (University of Durham PhD thesis, 1998).

Sharpe, J., 'Reapers of the Harvest: the Redemptionists in the United Kingdom, 1843–1898' (University of London PhD thesis, 1986).

Sloan, W., 'Aspects of the Assimilation of Highland and Irish Migrants in Glasgow, 1830–70' (University of Strathclyde MPhil thesis, 1987).

Tebbutt, M.J., 'The Evolution of Ethnic Stereotypes: An examination of stereotyping, with particular reference to the Irish in Manchester during the late nineteenth century' (University of Manchester MPhil thesis, 1982).

Tennant, L.M., 'Ulster Emigration, 1851–1914' (University of Ulster MPhil thesis, 1989).

Treble, J.H., 'The place of the Irish Catholics in the social life of the North of England, 1829–51' (University of Leeds PhD thesis, 1969).

Savage, D.C., 'The General Election of 1886 in Great Britain and Ireland' (University of London PhD thesis, 1958).

Woolaston, E.P.M., 'The Irish Nationalist Movement in Great Britain, 1886– 1908' (University of London MA thesis, 1958).

Wolffe, J., 'Protestant Societies and Anti-Catholic Agitation in Great Britain, 1829–60' (University of Oxford PhD thesis, 1985).

Ziesler, K.I., 'The Irish in Birmingham, 1830–1970' (University of Birmingham PhD thesis, 1989).

Notes on Contributors

JOHN BELCHEM is Professor of History at the University of Liverpool.

FRANK BOYCE teaches in the Department of Extramural Studies at the University of Liverpool.

CARL CHINN is Senior Lecturer in History at the University of Birmingham.

SHERIDAN GILLEY is Reader in Theology at the University of Durham.

JOHN HERSON is Head of History at Liverpool John Moores University.

MARY J. HICKMAN is Director of the Irish Studies Centre at the University of North London.

JOHN HUTCHINSON is an Associate Professor at Griffith University, Australia.

MARIE McCLELLAND is a Lecturer in Education at the University of Hull.

LOUISE MISKELL is a Research Assistant in Modern History at the University of Dundee.

GERARD MORAN is a Lecturer in History at Wolfson College, Oxford.

FRANK NEAL is Professor of Economic and Social History at the University of Salford.

ALAN O'DAY is Senior Lecturer in History at the University of North London.

PAUL O'LEARY is Senior Lecturer in History at the University of Wales, Aberystwyth.

YVONNE SIDDLE prepared the Index.

ROGER SWIFT is Director of the Centre for Victorian Studies at University College Chester.

JACQUELINE TURTON is a Librarian at University College Chester.

Index

Accrington 218, 221
Albert, Prince 233
Americas 170, *see also* United States of
 America, North America
Ancient Order of Hibernians 270–1
Anglican Church 109, 168, 206–7, 248,
 281–2
Antrim 207
Archdeacon, George 198, 227, 230–3

Armagh 56–7
Ashton-under-Lyne 220, 223, 233
Asian sub continent 245
Asylum for the Houseless Poor
 (Cripplegate) 129, 131–2
Auckland 79, 84
Australasia 170

Ballingarry 198
Ballymena 196
Baltimore 196
Bangor (Co. Down) 156
Barnett, T.A. (Chief Inspector of
 Schools) 118
Beames, Thomas 145, 154
Belfast 67, 196, 205
Benedictines, *see* Order of St Benedict
Benfieldside 88, 89, 90, 95
Bentley, Mr (Relieving Officer) 24
Bermondsey 105, 266
Binney, John 123
Birkenhead 222, 229, 231
Birmingham 7, 52–74, 180, 214, 227
Birmingham General Dispensary 61
Birmingham Town Infirmary 61
Birmingham Town Mission 56
Blackburn 94, 218, 220, 222, 224, 232
Black Country 63, 157
Bligh, Dr 208
Board of Education 110, 118–19, 121
Boase, W.D. (Poor Law Inspector) 25, 26

Bolton 215, 218–19, 230, 232
Boroimhe, Brian 230, 232
Boston (Mass.) 23
Bourne, Cardinal 270
Bowen, Father 57, 62–3, 72
Brea 38–9, 43, 48
Breslin, Michael 199
Bridgend 15
Bristol 15, 17, 34, 127–8, 132
Brooke, Canon R.E. 108
Brotherhood of St Patrick 10
Brotherhood of St Vincent de Paul 204
Brown, Bishop 201, 203
Brown, Bishop T.J. 29
Brown William 196
Bryant, Sophie 259
Bunce, John Thackray 62
Burnley 94
Bute, marquis of 19, 22
Byrne, 'Dandy' Pat 209

Cambourne 7–8, 31–51
Cardiff 7, 15–16, 19, 21–4, 26–7, 29–30,
 132
Cardiff Board of Guardians 22
Carlow 55
Carlyle, Thomas 245
Caribbean 245
Carrickfergus (Co. Antrim) 178, 188
Casey, Captain 17
Castlerea (Co. Roscommon) 156, 161,
 167, 173
Cathedral of Christ the King (Liverpool)
 293
Catholic Boys' Refuge (Liverpool) 208
Catholic Church 7–11, 22, 27–9, 42,
 45–6, 55–7, 71, 101–21, 147–52,
 156, 164, 169, 174–6, 182–3, 207,
 211, 219, 224–30, 234, 241, 247–53,
 255–6, 262–3, 265, 276, 278, 280,
 282–90, 295–7

Catholic Club (Liverpool) 200, 202–3, 208
Catholic Education Council 119
Catholic Institute (Liverpool) 204
Catholic League of South London 266, 269
Catholic Poor School Committee 248, 249
Catholic Young Men's Society 229, 287
Cavan 66
Channel Islands 129
Chepstow 22, 23, 24, 25, 28
Cheshire 233
Chester-le-Street 79, 80
Christian Brothers 104, 269
Church of Ireland 168
Clancy, J 209
Clare 66
Clerkenwell 130
Clifford (near Tadcaster) 104, 105
Cockburn, Revd G.A. 21
Commens, Dr Andrew 209
Congregational Church 180
Connacht 8, 56, 63–4, 70–1, 73–4, 160–2, 167, 171, 173–8
Connolly, Lawrence 208
Connors, John 27–9
Conservative Party 175, 192, 202, 205, 210, 248
Consett 83, 88
Conside-C-Knitsley 88–90, 95
Constable, Lady Chichester 104, 106
Coombe 37–9, 43
Corcoran, Bartholomew 174, 176
Corder, James (Clerk to Birmingham Poor Law Guardians) 69
Cork 8, 17–19, 21, 34, 56, 66, 71, 74, 126–9, 193
Corney, Daniel 42, 47–8
Cornish, Mr (Magistrate's Clerk) 41, 48
Cornwall 7–8, 31–51, 80
Council for Catholic Action 288
Courtmacsherry 21
Crosbie, Miss Jessie 288
Crowley, Thade 193
Cullen, James 196
Cullen, Michael 196
Cullen, Archbishop Paul 196, 225–7
Cumann na bPiobain 265

Cumann na Gaedheal 270
Cumberland 81
Cumbria 10

Dale, F.H. (HMI) 119–20
Daly, J. 209
Darwall, Dr John 60–1
Darlington 79
David, Bishop Albert Augustus 281–92
Davis, Thomas 214
Dawson, Mother Superior Stanislaus 118–21
Denvir, John 199, 207–9
Derry 55
Derryveagh (Co. Donegal) 223
De Valera, Eamon 271, 275, 281
Devon 279
Dickens, Charles 157
Donegal 55, 66, 223
Dowlais 28, 29
Down 65–6, 156, 180, 206
Downey, Richard 295
Driscoll, Lawrence 43, 48
Drogheda 25
Dublin 8, 9, 15, 25, 55, 66–7, 71–2, 74, 104–5, 127–8, 195–6, 198, 200, 203, 209, 213, 220, 222, 225, 231, 232–3, 262, 271, 286
Duffy, Charles Gavan 197, 198
Duncan, Dr W.H. 279
Dundalk 209
Durham 8, 76–83, 85, 88, 91, 96, 98

Easington 79, 83–5, 88–90, 99
Ebchester 88, 90, 95
Edinburgh 232
Edwards, Richard 42, 45, 50
Elley & Co Shoe Factory (Stafford) 168, 180
Elphin (Co. Roscommon) 64
Emmet Literary Club 218
Emmet, Robert 214, 228, 232
Endsleigh Training College 117
Engels, Friedrich 245

Fagan, Revd H.S. 46
Fahy, Frank 262, 263
Farley, John 218

Feeney, John Frederick 54
Fenians 10, 181, 198–9, 208, 212–13, 223, 228–9, 231, 234, 262
Fildes, Henry 220, 227–8, 230
Finigan, James Lysaght 199
Finigan, John, J. 214, 215, 229
Finigan, Thomas 56, 60, 63, 70, 72
Finigan, W.J. 224
Fisher, Revd M. 194
Fitzgerald, Lord Edward 214
Flat Holm Island 23

Gaelic Athletic Association 234, 259, 262
Gaelic League 234, 263, 265–6, 268–71, 273
Gaelic League of London 259
Galligan, Patrick 220
Galloway, Councillor R. 115
Galway 56–7, 63–6, 72, 74, 156, 161, 167–8, 185, 286
Garton, Patrick de Lacy 199, 209
Gateshead 78–9, 95
Gelder, Alderman Alfred 114
Geradot, Father Antoine 278
Geraghty, Patrick 222
German Catholics 289
Gibbons, John 43
Gibson, Hugh Woods (mayor of Stafford) 156, 180
Gibson, William 268
Gladstone, W.E. 168, 180, 241
Gory 66
Goss, Bishop 224–7, 283
Grattan, Henry 214, 228
Griffin, Canon 117
Griffith, Arthur 254, 262, 267
Gwithian 37

Harcourt, Sir William 41
Hall, Father J. 110–11, 116–17
Hall, Sir Benjamin 17
Harford, Austin 210
Harford, Frank 210
Hearne, Father Daniel 141
Her Majesty's Inspectorate of Schools 109–10, 115, 118–20
Heinrick, Hugh 73, 194, 254, 257, 260
Hibernian Society (Liverpool) 193, 210

Hodgson, Joseph 61
Hoey, Clinton 213, 228, 231
Hoey, Father 287
Holborn 130
Holland, Dennis 213, 215
Holland, Mark 106
Holme, Samuel 205
Holmes, E.G. (HMI) 118
Holy Cross Catholic Church (Liverpool) 285, 289
Home Rule Confederation 208, 255
Home Rule Movement 235, 256, 262, 265–6
Houghton-le-Spring 79, 83
Hull 8, 9, 101–21
Hull Catholic Union 116–17
Hull City Council 117
Hull Education Committee 112–15
Hull, Eleanor 259
Hull Irish National Club 117
Hull Literary and Philosophical Society 103
Hull School Board 108–12, 115–16
Hull Town Council 108, 114
Hume, Abraham 206–7
Hume, Canon Abraham 282
Huxtable, Mrs (Matron, Newport Board of Guardians' Lodging House) 24
Hyde (Cheshire) 233

Independent Irish Party 213
Irish-Americans 191–2, 199, 210
Irish Catholic Club 202–3
Irish Confederates 197–8, 217, 228, 231
Irish Folk Song Society 265
Irish Free State 281
Irish Industries Association 268
Irish Islington Church (Liverpool) 205
Irish Literary Society 259, 263
Irish Literary Theatre 263
Irish National Party 208–10
Irish National League of Great Britain 255
Irish National Society 266, 268
Irish Parliamentary Party 10, 265
Irish Policemen 66, 180
Irish Protestants 9, 10, 54–6, 149, 152, 160–3, 178–80, 182, 192, 205–7, 214, 253, 258

Irish Republican Army 272
Irish Republican Brotherhood 198, 199
Irish Self-Determination League 11,
    265, 271–5
Irish Soldiers 67, 91, 156, 179–80, 189
Irish Women 12, 25, 26, 71–2, 87–8,
    90–2, 94, 126, 133, 145, 153–4,
    219, 257, 272, 288
Islington 265
Italian Catholics 289
Ivestone 88–90, 95, 98, 100

Jalsk (Co. Roscommon) 64
Jameson, Robert (mayor of Hull) 109
Jesuits, *see* Society of Jesus
Johns, Revd John 280

Kay, James Phillips 245
Kelly, Archbishop Patrick 278
Kelly, Father 246
Kelly, Inspector 66
Kelly, Patrick 219
Kelly, T 209
Kennedy, James 224
Kennedy, Mother Superior 105, 107, 121
Kent 37
Kerry 135
Kildare, 37, 55, 67, 186
Kilkeevan (Co. Roscommon) 64
Killcommon (Co. Mayo) 57
King's County (Offaly) 55, 66
Kinsale 19
Kirby 290

Labour Party 210, 241, 251
Lacy, Bishop of Middlesbrough 115–16
Lambert, Canon Joseph Malet 114
Lambert, H. 109
Lancashire 8, 10, 77, 91, 93–4, 96, 98,
    142, 196, 212–35, 286
Lancaster 205
Langan, Jack 193
Lavelle, Father Patrick 213, 217, 220,
    223, 226, 229, 232
Leaf (HMI) 111
Leeds 102, 232
Leonard, Margaret 272
Leicester 169

Leigh (Lancashire) 191
Leinster 161, 183, 184
Leitrim 55, 63
Lewis, Cornwall 193
Liberal Party 41, 168, 180, 199–200,
    202–3, 207–10, 256, 269
Limerick 55, 127, 135, 209, 229
Liverpool 9–10, 11, 13, 15–16, 20, 25, 91,
    97, 101, 118, 127–8, 147, 182,
    190–211, 214–15, 218–20, 222–6,
    231–4, 260, 277–97
Liverpool Chamber of Commerce 196
Liverpool Corporation 280
Liverpool Domestic Mission 204
Liverpool Irish Rifle Corps of
    Volunteers 199
Llandaff 24
Llantrisant 27
Local Education Authority (Hull) 110,
    111, 112, 114
London 9, 11, 13, 15, 37, 76–7, 101, 122–
    55, 180, 203, 214, 232, 237, 254–76
Longford 157
Lomax, Mr J. Neale 283
Lowry, Henry Dawson 49
MacManus, Terence Bellew 197, 198,
    216, 221, 228
MacSwiney, Terence 274
McArdle, Charles 208
McArdle, John 193, 208
McCarthy, John 42, 47, 48
McCarthy, Justin 195
McCarthy, William 266
McDonald, Archbishop 255
McDonnell, J.H. 272
McGinty, Father 203
McGrath, Father 208
McGrath, Sean 272
McKey, Father 46
McManus, Deputy Chief Constable
    Michael 66
McNeile, Hugh 200, 205, 206
Madden, W 208–9
Malley, Henry 216
Manchester 12–13, 36, 182, 215–18,
    220–4, 226, 229–34, 242, 261
Manning, Cardinal 241
Martin, John 234

Martin, Thomas 266
Mathew, Father 146, 193
Mayhew, Henry 9, 122–55
Mayo 25, 34, 55–8, 63–7, 69, 72, 74, 97,
    102, 161, 168, 185, 213, 223
Meath 186
Meagher, Thomas Francis 216, 232
Mechanics Institute (Hull) 103
Merthyr Tydfil 16, 19, 25, 28–9, 144
Midlands 33, 37, 170
Milford Haven 20–1
Millea, Father 27–8
Miller, Superintendent 45
Mitchel, John 198, 216
Mitchell, Charlie 55
Moloney, Father 269
Monaghan 56, 197, 208
Monaghan, Peter 227
Monmouthshire 26, 77
Moore, George Henry 234
Moran, D.P. 254, 259, 262
Motler, Father John 103–4, 106
Mouchet, John 61
Mount Edgecumbe, earl of 46
Mount Pleasant Training College
    (Liverpool) 118–20
Muggeridge, R.M. 17
Murphy, Dr 54
Murphy, J.J. Finton 270
Murphy, Dr Patrick 197, 283
Murphy, William 53
Murray, John 43
National Brotherhood of St Patrick 198,
    212–35
National Union of Catholic Teachers 269
Neath 23–4
New York 13, 23
Newcastle-Under-Lyme 178, 188
Newcastle-Upon-Tyne 8, 13, 78, 95, 176,
    186, 214
Newland Avenue Board School (Hull) 110
Newlyn 47
Newport 17–24, 26, 29, 30
Newport Refuge for the Destitute 18, 23
Nolan, John 'Amnesty' 228
North America 23
North-east England 75–100
Northumberland 76–8, 81–2

North-west England 75–100
Nugent, Father 190, 204, 207–8
Nugent, Monsignor James 280

Oblates of Mary Immaculate 285, 289
O'Brian, Art 263, 271–2, 274–5
O'Brien, Dean Richard B., Limerick 229
O'Brien, J.F.X. 267
O'Brien, P.B. 226
O'Connell, Daniel 193, 197, 233
O'Connor, T.P. 208
O'Donavan Rossa Club 270, 271
O'Donoghue, The 234
O'Hara, O 209
O'Hara, Sister Anastasia 120–1
Oldham 94, 218, 220, 222–3, 230, 233
O'Neill, Arthur 269
O'Neill, Daniel J. 54
O'Neill, Thomas 215
Operative Conservative Association 206
Operative Protestant Association 206
Oran, Co, Roscommon 64
Orange Order 152, 206, 289
Order of St Benedict 197, 287, 285
O'Reilly, Bishop 283
O'Shea, Father James 289
O'Sullivan, Revd Canon 54
Our Lady of Mercy Convent, Hull 107

Paine, H.J. 22
Parnell, Charles Stewart 208–9, 262
Party (Co. Mayo) 223, 229
Peach, Revd Edward 55–6
Penarth 20
Pengegan 37–9, 43, 48
Penzance 47
Pike, Major Walter 44, 45
Pippard, Henry 201
Plunket, Bishop Thomas 220
Plunket, Oliver 214
Poland 230, 233
Police 19, 24–5, 27–9, 42, 45, 66, 224
Polish Catholics 289
Pontypool 20
Pontypridd 28–9
Potteries, The 157
Presbyterian Church 180, 196, 205–6,
    214

Preston 41, 216, 220, 222–3, 225–6, 229, 232
Priestley, J.B. 281
Protestant Association 200, 248
Purcell, Edward 199

Quebec 23
Queen's County (Laois) 55, 60

Rafter, Sir Charles Haughton 54
Randerson, Canon Benjamin 108, 109
Rathcarn (Co. Roscommon) 64
Raven, Canon Charles 281
Rawlinson, Robert 61
Redfern, George (Deputy Constable of Birmingham) 69
Redruth 33, 47
Repeal Association 227
Rhondda Valley 27
Ribbon Society 197–8
Ridell, Father Arthur 106–8
Rigby, Vernon 54
Rochdale 93–8
Roscommon 25, 56–7, 60, 63–5, 67, 72–3, 156, 161
Raith, Sir Randolph 20
Russell, Charles (Lord Russell of Killaren) 209
Ryan, John 198, 218
Ryan, Mark 270
Ryan, Thomas 213
Ryan, W.P. 254, 259, 262, 268

Taggart, J.G. 209
Teesdale 79
Thomas, Captain Charles 44
Tipperary 55, 66
Tocqueville, A. de 56
Tone, Theobold Wolfe 214–15, 232
Trappes, Father Michael 103–6, 108
Travers, Captain Robert 21
Tredegar 48
Tubercurry (Sligo) 60
Tuckingmill 40
Turner, Bishop 223

Tune, Galway 65
Tynemouth 8, 78, 179, 189

Ullathorne, Bishop 227
Ulster 65, 71, 132, 160, 180, 183–4, 192–3, 195–7, 205–6
Underwood, Thomas Neilson 213, 227–8
United Irish League of Great Britain 255, 264, 266–9, 271, 275
United Irishmen 214
Unitarian Church 200, 280

Vale of Glamorgan 15
Verdon, Peter 196

Wadebridge 49
Wales 14–30, 76–7, 82, 129, 157, 244, 249, 257
Wallasey 290
Warrington 218, 223, 232, 234
Waterford 127
Weardale 79
Wendron 42
Wesleyan Methodism 46
West Meath 53
Westmorland 81
Wexford 66, 127, 198, 203
Whitechapel, London 128
Whiteside, Archbishop Thomas 295
Whitty, James 203
Whitty, M.J. 203
Wicklow 55
Widnes 225
Wiseman, Cardinal 151, 246
Wolverhampton 214
Wood, Councillor S.P. 114
Worlock, Archbishop 292
Wrigglesworth, Edmund 101
Wright Steel Orphanage, Hull 111

Yeats, W.B. 259, 262–3
York 102, 132, 245
Yorkshire 76–7, 81, 214
Young Irelanders 214–15, 222, 231